D1480269

Richard Wilbur

a reference guide

A
Reference
Guide
to
Literature

Nancy C. Martinez
Editor

Richard Wilbur

a reference guide

FRANCES BIXLER

G.K.HALL&CO.
70 LINCOLN STREET, BOSTON, MASS.

Ref.
PS
3545
.I32165
.B59
1991

All rights reserved.
Copyright 1991 by Frances Bixler.

4-9-98 don Mr. & Mrs. James Faulkner in mem. of Judge Walter Hot
First published 1991
by G.K. Hall & Co.
70 Lincoln Street
Boston, Massachusetts 02111

10 9 8 7 6 5 4 3 2 1

Library of Congress Cataloging-in-Publication Data

Bixler, Frances, 1939-
    Richard Wilbur: a reference guide / Frances Bixler.
      p. cm. – (A Reference guide to literature)
    Includes index.
    ISBN 0-8161-7262-5
    1. Wilbur, Richard, 1921-   – Bibliography. I. Title. II. Series.
  Z8974. 15.B59   1991
  [PS3545.I32165]
  016.811'52 – dc20

                      91-11042
                      CIP

The paper used in this publication meets the minimum requirements of
American National Standard for Information Sciences – Permanence of
Paper for Printed Library Materials. ANSI Z39.48-1984.   ∞™
MANUFACTURED IN THE UNITED STATES OF AMERICA

Contents

The Author

Frances Bixler holds a Ph.D. from the University of Arkansas–Fayetteville, where Ben Kimpel was her major advisor. She has published articles on the fiction of Robert Penn Warren and Barbara Pym. Other publications include *Original Essays on the Poetry of Anne Sexton*, published by the University of Central Arkansas Press. In addition to editing this collection, she contributed two articles, "Anne Sexton's 'Motherly' Poetics" and "Journey into the Sun: The Religious Pilgrimage of Anne Sexton." Bixler has published other articles and presented several papers on Sexton's poetry. Another research interest is the poetry of Denise Levertov. Currently, she is a member of the Board of the Robert Penn Warren Circle and is developing a paper on his poems. Her work on Richard Wilbur has been ongoing since 1985 when she published her first article on his durable qualities. Since then she has written an extensive evaluative bibliographic article entitled "Richard Wilbur: A Review of the Research and Criticism" published by *Resources for American Literary Study*. At the present time she is teaching at Southwest Missouri State University.

Foreword

Most of what poets say about the criticism of their works should be warily heard. Frost was being disingenuous when he said, "I like to be crossed off people's lists from time to time, so as to be rediscovered." That is the sort of blithe thing one can say when reputation is firm and all danger of deletion has passed. I have known particularly sensitive poets to state that they "never read the critics," and in most cases I have been skeptical of the claim. It is easier to believe the amusing confession of one poet I know – that on entering a periodical room, he can *smell* whether or not there is an article on him in some magazine or other. For better or worse, the generality of poets do know and care what is being said of them.

Would it be a good thing if they didn't? The main function of criticism is to mediate between books and readers, not to instruct authors, and there are kinds of essay and review which it is unprofitable for poets to read. There is a sort of sweeping, shallow criticism which organizes the "poetry scene" into warring schools; there is a magisterial criticism much concerned with rankings, and with the enforcement of some canon; there is, in every poet's experience, the surprisingly venomous review which seems to be based on suppositions as to personality, politics, or manner of life. To encounter oneself in such writings is to be betrayed into thoughts of image and status which have nothing to do with the frame of mind in which poems are written.

E. M. Forster was once asked, during a conference at Harvard, whether criticism had ever helped him to improve his fiction, and his answer was a simple no. Most authors would say the same. While friends and editors may give valuable and specific aid when a work is in the manuscript stage, published criticism seldom offers counsels which one can apply. Yet I am deeply grateful to the best of those critics whose work Frances Bixler has so painstakingly listed and summarized. Whatever they have said of me, they have given me over the years a spelled-out assurance that my efforts are worth the attention of a number of bright, responsive people. Such an assurance can help to keep one trying.

Richard Wilbur

Preface

The need for an updated reference guide of works about Richard Wilbur has been sharply felt for some time. In the last decade, in particular, scholars and teachers have been dependent upon a patchwork of short bibliographies of critical works about Richard Wilbur. This annotated bibliography is intended to fill such a need by providing a record of all critical work relating to Richard Wilbur now in print. John Field's *Richard Wilbur: A Bibliographical Checklist* (1971.6), was and is a useful tool; however, its date creates a severe handicap for Wilbur scholars. The extensive number of entries in this bibliography are a tribute to a poet who has steadily given his best to the writing of poetry. In addition, they provide a means for assessing Richard Wilbur's critical reputation and for charting the often stormy course of the writing of poetry in the last half of this century.

Beginning with two early biographical entries in 1935, the bibliography jumps quickly to 1947, the year that *The Beautiful Changes* was published, and moves chronologically forward through 1991. Items are listed by year and item number: 1935.1, for example, means that the article was published in 1935 and is the first item to appear in an alphabetical list of articles published in that year. Included in *The Reference Guide* are all book-length studies, book reviews, critical articles, book chapters and shorter passages from books, dissertations, bibliographies, biographical notes, and works in progress. In addition, I have annotated all of the interviews granted by Richard Wilbur during these years, feeling that such information would be an aid to understanding the poet and the poetry.

Preliminary materials include a foreword by Richard Wilbur, an extensive chronology of major and minor publications, prizes and awards, and brief biographical facts, a table of contents, an introduction, and a short biographical item about the compiler. Under "Finding List" at the end of the bibliography is a description of the location of Richard Wilbur's papers. The index contains authors' names and titles of Wilbur's books in italics, titles of poems in quotation marks, and various topics in lowercase letters. All aspects relating directly to Richard Wilbur can be found under his name. Listings include items such as characteristics, craftsmanship, imagery, lyricism, or themes. Also included under Richard Wilbur are *his* comments on various topics taken from the annotations of the interviews. Users can locate these items alphabetically under Richard Wilbur and the subheading of "views on." I have distinguished book reviews from critical commentary under the titles of each volume of poems. For example, under *The Beautiful Changes*, a reader will find "commentary on" and "reviews of," each with different listings. Poems, plays, volumes of poetry, and Wilbur's literary criticism have been indexed only if they are treated in some depth. I have listed in the index all of the dissertations, interviews, critical articles, and articles commenting on Wilbur's critical reputation for the researcher's convenience. Cross-references in the index suggest possible alternatives for items.

I have attempted to annotate as faithfully as possible, using quotations, paraphrases and summaries to capture the salient points of each selection. In some cases when writers have discussed a large number of poems to support their views, I have not listed each poem in the annotation but have indicated that poems should be looked up individually in the index. In other cases, I have quoted very brief items in their entirety to provide quick reference for scholars. Asterisks preceding item numbers indicate that I have not been able to locate them. Cross-references at the end of annotations lead the reader forward to reprinted items and backward to the earliest publication date.

In compiling the bibliography, I have used the *International MLA Bibliography* (computer search), the *Essay and General Literature Index*, the *Humanities Index, American Literary Scholarship, Year's Work in English Studies, American Literature, Articles on Twentieth-Century Literature: An Annotated Bibliography 1954-1970*, "A Checklist of Explication" from several volumes of *The Explicator, Dissertation Abstracts*, the *Humanities Citations Index, Contemporary Poets*, and a host of short bibliographies.

Jack W. C. Hagstrom, who has been collecting Wilbur data for ten years, very generously lent me his extensive bibliography. I am most grateful for his generosity and encouragement. He is truly a patron of the arts in his dedication to the highest quality research and in his support of a number of scholars in arts and letters. I owe another debt of gratitude to John Lancaster, Curator of Special Collections at Amherst College Library where most of Richard Wilbur's papers are housed, who has gone out of his way to check sources, send me copies of items difficult to locate, and document facts. I wish both men well in their effort to complete a descriptive bibliography of Richard Wilbur's entire *oeuvre*. Bruce Michelson, a scholar whose insightful articles have added much to Wilbur criticism, has also kindly shared his ideas with me, especially those relating to his upcoming book on Richard Wilbur's poems. I would certainly be remiss if I did not express my special appreciation to Nancy Martinez for her interest and support. Her suggestions have been invaluable and her friendship most welcome.

Others who have made this project possible are Francie Rottmann, librarian in charge of interlibrary loan requests at Southwest Missouri State University, Robert Henigan, Professor Emeritus at Southwest Missouri State University, who gave my introduction a sympathetic but scholarly reading, and Vencil Bixler, who endured.

Chronology

1921	Born in New York City, 1 March.
1942	Married Charlotte Ward of Boston.
1942	Graduated from Amherst College, Massachusetts.
1943	Began active duty in the army, serving with the 36th (Texas) Division in Italy at Monte Cassino and Anzio, and along the Siegried Line in Germany.
1947	*The Beautiful Changes and Other Poems*. New York: Reynal & Hitchcock.
1947	M.A. from Harvard University.
1947-50	Junior Fellow, Society of Fellows, Harvard University.
1948	Harriet Monroe Memorial Prize (*Poetry Magazine*).
1950	*Ceremony and Other Poems*. New York: Harcourt, Brace.
1950	Oscar Blumenthal Prize (*Poetry Magazine*).
1950	"The Genie in the Bottle." In *Mid-Century Poets*. Edited by John Ciardi. New York: Twayne, pp. 1-15; reprinted in *Writing Poetry*. Edited by John Holmes. Boston: Writer, 1960: pp. 120-30.
1950	Briggs-Copeland Assistant Professor of English, Harvard University.
1952-53	Guggenheim Fellowship.
1954-55	Prix de Rome fellowship from the American Academy of Arts and Letters.

1954   Translator. "A Romance" by Jules Renard. In *French Stories and Tales*. Edited by Stanley Geist. New York: Knopf, pp. 263-72.

1954   "The Bottles Become New, Too." *Quarterly Review of Literature* 7:186-92; reprinted in *Quarterly Review of Literature* 19 (1974):138-44; reprinted in *Responses, Prose Pieces: 1953-1976*. New York: Harcourt Brace Jovanovich, 1983, pp. 215-23.

1954   Associate Professor at Wellesley College.

1955   Editor, with Louis Untermeyer and Karl Shapiro. *Modern American and Modern British Poetry*, rev. shorter ed. New York: Harcourt, Brace.

1955   Compiler, with Alexander Calder. *A Bestiary*. New York: Spiral Press for Pantheon Books.

1955   Translator. Introduction. *The Misanthrope* by Molière. New York: Harcourt, Brace. London: Faber & Faber, 1958.

1956   *Things of This World*. New York: Harcourt, Brace.

1956   "Poetry and the Landscape." In *The Landscape in Art and Science*. Edited by Gyorgy Kepes. Chicago: Paul Theobald, pp. 86-90.

1956   Edna St. Vincent Millay Memorial Award.

1957   *Poems 1943-1956*. London: Faber & Faber.

1957   Member of the National Institute of Arts and Letters.

1957   Professor of English at Wesleyan University.

1957   Pulitzer Prize for *Things of This World*.

1957   National Book Award for *Things of This World*.

1957   *Candide: A Comic Operetta*, lyrics by Richard Wilbur, book by Lillian Hellman, and score by Leonard Bernstein. New York: Random House.

1959   *Poems*. Spoken Arts. (Recording).

1959   Editor. Introduction. *Poe, Complete Poems*. New York: Dell.

1960   L.H.D. Lawrence College, Appleton, Wisconsin.

1960-1961   Ford Fellow, Alley Theater, Houston, Texas.

1960   With Louise Bogan and Archibald MacLeish. *Emily Dickinson: Three Views*. Amherst, Mass.: Amherst College Press.

1961   *Advice to a Prophet and Other Poems*. New York: Harcourt, Brace & World.

1961   Chancellor, Academy of American Poets.

1962   "Round about a Poem of Housman's." In *The Moment of Poetry*. Edited by Don Cameron Allen. Baltimore: Johns Hopkins University Press, pp. 73-98; reprinted in *A Celebration of Poets*. Edited by Don Cameron Allen. Baltimore: Johns Hopkins University Press, 1967, pp. 177-202; reprinted in *Responses, Prose Pieces: 1953-1976*. New York and London: Harcourt Brace Jovanovich, 1976, pp. 16-38.

1963   Guggenheim Fellowship.

1963   Translator. Introduction. *Tartuffe* by Molière. New York: Harcourt Brace & World; London: Faber & Faber, 1964.

1963   *Loudmouse*. Illustrated by Don Almquist. New York: Collier-Macmillan; London: Crowell Collier.

1963   *The Poems of Richard Wilbur*. New York: Harcourt Brace & World.

1963   Olin Chair in the English Department at Wesleyan University.

1963   Bollingen Prize for best translation of poetry.

1964   L.H.D. Washington University, St. Louis, Missouri.

1965   "On My Own Work." *Shenandoah* 17:57-67; reprinted in *Poets on Poetry*. Edited by Howard Nemerov. New York: Basic Books, 1966, pp. 196-72; reprinted in *Responses, Prose Pieces: 1953-1976*. New York and London: Harcourt Brace Jovanovich, 1976, pp. 115-126.

1965   Translator. *The Misanthrope and Tartuffe* by Molière. New York: Harcourt, Brace & World.

1966   Editor, with Alfred Harbage. *Poems of Shakespeare*. Revised and reprinted as *The Narrative Poems, and Poems of Doubtful Authenticity*. Baltimore: Penguin, 1974.

1967   D. Litt. Amherst College, Massachusetts.

1968   *Richard Wilbur Reading His Own Poems*. Caedmon.

1968   Sara Josepha Hale Award.

1968   *Complaint*. New York: Phoenix Book Shop.

1969   *Walking to Sleep: New Poems and Translations*. New York: Harcourt, Brace & World; London: Faber & Faber, 1971.

1969   "Poetry and Happiness." *Shenandoah* 20 (Summer):3-23; reprinted as "Poetry and Happiness" in *Responses, Prose Pieces: 1953-1976*. New York and London: Harcourt Brace Jovanovich, 1976, pp. 91-114.

1970   D. Litt. Clark University, Worcester, Massachusetts.

1970   *Digging for China: A Poem*. Garden City, N.Y.: Doubleday.

1971   Brandeis Creative Arts Award.

1971   Prix Henri Desfeuilles.

1971   Bollingen Prize (shared with Mona Van Duyn) for *Walking to Sleep*.

1971   Translator. Introduction. *The School for Wives* by Molière. Harcourt Brace Jovanovich.

1973   Editor. Introduction. *Poe, The Narrative of Arthur Gordon Pym*. Boston: David R. Godine.

1973   *Opposites*. New York: Harcourt Brace Jovanovich.

1973   Shelley Memorial Award (Poetry Society of America).

1973   "Poetry's Debt to Poetry." *Hudson Review* 26 (Summer):273-94; reprinted in *Responses, Prose Pieces: 1953-1976*. New York and London: Harcourt Brace Jovanovich, 1976, pp. 161-84.

1974-76   President, American Academy of Arts and Letters.

1974   Translator. *The Funeral of Bobò* by Joseph Brodsky. Ann Arbor: Ardis.

1974   *Seed Leaves: Homage to R. F.* Boston: David R. Godine.

1975   *Two Riddles from Aldhelm*. Derry, Penn.: Rook Press.

1975   L.H.D. Williams College, Williamstown, Massachusetts.

1976   *The Mind-Reader: New Poems*. New York and London: Harcourt Brace Jovanovich.

1976   *Responses, Prose Pieces: 1953-1976*. New York and London: Harcourt Brace Jovanovich.

1976   L.H.D. University of Rochester.

1977-78   Chancellor, American Academy of Arts and Letters.

1977   Writer in Residence, Smith College.

1977   D. Litt. American International College, Springfield, Massachusetts.

D. Litt. Marquette University, Milwaukee, Wisconsin.

D. Litt. Wesleyan University, Middletown, Connecticut.

1977   Translator. Introduction. *The Learned Ladies* by Molière. New York: Dramatists' Play Service; New York: Harcourt Brace Jovanovich, 1978.

1978   Editor. Introduction. *Selected Poems by Witter Bynner*. New York: Farrar, Straus, & Giroux.

1978   Harriet Monroe Poetry Award.

1981   *Seven Poems*. Omaha: Abattoir Editions, University of Nebraska Press.

1981   *Advice from the Muse*. Old Deerfield, Mass., and Dublin, Ireland: The Deerfield Press and The Gallery Press.

1982   "Poe and the Art of Suggestion." *University of Mississippi Studies in English* 3:1-13.

1982   Translator. Introduction. *Andromache* by Jean Racine. New York: Harcourt Brace Jovanovich.

1982   Translator. Introduction. *The Whale and Other Uncollected Translations*. Brockport, N. Y.: Boa Editions.

1982   Translator. *Four Comedies* by Molière. New York: Harcourt Brace Jovanovich.

1983   *On My Own Work*. Aquila Essay Series, no. 20. Isle of Skye, Scotland: Aquila Publishing Company.

1983   St. Botolph's Foundation Award.

1983   PEN Translation Prize.

1983   Drama Desk Award.

1984   Chevalier, Ordre des Palmes Académiques.

1986   Translator. Introduction. *Phaedra* by Jean Racine. New York: Harcourt Brace Jovanovich.

1986   Honorary Fellow, Modern Language Association.

1986	Foreword. *Strong Measures: Contemporary American Poetry in Traditional Forms*. Edited by Philip Dacey and David Jauss. New York: Harper & Row, pp. xix-xx.
1986	Retired as Writer in Residence, Smith College.
1987-88	Poet Laureate of the United States and Consultant in Poetry to the Library of Congress.
1987	*Lying and Other Poems*. Omaha: The Cummington Press.
1988	*New and Collected Poems*. San Diego, New York, London: Harcourt Brace Jovanovich.
1988	Aiken-Taylor Award.
1988	*Los Angeles Times* Book Prize for *New and Collected Poems*.
1988	Robert C. Bunn Prize (Seattle Public Library Foundation).
1989	Pulitzer Prize for *New and Collected Poems*.
1989	Robert Frost Library Fellow, Amherst College.
1990	*Some Atrocities*. Cleveland: Bits Press.

Introduction

Poetry is a matter of life and death, I think, simply because
there's no more miserable situation than muteness – being unable
to find words for one's sufferings and one's happiness – and so,
being inadequate to one's experience (1975.2).

Richard Wilbur

Wilbur criticism falls naturally into three periods, roughly equivalent to the
poet's creative periods. From 1947, the publication date of *The Beautiful
Changes*, to 1959, Wilbur enjoyed the approbation of many critics, though the
growing rumble of a critical war made itself known in a number of
derogatory reviews. During the 1960s and 1970s, the bardic wars,
characterized by Donald Hall as being between the Academics and the Beats,
played a major role in the reception of Wilbur's work by reviewers and critics
alike (1961.6). Though Hall himself admits that these labels are too simplistic
to suggest the variety of poetic endeavor in both camps, he documents the
intense loyalty poets and critics felt for one tradition over the other. Often
critics openly defended the poetics of one or the other camp under the guise
of writing about Richard Wilbur. Alongside these polemical pieces, however,
a number of valuable and illuminating articles appeared, contributing to a
steady increase in the quantity and quality of Wilbur criticism. To date,
however, only one book-length treatment is in print, Donald Hill's *Richard
Wilbur*, a part of the Twayne series (1967.4). It would appear that Wilbur
criticism is just beginning to come of age.

THE "GOLDEN" PERIOD

(1947-1959)

Richard Wilbur's acceptance as a powerful poet came early, with his first volume of poems, entitled *The Beautiful Changes* (1947). It was soon followed by a second volume, *Ceremony and Other Poems* (1950). The first of his witty translations of Molière's plays, *The Misanthrope*, appeared in 1955; and his most celebrated collection of poems, *Things of This World*, was published shortly thereafter in 1956. Such a dazzling amount of high-quality poems and translations was accompanied by three important essays which show Wilbur working out his own poetics.

"The Genie in the Bottle" is noteworthy in that Wilbur articulates for the first time several important standards for writing poetry.[1] In this essay, he asserts that "during the act of writing, the poem is an effort to express a knowledge imperfectly felt, to articulate relationships not quite seen, to make or discover some pattern in the world. It is a conflict with disorder, not a message from one person to another" (p. 121). He further affirms that he still finds it possible, even necessary, for a poet to "believe your own thought, to believe that what is true for you in your private heart is true for all men" (p. 124). Wilbur objects to the contemporary orthodoxy regarding the "deeply divided man" (pp. 126-27).

Several statements about the wedding of content and form appear in this article and have become staples of Wilbur criticism ever since: "A poem ought not to be fissionable. It ought to be impossible satisfactorily to separate 'ideas' from their poetic 'embodiment'" (p. 128). "I think it a great vice to convey everything by imagery, particularly if the imagery is not interrelated. There ought to be areas of statement. But the statement should not equal and abolish the 'objects in the poem'" (p. 128). "Rhyme, austerely used, may be a stimulus to discovery and a stretcher of the attention" (p. 129). Wilbur defends his use of poetic forms this way:

> The use of strict poetic forms, traditional or invented, is like the use of framing and composition in painting: both serve to limit the work of art, and to declare its artificiality; they say, "This is not the world, but a pattern imposed upon the world or found in it; this is a partial and provisional attempt to establish relations between things" (p. 129).

Over the years, Wilbur has repeated these elements of his poetics again and again; but he first articulated them as a young poet.

"The Bottles Become New, Too" is Wilbur's early assessment of the injustice of William Carlos Williams's criticism of formalism.[2] Wilbur takes issue with Williams because "he lays all the stress on structural reforms and inventions, as if structure were a practically separable thing, instead of talking about the need of a perpetual revolution of the entire sensibility, in the incessant task of achieving relations to the always changing face of reality" (p. 223). He agrees that a poet employing traditional forms must be aware of the danger of merely repeating what has already been said; however, he finds this danger a lesser one than the temptation for poets to create "a personal system of imagery, and then slowly retire within it." He argues that

> it is the province of poems to make some order in the world, but poets can't afford to forget that there is a reality of things which survives all orders great and small. Things *are*. The cow is there. No poetry can have any strength unless it continually bashes itself against the reality of things (p. 217).

Wilbur also objects to living either in the extreme of unknown reality or in "a vacuum-packed consciousness. . . . Neither the mysterious world nor the formative mind can be denied" (pp. 218-19). He then supplies his well-known example of the rain-dancer who can only be described as "trying to establish a *relation* to the rain" (p. 219). Just so, a poet must know that "in each art the difficulty of the form is a substitution for the difficulty of direct apprehension and expression of the object" (p. 220).

The most important statement in this article provides an explanation of Wilbur's poetic practice and helps to set aside the notion suggested by many critics that Wilbur is lazy or careless or inept because he insists on using traditional forms:

> The relation between an artist and reality is always an oblique one, and indeed there is no good art which is not consciously oblique. If you respect the reality of the world, you know that you can approach that reality only by indirect means. . . .
>
> So that paradoxically it is respect for reality which makes a necessity of artifice. Poetry's prime weapon is words, used for the naming, comparison, and contrast of things. Its auxiliary weapons are rhythms, formal patterns, and rhymes. It is by means of all these that poets create difficulties for themselves, which they then try to surmount. I cannot see that any of them needs or ought to be dispensed with (p. 220).

Wilbur concludes by insisting that

> if a poem arises from a dynamic relation with reality, it will be fresh whatever formal difficulties the poet chooses to overcome in the writing of it. . . . When this is so, one cannot say that the poets have surrendered to traditional forms. They have taken them over, rather (p. 223).

A third article written during this period, "Poetry and the Landscape," aids in understanding the role of nature in Wilbur's poems.[3] "The act of naming [objects in nature] is the essential poetic act," Wilbur says (p. 86). However, he senses that poets are no longer certain their naming work means anything, is *re*creative, as it once was:

> The suspicion that the landscape really belongs to the scientist has undermined the poet's confidence in the controlling, expressive and relating power of his nature-language. For most poets today, the idea is precisely a suspicion and no more – an unexamined concession, a habit of feeling, an inheritance from the literature of the later nineteenth century, which was so full of the shock of alienation and disinheritance (p. 87).

Wilbur finds that the "modern poet commonly writes through nature but not about it. He does not draw near the divine through natural analogies, nor pursue the self through the mazes of an oneiric landscape" (p. 88). Though contemporary poets have accepted quite readily "mills, railroads, airfields and bulldozers" as fit subjects for their poems, they need now to "repair [nature's] relations with the world." For Wilbur, "the landscape remains as always mysterious, and open to our intuitions" (p. 89). One of his own intuitions is that

> wherever I look in nature, I perceive fluid or energetic form – in soils and rock-formations seen from a plane, in any climbing vine, in club-moss, in dripping tapwater. . . . What I write, as my words energetically unravel and shape themselves, is a part of the truth of things, and a gesture toward the sources of form and energy (p. 90).

Many Wilbur critics acknowledged that he was, indeed, writing the kind of poetry he espoused, though they gave little evidence of having read his literary theory. The instant approval showered on him with the publication of *The Beautiful Changes* dominated the critical scene through the subsequent publication of *Ceremony* and *Things of This World*, creating what some have characterized as a "golden" period in Wilbur criticism. Critics praised Wilbur for his delightful imagery, his optimistic outlook, wit, and restraint. Pearl Strachan finds that "the imagery constantly refreshes" (1947.5). Wilbur's outlook is unique – light and optimistic, "healthy," according to Thomas Cole (1949.1). Louise Bogan agrees: "Wilbur has none of that monotonous pessimism that afflicts so many of his contemporaries" (1956.3). Wit, suggests Babette Deutsch, is one of Wilbur's outstanding characteristics (1948.2). Richard Eberhart observes that Wilbur is very tuned to "linguistic subtleties" (1948.3). "Word play, paradox, and diction based on Latin roots" merit attention from John Ciardi (1956.6). Both Donald Hall and Babette Deutsch comment on Wilbur's decorum and grace (1955.3, 1956.8).

A number of critics named Wilbur a lyric poet of the highest quality. For instance, Rolfe Humphries describes Wilbur as creating "grave music" in *Ceremony* (1950.2). Speaking of the same collection, Louise Bogan says that Wilbur displays the talent of an "authentic" lyric poet. His ability to "sing" suggests that "Wilbur points toward a time when tenderness will perhaps not be so rare, when a new freshness will restore modern poetry and a new strength sustain it" (1951.2). Equally warm in his praise is John Ciardi who says that Wilbur is "our serenest, urbanest, and most melodic poet" (1956.6). Donald Hall agrees, "On this particular level–the lyric level–no one in the twentieth century can equal Wilbur" (1951.9). Alonzo Gibbs makes note of the ample evidence of Wilbur's "ability to sing" (1957.10) while the Italian critic Alfredo Rizzardi speaks of Wilbur's "exquisite lyrical sweetness" (1959.8). Such strong agreement among early critics indicates that this was an easily recognizable talent.

Critics in this early period also found much to praise in Wilbur's "deft metaphors and masterful use of form" as Pearl Strachan puts it (1947.5). The fact that he was working well within the formalist tradition was a mark in his favor for Anthony Harrigan (1950.1). English critic Roy Fuller remarks that "Wilbur's poetry is usually technically impeccable, relying on a firm iambic line and certain but unmechanical rhymes. Mr Wilbur is excellent at inventing stanza forms, and his stanzas rhyming in pairs are particularly effective" (1957.8). After analyzing the meters of several poets, George Hemphill concludes that Richard Wilbur masterfully writes naturally artful verse that employs stress-verse as well as tight iambics (1957.11). Donald Hall emphatically affirms Wilbur's use of form: "The qualities of elegance, ornament, and artifice are opposite to the qualities which the imagists attempted to hammer into poetry." His comment, in context, is a complement to poetry that is "fully clothed" (1953.3). Clearly, these early critics had little cause to quarrel with Wilbur's choice of formal limitations. In fact, they saw these as enhancements to his thought.

A recurring comment appearing in many reviews and even some of the early criticism draws attention to the fact that Wilbur is both an artist and a thinker (Cahoon 1951.4). David Daiches represents a number of critics when he says that Wilbur "always keeps firm control over the shape of his poems, and it is a shape determined jointly by the ear and the mind, so that the poems absolve themselves to a conclusion both musically and intellectually" (1951.7; 1951.8; 1951.9). In a later review Daiches describes Wilbur's poetry as "imagism plus intellect" (1955.1). Ciardi sees Wilbur's great theme as artifice (1956.6), and Brewster Ghiselin and Joseph Langland note Wilbur's "unity of form and of essential substance" (1957.9; 1957.13). Wilbur is a "baroque rationalist," asserts Laurence D. Lerner (1957.14). James Tobin finds that "technical brilliance, similes and metaphors are handmaiden to the meaning" (1957.18). Donald Hall suggests that Wilbur has shown "steady intellectual growth, and a movement away from the destitution of formalism into the beginnings of something else" (1956.15). His comment is not meant to denigrate Wilbur's formalism but to praise his ability to renew the language while using traditional forms.

Though the dominant tone of most criticism in this period was laudatory, a group of critics had begun to articulate negative criticism which would grow in number and power through the two succeeding decades. Often scoffing at the very attributes others had praised, critics found fault with a relish. Wilbur is writing beyond his range, and his "modishness" is annoying, one critic complains (Francis C. Golffing, 1948.5). Roy Fuller, though largely appreciative of Wilbur's work, finds him at times exceedingly clever (1957.8). Richard Barksdale accuses Wilbur of indulging in "poetic calisthenics" (1958.1), and Horace Gregory damns with faint praise when he notes that Wilbur's poems are charmingly urban, catering to modern American suburban taste (1956.14). These critics see his "sunny landscapes" as childish (Byron Vazakas, 1951.13). John Logan notes the lack of a "night side" (1956.18) while Hyam Plutzik asks in exasperation, "How can he be so damnably good-natured in an abominable world?" (1956.23). Even so comparable a poet as Peter Viereck makes apology for the lack of darkness in Wilbur's poems. He assures the reader that *Ceremony* hints at a storm gathering beneath the surface and that the powerful tension between the "above-ground Apollo" and the "under-ground Dionysus" will save Wilbur from his greatest pitfall–"blandness" (1952.5). These critics appeared unable to believe that a poet could write honestly and affirmatively about the good things of this world, nor could they understand Wilbur's "reality."

Another group of critics, notable for their nasty jibes, found fault with several of Wilbur's characteristic methods. Francis C. Golffing says Wilbur "lacks wit," a remark that seems strangely out of touch with the poetry (1948.5). Bernard Heringman makes no secret of his dislike of Wilbur's heaviness of tone, of sound, of meter, of rhetoric, and even of grammar (1948.6). Most unkind of all are Joseph Bennett's comments that Wilbur's poems show lack of vigor and force, that they are insipid and sloppy. "There is much talent here, much native instinctive grace with language; and much laziness," Bennett asserts. He further suggests that Wilbur should have cut two thirds of *Ceremony*, but that his problem is that he doesn't know when to cut (1951.1). Thomas Cole echoes this harsh judgment (1953.1).

A few critics described Wilbur's choice of traditional stanzas and rhymes as mere emphasis on the mechanics of poetry (Byron Vazakas, 1951.13; Joseph Clancy, 1952.2). Frederick Eckman says Wilbur's poems have elegance without substance (1958.3). Francis Warlow characterizes Wilbur's poetry as having "a composite, temperately elevated style, a backward-looking modernism, that suggests a minor modern classicist at home in a silvery Sabine metier" (1958.9). Charging that Wilbur is attached "more to the forms and ceremonies of the metaphysical tradition than to the metaphysics of the tradition," Reed Whittemore suggests that empty formality is Wilbur's trademark (1951.14). G. S. Fraser speaks of Wilbur's "sheer craftsmanship" as if it were a bad word to be used in connection with a poet (1957.6) while Thomas Cole gets in the most cutting remark, about encouraging Wilbur to "stop writing prayers on pinheads" (1953.1). Here, the polemics are unmistakable.

After the publication of *Ceremony*, Randall Jarrell charged Wilbur with never including real people and real people's voices. Says Jarrell, "a reader after thirty or forty pages . . . would pay dollars for one dramatic monologue, some blessed graceless human voice that has not yet learned to express itself so composedly as poets do" (1951.10). Peter Viereck agrees that Wilbur "has all the qualities of the great artist except vulgarity" (1952.5). More unkindly, G. S. Fraser asks, "Is there a Wilbur 'world'? . . . Or is there only a Wilbur manner?" (1957.7). Most damning of all is Francis C. Golffing and Barbara Gibbs's comment that "the Wilbur type of poem may move us with its genuine pathos . . . but it is neither equipped nor desirous to deal with the human situation in its appalling complexity" (1959.2).

In this period, Frederick Faverty's "'Well-Open Eyes': or, the Poetry of Richard Wilbur" stands out as a sensitive appraisal of Wilbur's achievement (1959.1). Instead of concentrating on the three well-recognized collections of poetry, Faverty begins with an analysis of *A Bestiary* which contains thirty-three different poems about animals. It is his purpose to show the range of Wilbur's interest in animals, from centaurs to contemporary descriptions by Richard Eberhart and Marianne Moore. Faverty notes the allegorical beast fables of the Middle English *Bestiary*, but he suggests that "in definition and range . . . Wilbur's *Bestiary* goes far beyond its medieval original." Wilbur's original poems in *A Bestiary*, Faverty says, become "a medium through which he moves to larger, deeper issues." Faverty sees a second aspect of Wilbur's work in this small collection–the fact that "comic and serious themes" are equally of interest to the poet. Significant to Faverty is Wilbur's affinity with Molière and Voltaire as well as the many painters and paintings which appear in the major poems. He notes, "In the work of these painters it is evident that Wilbur finds principles operative that are of value, also, to him as a poet. There is, for example, the peculiar power the painter Pieter de Hooch has of making 'objects speak'. This power Wilbur also possesses." Faverty recognizes that "in his *Weltanschauung* Wilbur does not belong to the school currently in fashion," but he contends that one does not have to detract from such persuasive writers as Nietzsche or Kafka or Camus to hold a different worldview. Affirmation is also an acceptable and believable position for a poet, according to Faverty (1959.1). His work was an early exception to the rule of superficial treatment accorded Wilbur during this period.

Neither critics who applauded nor critics who deplored Wilbur's work paid attention to his own lucid statements about what he was trying to do. Though a number of critics accused Wilbur of writing poems with no substance, they failed to clarify how this was possible for a poet who thought "a poem ought not to be fissionable." Few bothered to question his statement that "art is a window" creating a dynamic relationship between the reader and the poem's reality. Yet an examination of his poems on this basis would have illumined the very substance that appeared to be lacking. Though many reviewers mentioned Wilbur's need to create order with his poetry, few really discussed the sort of order he was, indeed, creating. Their New Critical habits turned them toward analyzing the structures, the rhythms, the rhymes and meters without seeing the interpenetration of form and substance. Wilbur's assertion that "the relation between an artist and reality is always an oblique one" went largely unnoticed, while his certainty about "naming" as "an essential poetic act" passed over the heads of readers who did not quite understand what he was about, but liked the richness of the images and the descriptive detail. Perhaps it would be fair to say that though Wilbur enjoyed much acclaim during this period, his poems were being talked about but seldom carefully read. It is also clear that though praise appeared to be the dominant theme of critical response, a sufficient number of severely censorious articles provided a loud counterpoint.

By the close of the fifties, the golden period of Wilbur criticism was over. Existentialism was the favored philosophy in Europe. Nietzsche's proclamation that "God is dead" appeared to have become an accepted reality. Because Wilbur's focus was on hope, on celebration, on the metamorphsis of evil into good, he was often considered a bit naive or insincere. Readers found it impossible to forget the horror of the Holocaust, World War II, the atomic and hydrogen bombs, McCarthyism, and the Korean "police action." For many people, belief was no longer possible. "What was real" was being defined as only that which one could perceive through one's senses and emotional life. Personal, even private, responses to the dismaying realities of life were becoming the only fit subjects for poetry for many poets and critics. Several poets were, indeed, in the process of changing the direction of American poetry toward that which was intensely personal, largely written in free verse, and intent on shattering all traditions. Allen Ginsberg's *Howl* (1956), Robert Lowell's *Life Studies* (1959), W. D. Snodgrass's *Heart's Needle* (1959), and Anne Sexton's *To Bedlam and Part Way Back* (1960) confirmed that a new era in American poetry had, indeed, arrived.

BARDIC WARS, CRITICAL CONFUSION, AND EARLY MATURITY

(1960-1969)

Richard Wilbur was still a young man–thirty-five–when *Things of This World* brought him so much recognition. Clearly, he had many years left to develop his gifts. Writing the lyrics for *Candide* (1957) in collaboration with Lillian Hellman and Leonard Bernstein was one method he chose for enlarging his poetic skills. A fourth volume of poems appeared as *Advice to a Prophet and Other Poems* in 1961. Two years later, Wilbur completed a translation of a second Molière play, *Tartuffe* (1963). *Walking to Sleep*, his fifth volume of poems, was published in 1969.

During this same period, Wilbur wrote several pieces of literary criticism, two of which shed even more light on his poetic practice. "On My Own Work" contains important statements regarding the place of the poet in American culture and Wilbur's estimation of his poems.[4] Wilbur rejects the idea that he is creating in the body of his work a system of any kind; rather, he insists that "the unit of my poetry . . . is the single poem." His point is that he is "not a programmatic poet" (p. 118). Wilbur also disagrees with critics who feel that his early and later poems are very much the same. His estimation is that his early poems were an attempt to create order in the chaotic world following World War II, and sometimes he admits they may "at moments have taken refuge from events in language itself–in wordplay, in the coinage of new words, in a certain preciosity." However, he feels his "writing is now plainer and more straightforward than it used to be" (p. 118). Wilbur also notes a second change in his work "from the ironic meditative lyric toward the dramatic poem" (pp. 118-22).

In this article, Wilbur clearly states his position regarding the use of free verse and the "Imagist insistence that ideas be implicit in description, rather than abstractly stated." He objects to these limitations, calling them "reductive." Instead, he chooses to regard himself as "the grateful inheritor of all that my talent can employ. . . . So far as possible, I try to play the whole instrument" (pp. 122-23). Wilbur grants that one of his central themes has to do

> with the proper relation between the tangible world and the intuitions of the spirit. The poems assume that such intuitions are, or may be, true; they incline, however, to favor a spirituality that is not abstracted, not dissociated and world-renouncing. A good part of my work could, I suppose, be understood as a public quarrel with the aesthetics of Edgar Allan Poe (p. 125).

Rejecting completely the notion that poetry creates new systems of thought or new religions, Wilbur asserts that "what poetry does with ideas is to redeem them from abstraction and submerge them in sensibility" (p. 126).

"Round About a Poem of Housman's" is illuminating in its discussion of how to read a poem with "tact."[5] Wilbur insists that though Americans do not possess a literary tradition similar to that of the Japanese who are trained in the strategies of reading a haiku from an early age, they can respond to their poets with "tact." He defines a tactful reader as "one who understands not merely what is said, but also what is meant" (p. 180). His purpose in the essay is to show "how much of the meaning of any poem resides in its sound, its pacing, its diction, its literary references, its convention – in all those things which we must apprehend by tact" (p. 182). The bulk of the essay is taken up with a "tactful" reading of Housman's "Epitaph on an Army of Mercenaries" in which Wilbur demonstrates his method. His aim is to help a reader understand how to arrive "at a sure sense" of the meaning of the poem. He insists that a tactful reader must consider "the convention of the poem; the use of the convention; the sound, pace, and tone of the poem; its consistency with the author's attitudes and techniques in other poems; and the implicit argument of its allusions or echoes" (p. 191). Wilbur concludes the essay by arguing against Karl Shapiro's insistence that poets can no longer use history or myth in their work. Instead, Wilbur holds out for a "tactful" use of references to history, myth, and legend (p. 202).

Critical response to Wilbur's poems during the decade of the 1960s was mixed. On the one hand, it mirrored the continuing bardic wars which had broken out in the 1950s between the two central strands of American poetry. Critics loyal to Pound/Whitman/W. C. Williams's poetics found much to criticize and did so with vigor. To them, Wilbur was an academic poet, lacking all that was necessary to make poetry come alive. At the same time, the 1960s was a transition period for critics who had been steeped in New Critical principles. Fresh critical theories had not developed sufficiently to replace New Criticism completely, yet the best articles on Wilbur's poems show critics deliberately moving away from the often reductive analyses fostered by these older theories and moving toward careful readings employing some of Wilbur's ideas about the unity of form and idea. Their responses show that they were attempting to become "tactful" readers. Though the strident voices of Wilbur's detractors often left the impression that his work was not worth reading, in fact, many critics during this decade found much to praise; their work began to provide the much-needed illumination that had been lacking since the beginning of Wilbur's poetic endeavors. Though these critics appeared to be in the minority, their work provides evidence that Wilbur criticism grew steadily in quality and quantity during this period.

Several critics mentioned characteristics unique to Wilbur. For M. L. Rosenthal, humility best describes Wilbur's attitude toward his work. He finds "virtues of restraint, of yieldingness, of the deliberately unheroic" in the poetry (1962.23). "Wilbur is skillful, reflective, attractive and sweet" Charles Philbrick says (1963.18). Miller Williams suggests that Wilbur is "among our most innocent poets, and so among our most wise" (1969.21). Grace is the strength noted by Glauco Cambon who comments, "This 'graceful error' that changes the former impression of reality that we have received is the best definition of the poetry of Richard Wilbur" (1963.4). Wilbur's lyric, melodic sounds catch several critics' attention. "He writes a lyrical unpretentious verse whose very restraint and simplicity overlay a moving profundity" (Burton A. Robie, 1961.13). James Schevill agrees, "[Wilbur's] poems have a true, lyrical, melodic sound, rare in this age of conversational, hard-bitten tone" (1961.14). Noting his ability to write melodic poetry, Stephen Stepanchev speculates that "it is perhaps [Wilbur's] commitment to the forms, the nets, of tradition that enables him to sing. In this he is unlike many of his contemporaries, who merely talk" (1965.18).

Critics of this decade also enlarged on Wilbur's special talent for writing poetry of celebration and praise (William Meredith, 1962.13; James Dickey, 1962.5; Randall Jarrell, 1963.13; Stephen Stepanchev, 1965.18). Ralph Mills connects this talent to a spiritual dimension in Wilbur's thought: "A poet of endless celebrations, Wilbur is often concerned with the experience of life one must call religious. The natural world . . . becomes sacramental" (1962.14). Raymond Benoit's comments augment Mills's when he suggests that Wilbur is able, through his poetic craft, to change the natural world into a "sacramental reality." What many of his poems do is to "show the eternal through and in the temporal." This is poetry of "the secular as sacred," he concludes (1969.1).

It was John Holmes who described Wilbur as a "craftsman . . . and civilized thinker" (1961.8). Perhaps his comment arose out of a felt need to counter the accusations of other critics who were insisting that Wilbur's poetry was "mere craftsmanship" and empty of substance. Others joined Holmes in establishing the strong link between form and idea, apparent in much of the poetry (Glauco Cambon, 1963.4; P. N. Furbank, 1963.11; Arthur McGuiness, 1967.7). Gerald Reedy examines values inherent in Wilbur's poems, positing that Wilbur calls for

> a union of ideal and real. . . . He chooses as his own the difficult stance of the nuns, a perfect image of the poet, who must maintain his balance in two worlds, one of surrender to unorganized living, sense-experience, and disorder, the other of an ideal search for form, contemplation, and discipline (1969.11).

In his review of *Advice to a Prophet*, Dudley Fitts asserts that this volume contains poems of "elegance – a true elegance resulting from the fusion of form and idea which has nothing in common with the surface elegance of so much of the new formalism" (1961.4). William Dickey says that for Wilbur form is a part of the ceremony, a "means of understanding" (1969.3). Thom Gunn's comment is similar: "[T]here is a group of poems in which the famous skill has become an instrument of deepening precision, or rather an element inseparable from the statement of the poetry" (1962.8). For Henry Taylor, Wilbur's union of form and idea is very apparent: "Some readers have feared that [Wilbur's] well-wrought surfaces contain little more than themselves, and, in the broadest sense, this is true, for his forms and their content are finally inseparable. But his forms are made of words, words whose meanings have been carefully considered; thus the forms themselves become the ideas in Wilbur's poetry" (1969.18). These critics' perceptive understanding of a central element in Wilbur's poems did much to dismiss the charge of "empty craftsmanship."

In 1967 a noticeable shift in the direction of Wilbur criticism began with a strong emphasis on the substance – not the craft – of Wilbur's work. A few earlier critics had done preliminary work in this direction (Burton A. Robie, 1961.13; Stephen Stepanchev, 1965.18; Joseph Sittler, 1966.9), but Arthur McGuiness broke new ground by exploring Wilbur's ideas about the nature of reality. He suggests that Wilbur's view is that "the ordinary man lives an illusion. . . . His mind reads into the real world what it wants to find there: indeed, man's mind may be incapable of grasping what really exists. But there are moments in his experience when man can catch a glimpse of the reality behind the illusion." Such reality contains both dark and bright flashes of insight (1967.7). An article by Robert Sayre addresses Wilbur's unique relationship to nature. Sayre asserts that for knowledge of himself, Wilbur goes to nature, but one cannot make a system out of his ideas: "the distrust of both romanticizing and intellectual systematizing [is] stronger in Wilbur's poems than in the work of most 'beat poets'. . . . Yet the idea that nature draws life into itself, life which can be understood by the poet's discerning eye, . . . sets [Wilbur] apart from most nature poets" (1967.11). George Monteiro, in an attempt to explain an aspect of the poetry that had not been addressed by anyone else, argues that Wilbur's vision is that of the romantics, particularly Emerson and Thoreau and Frost. Monteiro also contends that for Wilbur unity with nature comes about by restoring nature's beauty, a function the poet serves through helping the reader see freshly (1968.16). Hyatt Waggoner picks up on these same ideas when he says, "Wilbur's basic assumptions and attitudes and his recurrent preoccupations have much more in common with those of both the American Transcendental and English Metaphysical poets than they have with the dominant patterns of assumption and attitude in Modernist poetry" (1968.21).

A. K. Weatherhead begins his article with a quotation from Wilbur's "The Genie in the Bottle" which conveys Wilbur's dislike of poetry made up solely of imagery and also confirms that critics had finally begun to read Wilbur's prose. He describes the method Wilbur employs to bring image and idea together and the strong sense of balance within which Wilbur works: balance between the faraway and the near at hand, between the chaotic imperfection of the world and the artistic perfection of poems. According to Weatherhead, "[Wilbur's] strategy is to work with facts and images subjected to interpretation, not presented bold and bald like a broken bottle in Williams." It is this action, the interpretation of the poet, which becomes a centerpiece of Wilbur's poetics (1968.23).

The year 1967 was also notable because of the publication by Twayne of the first book-length treatment of Wilbur's poetry. Reflecting the combative atmosphere surrounding criticism in this decade, Donald Hill carefully refutes the major claims of Wilbur's detractors. He notes Wilbur's apparent ability to live with the tension between the ideal and the real. Hill also analyzes the technical achievements in the first collection and the ensuing changes which occur in the next three volumes of Wilbur poems. Hill analyzes and interprets many poems for the first time. His final chapter examines several of Wilbur's prose pieces, especially those on Edgar Allan Poe and Emily Dickinson, and concludes that Wilbur must be free to find his own subjects and to remain within the "orthodoxy" of formal tradition. Finally, he reprints "Seed Leaves" as an example of Wilbur using the tradition, this time Frost's tradition, but still writing a "marvelously independent poem." Hill says, "the poem is about the necessity of self-definition, of coming to display a 'sure /And special signature,' of 'the doom of taking shape.' It represents the growth of a plant as a struggle between the desire for amorphous expansion and the fundamental 'urge' to become a thing of a certain kind." Such is the portrait of a poet who may not change what he was born to be (1967.4).

The negative voices were, however, remarkably strong; and their censure grew in quantity, if not in quality. Not surprisingly, a number of critics found great lack in Wilbur's work. He lacks intellectual rigor, Alain Bosquet says (1960.2). His poems lack wit and humor and moral certainty, complains Irvin Ehrenpreis (1961.3). Richard Foster finds a notable lack of "relevance" in the work of poets like Wilbur (1960.3). M. L. Rosenthal complains that Wilbur's poems "do not touch the imagination of their generation" (1960.6). R. W. Flint describes Wilbur as "essentially a Broad Church, Wordsworthian poet and Americans in general are not much given to either irony, elegance or pomp as a regular thing" (1962.7).

Another popular theme among Wilbur detractors was his impersonality. Theodore Holmes's strongly worded review of *Advice to a Prophet* suggests that "if Mr. Wilbur would fashion his poems from such stuff of the heart as a lived-in experience, and not simply the virtuosity of an intellectual mastery attained over it, then they would afford the reader a basis for giving a permanent meaning to life" (1962.12). Leslie Fiedler speaks even more bluntly: "[T]here is no personal voice – and there is no sex: the insistent 'I' and the assertion of balls being considered apparently in equally bad taste" (1964.6).

The predominant negative criticism during the 1960s, however, was the accusation that Wilbur wrote poems that were perfect, too perfect (Richard Foster, 1960.3; James Southworth, 1960.8; Barend Toerien, 1962.27; Richard Kell, 1963.14). Thus, many critics agreed with D. J. Enright that poems like "Stop" were "craftmanship at its emptiest" (1963.9). Beautiful but artificial, says Roger Asselineau about Wilbur's poems (1960.1). Randall Jarrell suggests that "[Wilbur's] impersonal, exactly accomplished, faintly sententious skill produces poems that, ordinarily, compose themselves into a little too regular a beauty." (1963.13). Reed Whittemore hears echoes of older poets and sees the poems as "mere exercises" (1962.29). Robert Bly calls Wilbur and others like him "jolly intellectual dandies" (1967.1). Richard Gustafson, more thoughtfully, finds that "in reading [Wilbur] one tends to become too conscious of the style, too enamored of the wit." Nevertheless, he credits Wilbur with giving "a higher tone to the language of the educated man of the world" (1966.3). Charles Gullans allows that Wilbur's achievements are in his impeccable craftsmanship; but to him, Wilbur's poems are "clever to the point of flipness, accomplished in craft, frequently witty, but so mannered as to be annoying" (1966.2). Displaying their assumptions about what poetry should be, Guy Davenport and John Ratti respond angrily to the new poems in *Walking to Sleep*. Davenport asks "When will this cool mastery collide with a theme worthy of it?" (1969.2). Ratti says, "Wilbur is enraging because he seems to wish to say so little with such infinite skill" (1969.10). These critics, though representing a minority view, managed to make themselves sound like a majority because of their bold and often strident remarks.

MATURE CRITICISM

(1970 - 1991)

Critics may have been discouraged by the cultural furor of the 1960s and the equally disturbing battles in literary criticism, but Richard Wilbur continued to write. A third Molière play, *The School for Wives* (1971), was met with delight. By this time, Wilbur's habit of interlacing the writing of original poems with long periods of translation had spilled over into his collections of poems where translations of a wide variety of authors and languages continued to enlarge his word store and broaden his formal range. *The Mind-*

Reader: New Poems (1976), Wilbur's sixth volume, contained strong new poems as well as translations from French and Russian poets. In 1976, Wilbur also collected and reprinted several important pieces of literary criticism and occasional speeches in *Responses, Prose Pieces: 1953-1976*. His fourth Molière translation, *The Learned Ladies*, appeared in 1977. He then turned to the much more difficult task of translating Jean Racine's *Andromache*, completing it in 1982. A second Racine play, *Phaedra*, appeared in 1986. The long-awaited volume of his collected poems finally appeared under the title *New and Collected Poems* (1988).

The tumult of the two decades prior to the 1980s had established a set of standards for poetry that had, in itself, become orthodoxy. Poetry must be personal, must reflect the tensions and frustrations of daily life, must be written in free verse without rhyme, must be highly autobiographical, and must agree with the prevailing worldview of despair and cynicism. Critics who had thoroughly endorsed these standards found Wilbur's poems unreadable, and their criticism reflected their inability to comprehend his meaning. In some cases, critics stopped reading and forgot that Richard Wilbur existed. For those who remembered, he was considered a leftover from the fifties who couldn't or wouldn't change with the times. Even those critics who should have been able to read his work with understanding allowed their own assumptions about poetry and their own anti-religious biases to get in the way of their reading accurately and well.

Another reason for the strongly negative responses of some critics is that they had failed to be, in Wilbur's words, "tactful" readers. That is, they had not discovered "the convention of the poem, the use of the convention; the sound, pace and tone of the poem; its consistency with the author's attitudes and techniques in other poems; and the implicit argument of its allusions or echoes." What Wilbur sets up for readers is the necessity for reading a poem "within" the boundaries established by the poet and the poem. Only after readers have moved through these steps are they prepared to discuss what is good and bad, what works and what doesn't. Some critics failed miserably to respect the poem and resorted, instead, to shouting down the poet.

Good scholarship did continue, however. Several useful aids to scholars appeared. John Field's *Richard Wilbur: A Bibliographical Checklist* became available (1971.6). Marcia Dinneen's annotated bibliography (1980.3) supplemented the *Checklist*, listing many of the valuable critical articles written during the intervening ten years. Richard Calhoun's biographical article in *Dictionary of Literary Biography* (1980.2) was the first attempt to pull together all the fragments available to scholars into an organized body of information. Equally helpful, though very different from Calhoun's more scholarly approach, was D. Van Diema's biographical article in *People Weekly* (1987.13), rich with anecdotes about Wilbur's life and full of details that had never surfaced before, such as the fact that the Wilbur's youngest child had suffered from autism. Bruce Michelson's bibliography and evaluative bibliographic article in *Contemporary Authors Bibliographical Series* (1986.7) was much needed and most helpful, though difficult to find.

The negative voices began to decline during the 1970s, but a significant number of critics continued to repeat their old charges. Robert Boyers was one of the critics who could not get past Wilbur's style. "The voice that pulses ever so lightly in Wilbur's verse," he says, "suggests a refinement of sensibility and a soundness of judgment so satisfying that one is hard-put to discern in it the contours of a man as we have been accustomed to men in our experience." Boyers finds that often "what [Wilbur] says is inscrutable, impervious to real analysis. His advice, his sense of radical possibility, leaves so much to our imagination that we wonder whether we are dealing with a serious man, or one who makes pronouncements from the proverbial top of his head" (1970.4). Calvin Bedient's review of *The Mind-Reader* shocks one with its caustic language:

> Richard Wilbur is a bell too conscious of its clapper, clapper-happy. Pert but proper, always safe rather than sorry, his poetry is completely without risks, a prize pupil's performance. His ideas are always cut exactly to the size of his poems, he is never puzzled. And the ideas are all sentiments; aware of their potential high-minded emotional value and determined to snuggle into it (1976.2).

Clearly, Bedient recognizes Wilbur's skill but is determined to denigrate it.

Another group of critics reiterated the charge that Wilbur's poems are beautiful displays of craftsmanship but that they have no substance, no evidence of the poet's "lived experience." In an extensive article, Kenneth Johnson attempts to show that "Wilbur's basic concerns – not his use of traditional forms or his lack of emotional intensity – are his major weakness." He asserts that, in essence, Wilbur has done exactly what Poe did, escaped to the world of the imagination. Johnson contrasts Keats's firm belief in both the tangible and the ideal world and his certainty that the tangible world contained "messages" for man with Wilbur's apparent inability to see "objects in the tangible world as valid messengers of the ideal world" (1970.11). Herbert Leibowitz's review of *The Mind-Reader* castigates the poet for his willingness to "mediate experience through reason." He characterizes this volume as similar to a visit with a friend "whose talk is genial but familiar – and occasionally dull" (1976.11). Colin Falck, also reviewing *The Mind-Reader*, takes a dim view of the book: "the range of life-experience that can authentically find its way into these poems is rarely more than a narrow, learned and high-art-ridden one. Life's elemental realities are urbanely gestured at while being left to seem quite remote from the literarily-upholstered world of the poetry itself: as indeed they are" (1977-1978.1). Geoffrey Thurley, employing the metaphor of the diaspora to stand for Wilbur's apparent Englishness, uses the minor poem "Stop" to represent Wilbur's entire poetic endeavor, which he characterizes this way:

> Wilbur has remained a poet without a core . . . and seems to represent a specific mid-century quality. Anglophile, academic, but with a metropolitan poise, correct, but with rushes of gaiety and exuberance that tend to come to nothing—Wilbur embodies better than any other of his contemporaries perhaps a style which we might call, simply, Ivy League (1977.18).

Here, it would appear, is a critic reading with little knowledge of the poet or the poems.

The most well-known of Wilbur's negative critics is Charles Altieri who asserts that the middle generation of poets inherited from the New Critics the "idea of pattern," but felt that they could not sustain such a vision and ended up working on "private balancing acts" in their own poetry. He admits that "incarnation provides a doctrinal basis by which an essentially symbolist poetic can assert the value of the mind's orders while insisting that universals are not mere fictions but contain the actual structure and meaning of particular experiences." He acknowledges that "pattern then iluminates [*sic*], but it also leads inexorably to the celebration of contemplative experience ultimately divorced from that flux." His complaint against Richard Wilbur is that "[he] has no metaphysical ground for the dynamic activities of mind exhibited in his poetry, so the poems have difficulty transcending their own elegance and becoming genuine spiritual experiences or witnesses of value." Altieri concludes that what Wilbur fails to do is "follow up the metaphysical implications of the priority he posits for the physical world and of the contradictions between fictive and physical orders with which he plays" (1979.1).

Four years later, James Breslin lodged a similar complaint: Wilbur has accepted the label of "New Formalist," but in doing so, he has "left no ground to stand on." The middle generation of poets, Breslin argues, "tried to counter strength with skill, energy with expertise." He takes issue with Wilbur's theory that "the difficulty of the form is a substitute for the difficulty of direct perception." Breslin says, "It was this conception of poetic form as autonomous, timeless, abstract, and therefore prior to its specific occasion—a form, moreover, that very likely will call attention to itself *as form*—that established authority in the late forties and early fifties." His final word on Wilbur's poetry is that it is "a poetry that seldom challenges its readers—or itself" (1983.3).

Martin Seymour-Smith had nothing quite so philosophical to fling at Wilbur. His reading of the poems, in general, indicates a mind-set determined to see Wilbur as "graceful, learned, civilized – but . . . he cannot be wild. . . . He observes well," Seymour-Smith says, "writes beautifully, translates exquisitely, but it is all just a little too good to be true" (1985.8). William Logan gives away his loyalties in his review of *New and Collected Poems*. Wilbur, he says, insists on writing poetry that indicates he would rather "intimate than be intimate." In comparison to Robert Lowell, he is second best. Logan does find weight in some poems, especially "in the autumnal poems, newly collected here, [in which] sadness and death are the suffusing themes, played against nature and its annual rebirths" (1989.7). Genevieve Stuttaford remarks about Wilbur's new work in *New and Collected Poems*: "the new material is mostly minor, though it confirms him as a versatile craftsman" (1989.24). Surely, by this time, one would think Richard Wilbur would not need confirming as a versatile craftsman. Taken together, only the Altieri and Brustein pieces present a considered and thoughtful approach.

Wilbur criticism also included appreciations that partake of the magic of Wilbur's poems. A number of critics took it on themselves to argue strongly and well against the charges leveled at Wilbur. Still others focused on the new directions they found in Wilbur's later work or on a consistent theme they perceived. Several scholars attempted an exhaustive survey of all Wilbur's collections of poems. The number and excellence of in-depth critical articles grew considerably. And, at long last, three critics chose to comment on Wilbur's translations. By far, the strength and number of critics who found Wilbur worth reading outweighed those who tried to deny him recognition as a major poet.

Three well-known literary figures – Joseph Brodsky, William Heyen, and Howard Nemerov – document this fact. Brodsky declares that Wilbur's

> is a pure, sometimes sardonic voice which speaks as a rule in a regular meter about the drama of human existence, and this narration, conducted according to the rather harsh laws of his *Ars poetica*, acquires an independent value and is transformed into one of those extremely vital "things of the given world."

He finds that "the formal perfection of Wilbur's poems is nothing more than a mask . . . [a mask that is necessary because] it is impossible to speak of life in an open text." The modern art of the mask is the "art of creating a scale against which things can be measured" (1972.4). William Heyen takes on several critics, asserting that "in Wilbur there is a dramatic confrontation between a center that cannot hold and a center that will. His rage, in a world of vertigo, is for the right word." Heyen objects strenuously to critics who would force poets into "programs" and finds that

> there is for me in the poetry of Richard Wilbur something always
> just past the threshold of realization, something elusive,
> something toward which his formal structures edge and with
> which they bump shoulders, something that criticism can only
> hope to graze. This something, I think, is feeling, passion"
> (1973.8).

Howard Nemerov suggests that Wilbur's response to Newton's scientific
theories which made the mind a recording instrument and to Kant's
philosophy which denied access to any "ultimate reality" was to return to myth
and legend in order to "see deeply into . . . truth." He says, "Wilbur's poem
about Merlin is his steadfast and poignant acknowledgment of what magic,
and what poetry, are about. It is part of the pathos, maybe, that this
acknowledgment can be made precisely and only because magic, and poetry,
have gone out of the world" (1975.9).

The number of critics defending Wilbur's practice testifies to the fact
that the battle of the bards had had a lingering impact on the literary world.
William Pritchard takes Calvin Bedient to task for a vicious attack on Wilbur.
Bedient, says Pritchard, "can't see the woods from the trees" (1976.18).
Robert Shaw quarrels with critics who object to Wilbur's continuing
formalism in *The Mind-Reader*, his willingness to remain "obdurately within
the boundaries defined by his earliest successes," and his "seeming" lack of
development. According to Shaw, the use of traditonal forms is "a calculated
means of confronting" the pressures of reality. Wilbur has "deepened," a term
deserving the designation of development. His "intricately patterned poems
reflect the discovery of patterns of natural beauty; and the poet's art thus
strives to be an adequate analogy to the surrounding creation." *The Mind-
Reader* is "a solid addition to his achievement" (1977.16). Charles Woodard
debunks the notion that Wilbur uses his imagination instead of his senses:
"Lowell and his followers, with their categories of 'cooked' and 'raw' poetry,
take it as a priori that the good poet suffers and, further, that good poetry
consists precisely in the reporting of this suffering." Woodard sums up his
argument by saying that "the uneasy ground of Wilbur's poetry is the
irreconcilable oppositions of appearance and knowledge. . . . The perceived
world, with its fine gauzy shimmer of fountains and its colored juggling balls,
is equally a world of the fine shimmer and juggling of mind" (1977.22).

In a lengthy review of *The Mind-Reader*, Frank McConnell corrects the
assumption that Wilbur's poems are full of the "easy assurance . . . and *self-
confident* sanity for which [Wilbur] is sometimes faulted." He cannot find a
single poem to support this assumption: "from toadstools to the end of the
world, his chosen subjects are unsettling and disorderly, those moments when
chaos erupts into the ordinary, and when it is mastered to 'sanity' again
because, frighteningly, it *needs* to be" (1978.11). Roberta Berke's commentary

addresses several familiar accusations. She acknowledges that at times Wilbur's intense concentration on objects leads to a sense that they are "abstract"–"nowhere in particular." However, such is not the case. Against the charge of a lack of passion and disinterest, she offers "The Pardon" and "Advice to a Prophet." As for the impersonality of which he has so often been accused, she explains, "There is a deliberate distance between blunt emotion and the finished poem, but it is the distance of craft, not callousness." Her especially sensitive reading and interpretation of "Junk" and the allusions to Hephaestus and Wayland are a tribute to her ability to read Wilbur with understanding (1981.2). Michael Hulse sees Wilbur's ability to "match subject to language" as one of his finest qualities. He contends that "this interpenetration of language and subject is Wilbur's most characteristic triumph, and his most characteristic failure, conversely, is made inevitable the moment he grabs over-hastily at such an effect, without the patience to set it up as carefully as he does in 'A Fire-Truck.'" As for the lack of response from the reading public, Hulse suggests that the public has rejected Richard Wilbur's work because they prefer confessional poetry; [the reading public] is showing itself to be anti-pluralist" (1981.7).

Brad Leithauser objects to the critics who have too often been willing to "scant the contents for the package or equate a 'conservative' use of old forms with a conservative or narrow outlook." This he finds too narrow an assessment of a "man of large, lively and mettlesome intellect." He lists the characteristic traits of Wilbur's work: "breadth of language," "an elevated grandness of both subject and style," "formal elevated lightness" kept in bounds by "a finely tuned ear and use of the colloquial," and a "sense of proportionality," that is, control of the poem (1982.9).

Peter Jones's comments seem especially pertinent as a corrective to misunderstandings that had become standard ways of thinking about Wilbur poems. He contends that Wilbur's "meditative argument and counter-argument, his attempt to turn raw events into experience, ensure a balance more complete and resonant than the rhetoric of poets more interested in effect and sensation than full apprehension." He also defends Wilbur's use of wit because it "is entirely functional, deepening rather than merely decorating the idea, enhancing and pointing rather than distracting from the meaning." He contradicts a large number of critics with his final statement that "most engaging is Wilbur's communicated sense of wonder and his formal skill. Grace and precision are not academic virtues in his poetry: the academic poet teases out meanings, while Wilbur's task is to discover forms. His is a warm art" (1980.8). Carol Simpson Stern's survey in *Contemporary Poets* contains equally valuable insights. She suggests that Richard Wilbur "continues to strike that difficult balance between solipsism and scientific objectivity upon which his best poetry depends." Moreover, she acknowledges the fact that some critics have chosen to "misunderstand" Wilbur by saying he is "restrained" or "too charitable" when the intent of his poems is to "rightly see the tensions which inform our sense of the world, to set isolated moments in a perspective" (1980.16).

Walter Freed's estimation of Wilbur's work also rejects a number of critical bromides. He finds that "Wilbur's keen interest in the tension between form and thought, between the known and unknown, between inner and outer lives, between reason and imagination mark him as a poet uniquely aware of the human condition." Freed insists that Wilbur's work "focuses on the enlightenment of the human spirit, but never denies the darker impulses or fears which are brought to bear when doubt, resignation, or apathy appear as challenges to the harmony that civilized man strives to achieve" (1982.3). Peter Harris chooses the metaphor of the equilibrist to describe Wilbur's activity as a poet for over four decades. For him, Wilbur's poetry "celebrates the power of metaphorical language to divine the human implications of natural patternment, and it affirms the capacity of strict metrics to contain both the dictates of civility and the promptings of joy." He notes that Wilbur demonstrates his ability as an "equilibrist" in poems that create "a yearning for a formal perfection beyond the depredations of time and an equally strong impulse to harrow the pleasures of the physical world" (1990.4).

Several critics abandoned the fight and chose instead to emphasize new directions they had perceived in their readings of *Walking to Sleep* and *The Mind-Reader*. Paul Cummins hints of new dynamics in the blank verse forms of "The Agent" and "Walking to Sleep," though he spots the "classic Wilbur" in "On the Marginal Way": this poem shows Wilbur "at his best – lyrical, passionate, yet superbly controlled, aware of life's inequities and tragedies, yet able to transcend ugliness and to offer us a celebration of the things of this world and a balanced vision of the range of man's potentialities" (1970.6). Carl Adkins notes the unusually heavy autobiographical content in "Running" and "Complaint" and theorizes that these poems are helping Wilbur come to terms with middle age (1972.2). John Edelman echoes William Heyen in his review of *The Mind-Reader* when he suggests that Wilbur's "range in form is matched by a comparable range in theme and emotion . . . [and] a sharply ironic wit." He concludes, "In Wilbur's work, discipline, agility, range and warmly human sensibilities are known and expected qualities" (1976.6). Clara Park chooses "The Eye" to bolster her contention that in *The Mind-Reader* Wilbur is "a poet of due regard, of the love which enjoins difficult balance between spontaneity and form, passion and precision, our needs and other people's, this world and another." She feels that this "poem . . . turns out to be about how visual and intellectual perception are separate from spiritual perception and moral responsibility, unless we pray for grace to join them" (1976.15). Bruce Michelson notes a new roughness in texture in this collection, more "defiant surfaces," best exemplified by "Children of Darkness." He describes the mind-reader of the title poem as having "the kind of sensibility that Wilbur's almost is—that is, one that hasn't found its way back [from the dark places of nightmare]" (1979.7).

Indicative of the maturation of scholars in their ability and willingness to understand Wilbur's poems was a steady increase in the number of articles that attempted an exhaustive treatment of all of Wilbur's volumes of poetry. Mary Mattfield surveys Wilbur's work from *The Beautiful Changes* through *Walking to Sleep* and draws the conclusion that he has grown in a "steady and quiet deepening and mellowing of vision. . . . Wilbur's latest work . . . continues and intensifies his mature vision while extending his range of subject matter and technique." The limitations she discovers are the "inevitable defects of his qualities: grace may on occasion seem facility, detachment may appear constraint. A scholarly cultivation risks pedantry; delicacy slightness" (1970.13). Stephen Miller also surveys Wilbur's first five volumes but comes to a somewhat different assessment. He feels that "Wilbur is at his ease and at his best when he is praising—in a genial and lyrical way—the beautiful changes of nature, the ceremonies of the mind's intellection, and the light that emanates from things of this world." For Miller, the mind is Wilbur's central subject because it is "always correcting the cave of reality." He does find the last two volumes disappointing (1970.15).

Paul Cummins's monograph was a valuable addition to Wilbur criticism because it brought depth to the discussions surrounding Wilbur's use of traditional forms, opened up the topic of Wilbur's relation to Poe, attempted to understand some of the philosophical underpinnings of Wilbur's poetry, defended poetry of celebration and praise, pointed up two major themes—the necessity for man to "work out his destiny amid imperfection and ambiguity" and the paradoxical idea that loss can be gain—and used "Love Calls Us to the Things of This World" as a metaphor for Wilbur's poetic practice (1971.2). Though Grace Schulman reviewed *The Mind-Reader*, her article incorporated comments on poems from all of Wilbur's collections. She describes Wilbur as a poet who "has conveyed with urgency and power the wonder of ordinary things and of the mind that perceives them." Her estimation of his overriding concern is that of "the creative process that lives in the mind and in the language, waiting to be released. . . ." She applauds Wilbur's attention to detail: "in Wilbur's poetry, the awareness of physical particularities intimates knowledge of a hidden world of absolute clarity: it recalls Baudelaire's work in its accumulation of facts that betray transcendent reality" (1976.22).

Ejner Jensen, commenting on all six volumes of poems, embraces Wilbur's vision: "the one that maintains the paradox [that man is both a rational and intuitive creature] and confronts it with full awareness of its extremes—as the more 'daring.'" He also locates a central theme in Wilbur's work as that of the idea of "stasis of any sort seems a condition out of nature:

the rule of life is movement dictated by the tension of opposites." A second powerful theme is that of a "cherished and tyrannical dilemma, that we must delight in evanescent things even as we recognize their transience." Jensen concludes that "The Mind-Reader," "In Limbo," and "The Writer" all testify to the unalterable fact that "each of us, finally, is alone." This condition is shared by the poet, and "he does this by helping us to see ourselves as we go on our curious, undirected pilgrimage" (1980.7).

In addition to the depreciation and appreciation by critics, found mostly in shorter pieces such as reviews and differing from the articles which attempt a thoroughgoing survey of Wilbur's poems, were a substantial group of critical articles which displayed an understanding of the poems as well as an ability to share that comprehension with a wider audience. Moving beyond the need to find what was good or bad, these critics offered new possibilities for reading and understanding Wilbur's meaning.

One such critic, William Pritchard, suggests that poets write two kinds of poetry—wild and tame. Pritchard defines a wild line of poetry as one which contains a close correlation between the sound and the sense of the word. On the other hand, a tame poem is one which contains no revelation or series of revelations, and a tame poet "takes himself so dead seriously that he cannot, evidently, afford to indulge in any recognizable tone of voice, with the result that . . . nobody is speaking to nobody." Wilbur, Pritchard argues, writes "wild" poems. In a poem containing the "wildness of logic" the utterance is deep and playful and made from "gestures of revelation *and reticence*" (1970.20). Charles Duffy isolates two aesthetic principles he feels Wilbur adheres to faithfully—the use of the "devout intransitive eye" of the poet who chooses to see in order to "guard and gild what's common" and the poet's clear allegiance to the power of the imagination which creates the world (1971.3). Though he does not adequately substantiate his claims, Duffy does help to sensitize readers to the need to understand Wilbur's poetics.

John Farrell makes a major contribution to Wilbur scholarship when he says, "Wilbur's poems envision two kinds of change, disintegrative and metamorphic. . . . Wilbur suggests that a genuine reverence for life can be attained if one has the capacity to see beyond disintegrative change, into the metamorphic and regenerative life of the universe" (1971.4). Such an understanding opens up a great many poems to an accurate reading. Henry Taylor points out what had been overlooked by everyone—the fact that Wilbur employs cinematic techniques such as rapid cutting, montage, fade-out, distortion of technicolor in several poems. Taylor's contention is that if one pays attention to how Wilbur presents his images, one is more able to understand his meaning (1974.12).

Mary Kinzie's review of *The Mind-Reader* is exceptionally thorough. Of the title poem, she says,

> The chief imaginative accomplishment of this poem is the
> rendering of the quirky, subjective mind as a place like the world
> into which things can disappear. The mind can and does literally
> absorb the concrete things with which it has engaged so that keys,
> photos, and ultimately lost eras of the heart reside in a *place* of
> thought.

She observes that "if [Wilbur's] poetry as a whole is flawed, in fact, it is so by
virtue of his measured, often playful refusal of 'majority,' and of his sense
that truths must be perfectly embodied" (1977.9). Michael Cooke's sensitive
reading and review of *The Mind-Reader* contributes yet another dimension to
Wilbur scholarship. He comments that "Wilbur has developed a voice more
truly Germanic than Gallic, that is to say, an unpretentious sacred voice . . . a
voice that addresses itself to and takes effect from the things that have
perennial power in and over us, generously binding us to our humanity." Part
II of "The Eye" is an example of this kind of voice and "In Limbo" is a sort of
counterpart to "The Eye" where the eye is useless and the ear must function
until both eye and ear are able to perceive reality accurately. A third poem,
"The Mind-Reader," centers on the human being who controls the ear and
the eye: "it confronts the problem that the content of actuality as well as the
content of the mind cannot be grasped, or retained, or controlled. All, in a
sense, is lost" (1977.3).

Anthony Hecht also expands the vision of the reader with his apt and
lengthy review of *The Mind-Reader*. A number of virtues "distinguish the
poetry of Richard Wilbur": "a superb ear," "a philosophic bent and a religious
temper," "an unfeigned gusto, a naturally happy and grateful response to the
physical beauty of the world, of women, of works of art, landscapes, weather,
and the perceiving, constructing mind that tries to know them." His central
contention, however, is that "most characteristic of all, his is the most kinetic
poetry I know . . . his poetry is everywhere a vision of *action*, of motion and
performance." Hecht argues that "this poet's recurrent subject is not only the
motion of change and transition but how that motion . . . is the very motion
of the mind itself" and calls this a "double fluency"–that of "style and subject"
(1977.5).

Though other critics had glanced at Wilbur's relation to Poe and Poe's
poetics, Bruce Michelson recognized that "the important and pervasive
presence of Poe in Wilbur's poetry, his impact on Wilbur's symbolism, his
language, and his understanding of imagination" was invaluable to
comprehending Wilbur's poems. Michelson asserts that the vortex is a central
image for Wilbur, as it is for Poe. However, where Poe chooses to enter the
doomed world of the imagination and thus to take the "vertiginous plunge"
[Wilbur's words], Wilbur chooses instead to live on the edges between the
"waking and hypnagogic state." Michelson also points up an important

difference between Poe and Wilbur in their view of the power of the imagination. Poe felt that the imagination *created* reality; Wilbur views the imagination as *re*creative (1978.12).

The major critical work of the 1980s was accomplished by readers whose work testifies to their willingness to read with care and to ponder the significance, the purport, the force, the argument, and the sense of Wilbur's poems. Wendy Salinger's introduction to her collection of reviews and criticism of Wilbur's work makes several valuable points. She distinguishes Wilbur's use of things from William Carlos Williams's in this way: "While Wilbur holds the imagist reverence for things . . . Williams's objects have a bare simplicity to which Wilbur can't confine himself–because his deepest instincts are metaphoric." She finds that "mind" is a problem for Wilbur: "one cannot render *things* totally free from *ideas*. . . . The resolution of these dichotomies has always been an implicit part of Wilbur's vision even as he has struggled with them." Her interpretation of the growing simplicity of tone in Wilbur's later poems is that it is the result of a "reconciliation of the pull of things with their spiritual/intellectual suggestiveness." Salinger defends Wilbur as a poet who has grown by "pursuing the *difficulty* in his work." She further contends that "it is easy to see . . . that the word-and-world correspondence in Wilbur's poetry is a manifestation of the intimate connection he sees between self and world. . . . We see that *he* is not the world, but his medium is the articulation of his relation *to* the world." Salinger concludes that Wilbur "has always been praised for his virtuosity but too often praised and *dismissed* because of it." She assesses his skill with words as the "function of intimacy, not formalism" (1983.18). Frances Bixler agrees with critics who see "high seriousness" in Wilbur's poems and argues that he "has demonstrated his ability to give a theme of consequence faithful articulation"–a standard he himself had raised. She proposes that the "devout intransitive eye" of the poet is what enables objects to "speak." It is the theme of seeing, not just the objects, but the reality beyond the objects which has run like a golden thread throughout Wilbur's canon. She concludes that "Wilbur's stature as a major poet of the twentieth century can no longer be considered doubtful. He is a fine craftsman; and he is a serious thinker, capable of sustaining a powerful theme over more than thirty years of poetic endeavor" (1985.1).

Virginia Levey's article addresses the notion that Wilbur is a Romantic at heart. She disagrees, saying Wilbur differs with the Romantics in that "he acknowledges the imperfection of things, not as a transient state, awaiting some resolution which would bring about a nebulous otherworldly perfection, but as a permanent state of things. . . . Imperfection cannot be avoided without avoiding perfection also and without avoiding an actual life." She also focuses on "the paradigm for this marriage of intuition and sense effected through redeeming love . . . [in] the Incarnation of divine love [abstraction] in the earthly form of Jesus [concretion]." This concept she places as central to Wilbur's poetics (1981.8).

Bruce Michelson contributed a second article defending Wilbur's language:

> I believe that Wilbur's use of language – especially his famous word-play – has everything to do with his urgent reasons for being an artist, that it is as daring an experiment in poetry as we have seen in the past three decades. Wilbur's language . . . is an attempt to use words as magical, incantatory, creative forces. His famous word-play is in fact the very essence of his imaginative transcendence of the world, as well as his reconciliation *with* the world. If we cannot understand this, the paramount seriousness of Wilbur's word-play, we cannot appreciate what Wilbur is doing. . . . Wilbur's word-play . . . expresses his conception of our ontological condition, his role as a careful, insightful nature poet, and his idea of the recreative power of language itself.

Michelson defends his position with powerful examples from the poetry and concludes that "living as we do in a time which confounds crudeness with passion, drabness with authenticity, and coherent, thoughtful art with superficiality, we can easily forget that artifice and intensity can have much to do with one another" (1982.11).

An article by John Reibetanz published the same year explores the course of Wilbur's poetic "evolution by following the progress of his concern with the process of seeing . . . devoting considerable initial attention to his early poems, for by showing so clearly the basic presuppositions of his art, they provide a basis for comprehending more recent work as it develops and modifies these presuppositions." Reibetanz establishes his view of Wilbur's basic beliefs: "that love is more powerful than hatred; that nature is a source of values and of reassurance; and that there is a strong creative urge in both man and nature which constantly seeks and finds expression in images of grace and plenitude." He closes with an interpretation of "The Eye" which he describes as "Wilbur's most explicit framing of the relationship between love and vision that has proved essential to his mature poetic achievement" (1982.12).

Peter Stitt argues that "in order to appreciate Wilbur's poetry fully, the reader must enter *its* world, and this requires more of a willing suspension of disbelief than is the case in reading most contemporary poetry." Further, he emphasizes that Wilbur stands in a class by himself: "the underlying worldview . . . is traditional and religious; admitting the existential primacy of material reality, Wilbur yet believes in a spiritual reality as well, and his goal as a poet – and, one feels, as a man – is to bring these two realms together into a unified whole." Crucial to fully understanding Wilbur's poems, Stitt contends, is the Christian idea that "through Christ, the Christian God gave physical manifestation to pure spirituality, thus uniting the two contrasting realms. And this is the way Richard Wilbur would have the two appear in his poetry, as in the universe he inhabits together, in interaction with one another, neither one alone." Stitt also claims that for Wilbur "sleep is allied with the spiritual realm, or provides a way into it, and waking is allied with the material, the everyday." He asserts that "a careful reading of several poems shows that Wilbur's injection of motion into a scene is his way of imagistically indicating the presence of the spiritual within the material." Finally, Stitt concludes that an understanding of Wilbur's definition of "grace" is central for accurate reading. Wilbur reverses the scripture in "Grace" by saying "flesh made word / Is grace's revenue." Stitt interprets this line to mean that "it is the poet's function, in his attempt to read God's mind, as it were, his attempt to match God's creative intelligence with his own pale version of the same thing, to change that manifest grace back into words" (1985.11).

Anthony Hecht's lengthy review of *New and Collected Poems* suggests that "this new work bears all the hallmarks of excellence that have stamped Wilbur's previous work: a kinetic imagination that is rare among poets, as well as an unusually rich and fertile gift for metaphor." Hecht also addresses the commonplace expressed by George Bernard Shaw that "a painter, a composer, an author, may be as selfish as he likes without reproach from the public if only his art is superb." Instead, Hecht asserts that "the work of art bears some important imprint of the spirit and inmost life of its maker." Hecht ends by saying that "there is nobility in such utterance that is deeply persuasive, and throughout Wilbur's poetry we are accustomed to finding this rare quality, usually joined to wit, good humor, grace, modesty, and a kind of physical zest or athletic dexterity that is, so far as I know, unrivaled" (1988.12).

At long last the critical silence on Wilbur's work as a translator was broken by Stanley Kunitz who discusses the challenges a translator faces in translating word-for-word from Russian into English. He compares his version of the last stanza of Anna Akhmatova's "Lot's Wife" to Wilbur's and notes that Wilbur attempts "something I wouldn't even try to do: he follows the original metrical pattern exactly" (1973.9). The first in-depth look at Wilbur's work as translator was Raymond Oliver's, calling Wilbur a master translator whose "best work is extremely faithful and it is fine poetry in its own right, achieving a kind of absolute in that it probably cannot be surpassed" (1975.10). John Simon addresses the differing methods of translation in "Translation or Adaptation?" Simon insists that Wilbur's "line-for-line verse translation" retains the timelessness of Molière's genius, whereas, Tony Harrison's adaptation allows several "damaging contradictions." He argues that "the trouble with modernization [of diction] is that what looks like an equivalent is nevertheless subtly different, and so manages to distort essential meanings" (1976.23).

Critical evaluations of Wilbur's translations remained very scarce in the 1980s. Rolf Fjelde credited Wilbur with helping to get rid of the old two-step method of translating a play into flat prose and then asking a writer to prepare a stageable script. He judges Wilbur's translation of *The Misanthrope* to be "pivotal in its encouraging example to theatre translators hoping for an authentic classic repertory stage in America" (1984.4). R. S. Gwynn's estimate of Wilbur's translation work is laudatory: "The best translations of poetry should be impersonal only in the sense that the translator's own voice is so effectively submerged in the translation that he writes himself into the persona of a Racine or a Molière and allows the original to speak to us as he might have done. Such is Wilbur's accomplishment" (1984.6). Alan Shaw's review of *Phaedra* notes that Wilbur's translation incorporates three arts: "the art of translation, the art of versification and the art of writing for the stage." He suggests that Wilbur is probably the only poet writing in English who has attempted to be faithful both to form and content of the original and has yet been able to create "speakable translations of verse drama" (1987.11). R. S. Gwynn echoes Shaw's opinion that Wilbur's translation is much more acceptable than Robert Lowell's (1961) because Wilbur's "is more in keeping with the tactful elevations of Racine's language." He concludes that "if ever there has been an ear worthy of Racine's, it is Wilbur's own" (1988.11).

As a new decade begins, evidence of a changing climate for poets becomes ever more insistent. X. J. Kennedy notes in his review of *New and Collected Poems*, that the younger poets have "rediscovered" Wilbur (1988.15). Wilbur scholarship too is changing. No doubt the crabbed, cranky critic who does not possess the emotional or psychological ability to understand Wilbur poetry will continue to harp away, but it is also clear that responsible scholars have begun the enormous task of responding seriously to a poet whose life's work has too often been denigrated or ignored. The University Press of Mississippi has released a reprinting of interviews with Richard Wilbur which represents in its own way a record of his life and thought (1990.2). *Resources for American Literary Study* has published an exhaustive evaluative bibliographic article by Frances Bixler (1991.1) that is complementary to Bruce Michelson's earlier one (1986.7). John Lancaster and Jack W. C. Hagstrom are in the process of completing a descriptive bibliography of the Wilbur canon (1991.2), and Bruce Michelson has completed the first book-length study of Wilbur's poems since 1967 (1991.3). The 1990s promise to be a decade of hard work, discovery, and reward for the readers of Wilbur's poems. In Richard Gustafson's words, Richard Wilbur has not only demonstrated the "courage of the quotidian" but has lived out the "courage of endurance" (1979.5).

NOTES

1. "The Genie in the Bottle," in *Mid-Century Poets*, ed. John Ciardi (New York: Twayne, 1950), pp. 1-15; rpt. in *Writing Poetry*, ed. John Holmes (Boston: Writer, 1960), pp. 120-30.

2. "The Bottles Become New, Too," *Quarterly Review of Literature* 7, no. 1 (1954):186-92; rpt. in *Quarterly Review of Literature* 19 (1974):138-44; rpt. in *Responses, Prose Pieces: 1953-1976* (New York: Harcourt Brace Jovanovich, 1983), pp. 215-23.

3. "Poetry and the Landscape," in *The New Landscape in Art and Science*, ed. Gyorgy Kepes (Chicago: Paul Theobald, 1956), pp. 86-90.

4. "On My Own Work," *Shenandoah* 17 (Autumn 1965):57-67; rpt. as "On My Own Work," in *Poets on Poetry*, ed. Howard Nemerov (New York: Basic Books, 1966), pp. 160-71; rpt. in *Responses, Prose Pieces: 1953-1976* (New York and London: Harcourt Brace Jovanovich, 1976), pp. 115-26.

5. "Round about a Poem of Housman's," in *The Moment of Poetry*, ed. Don Cameron Allen (Baltimore: Johns Hopkins University Press, 1962), pp. 73-98; rpt. in *A Celebration of Poets*, ed. Don Cameron Allen (Baltimore: Johns Hopkins University Press, 1967), pp. 177-202; rpt. in *Responses, Prose Pieces: 1953-1976* (New York and London: Harcourt Brace Jovanovich, 1976), pp. 16-38.

Writings about Richard Wilbur

1 "Meet Dick Wilbur, Times Correspondent!" *Montclair* (N. J.) *Times*, 5 July, pp. 1-2.
   Wilbur relates biographical details of his life. (He was in ninth grade at the time.)

2 "Times Appoints Jamboree Writer: Richard P. Wilbur, Eagle Rock Scout, to Serve as Special Correspondent-Artist." *Montclair* (N. J.) *Times*, 5 July, pp. 1-2.
   Reports on Richard Wilbur's appointment as Special Correspondent to the *Montclair Times* for the Scout Jamboree which he was to attend.

1947

1 BOGAN, LOUISE. "Verse." *New Yorker*, 15 November, pp. 133-34.
   Reviews *The Beautiful Changes*. Suggests that "Wilbur is still quite plainly entangled with the technical equipment of his favorite poetic forerunners, specifically Marianne Moore, Eliot, Rilke, and [Gerard Manley] Hopkins. . . . He has had the wit, however, to point up these influences from time to time with the invisible quotation marks of near-parody." Evaluates Wilbur as one who "surpasses the majority of his contemporaries in range of imaginative reference and depth of feeling." Says "Wilbur is a talent so sure of its bases that using the despised words 'the beautiful,' which he employs not as an adjective but as a noun in his title, does not harm it in the least." Suggests that he

is a young poet worth watching. Reprinted: 1970.3. Reprinted in part: 1983.18.

*2 KENNEDY, LEO. Review of *The Beautiful Changes*. *Chicago Sun Book Week*, 3 December, p. 8A.
   Listed in 1971.6, p. 71.

*3 *Kirkus*, 15 October, p. 594.
   Reviews *The Beautiful Changes*. Listed in 1971.6, p. 72.

4 KNIGHT, DOUGLAS. "New Verse." *Furioso* 3 no.2:61-64.
   Reviews *The Beautiful Changes*. Uses the adjectives "speculative" and "deliberate" to describe Wilbur's poems. Finds that Wilbur "has the power to see something clearly and then to build it into the rhetoric of his poem." "Mined Country" is an example "where the irony of the deceptive pastoral quiet might seem all too easy to exploit, [yet] the poem is able to reveal the nature of growth in human awareness and also the complexities which such a growth puts upon man."

5 STRACHAN, PEARL. "Poet's Eye." *Christian Science Monitor*, 29 November, p. 17.
   Reviews *The Beautiful Changes*. Says Richard Wilbur is a gifted young poet who delights with his deft metaphors and masterful use of form. Finds that "the imagery constantly refreshes with such delights as 'windless summer evenings, swollen to stasis,' a darkness which 'nibbles the last and crusty crumbs of sound,' and the 'small strict shape,' of a ballet dancer by Degas." Cites "First Snow in Alsace," "Objects," and "A Dutch Courtyard" as examples.

1948

1 DAICHES, DAVID. "Right and Wrong Tracks." *Saturday Review of Literature*, 10 January, p. 17.
   Reviews *The Beautiful Changes*. Suggests that though his first volume of poems is uneven, Richard Wilbur displays the right gift for writing poetry. "He has already perfected a less complex kind of poetry than he is apparently capable of: a poem like 'Tywater' is complete and perfect of its kind–more finished but less complex than 'Water Walker,' which is a potentially finer poem." In "Mined Country," for example, he moves into the feeling about the situation, managing to create a "sustained and comprehensive metaphor." Asserts that "this is the real poetic method, and, though there is a certain raggedness in

much of this volume, Mr. Wilbur is on the right track and is working his way towards impressive poetry."

2 DEUTSCH, BABETTE. Review of *The Beautiful Changes*. *Tomorrow* 8, no.2 (October):58-59.
    Reviews *The Beautiful Changes*. Points out that while attentive to senior poets' work, Richard Wilbur has not allowed their influence to overwhelm his own gift. Says "he is extraordinarily clever in the handling of his vocables and plays tricks with rhyme that I believe have appeared previously only in the most sophisticated Russian verse. His delight in language makes for provocative ambiguities, and if he is sometimes witty at the cost of the poem, he is more often finally suggestive." Thinks that his central preoccupation, like Gerard Manley Hopkins's, is with the "objectness" of things, a theme caught in the title poem, "The Beautiful Changes."

3 EBERHART, RICHARD. "Jewels of Rhythm." *New York Times Book Review*, 11 January, p. 4.
    Reviews *The Beautiful Changes*. Contends that Richard Wilbur's work falls halfway between the confessional and the projectionist mode. "What Mr. Wilbur has is a totality of esthetic awareness which uses both means, the impersonal more often than the other, and in a good many poems they are employed together." "June Light" displays his lyric, confessional mode. "Objects" makes clear his "esthetic preoccupations." The influence of Marianne Moore appears in "Cigales," "The Walgh-Vogel," and the second stanza of "Grace." Asserts that Wilbur's "art represents a fairly complex matter expressed in a thought-provoking and charming manner, with an admirable disinterestedness and with a certain wit." Finds Wilbur very tuned to "linguistic subtleties." "Occasionally, like pearls embedded in esthetic oysters, jewels of rhythm and recognition appear" ("Place Pigalle"). The problem he must face is the inability to "achieve unvarying excellence throughout a whole poem and in the sustaining of unified emotion." He pleases most with his "direct lyric feeling."

4 FIEDLER, LESLIE A. "Poetry Chronicle." *Partisan Review* 15, no. 3:381-85.
    Reviews *The Beautiful Changes*. Says Richard Wilbur's best poems are a conflation of his love of language, his delight in the shapes of objects, and the influence of Marianne Moore.

5 GOLFFING, F[RANCIS] C. "A Remarkable New Talent." *Poetry* 71, no. 4 (January):221-23.

1948

Reviews *The Beautiful Changes*. Criticizes Wilbur because he "too often spoils his chances by concessions to modishness . . . and by attempts at genres that are outside his range ("The Regata," "Superiorities"). . . . [Wilbur] apprehends sharply and justly; his metrical structures are often of great beauty; his diction combines cleanness with elegance. But he lacks wit and, when tapping the lighter vein, is capable of jejuneness." Asserts that Wilbur's "true domain is the borderland between natural and moral perception, his special gift for the genteel, non-metaphysical conceit which illuminates the hidden correspondences between natural and moral phenomena." Two of his favorite techniques follow Marianne Moore: the sharp eye for details and the insertion of anecdotes into narrative or meditative elements. Says "Grace" and "The Beautiful Changes" are "as good as any poetry written in English today, save Eliot and [Wallace] Stevens at their best." Reprinted in part: 1983.18.

6 HERINGMAN, BERNARD. "A Talent Definitely Worth Consideration." *Imagi* 4, no. 1 (Spring):13-14.

Reviews *The Beautiful Changes*. Observes that heaviness of tone, of sound, of meter, of rhetoric, and even of grammar spoil Richard Wilbur's first collection of poems. However, these failures must be compared to his successes. "His book introduces a talent definitely worth consideration, not only for its promise but for its accomplishment." "Grace" is a superb example of all that is good about his work, with its echoes of Gerard Manley Hopkins "transmitting the feeling of Hopkins's diction and sensibility, and in using that feeling for his own poetic purposes." Rhythm is often graceful. He demonstrates the ability to write light, moving, and "finely wrought" verse in "Poplar, Sycamore" and "The Beautiful Changes" and he "does this without sacrificing the perceptive intelligence which appears nearly everywhere in his work."

7 NIMS, JOHN FREDERICK. Untitled. *A Critical Supplement to Poetry* (Chicago), February, pp. 1-9.

Analyzes "Ceremony" and "A Simile for Her Smile" for this publication which was intended as a supplement to be used in conjunction with *Poetry* in the university classroom. Says "Ceremony" makes clear Wilbur's idea that "ceremony is a kind of graceful artifice which exists for the sake of concealing something, but which, in concealing it, makes its presence felt all the more strongly." Suggests Sabrina, "as opposed to the girl in the 'striped blouse,' . . . is a patroness more obviously associated with nature . . . so closely identified with nature that in her the nature-man distinction is no longer a clear one." However, "Sabrina's is a rather heavy-lidded vegetative beauty, like that of the goddess in Botticelli's 'Birth of Venus,' who looks half asleep, even less animated than the waves and roses behind her." Notes that the third stanza indicates this "is a boring kind of beauty. The poet prefers the 'wit and wakefulness,' the imagination or 'feigning' of the girl in the striped blouse, for her attitude shows a more real awareness of the relation between man and nature than Sabrina's does." Concludes that "the ceremony or artifice of her dress and attitude do not really cancel the natural and primitive vigor which man shares with nature; indeed, through contrast, they make us even more aware of them."

Praises Wilbur's skillful use of comparison in "A Simile for Her Smile." Says, "It is the freshness and unexpectedness of the contemporary imagery which rescues it from the now stale convention of the extended simile. There is no doubt about the descriptive excellence with which the image-episode is realized; the poet gives us not only the appearance but the very feel of such an incident." Feels that the form, pacing, details, and vocabulary all contribute to the effectiveness of the poem.

8 _____. Untitled. *A Critical Supplement to Poetry* (Chicago), December, pp. 1-10.

Lists ten student interpretations of "Driftwood" as a means of aiding students in developing interpretive skill. Adds Richard Wilbur's own comments on his intended meaning. Says the students were all wrong. Wilbur recalls that this "poem began when a friend tried to argue me into a revolutionary political party on the grounds that there are at present two choices only, Communism or Fascism." "Driftwood" was at first intended to be rebuttal to this argument but gradually took on more universal content.

Quotes Wilbur as identifying the poet in "To an American Poet Just Dead" as Phelps Putnam, "who died just before the Fourth of July weekend . . . and was given precisely three lines in the *Herald*. . . . I hope it is clear that the poem is not a calmly bitter suggestion that poetry throw in the towel, but a rapidly-written overflow of momentary despair and disgust." Says that copies of this poem and "We" "were distributed, anonymously, to two college classes in poetry who were given a period of fifty minutes to write down their reactions." Lists thirteen brief student interpretations and asks the student to "determine their rightness as interpretation and their relevance and correctness as criticism."

9 ROSENTHAL, M. L. "Speak the Whole Mind." *New York Herald Tribune Book Review*, 21 March, p. 8.

Reviews *The Beautiful Changes*. Says that "Richard Wilbur learns from many, but in the manner of the true original who seeks to master all techniques which will help him say just what he wants to on any level. . . . Wilbur is one of those rare poets who not only can think in verse but who are also a pure joy to read." Reprinted in part: 1983.18.

10 SWALLOW, ALAN. "Some Current Poetry." *New Mexico Quarterly* 18 (Winter):455-62.

Reviews *The Beautiful Changes*. Claims that "a poet may borrow, with little adaptation to his own individual insights, a style which is available to him. If the style is good enough and borrowed with enough completeness, the poet is likely to turn up with secondary poems which achieve significant insight, even if the poems be slightly mannered." Asserts that Wilbur does just this – borrows from "modern 'metaphysical' poetry." Sees that "Mr. Wilbur, although he appears more youthful in manner than the other two poets [Reed Whittemore and Howard Moss], is more arresting in his struggle to subdue his witty style when he needs to get down his appropriate insight. His title poem, 'The Beautiful Changes' is excellent evidence: much the quality of a fine poem peculiarly suited to his language, but still marred by some compulsion which he seemed to feel that he make the surface witty, as in 'a chameleon's tuning his skin to it.'"

1949

1 COLE, THOMAS. "Poetry and Painting: The Poetry of Richard Wilbur." *Imagi* 4, no. 3 (Winter):11-12.

Reviews *The Beautiful Changes*. Argues that contrary to many reviewers' assertions, Richard Wilbur is not overly influenced by older American and English poets; rather, "it does mirror the strong influence of such French impressionists as Gauguin (early Bretagne period), Monet, Renoir, and Degas. Also the *sunlight* Flemish painters such as Vermeer, de Hooch, and the more obscure Holderline" ("A Dutch Courtyard," "The Waters," "Museum Piece," "Ceremony"). Other poems that reflect Wilbur's interest in painting are "Five Women Bathing in Moonlight," "Wellfleet: The House," "Conjuration," "June Light," "My Father Paints the Summer," "Sunlight Is Imagination," "Sun and Air," and "The Beautiful Changes." Notes "fine poems on objects treated almost as a painter might treat them, making them central and yet elusive in the picture presented" ("Caserta Garden," "Attention Makes Infinity," "Poplar, Sycamore"). Sees Wilbur as a poet mainly influenced by painting. Clearly, he has developed his view of the world through studying the painter's art. His outlook is unique – light and optimistic, "healthy."

2 EBERHART, RICHARD. "The Muse – With the Yankee Accent." *Saturday Review of Literature*, 19 March, pp. 8-9, 36.

Argues that "the state of American poetry when looked at not of one year, or ten, but from roughly the First World War, justifies the notion that it is a life-giving body of work, informed with variety and depth, and bristling with tricky skills. . . . It is necessary to have a catholic approach to poetry. It is an ancient art always being adapted to new perceptions as these are essential to the lives of new poets, yet there is a central urgency about it which goes back to primitive needs in primitive man." Contends that young American poets, writing in their own idiom, display a great variety of features. Richard Wilbur's "The Death of a Toad" quietly suggests the importance of death. Never moving over into excess of feeling, Wilbur skillfully makes a mature statement about human existence and so represents an important feature of the poetic landscape today.

1950

1 HARRIGAN, ANTHONY. "American Formalists." *South Atlantic Quarterly* 49, no. 4 (October):483-89.

Argues that the reason critics and readers have failed to appreciate the work of the younger poets (those coming to prominence from 1945-50) is that their expectation is for the same "rage for poetic disorder" experienced by the poets who followed the romantic Victorians and Georgians. Such an expectation is not realistic. Trained in the literary theory and criticism of the New Critics, these younger poets have embraced their teachers' orthodoxy. Reminds readers that the formalist tradition demands of its practioners the ability to write in clear, lucid language. Points out that "reared in an atmosphere of critical orthodoxy, it was unlikely that our younger poets would embrace any radical technique, argue that rhyme and meter are archaic, and thereby deny their teachers' lively and learned doctrines. But the younger generation of American poets holds that the literary revolt of the recent past served to clear away the adjectival vagueness and imprecision that the Romantics introduced into our language."

Describes the formalist tradition "as that body of poetry in which emotion is defined with great scruple and care and in which the ideas involved in a poem, though not necessarily 'true' in a strict sense, are presented in a logical manner, precisely as if a poem were a prose work. This requirement of lucid expression renders one kind of obscurity out of order, namely, the obscurity which demands of a reader knowledge of the poet's personal experience or an act of literary charity in overlooking ambiguous syntax. Obscurity grounded in language and learning is permissible. In the formalist tradition is also that body of poetry which draws upon the traditional resources of the written arts: rhyme, meter, and stanzaic pattern. Poets who operate within the formalist tradition regard purely formal elements as necessary means of art rather than as impediments to the full artistic effect. . . . The essence of the formalist tradition is that the maximum of self-expression is achieved by the means of self-restraint."

Finds "a desire for poetic order as the chief characteristic of the work being done by the younger American poets." Among them are Robert Lowell, Peter Viereck, Richard Wilbur, William Jay Smith, and James Merrill. Wilbur is a poet of "sunlight and informed vision. . . . In his poetry are the reasonableness and precision that removes it far from the modernist subject matter of alienation and terror." His is a "healthy" poetry in the tradition of Robert Frost and Marianne Moore.

2 HUMPHRIES, ROLFE. "Verse Chronicle." *Nation*, 9 December, pp. 535-36.

Reviews *Ceremony and Other Poems*. Says that Richard Wilbur creates "grave" music in this new collection. "His poems are full of affirmation, delight in the shapes and colors of the visible world, water and light are favorite symbols." Warns that he may need to be careful of creating the easy, superficial poem.

3 KEITH, JOSEPH J. "'Giacometti' by Richard Wilbur." *Variegation* 5, no.1 (Winter):19.

Comments on "Giacometti." Finds that in "his longish poem written after the poet's visit to the artist's studio, [Wilbur] builds in rare qualities characteristic of modern poetry: masculinity without coarseness and vulgarity, robustness without abstruseness, artistic clarity without a telescoped simplicity. . . . Obviously serious and disciplined, Mr. Wilbur has avoided the temptations of many of his contemporaries, the cerebral poet and poetaster alike."

*4 *Kirkus*, 15 November, p. 690.

Reviews *Ceremony and Other Poems*. Listed in 1971.6, p. 73.

5 SPENDER, STEPHEN. "Rhythms That Ring in American Verse." *New York Times Book Review*, 3 September, p. 3, passim.

Recounts the meeting together at Harvard of a group of modern poets, among them Marianne Moore, John Crowe Ransome, Robert Lowell, Theodore Roethke, and Richard Wilbur to discuss such subjects as "Poetry and the Modern World," "The Poem and the Public," "The Poet and His Problems." This article is Spender's interpretive report. Says that Wilbur is "a poet of natural spontaneity (though disciplined within a perfectionist passion). . . one of those about whom it is difficult to say much, because he simply exists in his poetry."

1951

1 BENNETT, JOSEPH. "Five Books, Four Poets." *Hudson Review* 4, no. 1 (Spring):131-45.
    Reviews *Ceremony and Other Poems*. Claims that "Mr. Wilbur has stature. But he does not have enough ambition." Finds his poems lack "vigor and force." Says "Mr. Wilbur writes too much and he writes too rapidly; one has the feeling that everything he writes 'gets printed'. . . . There is much talent here, much native instinctive grace with language; and much laziness." Criticizes Wilbur because he "allows himself to be precious . . . to be sloppy . . . to be meaningless . . . to be insipid." Asserts further that "he has a 'conversational tone' that is lifeless. . . . His rhetoric is often gassy and 'put-on'. . . . He allows himself to be sentimental, with a stilted, off-key pathos . . . with a mushy, screechy 'moral,' as when he ruins the delicate Persian decoration of 'Marché aux Oiseaux'. . . . If Mr. Wilbur had left out two-thirds of this book and published a pamphlet instead, we would have a work of sustained brilliance, verve, and sophistication." Cites "Grasse: The Olive Trees," "Year's End," and "The Terrace" as "precise and brilliant . . . deft and elegant," as is "The Avowal." Sees "Five Women Bathing" as "an unblemished complex of modulated, serene and subtle observation." Notes that "A Glance from the Bridge," "A Simile for Her Smile," and "The Death of a Toad" are "miraculously phrased and constructed down to the last syllable." Concludes that "Wilbur's is the strongest poetic talent I can see in America below the generation now in their fifties." Reprinted in part: 1983.18.

2 BOGAN, LOUISE. "Verse." *New Yorker*, 9 June, pp. 109-10.
    Reviews *Ceremony and Other Poems*. Says this collection displays the talent of an "authentic" lyric poet. His ability to "sing" suggests "Wilbur points toward a time when tenderness will perhaps not be so rare, when a new freshness will restore modern poetry and a new strength sustain it."

1951

3 *Booklist*, 15 April, p. 291.
Reviews *Ceremony and Other Poems*. Notes the lyric quality of the poems. Richard Wilbur is a poet "who should not be overlooked."

4 CAHOON, HERBERT. *Library Journal*, 1 January, p. 49.
Reviews *Ceremony and Other Poems*. Contends that "Mr. Wilbur has in the past five years established himself as one of the best of a small group of fine American poets. His work is his mind and his heart, both profound, set out in poems of amazing skill and memorable beauty. True combinations of artist and thinker are not commonly met with in contemporary letters."

*5 *Cleveland Open Shelf*, March, p. 5.
Listed in 1971.6, p. 73.

6 COLE, THOMAS. "Poetry and Its Phases." *Voices* no. 145 (May-August):37-41.
Reviews *Ceremony and Other Poems*. Marks Wilbur's poetry as "controlled passion and precision, its complete awareness of being and its intelligent reaction to other states of being." Finds "form and clarity" notable as well as the "easiness and fluidity" of the poems. Says "in his best poems Wilbur is always clear and fresh and immediate, but it is the subtlety of rhythms which beguiles the reader and of which he is likely to be least consciously aware. There is also a subtlety of approach, of seeing, of presenting impressions to us." Several poems represent the best in contemporary poetry: "Castles and Distances," "Driftwood," "Giacometti," and "Ceremony."

7 DAICHES, DAVID. "Uncommon Poetic Gift." *New York Herald Tribune Book Review*, 18 February, p. 4.
Reviews *Ceremony and Other Poems*. Acknowledges that "at his best, [Richard Wilbur] writes with a beautiful gravity that combines a sensuous feeling for landscape and atmosphere with a quiet and even tense speculation that is far removed from the brittle intellectual exercises of so many of his contemporaries" ("Year's End"). Asserts that Wilbur "always keeps firm control over the shape of his poems, and it is a shape determined jointly by the ear and the mind, so that the poems absolve themselves to a conclusion both musically and intellectually." Concludes that "this is not 'metaphysical' poetry, though it is highly charged with ideas. The movement is from object to mood to idea (each suggesting the other) and the effects are achieved by deft modulation rather than by that hit-or-miss sparking of the central core meaning which so many modern poets aim at."

8 DEUTSCH, BABETTE. "Scenes Alive with Light." *New York Times Book Review*, 11 February, p. 12.

Reviews *Ceremony and Other Poems*. Says "some of these poems are pieces of pure gaiety, some present uncrossed felicity. Most of them are about gratifying objects. All of them are charged with responsiveness to the lusters, the tones, of the physical world, and show the poet alert to less apparent matters. The scenes are alive with light, be it the light coined by 'the minting shade of the trees' that shines on clinking glasses and laughing eyes, or one of a wintrier brightness." Suggests that though Wilbur greatly admires Milton and Robert Herrick, "he too can make enchanting music on a small theme, and he handles it with greater subtlety than was possible to the royalist vicar. If he cannot compass the grandeur of the republican poet, his lyrics show a finer moral fiber." Sees "Ceremony" as a deliberate statement of the "poet's preference for form and design, for that which defines the limits of a work of art, declares its artificiality, and invites the ingenuity of the artist." Concludes that "here is a poetry to be read with the eye, the ear, the heart and the mind." Reprinted: 1983.18.

9 HALL, DONALD. "Richard Wilbur and Others." *Harvard Advocate* 134, no. 5 (April):2-4,10-12.

Describes two schools of poets in America – the Wurlitzer Wits and the School of Elegance. Places Karl Shapiro, John Ciardi, Harry Brown, John Frederick Nims, and John Malcom Brinnin as Wurlitzer Wits. Lists William Jay Smith, James Merrill, and Richard Wilbur as belonging to the School of Elegance. Characteristics of this school are an "emphasis on ornamentation and poetical form: sweetness is the end of their poems, artifice the means. They are not satirical like the Wurlitzer Wits, and are more concerned with ideas than with the objects of ordinary life." Sees Wilbur as the best poet in this category. Praises Wilbur for the ability to "start poems with a full idea of the structure – that is to say the meaning." Says he calls Wilbur "the leader of this postulated school because he seems to me to combine intelligence and ornament to the highest degree, and to be second only to Robert Lowell among contemporary young poets. His work is sometimes playful, sometimes didactic, usually intelligent, usually beautiful, always elegant, and nearly always successful. He has the widest range of emotion and subject matter of any of the poets already mentioned, and is closer to the facts of our lives than Merrill or Smith is." Notes the lyrical quality of Wilbur's verse ("Then"). Says that "on this particular level of poetry – the beautiful and unprofound lyric – no one in the twentieth century can equal Wilbur." Notes Wilbur's use of humor, complicated stanza and rhyme patterns, and deliberate reach

1951

for artifice as part of his poetic technique. Concludes that "Wilbur usually finds the object more true when imagined than when perceived" ("Ceremony"). Predicts Wilbur will be remembered as a great writer if he keeps on writing this well.

10 JARRELL, RANDALL. "A View of Three Poets." *Partisan Review* 18, no. 6 (November-December):691-700.

Describes Wilbur's poems as "often gay and often elegiac – almost professionally elegiac, sometimes; funny or witty; individual; beautiful or at least pretty; accomplished in their rhymes and rhythms and language. . . . But generally his language has a slight incongruity or 'offness,' a skillful use of verbs and kinesthetic words, a relishable relishing texture, a sugar-coated-slap-in-the-face rhetoric, that produce a real though rather mild pleasure." Suggests Wilbur "seems to be a naturally lyric or descriptive poet" who writes only about scenes, never includes real people. Exclaims that a reader "after thirty or forty pages . . . would pay dollars for one dramatic monologue, some blessed graceless human voice that has not yet learned to express itself so composedly as poets do." Charges that "The Death of a Toad" turns out to be "only an excuse for some Poetry." Sees "Grasse: The Olive Tree" and "Poplar, Sycamore" as examples containing an "easy and graceful beauty." Claims that "Mr. Wilbur never goes too far, but he never goes far enough. In the most serious sense of the word he is not a very satisfactory poet. And yet he seems the best of the quite young poets writing in this country, poets considerably younger than Lowell and Bishop and Shapiro and Schwartz." His readers would like to encourage him to "take a chance," be willing to move into new territory. Reprinted: 1953.5. Reprinted in part: 1983.18.

11 NIMS, JOHN FREDERICK. "Poet Passes Second-Book Test of Critic." *Chicago Sunday Tribune Magazine of Books*, 11 March, pt. 4, p. 2.

Reviews *Ceremony and Other Poems*. Notes that in *The Beautiful Changes* Wilbur showed remarkable promise: "what was unusual was simply its distinction." Says Wilbur "wrote not amorphously but in the traditional rhythms of English poetry, tho [*sic*] with an unmistakable 20th century accent of his own." Finds that with *Ceremony*, Wilbur has managed to escape the pitfalls of too many poets' second books: "both like and unlike its predecessor, it shows the same distinction of diction and rhythm, but with a development in the direction of the simplicity which comes from superior organization and superior command of the forces of poetry. The least one can say is that Richard Wilbur is among the best poets of his generation."

12 *United States Quarterly Book Review* 7 (March):28.

    Reviews *Ceremony and Other Poems*. Argues that this collection "will establish Mr. Wilbur as one of the surest, and best, and most intellectually rewarding of the younger American poets." Says that "to watch Wilbur at his work of cool observation and annotation – his organizational raid on disorder – is like watching the most miraculously dexterous of anglers; not the least delightful of his assets being the 'textural' fineness of the net, in which, at the final moment, he comes up with his rainbow catch." Describes Wilbur's poetic process: "he phrases as immediately as he sees; he formalizes as swiftly as he phrases; and the result is a complex statement which is as satisfying to the ear as it is to the mind – a rare enough phenomenon in contemporary poetry." Compares Wilbur's poems to "the classic lightness of a young Herrick."

13 VAZAKAS, BYRON. "Eleven Contemporary Poets." *New Mexico Quarterly* 22 (Summer):213-30.

    Reviews *Ceremony and Other Poems*. Feels that Wilbur's second collection of poems makes clear that he has given in to childish games. He refuses to allow anything but "sunny" landscapes. His formal limitations are indeed limitations. Argues that "a disinfected feeling sugars phrases everywhere. . . . And coyness is extended, almost intolerably for our times, into quaint inversions forcing rhymes." Concludes, "One must watch out. Philistia has many disguises. The academic yardstick is one. Overemphasis on the mechanics of a specific form is another. Wilbur is a good student of poetry, but it's time he took it out of the classroom." Infers that Wilbur's stress on order and form has resulted in failure: "What if the genie doesn't come out of the bottle?"

14 WHITTEMORE, REED. "Verse." *Furioso* 6, no.2 (Spring):80-82.

    Reviews *Ceremony and Other Poems*. Contends that Richard Wilbur's second collection makes clear that his central preoccupation is a metaphysical one. Finds metaphysical dilemmas in "La Rose des Vents," "Conjuration," "A World Without Objects Is a Sensible Emptiness," and "Castles and Distances." Suggests that "in these poems Mr. Wilbur is saying that the ideal is to be found in the real, the essence in experience, God in the world; he is proposing an immanent, as opposed to a transcendental, principle of Being." Continues that "it is in this sense that tradition has become a profession that I am suspicious of it; and, suspicious as I am, I perhaps wrongly suspect Mr. Wilbur of being more attached to the forms and ceremonies of the metaphysical tradition than to the metaphysics of the tradition, of

1951

writing a book about Ceremony after all, and of writing it without
regard for the problem of the validity of traditional ceremony in these
here modern times." Partly retracts this criticism because of the many
good qualities of the book. Though these poems might in some places
appear "too neat," appear to be the product of another age and time,
Wilbur could reply that within the framework of the poem, his reality is
"real." Reprinted: 1983.18.

1951-1952

1 WEST, RAY B., Jr. "The Tiger in the Wood: Five Contemporary
Poets." *Western Review* 16 (Autumn):76-84.
Reviews *Ceremony and Other Poems* with Howard Nemerov's
Guide to the Ruins. Stresses that "the manner in which Nemerov and
Wilbur formalize their experience owes less to Pound and Eliot than it
does to the century against which these poets rebelled. Neither is as
willing as [Robert] Lowell to go the whole distance, nor does he strike
an individual note as strong as [Delmore] Schwartz's. There are times,
too, when Richard Wilbur approaches the bitter but thoughtful irony of
Schwartz, as in 'To an American Poet Just Dead.'" Cites "Ceremony" as
a good expression of "what's happening in poetry today." Thinks that
Richard Wilbur's obsession with ceremony and self-definition suggests
an "idealogical" approach to the themes of his poems. He is nearer to
Delmore Schwartz than to Robert Lowell in this respect.

1952

1 BENNETT, JOSEPH. "Poesia americana de la postguerra." *Insula:
Revista Bibliógráfica de Ciencias y Letras* (Madrid) no. 83, Supplement,
15 November, p. 4.
In Spanish. States that Richard Wilbur is the most promising of
the young American poets. Cites the first and last two verses of
"Grasse: The Olive Trees," as a poem of "sustained brilliance and
sophisticated inspiration." Says "Wilbur is a master of the art of
observation with serenity and perspicacity." Describes Wilbur's use of
language as delicate yet as lasting as that of Wallace Stevens.

2 CLANCY, JOSEPH. Review of *Ceremony. Thought* 27, no. 106
(Fall):590-92.
Reviews *Ceremony and Other Poems*. Says Wilbur's complex
forms, thoughtful tone, and "high degree of polish" make him one of

the most gifted of our youngest poets. He must be faulted for his unvarying tone and his too-ready acceptance of limits – limits which hamper his extraordinary talent. Nevertheless, he is not just a promising poet; he has "already arrived."

3 DEUTSCH, BABETTE. *Poetry in Our Time: A Critical Survey of Poetry in the English-speaking World 1900 to 1960.* New York: Henry Holt, pp. 284, 347-48.

Likens Richard Wilbur's poetry to that of Wallace Stevens because it "is charged with responsiveness to the lusters and tones of a physical world most happily furnished, and shows him alert to less perceptible matters." Says his "scenes are alive with light." He has a musical ear, and "more often and more intimately than that of [Wallace] Stevens, [his poetry] speaks of human beings." Sees a comparison between Wilbur's verbal play and that of Gerard Manley Hopkins's. Suggests that "The Beautiful Changes" is "a fresh asseveration of the way that the elder poet [Hopkins] saw the beautiful." Reprinted 1956.9; 1958.2; 1963.8.

4 MANENT, M. "La poesía norteamericana: ultimas tendencias." *Insula: Revista Bibliógráfica de Ciencias y Letras* (Madrid), no. 83, Supplement, 15 November, p. 3.

In Spanish. States that Richard Wilbur has published two books: *The Beautiful Changes* (1947) and *Ceremony* (1951). Situates Wilbur's poetry in line with "the rural themes which have such a brilliant tradition in North America." Compares the music of his verse to that of Gerard Manley Hopkins. Asserts that among the younger generation of North American poets, Wilbur is "perhaps the one who contemplates nature around him with the most fervent and limpid look and who responds to its mystery with less reticence and irony." Quotes several American reviewers.

5 VIERECK, PETER. "Technique and Inspiration: A Year of Poetry." *Atlantic*, January, pp. 81-83.

Contends that "Richard Wilbur . . . is the youngest of America's leading contemporary poets. He is also their outstanding perfectionist. Few surpass him in sensitivity of simile and in delicacy of rhythmic modulation. He has all the qualities of a great artist except vulgarity. By that I mean: he seems often to lack the human-all-too-human quality that gives a poet universal earthy humanity." Suggests that *Ceremony* hints at a storm gathering beneath the surface and that the powerful tension between the "above-ground Apollo" and the "under-

1952

ground Dionysus" will save him from his greatest pitfall–"blandness." Reprinted in part: 1983.18.

1953

1 COLE, THOMAS. "Wilbur's Second Volume." *Poetry* 82, no. 1 (April):37-39.

Reviews *Ceremony and Other Poems*. Says that "reading the majority of Wilbur's poems we find him, on close scrutiny, to be a highly gifted poet who too often repeats his failures in print. While the finest writing in the first book went into the most important poems, it is paradoxical that in *Ceremony* we should find most of his finest writing in the scantiest poems" ("In the Elegy Season," "The Sirens," "Years-End" [*sic*], "Grasse: The Olive Trees," "Clearness"). Charges that Richard Wilbur seems unable to tell what to cut and what to print in his second collection. Too many of the poems seem like "manufactured verse." An example is "Grasse: The Olive Trees." Not so "perfect" but more honest are "Giacometti" and "Castles and Distances." These poems show Wilbur thinking hard and welding his craft to the subject of the poem. They also display a certain philosophical bent: "the factual world we live in is the real thing; lose contact with it and we are lost." Suggests Wilbur should be called a classicist rather than a romantic because of his leaning toward concrete reality. Concludes that we should not ask Wilbur to stop creating perfection in his poems; rather we should ask him to write more serious poems and to stop making "prayers on pinheads."

2 GREGORY, HORACE. "The Postwar Generation in Arts & Letters." 3. Poetry. *Saturday Review*, 14 March, pp. 13-19, 64-65.

Remarks that "Wilbur's book *Ceremony*,...is poetry of understatement and lyrical poise. It has its own quiet felicities and charm; its deepest danger is that too many poems are afflicted by what Pound called 'the magazine touch,' by being the kind of verse that falls too inoffensively into the blank spaces below an article on 'Where is the World Going?' In reading a poet of Wilbur's sensibility, it is well to remember that Rilke's early lyrical poems lacked distinction; nor should Wilbur suffer too much unthinking patronage; at the moment it is enough to say that he stands at measurable distance from his contemporaries; he is not quite like them."

3 HALL, DONALD. "American Poets Since the War: II." *World Review* (London) n.s. 47 (January):48-54.

Says Richard Wilbur belongs to the "School of Elegance." He employs the speech and language of Americans, turning the poem into a "fine artificiality." Cites "Tywater" as one of his best early poems and "Then" as "a softer lyric, of a kind seldom practised well in our century." Says Wilbur's "technique is nearly faultless. . . . The whole speech and written language of America is open to him, and whatever he touches takes on a fine artificiality within the total articulation of the poem." Finds that one of Wilbur's obvious patterns of thinking lies between perceiving and imagining: "Wilbur usually finds the object more true when imagined than when perceived" ("Ceremony"). Mentions "A World Without Objects Is a Sensible Emptiness" as Wilbur's "most ambitious self-examination." Asserts that the "magazine verse by Wilbur since his last book is of consistently high quality" ("Beasts"). Concludes that "the qualities of elegance, ornament, and artifice are opposite to the qualities which the imagists attempted to hammer into poetry. The revolution here – for Elegance is the dominating theme of the younger poets in America – is similar to the revolution in the novel: from James T. Farrell to Truman Capote. . . . In poetry the pendulum has swung from the barren to the fully clothed."

4 ____. "Method in Poetic Composition (with special attention to the techniques of Richard Eberhart and Richard Wilbur)." *Paris Review* no. 3 (Autumn): pp. 113-19.

Observes that the method of composition practiced by Richard Eberhart is that of the *vates*, relying solely on the inspirational period when the poet works feverishly to get down the torrent of words coming to him. By contrast, Richard Wilbur, the craftsman, works slowly and deliberately, writing down only those lines which have already been polished to perfection in his head. Suggests that neither method guarantees quality nor denies it. What is gained through observation of their composing methods is insight into their personalities.

5 JARRELL, RANDALL. "Three Books." In *Poetry and the Age*. New York: Knopf, pp. 227-30.

Reprint of 1951.10.

6 PLATH, SYLVIA. "Poets on Campus." *Mademoiselle*, August, 290-91.

Mentions briefly Wilbur's philosophy regarding teaching writing. Lists most recent publications, the Harriet Monroe Prize, and the Oscar Blumenthal Prize from *Poetry*.

1954

1 CARGILL, OSCAR. "Poetry Since the Deluge." *English Journal* 43, no. 2 (February):57-64.

Suggests that "no one since Landor has written such quiet poetry." Finds that Wilbur's "real forte is to imbue the apposite descriptive phrase or image with expansible meaning." Discourages critics who worry about Wilbur's not realizing his potential: "there seems to be a consistent philosophy behind his writing which will force its way through and impart virility to his verse." Focuses on a small problem – the need to hide the tricks of his trade more carefully. Feels confident that because Wilbur has pledged himself to "wit and wakefulness," he will correct any problems.

2 VIERECK, PETER. "The Last Decade in Poetry: New Dilemmas and New Solutions." In *Literature in the Modern World: Lectures Delivered at George Peabody College for Teachers 1951-1954*. Nashville, Tenn.: Bureau of Publications, George Peabody College for Teachers, pp. 37-63.

Argues that "today the starting-point of free individualism is not at all in politics nor in philosophy but in poetry and art, though eventually its influence should permeate and redeem the rest of society. Hence, America needs the poet." Of the poets now in their thirties and forties, Theodore Roethke and Richard Wilbur are most unique. Says Wilbur is capable of "wonderful smoothness." He is an unusually gifted metrist with an equally large gift for simile. His only fault is his lack of "vulgarity"; that is, he tends to remove himself from the "earthy humanity" needed to save a poet from being too "bland." However, his second collection, *Ceremony*, shows signs of a "subsurface terror," that will be a saving grace. Reprinted in part: 1955.6.

1955

1 DAICHES, DAVID. "The Anglo-American Difference: Two Views." Part II. *Anchor Review* no. 1.: pp. 219-33, passim.

Argues that there is a difference between American and British poetry. Suggests that "America has achieved poetic independence not, as might once have been predicted, through following the Whitman road, but through absorbing in her own way and turning to her own purposes material common to the Western world. There *is* a modern American poetic idiom, and it does not consist of Whitman's epic catalogues or [Carl] Sandburg's hailing of the ordinary citizen." Cites lines from Richard Wilbur's "Statues" as an example. Says that young

American poets have distinguished themselves in writing poetry that is assured, artful, quietly controlled, unpoetic in its refusal to reach for the obviously beautiful phrase; "One might call this style imagism plus intellect: it moves from the fact to metaphysics easily, adroitly, the language always under control, the transitions assured." Richard Wilbur's work exemplifies this kind of poetry that looks at something until "idea is generated out of image." Such poetry is distinctly American. Compares British poet James Kirkup with Wilbur. Says Wilbur's poetry "is more sophisticated, more artful, more anxious to avoid any obvious poeticisms." Contends that poets like Wilbur prefer traditional meters and forms and more often write good poetry than do their British counterparts who, in reaching for the supereffect, often miss. Says "the American poet speaks today from the deepest and most mature layer of American consciousness." Concludes that "the whole anti-romantic trend in modern taste, together with the analytic demands of the 'New Criticism,' has encouraged control, craftsmanship, the clear gaze and the firm line, in recent American poetry, and when this is aerated with wit and spiced with the kind of ironic humor which comes from the poet's conviction that it is fatal to be wholly and naively the hero of one's own poem, the result is a deft and mature poetic utterance. But it is not necessarily great poetry." Sees Wallace Stevens and William Carlos Williams as brilliant American poets. Concludes that "the emphasis on the artifice, on craftsmanship in the handling of the medium, is now the most distinguishing feature of the American poetic scene."

2 GUIDICI, GIOVANNI. "Poesie di Richard Wilbur." *La Fiera Litteraria* (Rome), 4 September, p. 4.

In Italian. Introduces translations into Italian of "Beasts" and "The Terrace." Says Wilbur can be considered one of the most valid voices of American contemporary poetry. Notes that Wilbur is currently in Rome.

3 HALL, DONALD. "The New Poetry: Notes on the Past Fifteen Years in America." In *New World Writing: Seventh Mentor Selection*. New York: New American Library, pp. 231-47.

Suggests that in poetry "American letters has swung from the austerity of the vers librists to the lyrical elegance of Wilbur." Describes the characteristics of these poets as using "tight metrical and intellectual structures. Most of their poems are the development of an idea or a scene constructed to contain an idea; occasionally they will write a perfect simple lyric of the emotions, a kind of verse recently neglected in English" ("Then"). Argues that "critics who are irritated by

1955

[Wilbur's] finesse usually reveal themselves to be the conservatives of experimentalism, or the romantics of imitative fragmentation." Says that "to read Wilbur is to experience a tremendous delight in his precision, his unfailing decorum, his cleverness, and the subtle play of his mind. No one since [Robert] Herrick has written more exactly." Finds that "Wilbur's poems present us with the picture of the poet meditating on a problem; and the finished thought, formed so that it affirms its shape as a necessary part of its meaning, is the finished poem. The finished thought will not pretend to solve all our problems, but it may with both justice and neatness suggest our quandary" ("Tywater"). Cites "The Pardon," "Then," "Ceremony," "In the Elegy Season," "Epistemology," and "A World Without Objects Is a Sensible Emptiness" as examples of the various aspects of Wilbur's talent. Says *The Beautiful Changes* was spectacular in its perfection, but *Ceremony* shows Wilbur's ability to broaden his range of style. Concludes that "wherever he moves from here, Wilbur's survival as a poet of infinite delight is secure."

4 "Richard Wilbur." In *Concise Dictionary of American Literature*. Edited by Robert Fulton Richards. New York: Philosophical Library, p. 245.
   Mentions Wilbur's critical standing, education, literary prizes, and first two books of poems.

5 "Richard Wilbur." In *Twentieth Century Authors, First Supplement*. Edited by Stanley Kunitz. New York: H. W. Wilson, pp. 1079-80.
   In an autobiographical entry, Wilbur writes of his early childhood experiences, including writing poems. He goes on to recount briefly his high school and college years. During his years of service in World War II, he began to write poetry in earnest. He married, completed a degree at Harvard, and began teaching there while completing *The Beautiful Changes* and much of *Ceremony*. He accepts somewhat hesitantly the label of New Formalist.

6 VIERECK, PETER. "The Younger Poets and Conformity." *New Republic*, 21 February, pp. 16-18.
   Reprint of excerpt: 1954.2.

1956

1 ATKINSON, BROOKS. "Musical *Candide*." *New York Times*, 9 December, sec. 2, p. X5.
   Performance review of *Candide* at Martin Beck Theater in New York. Says "Richard Wilbur has written amusing lyrics that never

attempt to be clever but manage nevertheless to convey humor and drollery. . . . Whoever the individual authors may be, the lyrics are pithy and idiomatic, and *Candide* is in general a musical feast."

2 BECKER, WILLIAM. "Some French Plays in Translation." *Hudson Review* 9, no. 2 (Summer):277-88.

Reviews *The Misanthrope*. Declares that Molière's *Misanthrope*, as translated by Richard Wilbur, is surely one of the best in English. Suggests that "both in form and substance, it is a true translation, line by line into rhymed English couplets, capturing with astonishing success the intricate subtleties of tone and manner, the delicate alternations between parody, satire, farce, and high comedy, that make *The Misanthrope* not merely a great play, but a great poem." Wilbur's use of the rhymed couplet, though often troublesome in English, is exactly the right form for this play, though he has been unable to avoid the dominance of rhymes which the English language forces on a poet working in couplets. Admits that this presents a challenge for actors. However, these problems are not unworkable. "Wilbur's version is stage-worthy – and even durable." Actors in the Poets' Theatre in Cambridge presentation wisely avoided "the temptation that would obsess many actors to slur over the rhymes, or throw them away. . . . For it is precisely this strength that Wilbur has achieved so magnificently, thereby enabling a linguistic *tour de force* to be a workable theatre piece as well."

3 BOGAN, LOUISE. "Verse." *New Yorker*, 6 October, pp. 178-81.

Reviews *Things of This World*. Says this volume "makes [Wilbur's] involvement with the actual, as well as the spiritual, quite clear. Things exist for him in full density and circumstance, and he sees, hears, smells, tastes, and touches them with complete freedom. Wilbur has none of that monotonous pessimism that afflicts so many of his contemporaries." Claims that "Wilbur recognizes the terrible shadows in the human situation. But his poetry deals with the mystics' open mystery rather than the positivists' closed fact. His earlier work announced a lyric talent of the first order; in the last few years he has added new dimensions – humor and deep discernment – to his original endowment" ("A Baroque Wall-Fountain in the Villa Sciarra"). Reprinted: 1970.3.

4 *Booklist*, 1 September, p. 16.

Reviews *Things of This World*. Asserts that "these new poems by the author of *Ceremony and Other Poems* will be read and savored by all who follow the trend of contemporary verse. They give further evidence of Wilbur's variety of subject and form, his acute word sense, his motion-picture effects. The translations from French poets too are deft and musical."

5 CHAPMAN, JOHN. "*Candide* an Artistic Triumph; Bernstein's Score Magnificent." *Daily News*, 3 December.
    Performance review of *Candide* at the Martin Beck Theater in New York. Says only that Richard Wilbur has written some of the lyrics. Reprinted in *New York Theatre Critics Reviews 1956*, p. 176.

6 CIARDI, JOHN. "Our Most Melodic Poet." *Saturday Review*, 18 August, pp. 18-19.
    Reviews *Things of This World*. Says *The Beautiful Changes* by Richard Wilbur signaled that here was a unique poet. Always in his poems "things" are "ideas," and "ideas" are "things"–the mark of the true poet. Insists that Wilbur's great theme is artifice; and he continually wrestles with the limits between life and artifice, attempting to find that artifice which includes the most of life ("Year's End").
    Now that he has published *Ceremony and Other Poems*, a bestiary anthology, *The Misanthrope*, and *Things of This World*, Wilbur "emerges as our serenest, urbanest, and most melodic poet." Finds that four elements are nearly always apparent in a Wilbur poem: rhyme that closes a stanza, metaphors full of idea, word play and paradox, and diction based on Latin roots. Concludes that Wilbur's translation of *The Misanthrope* and many poems are extraordinarily good. Mentions *A Bestiary* as "a happy game of hunting out poems and prose passages dealing with animals [which] has caught the flavor, perhaps one should say the 'mystique,' of the medieval bestiary." Reprinted: 1983.18.

7 COLEMAN, ROBERT. "Musical *Candide* Is Distinguished Work." *Daily-Mirror* (New York), 3 December.
    Performance review of *Candide* at the Martin Beck Theater in New York. The lyrics for *Candide* by Richard Wilbur "have bite." Reprinted in *New York Theatre Critics Reviews 1956*, p. 179.

8 DEUTSCH, BABETTE. "The Grace and Wit of a 'Poet's Poet.'" *New York Herald Tribune Book Review*, 8 July, p. 2.
    Reviews *Things of This World*. Asserts that "grace, wit, a delighted and delightful interplay between the real and the imagined that can enlarge both, a brilliance that sharpens the shadows, have always marked Richard Wilbur's performance. They are the life of this volume." Admits that Wilbur's imaginative vision is not quite so all-encompassing as that of Wallace Stevens, "but is constantly active,

whether he is looking at children, turkeys, a fountain, or a railway station." Says that Wilbur's "skillfull interweaving of rhyme, assonance, and consonance, his puns and other poetic ambiguities make him a poet's poet. When his technical skill calls attention to itself, this virtue becomes a vice." Criticizes Wilbur for having "a few too many angels for comfort in so slender a volume, but these also Mr. Wilbur is able to domesticate."

9 ____. *Poetry in Our Time: A Critical Survey of Poetry in the English-speaking World 1900 to 1960.* New York: Columbia University Press, pp. 284, 347-48.
      Reprint of 1952.3. Reprinted 1958.2; 1963.8.

10 DONNELLY, TOM. "Best Musical News of Year Is Found in New *Candide.*" *New York World-Telegram and The Sun,* 3 December.
      Performance review of *Candide* at the Martin Beck Theater in New York. Says Richard Wilbur's "witty and graceful" lyrics are good balance to Bernstein's score. Reprinted in *New York Theatre Critics Reviews 1956,* p. 177.

11 EBERHART, RICHARD. "Strong, Sensitive and Balanced." *New York Times Book Review,* 24 June, p. 5.
      Reviews *Things of This World.* Grants that though Richard Wilbur employs traditional forms, he adds his unique touch. Argues that "one returns to the idea of balance, of orderliness, of excellence, of elegance, of a good centrality, nothing excessive, nothing divisive, which is to say that Wilbur has achieved a natural and full harmony in his poetry." "Event" may "come closest to pure confession of his central problem and realization. The poem is about the nature of the world and the poet's relation to it." Finds fault with some lines in translation. Concludes that "Richard Wilbur's best poems have a lasting look. The final poem ["For the New Railway Station in Rome"] asks 'What is our praise or pride / But to imagine excellence, and try to make it?' Wilbur has imagined excellence, and has created it."

12 ENGLE, PAUL. "Brilliant Pages." *Chicago Sunday Tribune Magazine of Books,* 16 September, p. 4.
      Reviews *Things of This World.* Maintains that "Richard Wilbur is the wisest, wittiest, cleverest, finest of poets establishing their careers in this country. Who should read him? All who value such attributes of our daily lives as our emotions, our language, our ear for sound and our eye for shape and sense happily welded, our feeling for the human scene and the natural landscape, our wonder at where hope comes

from, and our astonishment that one book can order and intensify so many of the qualities that we all partly find.

Indeed, there seems little in verse that Wilbur cannot do, from the gay decoration to the unanticipated weight of hard insight. His work is the sort that adds, in Frost's phrase, delight and wisdom to all who will turn his brilliant pages."

13 FERRY, DAVID R. "Poet on Campus." *Wellesley Alumnae Magazine*, March, pp. 151-52.

Writes about Richard Wilbur as a new faculty member at Wellesley College. Disagrees with the "wild men in the bushes proclaiming through their hair that the act of writing poetry and the acts of teaching, of criticism, of scholarship, are at heart opposed to one another and cannot be joined without mutual damage." Says "the poet who teaches must often be aggravated and annoyed with his lot, but this is because he is like everybody else, busy, harassed, and not over-paid. . . . Poetry is one of the forms of pursuing and capturing knowledge, one of the best, and the academy, in theory anyway, is a place where one can devote oneself to this pursuit and capture." Observes that "when Wellesley College hired the poet and teacher Richard Wilbur, it also got a critic, an anthologist, a short-story writer, and a translator." Explains that Wilbur's poetry "supports and exemplifies [the professional status of poetry]. It supports it explicitly in the subject-matter of poem after poem, and it exemplifies it implicitly in the carefulness and deliberateness, the knowledgeability, of their construction. [Wilbur] is almost always concerned with what we can know, and with the limits of that knowledge."

14 GREGORY, HORACE. "The Poetry of Suburbia." *Partisan Review* 23, no. 4 (Fall):547-53.

Reviews *Things of This World*. Sees the influence of suburbia on the academic world and on "verse written in this atmosphere." Says that Wilbur's *Things of This World* "should utterly charm the *Zeitgeist*. It is undoubtedly the best of [his] three books, and if his early reviewers have placed him among the better poets of his immediate generation, they have not been wrong." Suggests that "what Wilbur contributes to the verse of the *Zeitgeist* is an absolutely engaging personality with 'the desire to please' between the lines of every stanza. This is 'the something new' that he has offered to the *Zeitgeist*." Claims that a second reading calls up comparisons of several of Wilbur's poems with more famous writers, making one a bit uncomfortable. Nevertheless, his "charm should not be underrated."

15 HALL, DONALD. "Claims on the Poet." *Poetry* 88, no. 6 (September):398-403.

Surveys *The Beautiful Changes* and *Ceremony and Other Poems*. Reviews *Things of This World* and *The Misanthrope*. Judges that "Wilbur's delicacy of feeling, his poetical tact, is never more apparent than in his translations." Sees *The Misanthrope* as his "chef d'oeuvre." Says that though *Things* is a small book, it shows Wilbur working in a new way and "the best poems Wilbur has yet written are in this volume." Lists categories of Wilbur poems: those that "are responses to events," those that are "carefully constructed to contain and exemplify ideas," those that are a "simple lyric of direct emotional statement," and "the descriptive meditation on events." Says that "the made, considered, argued poem remains the center of [Wilbur's] work, and his best poems are these."

Claims that "until *Things of This World*, one set of ideas has dominated. It has been . . . an epistemology which approaches aesthetic nihilism. Objects, in *The Beautiful Changes* and *Ceremony*, are truer when imagined than when sensed." Sees "Epistemology" as "a highly successful self-critique." Suggests that "Wilbur has been negating as well as professing his interior gorgeosity and exterior asceticism, but the negations of *Ceremony* make no solution to the problem, only satirizing the contrary belief." Contends that Wilbur has allowed himself to be a user of language, but the delight is in the play of language – not in the idea. With this new book, Wilbur has attempted to rid himself of the cleverness of his verse. "The best poems . . . are not looking at themselves, but are looking at their subject matter." Wilbur, instead of employing his imagination to create a world without things as he has done in his first two books, celebrates the sensual pleasure of things, employing his imagination to make them even more enjoyable: "One feels, in this later book, Wilbur now subscribes to a hierarchy by which the dexterity of the juggler would be accounted less than the excellence of the architect. By extension, the intelligent poem is better than the brilliant one." Sees "A Voice from under the Table" as the best poem Wilbur has written. Argues that "it is pursuit of human satisfaction which is consistently Wilbur's subject" ("Love Calls Us to the Things of This World," "A Baroque Wall-Fountain in the Villa Sciarra"). Concludes "there has been a steady intellectual growth, and a movement away from the destitution of formalism into the beginnings of something else; from a self-delighting loveliness . . . not to any 'affirmation' as *Life* editors would have it, but toward the discovery of some 'things of this world.'" Reprinted: 1983.18.

1956

16 HECHT, ANTHONY. "Poetry Chronicle." *Hudson Review* 9, no. 3 (Autumn):444-57.

Reviews *Things of This World*. Notes that a constant theme in this volume is the "search for reality." Epiphanies occur, but they are extremely ephemeral and fragile. Affirms that "in truth, every poem in the book bears on this central subject, and it is Wilbur's virtue as a poet that, while he is able to take different positions in different poems, within any given poem he has a clear sense of the level of reality he is dealing with."

17 HOBSON, LAURA Z. "Trade Winds." *Saturday Review*, 8 September, pp. 10, 12.

Describes preparations for *Candide* and mentions several biographical facts about Richard Wilbur and the musical.

18 LOGAN, JOHN. "To the Silly Eye." *Commonweal*, 10 August, p. 474.

Reviews *Things of This World*. Grants that this volume "will certainly advance [Wilbur's] reputation, for it contains ten or a dozen fine poems." Confesses a lack of enthusiasm for it, however: "what I mean is this: few of the poems speak for me as the saint speaks for the sinner and the major poet for the needy fool." Suggests that "there is a night side of a man which civilization cows but which is itself indispensable to the progress and building of civilizations and to all the other arts of man as well." Sees little evidence of this "night side" in these new poems. Expresses surprise at Wilbur's use of images such as laundry and washwater. Admits that he finds Wilbur "at his best in poems where he employs stanzaic forms of widely varied line lengths, a practice he follows more generously in this book: the advantage of this is that it heightens the rhythm and action, through allowing more opportunity for enjambment, and breaks up the monotony of his deca-syllabic lines." Concludes that "these precious stanzas are a happy product of Wilbur's 'genie in the bottle' theory of poetry. But once in a while one wishes for more evidence of the alternate theory, 'the bottle in the genius.'"

19 McCLAIN, JOHN. "Fine, Bright – But Operetta Lacks Spark." *Journal-American* (New York), 3 December.

Performance review of *Candide* at the Martin Beck Theater in New York. Says "it is a thoughtful production and Miss Hellman's book is bright; so is the Bernstein music, and the lyrics by Wilbur." Reprinted in *New York Theatre Critics Reviews 1956*, p. 178.

20 McDONALD, G. D. *Library Journal*, 1 October, p. 2262.

Reviews *Things of This World*. Notes that "Richard Wilbur was awarded the Prix de Rome Fellowship in 1954, and some of the poems in this volume reflect Italian experiences. There are others that are translations from the French, and new original poems of superior quality. In conjunction with his earlier books, *The Beautiful Changes* and *Ceremony and Other Poems,* the evidence is now sufficient to place him among the major poets of our time."

*21 NORDELL, ROD. *Christian Science Monitor*, 28 June, p. 11.
Reviews *Things of This World*. Listed in 1971.6, p. 76.

22 PARK, BRUCE R. "Some Versions of Drama." *Accent* 16 (Winter):67-70.
Reviews *The Misanthrope*. Suggests that in this translation Wilbur manages very well to control the tension between "slang and archaism." Marvels that he has written a stageable play as well as very good poetry. Concludes that "Mr. Wilbur's *Misanthrope* upholds his reputation for work of edge and finish. . . . Comparisons between his *Misanthrope* and the 'standard' English versions – those in the Everyman Molière, for instance – are consistently odious. There is no *Misanthrope* to match this."

23 PLUTZIK, HYAM. "Recent Poetry." *Yale Review* n.s. 46, no. 2 (Winter):295-96.
Reviews *Things of This World*. Notes that Wilbur "walks among the devils that his fellow poets keep pointing out to him, but he doesn't see them. Instead, he persists in seeing angels" ("Love Calls Us to the Things of This World"). Finds that "it is astonishing how rarely Wilbur writes in the bleak, bitter or inconsolable mood. His visions of evil are muted, temporary, tentative" ("John Chrysostom," "After the Last Bulletins"). Feels that "a world so accustomed to the violent and the evil has trouble adjusting itself to Wilbur's consistent upbeat note." Asks "but what about his angels? How does he come by them? Those who stretch forth their hands like Tantalus might well ask upon what nectar he nourishes himself. What charm or exorcism does he use? How can he be so damnably good-natured in an abominable world?" Reprinted: 1983.18.

24 ROSENTHAL, M. L. "Tradition and Transition." *Nation*, 3 November, pp. 372-74.
Reviews *Things of This World*. Determines that contemporary poets are all trying to reach back behind the poets of sixty or seventy years ago in order to come to terms with themselves. Richard Wilbur is

one of these poets. His *Things of This World* makes clear that he is subject to a loss of spirit, "beset by a sort of ennui." His problem is that the older poets have said it better before him. The cure for this is to translate, which he does with some success. Says that "of the successful poems here that are *not* translations, the best are those most closely approaching the dream-atmosphere of the French Symbolist tradition" ("Merlin Enthralled," "Marginalia"). Reprinted in part: 1983.18.

25 WATTS, RICHARD, Jr. "Voltaire's *Candide* As an Operetta." *New York Post*, 3 December.

Performance review of *Candide* at the Martin Beck Theater in New York. Notes Richard Wilbur as a lyricist for *Candide* adds some "bite and pungency." Reprinted in *New York Theatre Critics Reviews 1965*, p. 393.

1956-1957

1 ASHMAN, RICHARD. Review of *Things of This World*. *Talisman* 10 (Winter/Spring):61-69.

Reviews *Things of This World*. Notes Wilbur's concern, in many of the poems, "is with the hiatus between things as they are imagined and as they are experienced; and in his lexicon things include not only the tangible, the physical, but the immaterial, the emotions, as well. He is so successful in leading the reader into his world that the reader can almost persuade himself that he shares the poet's imagination and sensitivity. Thus, the poems serve the most important single function of poetry. Once one has seen through another's eyes, understood with another's mind, he is changed, however imperceptibly. The effect of such poetry, therefore, is to civilize." Cites "Beasts" as evidence that Wilbur is concerned with people's ambivalence toward their human predicament. Points out that Wilbur has "a definite, inborn, advantage. This is his remarkable visual imagination" ("The Beacon"). Contends that "A Voice from Under the Table" "presents [Wilbur's] feeling of the transcendence of imaginative anticipation over experience." Judges this volume "to be an advance over most of his earlier work."

1957

1 ABBE, GEORGE. *You and Contemporary Poetry: An Aid to Appreciation*. North Guilford, Conn.: Author Audience Publications, pp. 24-25, 72-80.

Reprints "A Simile for Her Smile." Explicates "The Death of a Toad." Says Wilbur's "The Death of a Toad" is a fine example of his use of indirection to explore an idea. "All life is related and we, both the humans and the toad, die and revert back to a unity." Asks, "What does this poem have to do with religion or the cosmic? . . . And beyond this, what does the death of the toad mean?" Suggests that it reminds us that "we are all part of beginnings, a binding love . . . that goes much further back than this world . . . and that is our unifying, cosmic heritage." Feels that "in 'The Death of a Toad' we find the modern religious poem in which the private psyche lends its gifts to social vision, one that integrates man at a subconscious level with his inherent and noble ends and with meanings beyond time." Says "Richard Wilbur shows us that compassion is the *sine qua non* of a sensitive human being. . . . It is this peculiar spirit – the will to translate pity or compassion into an act – breaking through all form and technique, that persists as a cardinal criterion of the best verse, past or present." Reprinted 1965.1.

2 BOGARDUS, EDGAR. "The Flights of Love." *Kenyon Review* 19, no. 1 (Winter):137-44.

Reviews *Things of This World*. Sees "A Voice from under the Table" as a "rich poem, in which both the charms and dangers of the 'things of this world' are spelled out in terms of the character of the speaker, and the ending is an implicit hymn to the divine in the world that triumphs over the attempt of man to master it." Suggests that a "north pole" and "south pole" "define the drama of the book." One represents the sought-after reality of spirit, the other the richness of experience. The split between the poles is announced by the first poem, "Altitudes." In the title poem, the poet clearly sets forth the relationship between both poles – both the "angelic lightness" and the "heaviness of the world" are a part of human experience. Argues that though some poems are not as good as others, criticism of Wilbur that faults him for making much of an old building ("For the New Railway Station in Rome") arises from a misreading. Wilbur's interest is in praising those who attempt to "imagine excellence and try to make it." Concludes that "Mr. Wilbur is growing . . . . In this book we have hints of a Wilbur who wants to build, extend his range, and approach the grand manner."

3 COFFMAN, STANLEY, Jr. "American Poetry – 1927-1952." *Books Abroad* [changed to *World Literature Today*], Winter: pp. 5-14, passim.

Surveys poetic theories since the beginning of the century. Determines that "there are . . . two sides to the preoccupation with form: one – apparent and laudable from Imagism to John Ciardi's *Mid-Century American Poets* – an effort to improve the technique of poetry and a reaction against the sloppiness and looseness of much nineteenth century verse; the other – certainly less laudable and ultimately destructive – an effort to define for art a ground that would be unique, but doing so at the expense of the imagination." Surmises that "the age of criticism" has been a natural outgrowth of the latter preoccupation. Says John Crowe Ransom's theory of "poetry as knowledge . . . is probably the most thorough and convincing statement of the modernist position. . . . This poetic knowledge 'transcends' our ordinary practical and scientific knowledge only in that it apprehends the object in a different way and gives us a fuller, more complex perception of it." Says for Ransom, "the transformation of metamorphosis occurs not only through metaphor and analogy, but especially through adapting the language of the poem to the demands of meter and rhythm" – the "texture" of the poem. Traces the "ascendancy of this version of poetry [formalist poetry] as limited, as formal, as complex presentation of subjective states (demanding the short poem) – and as written by poets who in the form of their work tend to seek refuge against a world they cannot accept." Lists Hart Crane, Marianne Moore, William Carlos Williams, and e. e. cummings as a second group of poets who "are experimentalist, but they have not used the 'aesthetic' attitude as a basis for judging and rejecting the present for their attitudes are not restricted by a thorough going [sic] formalism or ritualism. They show the same disillusioned hatred of abstractions that we find in Hemingway but also the same attempt to front experience and from it to derive certain basic values."

Suggests that "the Thirties and early Forties in American poetry can be seen at once as a period of impressive technical achievement with a range of material that is seriously limited; as a time when formalist, basically experimentalist attitudes toward verse were still fruitful but beginning to lose their vitality." Marks World War II as having the effect of "drawing attention to the growing danger of formalism and isolation." Says that "Richard Wilbur is 'for wit and wakefulness' and there is little despair in his poetry; but for all its dexterity and promise . . . there is too much assent to what has gone before to provide the basis for a change."

4 DRAKE, LEAH B. "New Voices in Poetry." *Atlantic*, June, pp. 77-78.
    Reviews *Things of This World*. Says "Mr. Wilbur used to be a kind of backward-looking, forward-aspiring fellow. . . . But all is changed now. In his newest work he stands squarely in the midst of the things of this world and likes all of what he sees, smells, hears, touches, and tastes." Suggests that "now that Wallace Stevens is dead, Wilbur seems headed toward being the dandy of American verse."

5 EBERHART, RICHARD. "On Richard Wilbur's 'Love Calls Us to the Things of This World.'" *Berkeley Review* 1, no. 3:34-36.

Part of a symposium in print on Wilbur's "Love Calls Us. . . ." Says one should read Wilbur's poem enjoying the playfulness of it, even while it announces the victory of the "soul-state" over the "earth-state." Sees the poem "not a willful nor a dynamic one. It is static and a psyche poem. It makes nothing happen. . . . The soul must be put on the things of this world. The world cannot live by world alone but must hark back to the soul." Suggests that "fully awake man must accept full responsibility, . . . but it seems crucial with Wilbur that the sure-to-come knowledge does not overwhelm everyday reality with evil, pessimism, darkness or death, and that his view is optimistic." Reprinted: 1964.5.

6 FRASER, G. S. "Parnassian Grades." *New Statesman and Nation*, 18 May, pp. 649-50.

Reviews *Poems 1943-1956*. Says "Mr. Wilbur, one of the most famous of the younger American poets, is a deliberately rich, variegated, and ornate writer. He does not seem to me to have anything centrally interesting to say about life, but he is a superb verse craftsman who makes most of his English contemporaries – those between thirty and forty – look like fumbling amateurs." Cites "A Baroque Wall-Fountain in the Villa Sciarra" as a prime example of Wilbur's qualities. Urges that "Mr. Wilbur's book should be bought and read, both for sensuous pleasure, and as an example of what sheer workmanship in verse means."

7 _____. "Some Younger American Poets: Art and Reality." *Commentary* 23, no. 5 (May):454-62, passim.

Compares English and American poetic practice. Contends that English poets have been involved in social issues and in the argument about the "rival claims to our attention of the ideal and the actual." Contrasts them with American poets who, he finds, show "a far greater concern with what a poem is, with the shaping of a poem as an object. . . . American poems [also] strike me as being *luxury products* – that the American poet is expensively and deliciously adding something to life, rather than expressing, perhaps awkwardly, something urgently arising out of life."

Establishes a progression from a poet, Gene Derwood, whose poem ignores, in his opinion, tone and diction to Richard Wilbur's "Piazzi di Spagna, Early Morning." Says that "it is as an *object*, however, as a beautifully made small object, that one does tend to consider this poem rather than as a transcript and evaluation of experience. The feelings, outside one's feelings for the way the thing itself is shaped, that the poem appeals to are trite. . . . Our more intense emotional response is to the form, not to what the poem says, but to what it does." Poses the questions, "Is there a Wilbur 'world'? . . . Or is there only a Wilbur manner?" Concludes that "the world of Mr. Wilbur's little poem was, to make a crude distinction, a 'poetry' world and not a 'real life' world; his shaping of the poem became, for him and us, the relevant experience that the poem was about. "Summarizes by saying, "the current English worry about poetic content . . . and the English worry about tone, about the audience, about 'getting it across,' are worries with which young American poets could profitably burden themselves. But young English poets could certainly profit, even more strikingly, from sharing the concern of young American poets with form. . . . There certainly ought to be more intercourse between poets on both sides of the Atlantic, more exchange of ideas."

8 FULLER, ROY. *London Magazine* 4, no. 7 (July):72-75.
     Reviews *Poems 1943-1956*. Claims that "Mr Wilbur's reputation . . . is not in the least inflated, and this substantial collection contains many poems as good as, and better than, those by which he has been represented in anthologies." Sees that "Mr Wilbur's strength is undoubtedly that he founds his poetry on observation, the evidence of his senses." Notes also that "though his poems are usually short, they are substantial through having no superfluous fat, and the reports of experience are always being used to fathom the nature of experience itself, by observation being placed by disparate observation, by a constant awareness of the contrast between image and actuality." Praises Wilbur's craftsmanship: "[Wilbur's poetry] is usually technically impeccable, relying on a firm iambic line and certain but unmechanical rhymes. Mr Wilbur is excellent at inventing stanza forms, and his stanzas rhyming in pairs are particularly effective." Points out that "Mr Wilbur has his Hyde side: his exceeding cleverness sometimes degenerates into mere knowingness and he is not quite free of the sentimentality which is the occupational hazard of the American writer. Nor is one altogether happy about the development – or lack of it – which these selections reveal."

9 GHISELIN, BREWSTER. "The Best of Richard Wilbur." *Poetry Broadside* 1 (Summer):11, 14.
     Reviews *Things of This World*. Suggests that "on the whole, Mr. Wilbur's better poems are his more difficult, most likely to be misapprehended, but not because they appear opaque or complicated, as they hardly ever do. They are not highly elliptical in any of the

fashionable ways. Their life is no less concentrated and developed at the center of attention than at the peripheries of suggestion. In all of them abundant concrete substance engages the senses and satisfies the mind" ("Piazza di Spagna, Early Morning"). Argues that "the substance of ["Piazza"] is assembled in confirmation of a sense of pervasive necessities working in the concord of things. . . . The difficulty in reading this poem is that of passing beyond what is so abundantly presented in image and statement, to the whole import." A reader must apprehend the motion of the girl and the metaphor simultaneously in order to develop adequate understanding: "insight develops under a pressure simultaneously esthetic and intellectual, and it exists in full only so long as that pressure supports its life in the mind making use of the poem." Cites "Statues" as a poem that "by means of presenting a sequence of particular actions in a specific scene, and by means of some direct interpretations . . . develops a very manifest theme: the need for balanced interplay of order and disorder in all life." Asserts that "to perceive this design requires of the reader a full use of the finely fashioned sound – an aspect of poetry that poets and readers alike often misvalue" ("A Baroque Wall-Fountain in the Villa Sciarra"). Concludes that "the perfected surface is the very quick and unflayable substance of the poetry. . . . Such unity of form and of essential substance . . . is that of a poetry which wholly embodies the vision it purports to actualize."

10 GIBBS, ALONZO. "Four Abreast." *Voices* no. 163 (May-August):43-46.

Reviews *Things of This World*. Judges that this volume contains poems of "magnificent texture," daring experiments, and ample evidence of Wilbur's ability to sing. At times he sounds a bit like Yeats, but he is his own master.

11 HEMPHILL, GEORGE. "The Meters of the Intermediate Poets." *Kenyon Review* 19, no. 1 (Winter):37-55.

Analyzes meters of poets writing during the thirties, forties, and fifties. Notes that fifteen poets (Bishop, Eberhart, Jarrell, Robert Lowell, Miles, Nemerov, Plutzik, Roethke, Rukeyser, Schevill, Schwartz, Scott, Shapiro, Warren, and Wilbur) employ meters rather different from classical tradition. Says that "tight iambics seem to be their dress clothing, loose iambics and stress-verse their ordinary or business clothes, and freer verse their occasional escape from both." Notes that Richard Wilbur masterfully writes naturally artful verse that employs stress-verse as well as tight iambics.

1957

12 HORAN, ROBERT. "On Richard Wilbur's 'Love Calls Us to the Things of This World.'" *Berkeley Review* 1, no. 3:31-33.

Explicates "Love Calls Us to the Things of This World." Ascertains that the poem creates a little world in which the action of the soul accepts the "bitter" duty of the dailiness of life – a drama acted out in each of our lives daily. Yet the poem enlarges our understanding of this fact: "the poem is not difficult, nor its central observation, once reflected, surprising. . . . But the statement of the poem is focused like a changing chord or prism; and it does not merely reassert, it exfoliates. It enriches the poor, forgotten fact of that lovely title, which we so rarely animate in our lives." Admits that rhythms flow easily, sentences follow standard patterns, repetitions of sound are deftly handled. Wilbur is a fine lyric poet, yet the very "finish" of the poem tends to take away from the intensity. Admits he misses "a more urgent involvement, emotive, not sermonic; some real risk or riot of the head and heart and nerve." Perhaps the charge of "elegance" made by some lies in Wilbur's apparent lack of "rage and rebellion." Finally, though, one longs for a "real blaze of love" to overtake a poem of Wilbur's. Reprinted: 1964.10.

13 LANGLAND, JOSEPH. "A Contrast of Excellence." *Northwest Review* 1, no. 1 (Spring):56-60.

Reviews *Things of This World*. Describes Wilbur's world as "calm, cool, detached, elegant, poised, philosophically witty, beautiful in its shapes and forms and artifacts." Debunks the criticism that Wilbur is too "elegant, too good." Cites "Piazza di Spagna, Early Morning" as an example of "a typical excellence." Argues that "with the recent rise of a cruder, wilder, more elemental, jazzy poetry (typified most clearly by the "San Francisco Group" . . .) Wilbur's excellence has made him a natural target." Mentions "A Black November Turkey," "A Voice from under the Table," "Altitudes," "A Baroque Wall-Fountain," and "For the New Railway Station in Rome" as poems that "are so well contrived that [they] are blamed for lack of passion." Says Wilbur provides his own answer to his critics in the last stanza in the book. Ridicules the notion that "the world is in a mess, man is in a hell of a mess, the poets – if representative – must show the world to be in a hell of a mess." Says "this is too simple. . . . One reads the poets for other reasons."

14 LERNER, L[AURENCE] D. "Baroque Rationalist." *Listen* 2, no.3 (Summer-Autumn):23-26.

Reviews *Poems 1943-1956*. Acknowledges that "Mr Wilbur can do anything with words." However, this is not to say that he is the best poet in English today. He is a naturalist in that his interest lies in the ordinary, natural things of this world: "he immerses himself in the intensity of physical experience with a completeness that one sometimes wants to call 'negative capability.'" Adds that "parallel to his love of clarity in landscape is his feeling for verbal clarity." Allows that "his metre is so perfect not only because he likes to show off his skill but also . . . because, like Marvell and Pope, he sees it as evidence of the sway of Reason. He values reason for the same thing as he values art, that it asserts man's mastery over the world."

Contends that Wilbur is a rationalist in that he relies on form to shape the world of his poems. In other words, reason guides him. However, he is saved from becoming a mere writer of verse by his love for the baroque: "it involves the love of energy." Notes that he is also aware of the darker side of human nature, as is clear in "Beasts."

15 "Modern Wit-Poet." *Times Literary Supplement* (London), 17 May, p. 306.

Reviews *Poems 1943-1956*. Notes similarities between Wilbur's poetry and the "wit-poets of the early seventeenth century." Thinks that "Mr. Wilbur's achievement is to harness their form of expression to a peculiarly modern manner of feeling" ("The Terrace"). Suggests that Wilbur "achieves an effect through some form of contrast between actuality and the metaphysical conception of his imagination" ("The Good Servant," "Still, Citizen Sparrow," "Mined Country"). Notes that Wilbur also "shows a very unusual capacity for direct observation, unsentimental yet tender" ("The Death of a Toad," "He Was"). Finds that "the poems collected here over thirteen years show no particular line of development, only an increased technical ability and self-assurance. Mr. Wilbur seems to be one of those lucky (yet also limited) poets who know almost exactly what they want to say, and he has evolved a very interesting and effective way of saying it."

16 "Sketches of the Pulitzer Prize Winners for 1957 in Letters, Music, and Journalism." *New York Times*, 7 May, p. 28.

Briefly mentions biographical and literary facts.

17 SWENSON, MAY. "On Richard Wilbur's 'Love Calls Us to the Things of This World.'" *Berkeley Review* 1, no. 3:42-472

Explicates "Love Calls Us. . . ." Says that the poem, read first simply for sounds, is a pleasant physical experience. A second reading, however, discovers the philosophical content added in the last half of the poem – a content which adds layers of meaning, not easily uncovered. "The whole poem (in its material, structure and expression)

1957

is in fact an epitome of relative weight and equipoise." In the end the word *balance* is the clue to the meaning of the content and form of the poem. Concludes that the poem has much more depth than it would at first suggest. "Sonic deviccs" add much to the musical elements and imagery of the poem. Reprinted: 1964.15.

18 TOBIN, JAMES E. "The World and Beyond." *Spirit: A Magazine of Poetry* 23 (January):189-91.

Reviews *Things of This World*. Says that "six slow readings indicate that the genuine charm, the craftsmanship of simplicity, the underhillside stream of fresh thought are present – in enough of the thirty-two poems to make the volume worth while and the former promise of new poetry in this decade a reality." Cites "Digging for China," "He Was," "Boy at the Window," and "Statues" as examples. Finds that the "technical brilliance," similes and metaphors are "handmaiden to the meaning." ("After the Last Bulletins," "The Beacon"). Finds fault with "John Chrysostom" because of its lack of clarity and apparent misunderstanding of the saint's life.

1958

1 BARKSDALE, RICHARD K. "Trends in Contemporary Poetry." *Phylon Quarterly* 19, no. 4 (Winter):408-16, passim.

Assesses contemporary poets' endeavors as "poetic calisthenics" intended to be brilliant in their form and empty of meaning. These poets have nothing to say; so they say nothing brilliantly. Richard Wilbur belongs to this group. The central flaw among young poets is their "calculated devaluation of meaning and content." Suggests, however, that contemporary poets should not be blamed too much; American society has left them little that is meaningful to say.

2 DEUTSCH, BABETTE. *Poetry in Our Time: A Critical Survey of Poetry in the English-speaking World 1900 to 1960*. New York: Columbia University Press, pp. 284, 347-48.

Reprint of 1952.3 and 1956.9. Reprinted: 1963.8.

3 ECKMAN, FREDERICK. *Cobras and Cockle Shells: Modes in Recent Poetry*. Vagrom Chap Book Number Five. New York: Sparrow Magazine, 47 pp.

Divides up the poetry of the current generation into three modes: the decorative, the substantive, and the kinetic. Decorative poetry is that created by the New Formalists, the academic poets who rely on ornamentation and wit to create their desired effects. Adjectives and adverbs appear frequently. Creates sub-varieties of this mode: the elegant, the euphonic, the academic, and the apocalyptic. Says Richard Wilbur's work falls into the elegant category and that most of this kind of verse can rarely be called art at all. Characterizes the substantive or concretive mode by a lack of ornamentation, fictional or narrative qualities, and surreal images. Sees this mode as a reaction to the decorative mode. Describes the kinetic mode as poetry that relies heavily on verbs and verbals and ignores English metrics, fitting into the categories of conventional and modernist modes. Says that "the best poetry written today is in what (rather parochially, to be sure) I have called the modernist manner – by which I intend to suggest that it is the truest poetic voice of modern times. Though its ancestry is mixed, its chief predecessors seem to be, in the older generation, William Carlos Williams, . . . e. e. cummings, and Ezra Pound; in the middle generation Kenneth Rexroth and Louis Zukofsky." Defines the "outstanding characteristics of modernist verse" as the following: "(1) a prosody which studiously avoids conventional English metric, taking its rhythms from the spoken American idiom or from prose, its line structure either from the phrasing of everyday speech or from that of modern music; (2) a high degree of concentration, avoiding every sort of ornament and digression; (3) an awareness of the poem's graphic design – i. e., its appearance on the printed page: punctuation, vertical and horizontal spacing, indentation, grouping and fragmentation of lines – all as a guide to the poem's full intention; (4) generally, reliance on the verb as an ultimate source of kinetic power."

4 KIZER, CAROLYN. "Poetry of the 'Fifties': In America." In *International Literary Annual*. Edited by John Wain. No. 1: pp. 60-96 passim.

Surveys American poetry of the fifties. Suggests that Wilbur is attempting to loosen his control and allow himself more freedom of expression, perhaps to deepen the content of his poems.

5 "Richard Wilbur." In *Americana Annual 1958*. New York: Americana, p. 833.

Mentions a few biographical facts. Says, "Unlike many contemporary poets, Wilbur does not indulge in the pessimism and introspective self-pity so common to writers of his generation. Nor is he afraid to exhibit his profound understanding and love of nature. Frequently lyric, he is, nonetheless, highly conscious of the subtleties of his art."

1958

6 SANESI, ROBERTO. *Poeti Americani da E. A. Robinson a W. S. Merwin 1900-1956.* Milano: Feltrinelli Editore, pp. 929-30.

In Italian. Introduces Richard Wilbur to Italian readers. Notes that Wilbur was born in New York, was a student at Amherst College and Harvard University, and has published poems in many important American and international publications. Says that his is an original voice belonging to the generation of poets coming of age after World War II. Suggests that *The Beautiful Changes* contains poems about love and war. Describes Wilbur's poems as having the capacity to render social and moral reality. They are elegant, formal, and perfect; their strength lies in the union of the intellectual and the spiritual. Says Wilbur continues to write the same kind of poem in *Ceremony*, and that the rigid formality can become at times irritating. Concludes that Wilbur will occupy–with Robert Lowell–an important place in American literature for years to come.

7 SCOTT, NATHAN A., Jr. "Literalist of the Imagination." *Christian Century*, 19 March, pp. 344-45.

Reviews *Things of This World*. Says the 1957 National Book Award was rightly given to Richard Wilbur for this book: "[*Things*] from beginning to end, is a beautiful felicity and firmly secures for the poet of *The Beautiful Changes* and *Ceremony* the ranking position among our youngest poets (Daniel Hoffman, Anthony Hecht, W. S. Merwin and their generation)." Admits that "what makes me happiest about the direction Wilbur's career is taking is that he is unwilling, as his work increasingly shows, to practice those exercises in a hermetic ideography that our younger poets today are too often to be found addressing to their fellow poets. He is, on the contrary, a writer who has been learning the lesson that Marianne Moore has been teaching that 'poetry . . . must . . . take the risk of a decision,' and his own work moves more and more into the perilous but exhilarating regions of rhetoric." Suggests that "Wilbur's point of beginning is always where [Moore] has insisted the poet must begin, with the 'minute particulars,' with the stubbornly intransigent specificities, of this world. . . . I discern her influence throughout–which is to say that that which is most remarkably commendatory in these poems is that they are the offerings of a 'literalist of the imagination.'" Concludes, "[*Things*] is a splendid performance which he gives, and he makes us think that he begins to be in the full flower of what will be a great career."

8 WAKEFIELD, DAN. "Night Clubs." *Nation*, 4 January, pp. 19-20.

Reports on Jack Kerouac's reading of poetry at the Village Vanguard in New York. At the same time Richard Wilbur was reading four blocks away at New York University. Says that the difference between Kerouac and Wilbur, though they are nearly the same age, is that "Wilbur is a man and Kerouc a kid. [Kerouac] is now 'On the Town.' Lo and behold – it is Richard Wilbur who is on the road; who has been, all along."

9 WARLOW, FRANCIS W. "Richard Wilbur." *Bucknell Review* 7, no. 4 (May):217-233.

Attempts a preliminary assessment of Richard Wilbur's work. Shows that he belongs to the "silent" generation of young poets rather than to the "beats." These poets concern themselves with elegance in language and rhetorical skill. Argues that Wilbur's poetry appeals to a broad audience because "he is not a disturbing thinker." Says "Wilbur exploits the technical discoveries of twentieth-century poetry: he mutes and synthesizes them, blends them into an older, more regularly flowing and melodic line than that of any of his immediate predecessors, not excepting [Wallace] Stevens, and into more conventional forms, with the exception of traditionalists like Frost. . . . The result is a composite, temperately elevated style, a backward-looking modernism, that suggests a minor modern classicist at home in a silvery Sabine metier." Admits Wilbur "does seek and find belief and meaning in 'the opulent bric-a-brac' of a 'gay-pocked and potsherd world.'" Suggests that "in each volume one is struck by [Wilbur's] responsiveness to the variability of natural things, whose Maker, he puns, is a 'make-shift God.'" Allows that Wilbur "is aware of stultifying calms, of the fearful dark, of the violence of wind and sea; but they are all so beautifully rendered and so often bring us back to light, the weaving wind, and reassuring routines that we cannot quite take them seriously." Describes Wilbur's method as a poet who "moves from association to association, fusing statement, imagery, and verbal music as he circles in on his real subject, a fact at times, but more often a moral or a value that acquires a sobering or delightful solidity from the imaginatively rendered facts encountered on the way." Sees Wilbur as "preoccupied with diction, at times with etymology, and with word play." Says Wilbur is this generation's "refiner and to a certain extent one of its virtuosos and popularizers. He gives the impression of a composite style, at its very best one in which few if any joints show." Concludes that Wilbur's poetry suggests that "this is a time of constriction, of aspirations to the relatively near, of creative inbreeding, a time in which professionalism, craftsmanship, and form can be helpful stabilizers."

1959

1 FAVERTY, FREDERICK E. "Well-Open Eyes; or, the Poetry of Richard Wilbur." *Tri-Quarterly* 2, no. 1 (Fall):26-30.

Describes Richard Wilbur as a poet of affirmation who has not lost his sense of wonder. A special interest in animals is evidenced by his collection *A Bestiary*; through the physical animal Wilbur reaches for a larger meaning, a sense of the cosmic dance. Contends that Wilbur's enjoyment of both the comic and the serious is indicated by the wide range of authors he has read and translated, including Molière and Voltaire: "in Wilbur's English dress . . . Molière's epigrams retain their polish and their poison." Notes that "in the work of [many] painters it is evident that Wilbur finds principles operative that are of value, also, to him as a poet. There is, for example the peculiar power the painter Pieter de Hooch has of making 'objects speak.' This power Wilbur also possesses." Acknowledges that though able to find in things that which is odd and wonderful, Wilbur is keenly aware that he, like Wordsworth, is half creating and half perceiving his reality. Concedes that "for Wilbur . . . black is not the only color, nor anguish the only theme. . . . Essentially, Wilbur's note is one of affirmation. . . . Deep within the heart of reality . . . dwells the miraculous, requiring for its perception no perversion or distortion of things, only 'well-open eyes.'" Concludes that Wilbur "is an intellectual man who has not lost the sense of wonder." Reprinted: 1962.6; 1972.6.

2 GOLFFING, FRANCIS C., and GIBBS, BARBARA. "The Public Voice: Remarks on Poetry Today." *Commentary* 28, no. 1 (July):63-69, passim.

Builds a case for the fact that poets pass from one generation to another the techniques and strategies they have learned, yet each poet must decide what to do with his heritage. Proposes that the middle generation found itself in this "dilemma" and that "the only way out of the dilemma was (and still is) to construct poetic models that would be largely independent of what the masters of the preceding generation had furnished." Argues that Richard Wilbur's poetry was "one of the earliest of these new models to reach the market . . . with a *disastrous* success." Mentions Allen Ginsberg as at the opposite end of the spectrum. Arrives at three assumptions: "first, readers will put up with imitative poetry for a very long time, but not indefinitely. Second, for any new poetic model to take hold it is imperative that its producer be sure both of his means and his ends. Third, the latest model, in order to be successful, must be the polar opposite of the model preceding it." Contends Wilbur fits this paradigm perfectly because his poetry represents a complete about-face from Auden's. "The poetry of Wilbur and his fellows was built to consecrate pleasure, not hurt; pursuit of happiness through metaphor was its sole aim, and it achieved that aim with no apparent difficulty, with no flexing of muscles or other ostentation." Judges that "the Wilbur type of poem may move us with its genuine pathos (e. g. "The Death of a Toad") but it is neither equipped nor desirous to deal with the human situation in its appalling complexity." Suggests that "now at this very moment, it seems that two things are happening: . . . namely, that poets are seeking, in one gut-bursting effort, to finally break through that 'fence' which has plagued them through the centuries and has become unbearable, and on the other hand they are, at the same time, finding courage to simply assert the value of poetry through the act of writing it." Posits that in the future genres may disappear and that "poetry readers will come to center their attention increasingly on the nature of language, as symbology."

3 HALL, DONALD. "Ah, Love, Let Us be True, Domesticity and History in Contemporary Poetry." *American Scholar* 28, no. 3 (Summer):310-19.
   Suggests that a pattern is emerging among young poets of dependence upon the domestic in place of understanding one's own age and one's place in it. "Dover Beach" symbolizes the willingness of the younger generation of poets to substitute love for belief, either in a theory of history or in a philosophy of religion. Feels that Wilbur, however, seems somewhat impatient with this state of affairs. Suggests that "domesticity is the evasion of history, for us and for Matthew Arnold – but Arnold at least included history in his poem." Says that "if you wish to include the life of your own times in poems, you must avoid both barren subversion and phony affirmation." Suggests young poets now escape to mythology, not history, to avoid dealing with reality. Condemns young American and English poets: "we are a provincial generation, largely unaware of the past of our own tradition, or of the nature of our limitations. Most of us have sheltered in the protection of the intimate." Concedes that the solution to this problem is not just a recognition of failure or a desire to change. The poet must experience a change of character. If he wants to be a good poet, "he must see the new life." To avoid history in favor of domesticity is both a "moral and technical fault."

4 KLEIN, LUCE ARTHUR. "The Poems of Richard Wilbur." Commentary on jacket of the record *The Poems of Richard Wilbur Read by the Author*, Spoken Arts 744.

Comments that Wilbur "is a very spiritual poet at heart, only hides it with 'pudeur' and an anti-declamatory manner and masks it with wit, music and fantasy." Concludes that "tender, wistful yet vivacious, dreamy yet humorous, Wilbur's poetry roots grow deep in tradition, but it is also close to our modern nerves in need of a soothing crystalline voice."

5 KOPKIND, ANDREW P. "Poet Abhors Chores and Chooses Muses." *Washington Post Books*, 5 May, p. 8.

Discusses Wilbur's activities as a lyricist for *Candide*, a lecturer, a teacher, and a translator.

6 KUNITZ, STANLEY. "Poems Recorded by Richard Wilbur." *Evergreen Review* 2 (Spring):201-2.

Admits that Wilbur is certainly not an avant-garde poet, but he writes "with a grace, a dignity, a discipline that are currently out of fashion among those who consider fashion to be a matter of literary consequence. Though he can be witty, ironic, and even acerbic on occasion, he is not one given to rant and rage." Describes Wilbur as "one of the few masters of stanzaic structure; and far from cramping his style, meter and rhyme seem actually to liberate it. A clean wind of the spirit blows through these lines. It is not a wild impulse, it is not a hurricane, but it comes from a far quarter, and it blows. . . . The recording . . . is brilliantly alive."

7 LANGBAUM, ROBERT. "The New Nature Poetry." *American Scholar* 28, no. 3 (Summer):323-340.

Argues that Joseph Beach (*The Concept of Nature in Nineteenth-Century English Poetry*) is wrong when he says that nature poetry has disappeared in this century. Rather, nature poetry has taken on a new form "and is better than it has been for a long time." Mentions Wallace Stevens, Marianne Moore, Robert Frost. Sees Frost's "sense of nature as manageable and very like Wordsworth's, as is his method of conveying that sense." Finds Frost "our best nature poet since Wordsworth." Says that contemporary poets are becoming adept at portraying nature in its "nonhuman otherness": "for the new nature poetry is really about that concept by which living unconsciousness has come to be understood as a form of consciousness and, paradoxically, the most vital form of it." Asserts that "there seems to be a direct proportion between our sense of nature as wild and nonhuman, and our appreciation of just the artificial surface, the distinctively 'aesthetic' quality, of art and civilization." Describes Richard Wilbur's "Death of a Toad" as moving from the event outward to larger concerns. Finds that

Wilbur and others of his generation "show how animals operate in . . . poetry to connect inanimate nature with civilization through our current ideas about the vitality of the unconscious life and the origins of culture in the worship of animals, the contemplation of the vegetation cycle, and the killing of gods to renew the fertility of the soil." Concludes that the new poets' work shows "the point where nature poetry comes full circle from the rejection of the old religion of nature to the discovery of an inevitably re-emerging religion of nature at the source of things."

8 RIZZARDI, ALFREDO. *La Condizione Americana: Studi su Poeti Nord-Americani*. Rome: Capelli Editore, pp. 209-12.

In Italian. Describes Richard Wilbur's work as having exquisite lyrical sweetness trusted to an incredible formal perfection. Says he abandons himself to an intense intellectual pleasure and to the heart in order to discover the essential measure of things. Finds that Wilbur's elevated style, internal and serene harmony, a clear intelligence, and a sense of moral responsibility form the backbone of the poetry of Richard Wilbur. Says Wilbur represents the best of American university poets and American poets who employ traditional forms. Suggests that Wilbur's technique allows delicate lines to appear: the spark of his style is a way of seeing, hearing, feeling, and thinking originally. Mentions *Candide*. Suggests that "Still, Citizen Sparrow" reveals the nature of Wilbur: tragic tones easily disappear. Compares the railway station in Rome to the ruins of great civilizations; Wilbur illuminates each in a similar way, creating an unusual beauty ("For the New Railway Station in Rome").

9 SHAPIRO, KARL. [New American Poetry]. *America Illustrated* no. 28 (January):8-11.

In Russian. Wilbur's use of symbolism in "The Death of a Toad" suggests a relation between a human being and his responsibility for the well-being of all that lives and a toad. The message in the poem is that people can or should care when a toad dies. Poetry from all countries suggests that these meetings (people and toads) take place, and these hard deaths assume an important place, though at first sight they make little sense.

1960

1 ASSELINEAU, ROGER. "Les Fleurs de Verre de Richard Wilbur." *Critique* (Paris) 16, no. 161 (October):844-848.

In French. Reviews *Poems 1943-1956*. Suggests this collection provides an invitation to examine Wilbur's canon. His technique can be compared to his poem "Grace" about the ballet dancer, Nijinsky, who dances with grace. Each of his poems is a classic ballet of words and phrases which are a mixture of discipline and lightness. The supreme accomplishment of his art is his ability to maintain his "difficult balance" between the order of art and the disorder of his emotions. He is also able to capture the fragile and ephemeral in his poems. Above all, he is interested in objects, rejecting the mirage and the dream. The work of Richard Wilbur transports us to a world more pure and more beautiful than the one our senses habitually perceive. The flaw in his work, however, is just this; it is too perfect. Thus we are presented with that which is beautiful but artificial.

2 BOSQUET, ALAIN, ed. Preface. In *Trente-Cinq Jeunes Poètes Américains*. Paris: Gallimard, pp. 9-37, 345-52.

In French. Criticizes mid-century American poets because they lack intellectual rigor. They concentrate on form rather than content. (Three of Richard Wilbur's poems, "John Chrysostom," "Mind," and "Boy at the Window" are included in this anthology. No specific mention is made of Wilbur's work.)

3 FOSTER, RICHARD. "Debauch by Craft: Problems of the Younger Poets." *Perspective* 12, no. 1 (Spring-Summer):3-17.

Suggests that the poetry represented in the anthology *The New Poets of England and America*, edited by Donald Hall, Robert Pack, and Louis Simpson, "was bad not because its subjects were 'suburban' or its manners 'Alexandrian,' but because its perceptions were *sentimental*." Cites examples of poems by Robert Pack, Robert Mezey, W. D. Snodgrass, Anthony Hecht, James Wright, Wesley Trimpi, Alastair Reid, Jon Silkin, and Louis Simpson. Accuses young poets of being "trained up in craft" and of finding it "difficult . . . to keep their imaginations intact." Says that "the result is the debauch of sensibility by craft."

Argues that "another and more generalized deleterious effect of craftsmanly exercise is the smothering or diluting of individual talents by 'influences.'" Sees Richard Wilbur as "a kind of summa of the welter of influences today's young poet inherits, and of the costs to the individual sensibility when that inheritance becomes a burden, even a tyranny." Says the voice of Auden is plainly heard in Wilbur's "Love Calls Us to the Things of This World." John Crowe Ransom, Gerard Manley Hopkins, Marianne Moore – all appear frequently in Wilbur's work.

Finds "a notable lack of 'relevance' in the work of *The New Poets.*" Uses Wilbur's "Merlin Enthralled" as an example "where a construction out of Arthurian materials presents a more or less 'pure' or essential myth of the loss of magic and imagination in the enthralling of Merlin by Niniane." Dismisses it as "merely a sweetly moving attitude existing in a vacuum, withal very beautifully." Concludes by saying, "My own notion of the new poet is a paradox and a monstrosity – the joining somehow together of the greatest intensity with the greatest skepticism."

4 GREENE, GEORGE. "Four Campus Poets." *Thought* 35, no. 137 (Summer):223-246.

Grants many poets are connected to the academy and are thus open to the charge that they write to please the academic journals and political powers. Argues, however, that "from the financial point of view, . . . American education constitutes the central and sometimes solitary patron [of poets]." Argues further that the fact that poets work within the academy makes "unquestionable the value of the literary act." Says Richard Wilbur, the artificer, writes poetry that has "appreciably widened our consciousness of the local, the deliberately circumscribed." He also knows "that, above all else, a text should not be fissionable. The better the performance, the more impossible it becomes to separate ideas from embodiment." Describes Wilbur's sensibility as "the keenest perception of epiphanies granted on the neighborhood sidewalk or along one's back fence."

5 "Richard Wilbur." In *A Library of Literary Criticism*. Edited by Dorothy Nyren. New York: Frederick Ungar, pp. 525-27.

Contains brief summaries of several critical articles and bibliographical information.

6 ROSENTHAL, M. L. *The Modern Poets: A Critical Introduction*. New York: Oxford University Press, pp. 8, 248, 253-55.

Contends that out of the many fine poets writing today, relatively few have opted for the "perfectionistic and aesthetic-centered lead of poets like Marianne Moore and Wallace Stevens." Elizabeth Bishop and Richard Wilbur have been influenced by these two poets. Notes that "although these two writers have done exquisite and richly suggestive work they have touched the imagination of their generation very little. The reason seems to be that they remind us only of what we have already been taught to value: elegance, grace, precision, quiet intensity of phrasing" ("Marginalia"). Concedes that Wilbur does not "wear a mask all the time." "Juggler" and "Mind" state clearly that his "aim is to do his work so skillfully, . . . that it will 'shake our gravity up' and we shall, for the moment have 'won for once over the world's weight.'" Sees that "in the poems that move with a weary splendor to the full assumption of their Existential burden ("Marginalia," for instance, and "Beasts," "After the Last Bulletins," and "Merlin") we feel, if still no irresistibly new perceptions, the breath of a true diver into his own meanings. And curiously enough, we feel it as strongly in those poems which, with a joyous connoisseurship, give praise to beauty and to the variety of worldly possibility."

7 SHAPIRO, KARL. [Writer-on-Campus in America]. *America Illustrated* no. 49 (October):20-22, 27.

In Russian. Wilbur is mentioned as an academic poet.

8 SOUTHWORTH, JAMES G. "The Poetry of Richard Wilbur." *College English* 22, no. 1 (October):24-29.

Reviews *Poems 1943-1956*. Contends that "Wilbur's contribution to date lies essentially in his craftsmanship." Finds that a close analysis of his poems supports this thesis and also makes clear that rhythm is just as important as metrics. Finds most notable his sense of the importance of rhythm as opposed to the easy use of rhyme. Wilbur also employs his imagination to "wrench things awry" in order to see more clearly what this world is about. He displays psychological strength in his willingness to concentrate on the present. Criticizes Wilbur, however, because too large a group of his poems do not carry much meaning. A second reading of them is often a disappointment. Asks, "Has he subsided into too equable a life?" Concludes that "Wilbur is a deft translator, capturing the wit and grace of his original. The release from having to furnish both the subject and the technique enables him to concentrate on the technical aspects of his task and he succeeds admirably. His translation of Molière, for example, is witty, fluid, and urbane. Unwillingly I am reminded of Ezra Pound, who was only at his best when he had the thought from another, such as Propertius, and needed only to furnish the technique."

1961

1 AMACHER, RICHARD E. "Poe's 'The City in the Sea.'" *Explicator*
19, no. 8 (May):item 60.
Disagrees with Richard Wilbur's suggestion that Poe's "The City
in the Sea" is "so thoroughly pictorial, so lacking in narrative or
argumentative structure, that all evidence of Poe's true meaning must
be drawn from external sources; largely from prose pieces of later
composition." Argues that "this poem contains within itself sufficient
dramatic movement and well-established order in its part-whole
structure to constitute highly pleasurable poetry." Explicates the poem
by analyzing images.

2 DEUTSCH, BABETTE. "Seasonal Miracles and Permanent Truths."
New York Herald Tribune Book Review, 3 December, p. 4.
Reviews *Advice to a Prophet and Other Poems*. Feels that "it is
[Wilbur's] emphasized refusal to unlearn 'Anxiety and hate / Sorrow
and dear concern' that gives this collection a greater strength than its
predecessors while it retains the agile grace that has always been a
notable feature of Mr. Wilbur's work." Mentions "Two Voices in a
Meadow" and "The Aspen and the Stream" as meaningful dialogues.
Notes other poems on "seasonal miracles and permanent truths": "A
Summer Morning," "A Fire-Truck," "Shame," "Stop." Observes that his
translations also show remarkable power.

3 EHRENPREIS, IRVIN. "Four Poets and Others." *Minnesota Review*
2:397-410.
Reviews *Advice to a Prophet and Other Poems*. Says that the
poems in Richard Wilbur's new collection contain the positive
characteristics of good taste, refinement, and charm. However, these
poems also show the poet limited by his own skill, his inability to be
personal, his lack of wit and humor, and his "moral uncertainty."

4 FITTS, DUDLEY. "A Trio of Singers in Varied Keys." *New York
Times Book Review*, 29 October, pp. 16-17.
Reviews *Advice to a Prophet and Other Poems*. Suggests this
collection contains poems of "elegance – a true elegance resulting from
the fusion of form and idea which has nothing in common with the
surface elegance of so much of the new formalism that seems obsessed
by its own shapes." Defends this collection as having "a tremendous
amount of excitement: the concentration upon physical detail, the
analogical play, the amused perception of the extraordinary in the most
humble and humdrum *données* – these insights and operations release a

memorable energy, vibrating far beyond the apparent scope of any one of the poems."

5 FLINT, R. W. "The Foolproof Style of American Poets." *Audience*, 20 May, pp. 1-5.

Argues that though David Daiches's critique of American poets as having more "maturity" and "craftmanship" than English poets may have some basis in fact, his judgment that American poets have not produced great poetry can be contravened by looking at the work of Robert Lowell and Richard Wilbur. Argues that both poets have shown an authoritative use of traditional conventions to create unique styles. Says that "Wilbur's voice is somewhat different [from Lowell's], 'broad church' in contrast to Lowell's Augustinianism. He also mixes lyricism, prophecy, ironic commentary, semi-allegory and most of the other forms and manners we expect from a wide-ranging younger poet. He is probably more uneven, more 'poetical,' less sure of himself than Lowell, less a maker of uniform single poems and more startling in his sudden successes within a poem." Concludes that "what we find here [in the work of Lowell and Wilbur] is a nimble kinaesthesia held powerfully in check by a seasoned imagination; a poetry full of echoes, rejoicing in its own display but also entirely individual and local."

6 HALL, DONALD. "The Battle of the Bards." *Horizon* 4, no. 1 (September):116-21.

Acknowledges that evidence of American poets separating into two groups is strong. Two anthologies support this opinion. One selects poets whose work is similar to that of Richard Wilbur and other academic poets. The other follows the dictums of Pound and Williams Carlos Williams. Characterizes some attacks as silly, especially those in regard to the lifestyles of poets. However, serious differences lie in the use of language and a poet's concern for form, but suggests the differences may be overstated since "all American writers are obsessed with their techniques." Notes, however, that these two traditions reflect the extremes of American "thought and feeling" and need to be synthesized. Finds that much good exists in both camps and argues that the best poets will be able to combine the virtues of both the "palefaces and the redskins."

7 HAZO, SAMUEL. "A Clutch of Poets." *Commonweal*, 22 December, p. 346.

Reviews *Advice to a Prophet and Other Poems*. Finds that it displays much the same high quality as Wilbur's prior collections. Says he retains his ability to create freshly. Critics who fault him because he has not written dramatic poetry overlook the fact that the "quality of excellence is omnipresent."

8 HOLMES, JOHN. "Wilbur's *Advice.*" *Christian Science Monitor,* 21 December, p. 7.

Reviews *Advice to a Prophet and Other Poems.* Calls Richard Wilbur "craftsman . . . and civilized thinker," who has again given the world an admirable group of poems. Notes that the control in these poems is deceptive; this is not a "quiet book" ("Two Voices in a Meadow"). Finds two different kinds of poems here and elsewhere in Wilbur's work: the serious, substantive poem and the clear-sighted evocations of daily things such as "A Fire-Truck," "In the Smoking-Car," and "October Maples." Cites "She" as a poem which "undertakes to say all there is to say, no less, about woman from Eve to now, and succeeds." Sees "Advice to a Prophet" as another example of the "serious, substantive poem." "Stop," "A Hole in the Floor," "Summer Morning," and "Next Door" are "striking, delightful, perceptive" but ultimately "less formal, and seemingly less serious." Agrees that Wilbur's translations are excellent.

*9 *Kirkus,* 1 September, p. 824.

Reviews *Advice to a Prophet and Other Poems.* Listed in 1971.6, p, 80.

10 LAWNER, LYNNE. "Tre Nuovi Poeti Americani." *L'Approdo Letterario* (Rome) 7, no. 13:39-57.

In Italian. Prints translations of "First Snow in Alsace," "On the Eyes of an SS Officer," "Sunlight Is Imagination," "Museum Piece," "Ceremony," "Piazza di Spagna, Early Morning," and "Love Calls Us to the Things of This World." Says "this poet, who hasn't yet reached forty, has the acute sense of simple discoveries that nature offers us: water, leaves, grass, sunlight, lakes, weather. Even something like snow is transformed under the pressure of his imagination into something beautiful" ("Alsace"). Notes Wilbur is able to remove himself from the horrors of his subjects and describe the experience more acutely than the reader would himself ("SS Officer"). Says he possesses a finely tuned ear able to create a perfectly measured cadence in his verses, feels an evident pleasure in playing with words and developing difficult stanza forms and occasionally allows his technique to overwhelm the poem ("Sunlight"). Finds a sense of irony more apparent in *Ceremony.* Describes Wilbur as being able to write well about superficial things, but also able to write about more difficult subjects without the direct and passionate rhetorical slant of Robert Lowell ("Still, Citizen

Sparrow," "Year's End"). Suggests that in "Ceremony" form is celebrated for itself in that it is a form exquisitely chiseled. Thinks that *Things of This World* was greatly inspired by Rome and its citizens and nature.

11 LOMBARDO, AGOSTINO. "L'Arte Parnassiana di Richard Wilbur." In *La Ricerca del vero: saggi sulla tradizione Litteraria Americana*. Rome: Edizioni Di Storia e Letteratura, pp. 385-96.

In Italian. Expresses disappointment in the lack of power in the poetry of middle-generation American poets. Says their poetry is grey, academic, technically perfect, boring, bloodless, and unreal. The poetry of the beats contains blood and reality in abundance but is spoiled by childishness. Thus, the inheritance available to these poets of their own tradition and the English and European traditions has been dissipated.

Says Wilbur has contributed to post-war poetry with technical perfection that lacks substance. The fact that his *Things of This World* was chosen for the National Book Award is an indication of the level of American standards. Contends that *Things* is the completion of a process that began in Wilbur's first works. Characterizes "Ceremony" as the poet's statement about poetry and life. Says behind the ceremony is a mask, which resolves nothing and attenuates the impact of violence on reality. The ceremony is also incapable of autonomous life; it can have only illusionary and formal reality. Argues that *Things* deepens the premise inherent in "Ceremony." Finds psychological and sentimental limits in Wilbur's work. Says that reading the poems is very pleasant, but they don't satisfy one completely. Feels that Wilbur does not risk enough.

12 MILES, JOSEPHINE. "The Poetry of Praise." *Kenyon Review* 23, no. 1 (Winter):104-25, passim.

Suggests that "the Protestant-democratic style is not the plain English but the high Biblical style; second, that of two major and almost opposite Romantic styles it was again not the dramatic one of Coleridge but the high one of Thomson and Blake that most affected American nineteenth century romanticism; third, that the prevalent balanced style in America, often called classical, represents a steady and conscious effort at a compromise between extremes: between the lowly and plain in poetry, ... and at the other extreme the sublime, the worshipful Sunday poetry early adopted and enthusiastically maintained; and fourth, that when the two nations separated politically at the end of the eighteenth century, it was America, not England, that carried on the eighteenth century poetic tradition, and it is now America which is taking the lead in returning this tradition to England, with an increasing consolidation of interests and powers." Cites Richard Wilbur's *Things of This World* as a prime example of a younger poet who is carrying on this tradition.

13 ROBIE, BURTON A. *Library Journal*, 1 December, p. 4192.

Reviews *Advice to a Prophet and Other Poems*. Says "one reads the poetry of Richard Wilbur as one listens to the single lilt of a rare birdsong in the stillness of a quiet summer morning. Versatile though conservative in form, he writes a lyrical unpretentious verse whose very restraint and simplicity overlay a moving profundity as in 'Stop,' where the plain description of a railroad station in winter summons 'A purple, glowing blue / Like the phosphorus of Lethe,' or 'The Agrigentum Road,' which distills the entire tragedy of the ruin of the classical world. In his quiet, original, not infrequently subtle and witty lines describing 'A Hole in the Floor,' 'October Maples,' a home for the aged, or 'A Summer Morning' there is manifested a rare gift of making much from little and the power of transforming past, present, and future into a timelessness which is the essence of all real poetry."

14 SCHEVILL, JAMES. "Contemporary Poetry–Lowell, Wilbur, Gunn and Others." *San Francisco Sunday Chronicle: This World Magazine*, 3 December, pp. 31-32.

Reviews *Advice to a Prophet and Other Poems*. Notes that Richard Wilbur's new book, "although it contains no fresh advances in style, demonstrates once again his mastery of formal, classical techniques. His poems have a true, lyrical, melodic sound, rare in this age of conversational, hard-bitten tone. His range in subject matter is wide. . . . He is brilliant at handling rhymes and renews one's interest in the possibilities of this technique. His images are full of humor and subtle, objective precision. Reading his work, I think of such words as 'honor,' 'dignity,' 'decency,' 'wit,' 'grace'–words, perhaps, with more of an 18th-Century than a 20th-Century ring. He is a poet with a rare and balanced temperament. The one reservation I have is that sometimes his diction seems a little artificial and glassy."

15 THORP, WILLARD. "Richard Wilbur." In *American Writing in the Twentieth Century*. Cambridge (Mass.): Harvard University Press, p. 225.

Lists Richard Wilbur as one of several new poets.

1962

1 BERMEL, ALBERT. "Adventures in Translation." *Kenyon Review* 24, no. 1 (Winter):168-73.
　　Reviews *The Classic Theatre*, Vol. IV, edited by Eric Bentley, which includes Richard Wilbur's translation of Molière's *The Misanthrope*. Suggests Wilbur "as good as duplicates" the original play "in self-contained heroic couplets." Praises Wilbur's prosody as an outstanding accomplishment. Also notes Wilbur's ability to vary "the pitch and rhythm of his lines without ever losing the feel and beat of the pentameter, even when the lines are extended from ten to fourteen syllables." Argues that "his meter is no handicap; it works for him. So does his rhyme, which becomes an integral part of the humor." Calls Wilbur's *Misanthrope* "a great play in English."

*2 *Bookmark* 21 (June):258.
　　Reviews *Advice to a Prophet and Other Poems*. Listed in 1971.6, p. 80.

3 CAMBON, GLAUCO. *Recent American Poetry*. University of Minnesota Pamphlets on American Writers, no. 16. Minneapolis: University of Minnesota Press, pp. 5-17.
　　Surveys poets who have come to prominence since World War II. Excludes Robert Lowell, Karl Shapiro, Theodore Roethke, and Stanley Kunitz. Begins with Wilbur who is characterized as an artist of high standards who is consistently good, who works within patterns already well-established in English poetry. Notes his debt to Marianne Moore ("Objects"). Sees the "effect of expansion and recoil" of the "elastic stanzas" of "Water Walker." Credits the use of "American speech" for Wilbur's success in "Tywater." Suggests several poems which testify to Wilbur's awareness of modern reality. Cites "Epistemology" and other poems as a clear link to Wallace Stevens. Says, "An intellectual poet who delights in the visible, Wilbur is as subtly aware of history as Henry James was; a look at 'Years-End' [*sic*] will easily prove it." A self-conscious artist, he is "relatively immune to artiness" ("The Death of a Toad," "&," "O," "Games One," and "Games Two"). Cites "Juggler" and "Grace" as poems with "pictorially dynamic sensibility." Concludes, "A 'graceful error' which modifies our received notion of reality: that is an apt definition of Richard Wilbur's poetry, if not of all poetry."

4 CURRY, DAVID. "An Interview with Richard Wilbur." *Trinity Review* 17, no. 1 (December):21-32.

Wilbur defends his use of traditional meters, rhymes, and rhythms and discusses the weakness of free verse. He talks about his connection to the academy as neither a strength nor a weakness. Discusses courses he teaches in writing poetry. Says that poetry readings have a positive effect on the poet, encouraging him toward the dramatic and the melodic. However, a poet cannot allow his audience to limit his field of reference. Talks about the quality of magazine verse in various publications. Comments on Randall Jarrell's criticism of his writing. Feels that translating *The Misanthrope* and *Tartuffe* has been stimulating and instructive. Likes a wide variety of poets. Says he wanted Robert Frost to get the Nobel Prize for this year. Reprinted: 1990.2.

5 DICKEY, JAMES. "The Stillness at the Center of the Target." *Sewanee Review* 70, no. 3 (Summer):484-503.
    Reviews *Advice to a Prophet and Other Poems*. Notes that his ability to celebrate and to praise marks Richard Wilbur's *Advice to a Prophet* as it has all of his other work. Contends that though one could suggest that this poet shows no growth, his extraordinary talents affirm that he has found his subject and his method. "Even in this book, which is not Wilbur's best, there is, underlying the grace and intelligent mastery, the things that should eventually make him the truly important poet that he deserves to be: the thing which his superlative manipulation of verse forms, his continuous and unobtrusive skills never fully state but never lose sight of. This is the quietly joyful sense of celebration and praise out of which Wilbur writes: the kind of celebration that is done, usually, without anyone's being told, and of the things that cause joy to rise unexpectedly, excessively, and almost always voicelessly in the human breast." Admits that Wilbur does not perceive the world darkly, and that this trait will probably prevent his being named a great poet by the literary establishment. Yet his poems "are as true and heartening a picture as we are ever likely to have of the best that the twentieth-century American can say of himself or have said about him." Reprinted: 1968.6.

6 FAVERTY, FREDERICK E. "Well-Open Eyes; or, the Poetry of Richard Wilbur." In *Poets in Progress*. Edited by Edward Hungerford. Evanston, Ill: Northwestern University Press, pp. 59-72.
    Reprint of 1959.1; reprinted 1972.6.

7 FLINT, R. W. "The Road From Rome." *Partisan Review* 29, no. 1 (Winter):147-48.

1962

Reviews *Advice to a Prophet and Other Poems*. Argues that "[Wilbur] offers some whacking paradoxes to criticism. On the platform he looks like someone in a Civil War photograph, yet elegance is the word most commonly used of his poetry. He reels in sonorous Johnsonian epithets like ' . . . gulls colonial on the sullied ice' or 'The bronze annals of the oak tree. . .' but the most affecting poem in this book finds him peering domestically under the ripped-up floorboards of a room in his house" ("A Hole in the Floor"). Feels that "much of Wilbur . . . stifles criticism by swinging along a broad noonday highway of common feelings and common ideas, followed by a baggage-wagon of loot from all over the world." Describes Wilbur as "essentially a Broad Church, Wordsworthian poet and Americans in general are not much given to either irony, elegance or pomp as a regular thing." Contends that "his appeal derives as much from his ability to undermine his Latin kingdom of the mind as from his skill in conjuring it up." Says he likes the poems of *Ceremony* better than those in this new collection. Suggests that *Advice* "shows an advance in domestication as well as a growing tendency, like Lowell's, to draw his themes from other poets." Though he "regrets" that Wilbur appears to be "mellowing," he finds him still "a poet to be savored – and reckoned with."

8 GUNN, THOM. "Imitations and Originals." *Yale Review* n.s. 51, no. 3 (Spring):480-89.
Reviews *Advice to a Prophet and Other Poems*. Says this collection is Wilbur's best yet: "there is a group of poems in which the famous skill has become an instrument of deepening precision, or rather an element inseparable from the statement of the poetry." In this book his technical skill is put to use to strengthen meaning; the result is a tight interweaving of form and content. Observes that "Wilbur's progress has been in exactly the opposite direction to that of Lowell, who has tended to particularize more and more closely. In *Advice to a Prophet* symbol and perception have started to take on a general force. . . . The generalizing power is most successfully in evidence at the start of 'The Aspen and the Stream'. . . . [Wilbur's work] is writing both nourished by and nourishing a tradition." Reprinted in part: 1983.18.

9 GUTTMANN, ALLEN. "Images of Value and the Sense of the Past." *New England Quarterly* 35, no. 1 (March):3-26.
Suggests that in addition to the images of the Virgin and the Dynamo, a third image of value should be added to understand American literature – the house. Surveys several American writers from

Anne Bradstreet up to and including Richard Wilbur. Reprints and cites "Altitudes," as Wilbur's "way of saying that America does have a past. We do have our houses now, and our traditions. We have poets to cherish and shrines to visit."

10 HALL, DONALD. Introduction to *Contemporary American Poetry*. Baltimore: Penguin, pp. 17-26, passim.

Reprints "Tywater," "A World Without Objects Is a Sensible Emptiness," "Museum Piece," "After the Last Bulletins," "She," "The Undead," "In the Smoking Car," "Shame." Includes a paragraph of brief bibliographic facts in the Table of Contents. Creates a context in the introduction for the poets included in this anthology. Suggests that "for thirty years an orthodoxy ruled American poetry. It derived from the authority of T. S. Eliot and the new critics; it exerted itself through the literary quarterlies and the universities. It asked for a poetry of symmetry, intellect, irony, and wit." Asserts that "from the mid-twenties until very recently, American poetry has functioned as part of the English tradition." Divides the poets of the thirties into "those who admired the tough density of Donne, and those who preferred the wit of Marvell or the delicacy of Herrick."

Argues that "immediately after the war, two books were published which were culminations of the twin strains of density and delicacy"–Lowell's *Lord Weary's Castle* and Richard Wilbur's *The Beautiful Changes*. Says that "these two poets, though they are not the oldest here, form the real beginning of post-war American poetry because they are the culmination of past poetries."

Notes a "contrary direction . . . endured throughout the orthodoxy [which] was the direction . . . or the line of William Carlos Williams." Finds that what unites all the poets writing in this direction is the conviction that an "alternative to the traditional poetry of the last decades was necessary."

Mentions the New York school of poets as a fourth group that is attempting to write in a new way. Concludes that "one thing is happening in American poetry . . . which is genuinely new, and so new that I lack words for it. . . . A new kind of imagination seems to be working. . . . This imagination is irrational yet the poem is usually quiet and the language simple. . . . This imagination reveals through images a subjective life which is *general*, and which corresponds to an old objective life of shared experience and knowledge."

11 HOLMES, JOHN. "Surroundings and Illuminations." In *The Moment of Poetry*. Edited by Don Cameron Allen. Westport, Conn.: Greenwood Press, pp. 4-26.

1962

Discusses the various rings of influences which surround poets: giant figures of the past (Dante, John Donne, Andrew Marvell), the Master, personal life experiences, editors and publishers, critics, the university (where poets like Wilbur earn their living), the watcher who analyzes the poet's method. Argues that "these other books, these companies and hosts at the ritual of writing the poem, do not interfere with, or become substitutes for, or in any way thin or distort, the poetry itself. Instead, they take up poetry's life and carry it outward, prolonging it in time, adding to it weight and worth it hardly had when it was new." Reprinted: 1967.5.

12 HOLMES, THEODORE. "A Prophet Without a Prophecy. Part I of Wilbur's New Book: Two Views." *Poetry* 100, no. 1 (April):37-39.
Reviews *Advice to a Prophet and Other Poems*. Views this collection negatively: "the poems supply no deeper resource in understanding by which life may be led with dignity and compassion for our frailties – they are like a ceremony gotten up by the mind to distract us from truth they represent." Accuses Wilbur of "holding up the things of this world in their own ultimate status in ontology as a solution to the dilemmas of human existence." Says such a worldview grows out of "things seen from Parnassian heights of wealth, privilege, ease, refinement, and education, looking down on the permanent sufferings of humankind without being part of them."
Observes "this latest book of Mr. Wilbur's is chiefly the kind of thing that is so often the end of an essentially formal attachment of truth that eventuates in a waning of interest. . . . All that had been his skill, his precision, his sense of grace, the *élan* of his mind, here becomes tired of itself and caves in to a mere posturing." Grants that a few poems hint of a new direction toward "openness, a straightforwardness, a giving voice to his own heart." Especially sees this in the title poem. Concludes, "If Mr. Wilbur would fashion his poems from such stuff of the heart as a lived-in experience, and not simply the virtuosity of an intellectual mastery attained over it, then they would afford the reader a basis for giving a permanent meaning to life." Reprinted: 1983.18.

13 MEREDITH, WILLIAM. "A Note on Richard Wilbur. Part II of Wilbur's New Book: Two Views." *Poetry* 100, no. 1 (April):40.
Reviews *Advice to a Prophet and Other Poems*. Thinks that "for people who know and care about Wilbur's work, this is just the excellent book they had hoped for and expected. For other readers it is something of a booby-trap. It invites careless reading: how genteel this all is, they think, how cheerful and Episcopalian, how very damned

elegant. But these accusations, the ones that are actually derogatory anyhow, are self-generated. The poems will not support them." Asserts that "Wilbur's poetry (like most good art, could you say?) explores the human capacity for happiness. The human capacity for despair (not to be confused with tragedy) is very big now with a lot of artists, and even novelists and poets who are not gifted in despair sometimes feel impelled to fake it."

Concludes, *Advice to a Prophet* strikes me as the strongest assertion yet, by this poet, that the universe is *decent*, in the lovely derivative sense of that word. Like that word, the book is unfashionably quiet in what it asserts, and subject to misuse." Reprinted: 1983.18.

14 MILLS, RALPH J., Jr. "The Lyricism of Richard Wilbur." *Modern Age* 6, no. 4 (Fall):436-40.

Reviews *Advice to a Prophet and Other Poems*. Contends "it is clear that, from the outset of his poetic career, Wilbur was tempted neither to write surrealist poems nor to imitate Robert Bridges – or if he was, these temptations were overcome in secret – but that, instead, his gifts and inclinations drew him toward the tradition of English lyricism which maintains its center in formalism and wit and musical grace." A poet of "endless celebrations," Wilbur is often concerned with the experience of life one must call religious. Says, "experience, and the spiritual threads deep within it, usually comes to Wilbur through his amazing sensitivity to the phenomenal world, to every fluctuation of nuance in his surroundings, and to the incredible beauty he perceives there." Observes that "the natural world in its particular mood and season becomes, through the poet's eye, through a wealth of analogy and allusion, sacramental; though with Wilbur this awareness of the spiritual possibilities inherent in the physical order never reaches to the level of visionary or mystical intuition." Nor is Wilbur a poet of systematic vision ("A Hole in the Floor").

Sees one additional characteristic in Wilbur's work – the moral element. "He tends to handle the poetic events he creates in a way that involves his own deepest instincts and considered judgment" ("Advice to a Prophet"). Expanded and reprinted in 1965.12. Reprinted 1962 version: 1983.18.

15 MORSE, SAMUEL F. "A Baker's Dozen." *Virginia Quarterly Review* 38, no. 2 (Spring):324-30.

Reviews *Advice to a Prophet and Other Poems*. Notes that "Richard Wilbur underscores his earlier achievements in *Advice to a Prophet*. The skill with which he handles almost anything that his imagination touches is everywhere apparent, in 'A Stone' and 'A Fire-Truck,' and also in 'The Undead' and 'Shame.' Each of his books has defined his range; the depth of his perception and feeling, for all the delicacy of his touch, is remarkable. Although *Advice to a Prophet* contains no particular surprises, it offers no disappointments. A handful of beautifully wrought translations (including a marvelously disciplined scene from *Tartuffe*) rounds out the volume. As always, Wilbur sets a standard of excellence that those poets who in one way or another acknowledge him as a master strive to maintain."

16 O'CONNOR, WILLIAM Van. "The Recent Contours of the Muse." *Saturday Review*, 9 January, pp. 68-71.

Reviews *Advice to a Prophet and Other Poems*. Comments that "Richard Wilbur is in most of the anthologies nowadays and may soon make the permanent canon. *Advice to a Prophet* . . . ought not to disappoint his admirers. The early Wilbur is here, as in 'Loves of the Puppets'; he can catch a paradox as neatly as anyone writing poetry. And there is something new in *Advice to a Prophet*. Wilbur manages to conceive an almost unimaginable world. The essential neatness and perceptiveness of his mind do not click off; they move to a new register."

17 OHMANN, RICHARD M. "A Verbal Artifact." *Commonweal*, 29 June, pp. 358-59.

Reviews *The Moment of Poetry*, edited by Don Cameron Allen (1962.11). Suggests that several of the poets' comments in this anthology are "irrelevant or pernicious buzzing." Judges that "the volume is redeemed by the contributions of Randall Jarrell and Richard Wilbur." Thinks that Wilbur makes a contribution in "explaining Housman's 'Epitaph on an Army of Mercenaries'; he reaffirms an old principle – the poet's right to draw on the past – so freshly, so clearly, so *memorably*, that the familiarity of the idea scarcely matters." Concludes, "[Wilbur's] talk, like Mr. Jarrell's, belongs to the more lasting dialogue of culture."

18 OSBORN, CHARLES. "Among the Poetmen." *Spectator* (London), 21 December. p. 969.

Reviews *Advice to a Prophet and Other Poems*. Argues that "though his thought is often complex, Mr. Wilbur is nowhere difficult to read. A surface clarity helps one to see the depths below" ("Ballade for the Duke of Orléans"). Concludes that "this man is surely one of the most considerable poets writing in English today."

19 PUGH, GRIFFITH T. "From the Recent Books." *English Journal* 51, no. 5 (May):375.

Reviews *Advice to a Prophet and Other Poems*. Describes this collection as a "book of sensitive, beautiful poems." Says "the poems are a joy to read. They exhibit a technical skill, a precision of thought, a tender care for life, and a delicacy of language that lift them above the poems of most of his contemporaries. His 'Two Voices in a Meadow,' a poem of a single page, shows a calm and a reverence that appeal to both thought and feeling."

20 Review of *Advice to a Prophet and Other Poems*. *Christian Century*, 16 May, 631.

Reviews *Advice to a Prophet and Other Poems*. Notes that lines in the title poem: "Nor shall you scare us with talk of the death of the race. / How should we dream of this place without us?" come close to condensing the main themes of this varied collection. Says Wilbur is one of the better craftsmen around today, a poet used to taking conventional forms and expressions and investing them with profounder meanings than his more esoteric colleagues can offer. He can have fun, too.

21 "Richard Wilbur." In *American Authors and Books: 1640 to the Present Day*. Rev. ed. New York: Weiss-Crown, pp. 803-4.

Lists biographic and bibliographic information: *The Beautiful Changes* (1947); *Ceremony* (1950); *A Bestiary* (ed., 1955); *Things of This World* (1956; Pulitzer prize for poetry, 1957); *Candide* (comic opera, with Lillian Hellman, 1957); *Poems 1943-1956* (1957); *Advice to a Prophet* (1961). Translator: Molière's *Misanthrope* (1955). Professor of English, Wesleyan University since 1957.

22 "Richard Wilbur." In *The Reader's Encyclopedia*. 2d ed. Cambridge (Mass.): Thomas Y. Crowell Co., p. 1229.

Lists biographic and bibliographic information: "Wilbur studied at Harvard University, taught there for some years, and then began teaching at Wesleyan University in 1957. His poetry, which owes something to Marianne Moore as well as to the metaphysical school, is formal, polished, yet lively, witty, and full of ingratiating detail. His collections are *The Beautiful Changes* (1947); *Ceremony and Other Poems* (1950); *Things of This World* (1956); *Poems* (1957); and *Advice to a Prophet and Other Poems* (1961). He also translated Molière's *The Misanthrope* (1955), and provided songs for the Broadway production of Voltaire's *Candide* (1957)."

1962

23 ROSENTHAL, M. L. "An Unfair Question." *Reporter*, 15 February, pp. 48-51.

Reviews *Advice to a Prophet and Other Poems*. Regards Richard Wilbur "as perhaps the most quietly effective poet now writing in America." Says that "'humility' is one right word for Mr. Wilbur's approach to his own work. It requires artistic humility to sink himself in the lyric tradition as he does. He understands, of course, that he finds his truest music in this way. Moreover, several of his poems speak explicitly for the kind of triumph that can follow upon the humble virtues of restraint, of yieldingness, of the deliberately unheroic" ("Two Voices in a Meadow"). Compares Wilbur favorably with Andrew Marvell. Says that Wilbur's "Advice to a Prophet" demonstrates Wilbur's concern with the "larger issues of life." Notes that he asserts "the sweetness of our world as we know it, its hidden beauties that blaze into view unexpectedly, and its worth despite the harsh and tragic discipline it imposes on most of us on occasion." Concludes by asking, "Why, with so much to go on and such depths of insight, can these poets [Richard Wilbur and John Ciardi] not strike out for the main chance and take the great risk of 'making it new'?"

24 SCHOTT, WEBSTER. "Plain Vanilla." *Prairie Schooner* 36, no. 1 (Spring):88-90.

Reviews *Poets at Wesleyan*, an anthology which contains some of Richard Wilbur's poems. Observes that "the work by Richard Wilbur in this book seems distantly metaphysical beside Mr. Garrett's."

25 SIMON, JOHN. "More Brass Than Enduring." *Hudson Review* 15, no. 3 (Autumn):455-68.

Reviews *Advice to a Prophet and Other Poems*. Says that Richard Wilbur's new collection is disappointing. Only three poems really deserve mention: "A Summer Morning," "A Hole in the Floor," and "In the Smoking-Car." The rest of the poems do not live up to Wilbur's reputation for excellence. Observes that "a poet of Richard Wilbur's distinction need not continually surpass himself, but neither should he fall disconcertingly short of his standard. Mr. Wilbur's current problem seems to be (not unlike Robert Lowell's) one of transportation. He is trying to transport his verse from the poetic trance to ports of call of reality, but whereas in the demesne of pure poetry his excellence remains unchallenged, in the domains of contemporaneity his assurance is less than complete." Grants that the translations are, "as usual, deft and commendably faithful."

26 STEPANCHEV, STEPHEN. "In Praise of Craft." *Spirit: A Magazine of Poetry* (New York) 28 (January):163-65.

Reviews *Advice to a Prophet and Other Poems*. Says that Richard Wilbur "maintains his standard of excellence in thirty-one lyrics representing a wide range of subjects, from the great to the small and even trivial. He has given them all the sort of closeness of attention that discovers diamonds in an ash-heap or the macrocosm in the microcosm" ("Junk"). Notes that "Wilbur's voice is individual even as it sings with a tradition." Suggests that his ear for melody and his metaphor-making ability set him apart. Warns, however, that "Wilbur's formal excellence carries, intrinsically, one of his weaknesses, a too confining commitment to the rigors of his technique." Notes that "it is also true that Wilbur does not exhibit much passion." Discusses "The Undead" as unsuccessful. Mentions "Advice to a Prophet," "Stop," and "A Hole in the Floor" as exceptional. Concludes that Wilbur remains a poet of distinction who submits himself to his craft, a reason for much admiration.

27 TOERIEN, BAREND J. "Verse van Richard Wilbur: met opmerkings oor moderne Amerikaanse poësie" [Poetry by Richard Wilbur with Remarks about Modern American Poetry]. *Tydskrif vir Letterkunde* [Journal for Literature] (Johannesburg, South Africa) 12, no. 2 (June):13-20.

In Afrikaans. Translates into Afrikaans "The Death of a Toad," "Exeunt," "Two Voices in a Meadow," and "Digging for China." Makes general comments about American poetry which he characterizes as "among the richest in the world." Lists top ten American poets; among them is Richard Wilbur. Praises Americans for their diversity and willingness to experiment, though he finds that most do write in the Anglo-Saxon tradition.

Says he is "charmed" by Wilbur's work, but finds it is "lacking the element of the unexpected, of wonder." Criticizes Wilbur because his "work is neatly ordered, perhaps too neatly. The technique is conventional, with preferences for the quarto, rhyme, and the regular, steady rhythm of reflection. Rare are the images that open up vistas." Praises him because "his diction is aristocratic, mandarin, and is not connected to any period as such; it has a touch of the immortal – something that is very rare indeed." Says that a bit too much "book-learning" shows in the poems. Discusses the difficulty of translating "The Death of a Toad" accurately, especially the phrase "castrate lawn." Compares Wilbur's poem with Ernst van Heerden's "Dood van die Akkedis" (Death of the Lizard) in his volume *De Klop*

1962

(The Knock). Sees similar themes, forms, and even rhyme schemes. Yet, Wilbur's poem is uniquely his.

28 WALSH, CHAD. *Doors into Poetry*. Englewood Cliffs, N.J.: Prentice-Hall, pp. 173-76.

Contains a critical note on the genesis of the poem "Then" with three versions of the manuscript reproduced.

29 WHITTEMORE, REED. "Packing Up for Devil's Island." *Kenyon Review* 24, no. 2 (Spring):372-77.

Reviews *Advice to a Prophet and Other Poems*. Feels the poems in this volume are a blending of echoes of older poets such as Auden, Yeats, John Crowe Ransom, and Paul Engle. Argues that the echoes are so strong as to exert "a measure of control over the whole sound and statement of the poem." Says that "the Wilbur voice is, at least for me, a mixture of voices." Admits to being bewildered by the final lines of "Advice to a Prophet" which remind him of no other poet and thinks that perhaps he has carried his search too far. Concludes, "Still, as a result of the constant echoes, I keep reading the poems as exercises – exercises in various forms, various manners, various kinds of statement – excellent exercises but exercises; and I keep wishing, no doubt romantically, that I'd occasionally find instead a great big personal Wilburian yawp, or burp."

1963

1 ABSE, DANNIE. "Variety and Obsession." *Poetry Review* n.s. 54, no. 2 (Spring):108-10.

Reviews *Advice to a Prophet and Other Poems*. Acknowledges that Richard Wilbur defies the critic who wants to find "repetitive themes, or even repetitive shapes in a book of poems." Says *Advice to a Prophet* contains a wide variety of poems, all exhibiting "the voice of an adult American poet, direct and clear in enunciation, frequently witty or ironic, lyrical when the occasion demands, and almost always verbally tactful. . . . A rich variety results that is the despair of the critic intent on finding single obsessive motifs." Sees as most typical poems such as "A Hole in the Floor," "Advice to a Prophet," "Stop," and "The Undead."

*2 "Biographical Sketch." *Poetry in Crystal, by Steuben Glass*. New York: Spiral Press, p. 70.

Cited in 1971.6, p. 31. Field says this entry contains "interpretations in crystal of thirty-one new poems by contemporary American poets."

3 BLACK, IRMA SIMONTON. "Helping Beginners Find Fun and Wonder." *New York Times Book Review*, 10 November, p. 51.

Reviews *Loudmouse*. Contains a summary of the narrative of *Loudmouse*. Suggests second- or third-grade children will find it good reading.

4 CAMBON, GLAUCO. *Literatura Norteamericana de Hoy: Poesía – teatro – novela*. Madrid: Gredos, pp. 11-22.

In Spanish. Mentions *The Beautiful Changes, Ceremony and Other Poems*, and *Things of This World* to show the consistency of Wilbur's style. States that Wilbur's strict adherence to form provides the resistance which stimulates his poetry. Analyzes "Objects" to illustrate this point as well as to demonstrate Wilbur's great ability and freedom within a prescribed form. Uses "Water Walker" to describe the poet himself as one moving between two opposite environments "feeling foreign in both of them" and discovering "hell and heaven in the equilibrium between living and understanding." Comments that the force of North American speech contributes to the success of poems such as "Tywater." Argues that faithfulness to the academic does not mean that Wilbur ignores modern reality and that poems such as "Mined Country," "First Snow in Alsace," "On the Eyes of an SS Officer," "To an American Poet Just Dead," "He Was," and "For the New Railway Station in Rome" are a defense against the accusation of "aesthetic sterility."

Compares Wilbur favorably to his master/teacher, Wallace Stevens. Shows Stevens's influence in such areas as the titles of poems ("A Simile for Her Smile," "Five Women Bathing in the Moonlight," "La Rose des Vents," "A World without Objects Is a Sensible Emptiness," "My Father Paints the Summer," "Sunlight Is Imagination," "Praise in Summer," "Attention Makes Infinity"), the calling into question of poetic language as "a distortion of reality" ("Praise in Summer"), the "rich effects of alliteration" ("A Simplification," "The Beautiful Changes").

Notes that Wilbur's preoccupation with understanding and the act of knowing stems from "the transcendentalist and Puritan tradition of New England which the New York poet recovered with no difficulty." Remarks that this is what makes French sources so attractive to Wilbur. Notes that "Year's End" demonstrates Wilbur's deep awareness of history in spite of his delight in "all that is visible."

1963

Says that "for a poet so conscious of his art, Wilbur shows himself to be relatively immune to the disease of the 'trade,' as in 'The Death of a Toad,' and acrobatic exercises like '&,' 'O,' 'Games One,' and 'Games Two.'" Lists traits, as seen in particular poems, which characterize Wilbur's works: "the perfect dexterity of 'Juggler,' the irony of verbal inversion in 'Grace,' the grace and flow of phrase in 'Lightness,' the sensuality, ingenuity, and supplication, 'Bell Speech.'" Concludes by referring to the line from "Grace," "A graceful error may correct the cave. . . ." and stating, "This 'graceful error' that changes the former impression of reality that we have received, is the best definition of the poetry of Richard Wilbur."

5 "Contemporary Poets Who Deserve a Reading." *Sunday Times* (London), 14 March, p. 17.

Reviews *Advice to a Prophet and Other Poems*. Says that "clarity, beauty, and a fresh intelligence" are words that describe the work of Richard Wilbur. His latest collection gives the reader much enjoyment. "Every poem here has a clear structure of orderly description, illustrated thought, or controlled fancy." Adds, "The descriptions . . . have the lucid composure of a Dutch painting, delicately played on by more romantic light." Describes Wilbur's thought as "simple, noble." Notes that his wit comes through in the reworking of fourth-century Latin riddles, though one is a bit uncomfortable with such an ignoring of the high modern seriousness. Concludes that "there is no doubt that *Advice to a Prophet* is poetry of a high order."

6 "Cowboys and Indians." *Times Literary Supplement* (New York), 18 January, p. 42.

Reviews *Advice to a Prophet and Other Poems*. Asserts that the war between the "palefaces and the redskins" is nowhere more clearly exemplified than in the concurrent publication of Richard Wilbur's *Advice to a Prophet* and Gregory Corso's *Selected Poems*. Suggests that "never did a United States Marshal appear more immaculate among the roughnecks of the West, not to mention the even scruffier Indians, than Mr. Wilbur does among the generation of the 'beats.' An imposing, elegant figure, he indubitably stands for Law and Order." Wilbur's work also lacks humor unless he is translating Molière. Says that "almost all serious poets today seem to feel compelled to be very serious indeed, to enlighten us or preach at us from whatever rostrum they find handy, even if it be no more than, in one of Mr. Wilbur's poems, 'A Hole in the Floor.'" Feels that contemporary poets "smother simple observation under a smog of words." Wilbur, too, is guilty of this. Conversely, "Mr. Corso is an Indian." He attempts to bring a corrective to these tendencies. Reprinted: 1964.3.

7 DERRICK, CHRISTOPHER. "Power and Laws." *Tablet* (London), 16 February, pp. 169-70.

Reviews *Advice to a Prophet and Other Poems*. Though we are every day confronted with huge waves of words, we "tend to be left impervious to the other thing when it comes, words used needle-like, precisely and a few at a time." Richard Wilbur is one of three poets "of the Desert, refugees by intention: their starting-point is the Fall (though not all of them would relish that terminology), their instincts are compassionate, their main subject is the World, and their conclusions are therefore what some might call negative or reactionary." Quotes Wilbur's echoes of St. Augustine and lines from "Advice to a Prophet" to back up his claims. Suggests that "all three writers [see] a kind of strangulation with abstract nouns, a crushing of soft humanity under Babels of power and organisation."

8 DEUTSCH, BABETTE. *Poetry in Our Time: A Critical Survey of Poetry in the English-speaking World 1900-1960*. Garden City, N.Y.: Anchor Books, Doubleday, pp. 284, 347-48.

Reprint of 1952.3; 1956.9; 1958.2.

9 ENRIGHT, D. J. "The Greater Toil." *New Statesman*, 4 January, pp. 21-22.

Reviews *Advice to a Prophet and Other Poems*. Remarks that Richard Wilbur "is, with reason, celebrated for his craftsmanship – this new collection is full of it – but some readers may have their doubts about the materials in which he works. Considering its subject . . . the title-piece here strikes me as unseasonably marmoreal." Says lines in "Stop" are typical of "craftsmanship at its emptiest." Admits, however, that several poems in this collection stand out as very successful ("The Undead," "Shame," "A Grasshoper"), enough to redeem the value of the book. Concludes that "Mr. Wilbur cannot be used, as some critics have tried to use him, as a definitively effective reproach to the 'fumbling amateurs' of British verse."

10 FREEDLEY, GEORGE. *Library Journal*, 15 October, p. 3859.

Reviews *Tartuffe*. Suggests that "this new translation by Richard Wilbur, a distinguished poet, is as brilliant and informative as his earlier reworking of *Le Misanthrope*, which was so justly acclaimed. Molière can have a renaissance on the English-speaking stage now that an inspired translator has appeared on the scene who knows how to turn into modern poetic English the bittersweet quality of Molière's French. I hope Mr. Wilbur continues until he has newly translated all of the dramatic comedies of France's greatest dramatist."

11 FURBANK, P. N. "New Poetry." *Listener* (London), 7 March, p. 435.
  Reviews *Advice to a Prophet and Other Poems*. Says that Wilbur's poetry rightly places him in the "school of urbanity" as Donald Hall suggests. His elegant phrasing and obvious control of the language often covers over his subjects, which, in this collection, do seem like odds and ends. Suggests that a better way of testing the power of Wilbur's work is to ask "whether the whole argument and fiction of his poems can really bear scrutiny." Analyzes "Next Door" and concludes that the poem "stood up well."

12 "In the Twilight of an Old Order, the Promising New Poets." *National Observer*, 8 April, p. 20.
  Contains commentary on several younger poets, including Richard Wilbur. Says that he "is easily our first poet in technical skill. No one rhymes better, handles meter more skillfully, or translates so delightfully. He lent his talents to the Broadway stage with equal facility in 1956, when he contributed most of the lyrics for the musical *Candide*. His honors are many – including the Pulitzer Prize, Melville Cane Award, and Prix de Rome." Admits that "many feel Mr. Wilbur lacks 'depth,' . . . that he will never be able to deal successfully with serious subject matter." Cites Theodore Holmes's "scathing review" (1962.12) in which he "made the classic case against Mr. Wilbur's kind of poetry. It is mannered and artificial, he [Holmes] said, lacking any real contact with the great verities of life and death." Suggests that "Mr. Wilbur's supporters are by now hardened to such attacks. There is nothing wrong with technical facility, they feel. Wilbur could not write any differently if he tried, nor should he."

13 JARRELL, RANDELL. "Fifty Years of American Poetry." *Prairie Schooner* 37, no. 1 (Spring):1-27.
  Criticizes Wilbur's work. Says "Petronius spoke of the 'studied felicity' of Horace's poetry, and I can never read one of Richard Wilbur's books without thinking of this phrase. His impersonal, exactly accomplished, faintly sententious skill produces poems that, ordinarily, compose themselves into a little too regular a beauty – there is no eminent beauty with a certain strangeness in the proportion." Concedes that "A Baroque Wall-Fountain in the Villa Sciarra" "is one of the most marvelously beautiful, one of the most nearly perfect poems any American has written." Sees "A Black November Turkey" and "A Hole

in the Floor" "are the little differentiated, complete-in-themselves universes that true works of art are." Remarks that Wilbur "obsessively sees, and shows, the bright underside of every dark thing. . . . This compulsion limits his poems; and yet it is this compulsion, and not merely his greater talent and skill, that differentiates him so favorably from the controlled, accomplished, correct poets who are common nowadays." Reprinted: 1969.6. Reprinted in part: 1983.18.

14 KELL, RICHARD. Review of *Advice to a Prophet and Other Poems*. *Critical Quarterly* (London) 5 (Autumn):283-84.

Reviews *Advice to a Prophet and Other Poems*. Observes that the craftsman prevails in Richard Wilbur's new collection and that the subject matter of these poems is slight. Imaginative vision appears only now and then to surprise and delight the reader. Concludes that, on the whole, it is a dull book.

15 *Literary History of the United States*. Edited by Robert E. Spillers, et al. 4th rev. ed. New York: Macmillan Publishing Co., p. 1433.

Asserts that Richard Wilbur has created order in the world through his poetry. Notes that his particular bent is to exclude from his verse the "madness" of the twentieth century, yet he recognizes the need for keeping in touch with the "flux of life," as the titles of his work, *The Beautiful Changes* and *Things of This World*, suggest. Finds that he consistently rejects *le poésie pur*, subjecting himself, instead, to the rigors of traditional form.

16 MATTHEWS, JACKSON. "A New *Tartuffe*." *New York Review of Books*, 26 September, pp. 19-20.

Reviews *Tartuffe*. Notes that because people are generally annoyed by English rhymes, Molière's plays have been adapted to the English stage or translated in prose. Richard Wilbur's translation of *Tartuffe* is proof that it is possible for a fine poet to catch the nuances of the full meaning of the play in rhymed couplets. Says that "the superiority of Mr. Wilbur's verse does not come, of course, solely from the presence of rhyme. It comes from his superior sense and use of language as a whole. It comes from his being the better poet." Concludes that "Mr. Wilbur has given us, with great fidelity and charm, the nearest thing to Molière that we have."

17 MYERS, JOHN A., Jr. "Death in the Suburbs." *English Journal* 52, no. 5 (May):377-79.

Suggests methods for teaching Richard Wilbur's "To an American Poet Just Dead" to high school students. Urges that students must concentrate on the tone of voice of the speaker of the poem. Students will then be able to recognize the heavy irony imbedded in the poem. Asserts that students must also be able to separate the "I" of the poem from the actual poet. Explains that "in the [last] three stanzas of the poem, Wilbur uses a multitude of primarily tonal devices to paint a picture of the spiritual inertia and complacency that characterize American suburbia." Argues that "the irony [in the last two lines of the poem] matches the speaker's final state of resignation." Hopes to awaken students to the rich imagery and sound patterns of the poem through using these methods.

18 PHILBRICK, CHARLES. Review of *Advice to a Prophet and Other Poems. Mutiny: A Magazine of the Arts.* 12:62-63.
    Reviews *Advice to a Prophet and Other Poems.* Grants that Richard Wilbur "is a poet whose work one associates with aesthetic intelligence, with address, sensitivity and civility, in the best sense of each of those words. His strength is like that of one's favorite and most feared-for athlete: it is the strength of control and gracefulness. Wilbur is skillful, reflective, attractive and sweet: if these are old-fashioned qualities, may he make the most of them, for they cannot stay long out of fashion." Disputes the validity of questions such as "Where is the big poem?" or "Is he a *major* poet?" Says these questions "somehow don't dare raise their heads in this clear light."

19 "Richard Wilbur." In *The Author's and Writer's Who's Who.* London: Burke's Peerage, pp. 519-20.
    Lists Wilbur's educational experience, marriage to Charlotte Hayes Ward, teaching positions at Harvard University, Wellesley College, and Wesleyan University. Lists several important prizes and awards. Includes a brief primary bibliography beginning with *The Beautiful Changes* (1947) and ending with *Complete Poems of Poe* (edited by Wilbur) and *Poems 1943-1956.*

20 "Richard Wilbur." In *The Concise Encyclopedia of English and American Poets and Poetry.* Edited by Stephen Spender and Donald Hall. New York: Hawthorn, p. 357.
    Mentions biographical facts about Wilbur's upbringing, education, awards, and present occupation. Also lists publications to date. Asserts that Wilbur is known for his adherence to artifice, his elegance, use of classical references, and "accurate epithets." Suggests that currently, Wilbur has moved from a created imaginary world to writing about more earthy subjects.

*21 "Richard Wilbur." In *The Concise Encyclopedia of Modern World Literature*. Edited by Geoffrey Grigson. London: Hutchinson of London, pp. 484-85.

    Item listed in unpublished bibliography.

22 ROSENTHAL, M. L. "New Singers and Songs." *New York Times Book Review*, 30 June, pp. 1, 26-27.

    Reviews several poets who are close to fifty. Turns up a number of fine poets writing various kinds of poetry. Among them is Richard Wilbur who writes poems, "sometimes of incomparable richness and deftness [that] stand by themselves in their own modest perfection. He shares the concerns of the age, of course, as his poem against the McCarran Act and his 'Advice to a Prophet'–concerning the right way to shock ourselves awake to the horror of the Bomb–show clearly. A very pure, vivid intimacy with language and the possibilities of traditional form have made him a poet of almost Classical cast." Admits that "one may quarrel, as I have, with this self-limiting quality . . . ; and yet, in another mood, I am sure the quarrel is presumptuous, for one should be grateful to have what Wallace Stevens called the 'noble accents' and the 'lucid, inescapable rhythms' of the true 'bawds of euphony.'"

23 WALLACE, ROBERT M. "Second Impressions, Review of Paperbacks." *Nation*, 28 December, p. 463.

    Reviews *The Poems of Richard Wilbur*. Says these are "poems of great virtuosity, insight and feeling from four volumes."

1963-1964

1 MERCIER, VIVIAN. "No Second Miracle." *Hudson Review* 16, no. 4 (Winter):634-36.

    Reviews *Tartuffe*. Says Wilbur's translation of *Tartuffe* is a disappointment: "it is very hard for the modern reader to accept as the first line of a heroic couplet Richard Wilbur's 'It looks to me as if you're out on a limb,' yet, once he had assumed the hero's task of producing a line-by-line verse translation of *Tartuffe*, Wilbur was almost forced to write like this at regular intervals." Notes that "the most Wilbur claims for his diction is that 'at best' it 'mediates between then and now, suggesting no one period.'" Grants that "Wilbur's verse is natural to the extent that it very rarely misplaces a stress for the sake of scansion or rhyme. And he is right in claiming that a verse translation makes the long, logical speeches far more acceptable than a prose one would." Admits that the critical acclaim given to Wilbur's translation of *The Misanthrope* is well deserved and concludes that the "blame for the unsatisfactoriness of Wilbur's *Tartuffe*" must go to Molière. "It is far from being a great play."

1964

1 BRUNS, GERALD L. "The Obscurity of Modern Poetry." *Thought* 39, no. 153 (June):180-98, passim.

Discusses two problems related to modern poetry–isolation of the poet and obscurity. "We should understand that, so far as modern poetry is concerned, obscurity is necessary, but that for more than one reason many poets are more obscure than they need be. And, secondly, in order to see the relationship between obscurity and isolation, it will be necessary to inquire into the relation of the poet to society–a matter which will plunge us directly into a discussion of myth, since it is in terms of myth that the poet is related to society, and since it is precisely society's loss of myth which has played a large part in severing this relationship."

2 Commentary. *Virginia Quarterly Review* 40, no. 1 (Winter):xxv-xxvi.

Review of *Tartuffe*. In mastering the heroic couplet, Wilbur has done Molière good service. His translation of *Tartuffe* is brilliant.

3 "Cowboys and Indians." *Times Literary Supplement, Essays and Reviews from the Times Literary Supplement, 1963*. Vol. II. London: Oxford University Press, pp. 133-36.

Reprint of 1963.6.

4 CROWDER, RICHARD. "Richard Wilbur and France." *Rives* (Paris) no. 25 (Spring): pp. 2-8.

Introduces Wilbur's poems, in their urbane wittiness, to the French. Provides a basic overview of Wilbur's career, designed for the neophyte. Also encourages the French to read Wilbur because of Wilbur's indebtedness to a number of French poets and painters and his various translations of French poets.

5 EBERHART, RICHARD. "On Richard Wilbur's "Love Calls Us to the Things of This World."" In *The Contemporary Poet As Critic and Artist*. Edited by A. J. Ostroff. Boston: Little, Brown, pp. 4-5.

Reprint of 1957.5.

6 FIEDLER, LESLIE A. "A Kind of Solution: The Situation of Poetry Now." *Kenyon Review* 26, no. 1 (Winter):54-79.

Surveys contemporary poets' work. Says that the process of generations of poets begetting new generations of poets continues. The generation of the New Critics and their star poets, T. S. Eliot and Ezra Pound, has given way to a group of poets best represented by Oscar Williams's *New Pocket Anthology of American Verse*. Contends that "best of the group by far . . . is Richard Wilbur. . . . [He] is a versatile craftsman, capable of assimilating to his own uses the techniques of poets as peculiar and difficult as Marianne Moore; and he controls always with deceptive ease whatever he sees, . . . feels, . . . imagines, . . . or muses upon. His language is never banal and never outrageous; his music never dull and never atrocious; what he can do he knows, and is never tempted to exceed it." Suggests that Wilbur has "tried to extend his range in the theatre" by translating Molière and writing lyrics for *Candide*. Contends that "not only his example but his taste is helping to determine the shape of poetry at the present moment; for he is one of the editors of a series of volumes of new poetry published by the Wesleyan University Press." Quotes "Museum Piece" as a poem which demonstrates Wilbur's "special qualities." Admits that "there is wit in these lines and grace, as well as an impulse – far from ignoble – to write at every moment as well as one can; but there is no personal voice – and there is no sex: the insistent 'I' and the assertion of balls being considered apparently in equally bad taste." Concludes that "there is more sense of the aroused and living flesh, of bodies savored and seed sown, and, therefore, of a creating 'I,' in the work of certain women poets, especially Ruth Stone, whose debut was simultaneous with Wilbur's." Reprinted: 1964.7.

7 ____. *Waiting for the End*. New York: Stein and Day, pp. 218-221.
   Reprint of 1964.6.

8 FOWLER, NANCY B. Untitled. *Daily Hampshire Gazette* (Northampton, Mass.), 10 March, p. 10.
   Reports on a poetry reading by Richard Wilbur at Smith College in the Vanderbilt Series. Lists some of his achievements at the end of the article.

9 FRANK, ROBERT, and MITCHELL, STEPHEN, eds. "Richard Wilbur: An Interview." *Amherst Literary Magazine* 10, no. 2 (Summer):54-73.
   Wilbur discusses the interaction of his teaching and his writing, his "painless" introduction to publication, his broad reading of other poets – including George Herbert, Andrew Marvell, the prose of Thomas Traherne, and William Carlos Williams. He defends himself

1964

against Randall Jarrell's criticism of not "going far enough," describes the audience he writes for, discusses his method of writing poetry, and defends the formal poem as opposed to free verse. Being called a religious poet is a label he accepts, suggesting several ways one could support such a description. He discusses the role of metaphors in poetry, especially poetry containing "concrete reality." Wilbur disavows any notion of belonging to or founding a school of poets or critics. The joy of translation, for him, is to try to bring the poem "back alive" rather than to assert some of himself into the original poem. Argues that "the issue of reading the poem is not conversion, but enrichment of experience." Reprinted: 1990.2.

10 HORAN, ROBERT. "On Richard Wilbur's 'Love Calls Us to the Things of This World.'" In *The Contemporary Poet As Critic and Artist.* Edited by A. J. Ostroff. Boston: Little Brown, pp. 6-11.
Reprint of 1957.12.

11 LERNER, LAURENCE D. "Molière's *Tartuffe*." *Listener* (London), 14 May, p. 809.
Reviews *Tartuffe*. Asserts that "the translator of Molière must be elegant, witty, supple: able to write formal and polished couplets that retain speech rhythms. No living poet is better able to do this than Mr Wilbur, who has the technical mastery and – at times – the bite of Pope himself." Contends that "this translation is not uniformly satisfying. Too often Mr Wilbur fills up a couplet with a word or a phrase that seems there simply to add syllables; . . . occasionally – very occasionally – he seems to get an effect wrong." Notes two other serious faults. Finds it "embarrassing" to move from Augustan couplets to "schoolboy slapstick" of modern America. Also finds the most serious fault in the play itself. Concludes the play is "botched."

12 "Molière Then and Now." *Times Literary Supplement* (New York), 23 April, p. 35.
Reviews *Tartuffe*. Says that "when Mr. Wilbur's verse translation of *The Misanthrope* was published in 1958 a reviewer described it in these columns as 'brilliantly successful in the scenes of high comedy,' but had reservations about the translator's handling of the more pedestrian scenes. His translation of *Tartuffe* invites a similar judgment. It does not, as Mr. Wilbur remarks in his preface, provide the translator with the same opportunities as *The Misanthrope*, but he is highly successful with the principal speeches of Cléante and Dorine."

13 "Richard Wilbur." In *Books U.S.A.* (London) n. 10, June, pp. 14-15.

Lists Richard Wilbur's accomplishments, prizes and awards, his translations from French poets Molière, Baudelaire, Valéry, Francis Jammes, and Philippe de Thaun. Gives biographical details of his early life and army service as well as his educational experience and teaching assignments. Lists published works. Notes that "Wilbur is editor of the Laurel Poetry Series of Dell Books and is a member of the American Academy of Arts and Sciences and the National Institute of Arts and Letters." Reprints "Loves Calls Us to the Things of This World."

14 "Richard Wilbur." In *The National Cyclopaedia of American Biography – 1960-63*. Vol. J. New York: James T. White, pp. 314-15.

Includes biographical data, education, teaching assignments, and marriage to Charlotte Ward. Notes the names of the Wilburs's four children. Also lists major publications, including editorial work, from *The Beautiful Changes* (1947) through *Emily Dickinson: Three Views* (1960) and *Poe: Complete Poems* (1959). Mentions several prizes and awards and his membership in the American Academy of Arts and Sciences, National Institute of Arts and Letters, the Dramatists' Guild, and Chi Psi fraternity. Notes Wilbur's religious affiliation is Episcopalian.

15 SWENSON, MAY. "On Richard Wilbur's 'Love Calls Us to the Things of This World.'" In *The Contemporary Poet As Critic and Artist*. Boston: Little Brown, pp. 12-16.

Reprint of 1957.17.

1965

1 ABBE, GEORGE. *You and Contemporary Poetry: An Aid to Appreciation*. Peterborough, N.H.: Noone House, pp. 32-33, 98-105.
Reprint of 1957.1.

2 BEATY, JEROME, and MATCHETT, WILLIAM H. *Poetry from Statement to Meaning*. New York: Oxford University Press, pp. 208-9, 239-40.
Contrasts Wilbur's "Mind" to Marianne Moore's "The Mind Is an Enchanting Thing." Says "Mind" is a poem based on a simile used to explain the human mind. The simile falls short, and the poet reaches beyond its comparisons to say something more about the human mind. Notes "how the poem moves from the disparagement of mind implied in 'some bat' to the respectful recognition that the mind's very errors can bring about advancement. The bat's environment is independent of the bat, but the mind's is subject to the mind conceiving it."

*3 BRUSTEIN, ROBERT. "Health in an Ailing Profession." *New Republic*, 20 January 1965: pp, 32-35.
Listed in 1971.6, p. 81.

4 CHAPMAN, JOHN. "*Tartuffe* a Rollicking Big Romp; Best Yet for Lincoln Center Co." *Daily News*, 15 January.
Performance review of *Tartuffe* produced by the Repertory Theater of Lincoln Center. Says that "Richard Wilbur's translation of Molière's text into clear, direct and even colloquial rhymed couplets, is admirable and seemingly effortless. It is to the point and never labored or cute, and the entire company speaks the verse with an offhand ease which is remarkable." Reprinted in *New York Theatre Critics Reviews 1965*: p. 393.

5 FUSSELL, PAUL, Jr. *Poetic Meter & Poetic Form*. New York: Random House, pp. 73, 153, 65-66, 99-100.
Notes that Richard Wilbur, along with other modern American and British poets, "has returned to a more or less stable sort of Yeatsian accentual-syllabism." Cites "Junk" as a "successful suggestion of the tonality of Old English versification . . . possible when the poetic subject seems more appropriate." This poem "gives a contemporary twist to a favorite Old English subject, the power of good workmanship, and we end with a feeling that spirits of two distinct ages have momentarily almost been joined." Contends that, in the end, "Old

English verse can be imitated, [but] nothing really like it can be recovered." Says Richard Wilbur "displays his accuracy and tact as a metrist in 'A Simile for Her Smile,' where almost every variation convinces us that it issues from the pressure of the poem's internal dynamics." Thinks that Wilbur "reveals that he knows what density of texture is, and he reveals a mastery of one of the main techniques for attaining it, the interfusion of predication and rhythm."

6 GARRETT, GEORGE. "Against the Grain: Poets Writing Today." In *American Poetry*. Edited by Irvin Ehrenpreis. Stratford-Upon-Avon Studies, no. 7. London: Edward Arnold, pp. 220-39, passim.

Surveys the state of modern poetry. Says that all the fireworks engendered between the "academics" and the "beats" are "utterly bogus." Both camps have considerable academic backgrounds, both camps have been influenced by Eliot, Pound, and William Carlos Williams; the fight has been an "internecine war" amounting to nothing. Cites the anthologies *The New Poets of England and America* (1957), edited by Donald Hall, Robert Pack, and Louis Simpson, and *The New American Poetry 1945-1960*, edited by Donald M. Allen, as the "main battleground." Thinks that neither camp has as yet produced a poet who can speak to human beings outside the confines of their little worlds and make his speech matter. Summarizes, "We are still in the post-war period, but now a second 'generation' has arrived upon the scene. Their internecine wars brought nothing about, except, of course, sufficient ferment and excitement to alleviate some of the essential loneliness of being a poet. That precisely because of their internal squabbles they have at once increasingly isolated and become increasingly aware of the isolation of the American poet from any audience." Concludes that "it remains to be seen if one or many of our new poets will learn enough human charity to speak to another human being and have it matter." Places Richard Wilbur in the academic camp.

7 "God of Common Sense." *Time*, 22 January, p. 46.

Performance review of *Tartuffe* produced at Lincoln Center's off-Washington Square theater. Says "[Wilbur's] springy, intelligent couplets turn Molière's French into speakably idiomatic English."

8 HESTER, Sister MARY. "'The [*sic*] Juggler' by Richard Wilbur." *English Journal* 54, no. 9 (December):880-81.

Recounts analyzing "Juggler" with a group of high school students. Says her approach proved to be a rewarding experience as students became aware of the tone, the symbols, the kinetic action, the extended metaphor of the juggler, and the fresh use of words like "gravity" to renew one's sense of its meaning.

9 HEWES, HENRY. "Broadway Postcript." *Saturday Review*, 6 February, p. 44.
     Performance review of *Tartuffe* produced at the Lincoln Center Repertory Theater. (Wilbur is briefly mentioned as an "adaptor.")

10 KERR, WALTER. *New York Herald Tribune*, 16 January.
     Performance review of *Tartuffe* produced by the Lincoln Center Repertory Theater. Says "Richard Wilbur has provided an excellent, sorely needed, translation and provided it on Molière's verse terms. That the couplets can be managed easily, without any sense of being boxed in by recurring sound, was demonstrated several years ago in an off-Broadway production of *The Misanthrope*." Suggests that "here, however, the end-stops are stressed, even when they are not end-stops. The players swallow breath just in time for every rhyme so that melody dominates and sometimes strangles, sense. What might have been treated as a sub-surface echo becomes as strong as a strict conductor's beat, and even the excellent actress Sada Thompson, who sweetly subdued the metrics in *The Misanthrope*, is bound by it." Judges that "Miss Thompson's eyes flash so impertinently, and she so thoroughly knows her sassy, common sense maidservant, that her quality comes through anyway. But neither it nor Molière's irony should have to work quite so hard to pierce a deliberately picturesque overcast." Reprinted in *New York Theatre Critics Reviews 1965*, p. 392.

11 LEWIS, THEOPHILUS. "Theatre." *America*, 6 March, p. 336.
     Performance review of *Tartuffe* produced by the Lincoln Center Repertory Theater. Mentions Wilbur as translator in passing.

12 MILLS, RALPH J., Jr. "Richard Wilbur." In *Contemporary American Poetry*. New York: Random House, pp. 160-75.
     Expanded version of 1962.14. Reprinted 1962 version: 1983.18.

13 NADEL, NORMAN. "Five Words from *Tartuffe*, and *Tartuffe* Is Saved." *New York World-Telegram and The Sun*, 15 January.
     Performance review of *Tartuffe* produced by Lincoln Center Repertory Theater. Says, "I hope that Richard Wilbur's translation of *Tartuffe* into English isn't the last word in this language. It's workable for the stage, but not always artful. The use of colloquial speech, not of Molière's time, sounds out of key." Reprinted in *New York Theatre Critics Reviews 1965*, pp. 391-92.

14 QUASHA, GEORGE. "A Reading of 'The Beautiful Changes.'"
Washington Square Review 1, no. 2 (Spring):34-40.

Employs New Critical methods in Part I for analyzing "The Beautiful Changes." Attempts to create "a *ménage à trois* of content, form, and critical terminology. That analysis is perhaps a necessary evil for one who holds that a good poem may seem simply conceived in both its prose meaning and its structure yet reveal, upon a close look at its argument and the technical devices enforcing it, a certain functional complexity." Reads each stanza of the poem closely to isolate levels of meaning in words and lines of argument. Says that "it is clear that the poet has presented a subtle argument on the nature of the beautiful. In the first stanza, he presents the evidence; in the second stanza, he presents the idea and illustrates it; in the third stanza, he begins by restating, adjusting, and completing the idea begun in Stanza 2; and, in the last three lines, he clarifies the implications of this idea." Suggests that "on another level, [the poem] embodies a progression from a state of lost inocence to a state of regained innocence or salvation." Sees a threefold argument: "there are changes in nature which are beautiful; that which is beautiful changes; and the beautiful changes things and people."

Analyzes structural and formal details of the poem in Part II.

15 "Richard Wilbur." In *Oxford Companion to American Literature*. 4th ed. Edited by James D. Hart. New York: Oxford University Press, p. 923.

Lists Richard Wilbur's education and teaching assignments; notes influences of the French symbolists, Marianne Moore, and Wallace Stevens. Lists major works beginning with *The Beautiful Changes* (1947) through *Candide* (1957).

16 SHEED, WILFRID. "The Comedy of Quaintness." *Commonweal*, 5 February, pp. 611-12.

Performance review of *Tartuffe* produced by the Lincoln Center Repertory Theater. Contends that "Richard Wilbur has translated the play into English couplets, some of them ingenious, and some of them pretty bad (with rhymes that a popular-song writer would blanch at), and the actors don't throw half enough of them away, because they are playing it all with too much feeling."

17 "Songs Around the Mountain." *Times Literary Supplement* (London), 25 November, p. 1070.

Focuses on the tension between "the radical poets and the lapidary antiquarians." Says that the new anthology of contemporary poetry, *A Controversy of Poets*, edited by Paris Leary and Robert Kelly,

1965

highlights the chasm between poets practising a new orthodoxy and apparently "relinquishing a grand and flexible instrument – and narrowing their scope, while sharpening their handling of certain devices – for inadequate reasons" against poets, like Richard Wilbur, who appear to be writing "English as if it were a dead language."

18 STEPANCHEV, STEPHEN. *American Poetry Since 1945: A Critical Survey.* New York: Harper & Row, pp. 93-106.

Surveys Wilbur's first four collections of poems. Says Richard Wilbur has the "gift of metaphor-making," and "the patience and perseverance of the craftsman, the carpenter, who respects his medium and submits himself to the slow task of fitting matter to design, theme to object." Suggests that it is "perhaps [his] commitment to the forms, the nets, of tradition that enables him to sing. In this he is unlike many of his contemporaries, who merely talk." Characterizes *The Beautiful Changes* (1947) as a book of "joyous celebration of all that is wild and free and full of life," though he notes a number of war poems ("Mined Country," "Potato," "Place Pigalle"). Cites the sonnet "O" as an example of Wilbur's "love of the things of this world, their textures and colors, and his distrust of fleshless abstraction." Sees evidence of similar qualities in *Ceremony* (1950), "a deftly written, fluent book full of the poet's experience of objects under varying conditions of light and weather ("La Rose des Vents," "Castles and Distances"). Finds "A World without Objects Is a Sensible Emptiness" a poem disclosing Wilbur's sense of the value of "the embodiment of spirit even though the body is maculate." Notes that "'Epistemology' teases one into conceding the possibility that the celebration of the things of this world is, in reality, a celebration of the individual imagination, the power of mind that creates the world" ("The Terrace"). Counters this view by citing "Giacometti" as a poem showing "Wilbur's ability to see man as ['unspeakably alone'] as well as in the positive terms of creative power." These paradoxical views make clear "the range and complexity of the tensions out of which [Wilbur's] poems are made."

Describes *Things of This World* (1956) as a collection in which the poet "speculates about the reality of this world he renders with such love and precision. Is he dreaming it? Is he alone in space and imagining the properties of reality? . . . Over and over the poet speaks of dream, of 'dreamt land,' of dream-laden reality" ("Merlin Enthralled," "For the New Railway Station in Rome," "Love Calls Us to the Things of This World"). Asserts that Wilbur continues to work on his epistemological concerns in *Advice to a Prophet* (1961) ("Two Voices in a Meadow"). Says that "the contrast between appearance and reality is at the center of 'Junk' and 'A Summer Morning.'" Finds

"Advice to a Prophet" "a brilliant paradox [which] suggests the wit of a poet who sees the world as both shadow and substance, subject and object." Concludes that Richard Wilbur "is unquestionably one of the most accomplished of contemporary poets. . . . His excellence, within his limits, is real. His achievement is due to his submission to his art, his craft; it is an effect of will, patience, and love."

19 SUTTON, WALTER. "Criticism and Poetry." In *American Poetry*. Edited by Irvin Ehrenpreis. Stratford-Upon-Avon Studies, no. 7. London: Edward Arnold, pp. 175-95, passim.

Notes that Pound and Eliot are the leaders of two traditions in American poetry, each having interaction with the other on critical theory. Descending directly from Eliot's tradition are the articulators of the New Criticism, the first generation of disciples. The second generation is made up of the poets of Richard Wilbur's period who have largely chosen to adopt the values of the New Critics. Sees a third, less well-defined generation as that of the "beats" and Black Mountain poets who descend directly from Pound and William Carlos Williams. Concludes that "critics and theorists, as well as poets themselves, have been moving towards a conception of organicism that recognises the necessary interpenetration of literary form and cultural environment, and the corresponding interdependence of formalist or aesthetic and historical criticism. . . . At this point in history we are badly in need of a poetry, of a literature, that can speak powerfully as a champion of positive social and political ideals and as a critic of their neglect."

20 TAUBMAN, HOWARD. "The Theatre: *Tartuffe*." *New York Times*, 15 January.

Performance review of *Tartuffe* produced by the Lincoln Square Repertory Theater. Says that the actors have mastered Wilbur's excellent English couplets, reading them with skill in order to appear natural. Agrees that Wilbur has boldly employed contemporary English without resorting to cleverness in his translation. Reprinted in *New York Theatre Critics Reviews 1965*, pp. 390-91.

*21 *Variety*, 20 January.

Listed in 1971.6, p. 82.

22 WATTS, RICHARD, Jr. "Notable Production of *Tartuffe*." *New York Post*, 15 January.

Performance review of *Tartuffe* produced by the Lincoln Square Repertory Theater. Praises "Richard Wilbur's translation into English rhymed couplets [because it] soon loses any suggestion of self-consciousness and seems to strike just the right note in humor and grace." Reprinted in *New York Theatre Critics Reviews 1965*, p. 393.

1966

*1 GEIGER, Sister MARY LORETTA. "Structure and Imagery in the Poetry of Richard Wilbur." Master's Thesis, Villanova University, 87 pp.
    Listed in unpublished Hagstrom bibliography.

2 GULLANS, CHARLES. "Edgar Bowers' *The Astronomers*, and Other New Verse." *Southern Review* n.s. 2, no. 1 (Winter):189-209.
    Reviews *Poems*. Compares Edgar Bowers, Robert Lowell, and Richard Wilbur, and finds Wilbur to be the least exceptional. Says his poems lack the "concentration, intensity, and vigor" of the other poets. Asserts that "his scope of idea is more limited, his range of subject matter less absorbing. There is little that could be called experimental about his poems, unless it be his early interest in accentual meters and his early command of them." Suggests that Wilbur's "tolerance of accentual meter has sometimes loosened his handling of standard meter to awkwardness." Finds strong echoes of T. S. Eliot and Auden in early poems. Criticizes Wilbur by saying "a number of poems seem to me destroyed by the affectation of an offhand manner in dealing with serious material, a kind of latter-day romantic irony." ("Ceremony," "To An American Poet Just Dead," "The Pardon"). Calls "Death of a Toad," "A Baroque Wall-Fountain at the Villa Sciarra," "Beasts," "After the Last Bulletins," and "Shame" "some of the most fashionable poems of two decades." Says "they are clever to the point of flipness, accomplished in craft, frequently witty, but so mannered as to be annoying." Cites "Caserta Gardens," "First Snow in Alsace," "Grasse: The Olive Trees," "Year's End," "A Voice from under the Table," "Lamarck Elaborated," and "She" as "good or interesting poems" because they are "serious in subject, show less affection of manner and diction than other poems . . . and are his most impressive craft achievements." Concludes, "Wilbur maintains a vital tradition cleanly and honestly. We need more poets with his virtues and strengths."

3 GUSTAFSON, RICHARD. "Richard Wilbur and the Beasts." *Iowa English Yearbook* no. 11 (Fall): pp. 59-63.
    Argues that Richard Wilbur's poems do much to renew the language, and at times, move us to feel a new excitement about something familiar. Says poems from *Things of This World*, in particular, are "characterized by crisp diction, surprising phrases,

masterful total form, and graceful, rather epigrammatic, endings. But these qualities are dangerously dominant in Wilbur's work. In reading him one tends to become too conscious of the style, too enamored of the wit." Criticizes Wilbur because he "never seems to get out of the drawing room nor put down the martini of his wit." Finds his exploration into the human mind reveals "a bestial terror grinning there." Says "poems about people fall into two categories: exaltation of the very humble, or terror at the very passionate" ("A Prayer to Go to Paradise with the Donkeys," "A Plain Song for Comadre," "Beasts"). Notes that "Mind" presents "some hope" but questions the meaning of 'happiest intellection.'" Notes the publication of bestiary poems and questions "why he allegorizes the mind so." Says that even when Wilbur writes of "people in the mass, he . . . tends to make them bestial" ("Still, Citizen Sparrow"). Maintains that Wilbur "shows himself to be somewhat of an eighteenth century recluse, whose scorn for and fear of the world drives him to the enclosed garden, the *hortus* conclusion. And Wilbur has all the virtues of a classical Augustan; the scorn and fear and escape into a conventional retreat; a very eastern professorship, an episcopalianism, an elegance, a wit, a tendency to latinism in style."

Grants that there is love in Wilbur's work, but "it is a special form of love" ("Love Calls Us . . ."). Love poems to women are much more "restrained." Concludes that "Wilbur's virtues are his defects. But he is a viruous [*sic*] example of a seemingly typically American malaise. Most suburbanites don't write poetry, and their imaginations get no further than thinking up clever Christmas cards. We admire Wilbur's grace, his wit, his sweet elegance, but we miss the four fiery horsemen. . . . But Richard Wilbur must be read. He has polished our diction and advanced our idiom. He has given a higher tone to the language of the educated man of the world, a finer timbre and a deeper resonance. In these matters, he is an important modern poet."

4 HEWES, HENRY. "Broadway Postscript." *Saturday Review* (5 March): pp. 54-55.

Recounts the production of *The Misanthrope* in Chicago. Does not mention Richard Wilbur's work specifically.

5 LEVIDOVA, I. [On American Poetry of Our Days]. *Inostrannaya Literatura* (Moscow), 9 (September):200-207.

In Russian. Surveys the work of several contemporary American poets, but says she cannot forget Richard Wilbur because he has more poetic talent, more ability to create good poetry. Other poets are interested in progress and in technique, but he has a large interest in nature. Finds that at times Wilbur uses irony with nature imagery. At other times nature is a metaphor for a larger meaning; he uses nature, in other words, as a vehicle for ideas. Sometimes nature is simply image. Concludes that Richard Wilbur is a well-known twentieth-century poet whose poems are read by many Americans.

6 McNIGHT, PAUL, and HOUSTON, GARY, eds. *Thistle* 9, no. 1 (December): 22-27.

The following interview took place from 9:15 to 9:45 A.M. on April 30, 1966, in a parlor at the Wooster Inn, shortly before Mr. Wilbur was to participate in a panel discussion with Lewis Mumford and Howard Hanson.

Richard Wilbur admits to being influenced by many poets. Says "it's no shame to confess that one's been influenced, because no poet has ever thought up the idea of poetry for himself." Resists being "against" any particular poet. Insists he enjoys and profits from "the very prosaic poetry of William Carlos Williams." Lists his country upbringing, his father's work as a painter, and World War II as formative influences on his poetry. Notes that "the relationship between the poet and the reader is a very oblique one. . . . You do not write for an audience directly. . . . You have the audience and your likely effect on it, and your commerce with the audience is your sense of the language and of its range of experience. In the back of your mind, as you write, what you're really thinking about is how you can get down on paper what it is that's eating you at the moment, in a form satisfactory to you. . . . From the point of view of the reader, I should like poetry to have the effect of putting everything into one language, as it were, of introducing the aspects of life which are likely to be separate in everyday, scattered experience – of introducing these aspects of life to each other, yoking them together with grammar, making some kind of unity of sensibility possible at least for a moment." Feels that poetry is "something to be permeated by." On philosophy and poetry, he argues that "philosophical poetry, at its best, manages to be abstractly orderly and at the same time to test its abstract ideas in something that looks like the felt world of experience." Mentions wanting to be a painter, a newspaper cartoonist, a political cartoonist, a general journalist, and a teacher before he ever came to think of himself as a poet. Contends that though many people dislike "close reading," "it seems to me that that's about all you can do in class, unless you resort to a lot of generally irrelevant historical and biographical background, or unless you restrict yourself to OH's and AH's – unless you place yourself, as one of my Amherst teachers said, in the 'wet pants' school of literary criticism." On the use of sound in poetry, Wilbur says he has matured since his early days: "I started out writing under the influence of that kind of stress in criticism and classroom teaching. And I think, therefore, that some of my early poems are written with a tin ear or with no ear at all. I was interested in the words, in the interaction of the words, but not in the dramatic tone of the poem and with no interest in the matter of articulation." Reprinted: 1990.2.

7 PERRINE, LAURENCE. "Richard Wilbur." *100 American Poems of the Twentieth Century*. Edited by Laurence Perrine and James M. Reid. New York: Harcourt, Brace, & World, pp. 253-61.
   Reprints "A Baroque Wall-Fountain in the Villa Sciarra," "For the New Railway Station in Rome," and "The Mill" with critical interpretation of each. Says in the first poem, Richard Wilbur contrasts two life styles – that of the pagan delight in the life of the senses and the Christian life of struggle toward the ideal. In the end he synthesizes these two views of the world in the image of St. Francis of Assisi, praying in the snow. Interprets "For the New Railway Station in Rome," as celebrating the ability of the imagination to "create excellence." Says "The Mill" asks about the meaning of life. It is the perfect symbol of the questions one asks in the face of death. Though the wheel continues to turn, the memory of it will disappear with the death of the viewer and of the poet.

8 "Richard Wilbur." In *The Biographical Encyclopaedia & Who's Who of the American Theatre*. First Edition. New York: James H. Heineman, p. 917.
   Mentions Richard Wilbur as poet, translator, teacher, critic, lyricist. Gives important historical dates. Recounts Wilbur's work as translator of Molière and writer of lyrics for *Candide*. Lists books of poetry from *The Beautiful Changes* (1947) through *Advice to a Prophet* (1961). Lists editorial work on several poets. Numerates various prizes, awards, and honorary degrees.

9 SITTLER, JOSEPH. "The Care of the Earth and the Future of Man." *Colorado Quarterly* 14, no. 3 (Winter):197-208.
   Argues that Wilbur's work defies the commonly held belief that "there is no necessary connection between the thoughts in the mind and the way things are." Instead, Wilbur works within the theological pattern of finding man in relation to God, his fellow man, and "the great garden of nature." Contends that his work is deeply theological. Asks "What . . . in the great tradition of Western Christian and Judaic

thought . . . is diagnostically as penetrating as that poem ["Advice to a Prophet"] and as salvatory as the exposed predicament?"

10 WHEELER, CHARLES B. *The Design of Poetry.* New York: W. W. Norton & Co, pp. 197-201, passim.
   Uses Richard Wilbur "Year's End" as an example of a poet employing symbol inductively. From the beginning scene to the end of the poem where the end of a new year is compared to the end of Pompeii, the poet works with symbol to enlarge the import of his poem.

1966-1967

1 "Richard Wilbur." In *Current Biography Yearbook – 1966.* Edited by Charles Moritz, Vol. 27. New York: H. W. Wilson, pp. 440-42.
   Quotes critics who regard Richard Wilbur as "the most skillful master of poetic technique in the United States today." Mentions critics' discussion of Wilbur's "formalism at the expense of content." Recounts Wilbur's boyhood and family background, spent in New Jersey in a farm environment. His father encouraged him to paint and his mother to write. Lists high school and college writing activities. Cites Wilbur's assertion that "the business of poetry is to make some sort of sense out of everyday experience." Includes wartime experience, Harvard graduate study, publication of *The Beautiful Changes* (1947), *Ceremony and Other Poems* (1950), *Things of This World* (1956), *Advice to a Prophet* (1961), *The Misanthrope* (1955), lyrics for *Candide* (1956), *Tartuffe* (1963), *The Poems of Richard Wilbur* (1963), and significant critical responses to each of these works. Mentions Wilbur's editorial work including *A Bestiary* (1955), *The Complete Poems of Poe* (1959), and literary criticism – *Emily Dickinson: Three Views* (1960). Lists numerous prizes and awards given to Wilbur as well as his honorary degrees and memberships in professional groups. Concludes by describing Wilbur as tall, with brown hair and eyes, in politics an independent, in religion an Episcopalian.

1967

1 BLY, ROBERT. "The First Ten Issues of *Kayak.*" *Kayak,* no. 12, pp. 45-49.
   Reviews the effectiveness of the first ten issues of *Kayak.* Says that these issues "have been on the whole clogged and bad. As an editor, George Hitchcock is too permissive. Poets are encouraged to continue in their failures as well as in their fresh steps." Contends,

however, that *Kayak* has been "a valued and much-loved magazine." Notes that "at first *Kayak* raised its hand against stuff like this, crystallized flower formations from the jolly intellectual dandies." Quotes lines from Richard Wilbur's "Mind." Implies that Wilbur can never be considered a *Kayak* poet.

2 CLOUGH, WILSON O. "Poe's 'The City in the Sea' Revisited." In *Essays on American Literature in Honor of Jay B. Hubbell*. Edited by Clarence Gohdes. Durham, N.C.: Duke University Press, 77, 84-89.

Argues with Wilbur's critical stance on Poe. Objects to Wilbur's finding in Poe "all one story of the mind's escape from corrupt mundane consciousness into visionary wholeness and freedom." Quotes Wilbur as saying, "My suggestion is that 'The City in the Sea' is simply a version of the star Al Aaraaf." Says the word *simply* cannot "go unchallenged" and asserts "that the injection of 'passionate excitement' and intoxication into Poe's 'City in the Sea' is quite out of tune with its 'eternal rest' and its utter motionlessness of silence, and the atmosphere can only be that of post-annihilation of the dreamers."

3 CUMMINS, PAUL F. "'Difficult Balance': The Poetry of Richard Wilbur." Ph.D. dissertation, University of Southern California.

Says Wilbur sets himself apart by employing form to create meaning. Many poems set up a thesis, anti-thesis, and sometimes a synthesis. Analyzes poems to show that Wilbur employs more rhythm than meter, end rhyme, diction betraying classical training, humor, and images drawn from nature. Says Wilbur's theory of poetry leans toward Marianne Moore's idea that "poets must be literalists of the imagination," that poets should steer away from abstraction. Sees that imagination, for Wilbur, is the door to reality. Compares many of his ideas to those of Teilhard de Chardin who also saw a force within nature which unites man and the universe. Concludes that love, for Richard Wilbur, is the way man can redeem man.

Includes a section called "Questionnaire to Mr. Wilbur." Wilbur responds to a question about the absence of Christian symbols in his poems by saying, "my view of things, though not steady, is some sort of Catholic Christian, but I don't . . . make much use of Christian symbol or doctrine. This is because I cannot bear to borrow the voltage of highly charged words. . . . Poetry full of ready-made emotional value will also not represent the movement of the mind and heart toward understanding and clarification, and poetry has to be discovery rather than the celebration of received ideas." Asserts that his poems deal with socio-political matters and have an "implicit political dimension." Lists Augustine, Thomas Traherne's "Centuries," and Pascal as the philosophers and theologians who have had the greatest influence on him. "Questionnaire to Mr. Wilbur" reprinted: 1990.2. See *Dissertation Abstracts International* 28 (1967):3176A.

4 HILL, DONALD L. *Richard Wilbur*. Twayne's United States Authors Series. New York: Twayne, 192 pp.
     Covers *The Beautiful Changes, Ceremony and Other Poems, Things of This World,* and *Advice to a Prophet and Other Poems.* Discusses significant poems in each collection in some detail. Suggests that a major theme for Wilbur is the complementary quality of the ideal and the real. The poet does not attempt reconciliation of these extremes, but rather enjoys the tension created by them. Notes technical achievements in the first collection and subsequent changes. Defends Wilbur against the attacks of critics who regard his work as too mannered or too allusive. Establishes Wilbur within the framework of continuing orthodox poetic practice, though contributing his own unique work. Locates Wilbur ideologically as a poet who accepts the flaws of this world, yet thirsts for the perfection of the eternal. Reprinted in part: 1983.18.

5 HOLMES, JOHN. "Surroundings and Illuminations." In *A Celebration of Poets.* Edited by Don Cameron Allen. Baltimore: Johns Hopkins Press, pp. 108-31.
     Reprint of 1962.11.

6 *Literary and Library Prizes.* 6th ed. Revised and enlarged by Olga S. Weber. New York & London: R. R. Bowker, pp. 13, 67, 101, 124, 207, 210, 211, 214, 216, 219.
     Lists prizes and awards received by Richard Wilbur.

7 McGUINNESS, ARTHUR E. "A Question of Consciousness: Richard Wilbur's *Things of This World.*" *Arizona Quarterly* 23, no. 4 (Winter):313-26.
     Analyzes poems from *Things of This World.* Feels that in this collection Wilbur makes clear that "the ideal world of the imagination . . . is the world of art. . . . Kinetic art . . . has value as metaphor because its movement is the movement of life." Two poems "contrast the static and perfect world of art with the changing and imperfect world of experience" ("Altitudes," "A Baroque Wall-Fountain in the Villa Sciarra"). Suggests that Wilbur deals with the static and the kinetic again in "Statues." Contends that he "has little sympathy for those who would make the ideal world a possible achievement for man" ("Beasts"), though "A Voice from Under the Table" presents "a more

tolerant attitude toward the frustrated idealist." Argues that "Digging for China" is "clearly an indictment of the escapist mentality. . . . For Wilbur, man is movement. He expresses this insight in symbols and metaphors of motion."

Interprets Wilbur poems about love as suggesting that "truly human consciousness develops out of a love of what is real" ("Love Calls Us to the Things of This World"). Finds that though Wilbur "does not deny that transcendent experience is possible, he does insist, however, that such transcendence can develop only out of a deep love of the world's things" ("A Plain Song for Comadre," "John Chrysostom"). Sees "Merlin Enthralled" as a "failure to learn this lesson of love."

Explores Wilbur's ideas about "the nature of reality." Asserts that Wilbur's view is that "the ordinary man lives an illusion. . . . His mind reads into the real world what it wants to find there; indeed, man's mind may be incapable of grasping what really exists. But there are moments in his experience when man can catch a glimpse of the reality behind the illusion" ("The Beacon," "Beasts"). Reality is both dark and light. Says, finally, that Wilbur shows man as "capable of achievement as well as destruction" ("For the New Railway Station in Rome"). Interprets this poem to mean that "consciousness is uniquely man's possession. It can cause him to seek escape from what is all around him, an escape he can never really achieve, but only dream of. But consciousness can also move man to embrace this paradoxical, constantly changing thing called life and make it into his own likeness."

8 "Richard Wilbur." In *Contemporary Authors*. Vols. I-IV. 1st rev. ed. Detroit: Gale, p. 1002.

Lists major biographical facts such as birth date, wife's and children's names, education, politics, religion, and address. Mentions under CAREER Wilbur's graduate study at Harvard University, his teaching assignments at Harvard, Wellesley College and Wesleyan University. Lists travel and military service, memberships in professional organizations, various prizes and awards. Includes a primary bibliography of works by Wilbur beginning with *The Beautiful Changes* (1947) and ending with *The Poems of Richard Wilbur* (1963). Lists WORK IN PROGRESS as lyrics for "The Mad-woman of Chaillot," a musical based on Jean Giraudoux's fantasy. Mentions comments by John Holmes and Alonzo Gibbs. Concludes with a brief list of Biographical/Critical Sources.

9 ROSENTHAL, M. L. *The New Poets: American and British Poetry Since World War II*. New York: Oxford University Press, pp. 328-30.

1967

Mentions that Richard Wilbur represents a group of poets who have avoided "personalist immediacy" in favor of working with more objective structures.

10 SANDERS, THOMAS. *The Discovery of Poetry*. Glenview, Ill.: Scott Foresman, 182-86.
    Interprets "The Death of a Toad" as an example of a poem which establishes a metaphysical relationship between the life of the toad and the life of human beings. Follows New Critical principles in developing a close reading.

11 SAYRE, ROBERT F. "A Case for Richard Wilbur as Nature Poet." *Moderna Språk* (Stockholm) 61:114-22.
    Suggests that nature is Richard Wilbur's "most important subject." Wilbur shares with the Transcendentalists a "sense of correspondence" between nature and man. Yet, Wilbur does not make a religion of nature. For knowledge of himself, the poet goes to nature. Argues that his confidence in nature cannot be turned into anything systematic or romantic: "the distrust of both romanticizing and intellectual systematizing [is] stronger in Wilbur's poems than in the work of most 'beat' poets." It is Wilbur's "live formality," the idea that nature draws life into itself, life which can be understood by the poet's discerning eye, that sets him apart from most nature poets. For Wilbur, "intelligence and imagination animate nature, and nature gives back spirit and power to art and self." Finds that the "New Formalism" is much more than a turning back to old traditions. It is a recognition of the poet's relationship to nature: "Wilbur is at present America's most profound moralist of man's relations with nature." Reprinted: 1983.18.

1968

1 BARNES, CLIVE. "The Theatre: A Timely *Misanthrope*." *New York Times*, 10 October.
    Performance review of *The Misanthrope* performed by the Association of Producing Artists at the Lyceum. Says that "what often stands in the way of Molière in English is the incredible difficulty of translating the poet's rhymed couplets while preserving rhyme, sense, rhythm, wit, and sensibility. Richard Wilbur's marvelous translation does this. It is supple and subtle, it trips affectionately off the tongue with the rise and fall of natural speech to it, and the wit shimmers at its heart like a priceless diamond on a bed of velvet." Reprinted in *New York Theatre Critics Reviews 1968*: pp. 216-17.

2 CHAPMAN, JOHN. "*Misanthrope* Sparkles at APA." *Daily News* (10 October).

Performance review of *The Misanthrope* performed by the Association of Producing Artists at the Lyceum. Calls Richard Wilbur's translation "airily rhymed." Reprinted in *New York Theatre Critics Reviews 1968*: p. 216.

3 CLURMAN, HAROLD. "Theatre." *Nation*, 11 November, p. 510.

Performance review of *The Misanthrope* performed by the Association of Producing Artists at the Lyceum. Says this play would make a "first-rate radio show." Praises Richard Wilbur for his "admirably ingenious translation (less sprightly than the original French, which is mostly a matter of the difference in languages)." Says the play "is well spoken by the entire company." Finds that "it is all quite sensible and easy to take."

4 COOKE, RICHARD P. "Rebounding with Molière." *Wall Street Journal*, 11 October.

Performance review of *The Misanthrope* performed by the Association of Producing Artists at the Lyceum. Contends that the success of the APA Repertory Company's *Misanthrope* can be attributed to the skill of the translator in producing excellent rhymed couplets and reproducing Molière's seventeenth-century wit. Reprinted in *New York Theatre Critics Reviews 1968*: p. 218.

5 CUMMINS, PAUL. "Richard Wilbur's 'Ballade for the Duke of Orléans.'" *Concerning Poetry* 1, no. 2 (Fall):42-45.

Analyzes "Ballade for the Duke of Orléans." Argues that "Richard Wilbur's poetry "reflects a tough minded confrontation with the timeless problems of human experience." Interprets this poem as a statement about the "cycle of love begetting life followed inevitably by death." Understands Wilbur to mean that "it is both man's fate and his blessing that he must work out his destiny amid imperfection and ambiguity. This paradox, of affirming life amid suffering and deprivation, is at the center of [the poem]."

6 DICKEY, JAMES. "The Stillness at the Center of the Target." In *Babel to Byzantium: Poets and Poetry Now*. New York: Farrar, Straus & Giroux, pp. 170-72.

Reprint of 1962.5.

1968

7 FAUCHEREAU, SERGE. "De Lowell à Wilbur par Berryman."
Lecture de la Poésie Américaine. Paris: Les Éditions de Minuit, pp. 149-74.

In French. Compares Richard Wilbur to Robert Lowell and John Berryman. Notes that Wilbur is very cultured and interested in the technique of poetry like the strict prosodists of the Modern period. Says that little change occured from *The Beautiful Changes* (1947) to *Things of This World* (1956). Quotes Wilbur as saying the unit of his work is the single poem. Notes that *The Beautiful Changes* was published after the war when Wilbur felt the need to create order in his life. Says that the "préciosité" of Wilbur's work is markedly different from that of Berryman's. Quotes Gottfried Benn who characterizes Wilbur as a poet who is an artisan, who works with the materials of his poem as a sculptor works with his medium ("Ceremony"). Says Wilbur is not an inferior poet to Lowell or Berryman; he simply writes in a different manner, principally in rhyme and meter because he feels it is the most effective method ("Juggler"). The consequence is that he achieves a remarkable demonstration of skill, but the reader often becomes very aware of his technique. Suggests that *Advice to a Prophet* (1961) marks a change in Wilbur's orientation. In these poems he introduces more human interest. Cites "Shame" as a poem that is a transparent allegory of the people of the United States. Cites the last stanza of "Loves of the Puppets" as an example of the new ideas that have entered Wilbur's thought.

8 GILL, BRENDAN. "Poets and Others." *New Yorker*, 19 October, pp. 159-60.

Performance review of *The Misanthrope* performed by the Association of Producing Artists at the Lyceum. Contends that an absolute requirement for *The Misanthrope* is that it be excellently translated and that Richard Wilbur has done so, with a wise choice of using English iambic pentameter instead of the French Alexandrine. Says Wilbur "has performed a miracle that . . . is surely more difficult than turning ordinary water into ordinary wine: he has turned one rare wine into another without causing the first to lose its identity." Contends that "Mr. Wilbur's employment of rhyme is masterly; it refreshes our recollection of the sheer utility of rhyme in raising the internal tension of a play, especially of a comedy, and in adding to the complex pleasure we derive from the sense of words the simple pleasure of the sweet collision of their sounds."

9 GOTTFRIED, MARTIN. "*The Misanthrope*." *Women's Wear Daily*, 10 October.

Performance review of *The Misanthrope* performed by the Association of Producing Artists at the Lyceum. Grants that the cast had a challenge before them in trying to speak Richard Wilbur's rhymed couplets and make them sound like ordinary conversation. Rhymed couplets may not be the ideal form for this play because of the trouble they present to actors. "Only a few of the cast could properly handle the rhymes." Reprinted in *New York Theatre Critics Reviews 1968*, p. 218.

10 HARRIS, LEONARD. *"Misanthrope."* WCBE TV 2, 9 October.
Performance review of *The Misanthrope* performed by the Association of Producing Artists at the Lyceum. Complains that though Richard Wilbur's translation is good, it is "almost jarring because the rhymes break one's concentration on the sense of dialogue." Reprinted in *New York Theatre Critics Reviews 1968*, p. 218.

11 HEWES, HENRY. "The Theatre." *Saturday Review*. 2 November, p. 53.
Performance review of *The Misanthrope* performed by the Association of Producing Artists at the Lyceum. Remarks that "Stephen Porter has avoided the temptation either to choreograph [the play] breathtakingly or to increase its emotional voltage more than a comedy can bear. Thus undistracted, we listen more intently to Richard Wilbur's remarkably rich translation of Molière's rhymed couplets."

12 HUTTON, JOAN, ed. "Richard Wilbur: Talking to Joan Hutton." *Transatlantic Review* no. 29 (Summer): pp. 58-67.
Richard Wilbur discusses his love of painting and music and gardening. He says that good poets never lie in order to rhyme. His method of writing poetry begins with a "trajectory" and the form of the poem in mind. He admires Borges for his ability to represent the whole of society in his verse, not allowing an obsession to be original to color this thinking. On the Beat poets, Wilbur suggests that they have set themselves up as "supersane." When they suggest that institutions of our society are sick, Wilbur disagrees. He is "all for institutions, for working in and through institutions." Regarding central themes in his work, Wilbur admits that he has often reached for a "clarified contradiction, or balance" because he likes to feel the "resistance" of reality against his ordering of ideas.
In answer to the suggestion that "Poets must keep telling us what's true," Wilbur says, "Yes and if you think . . . of the poet as an agent of society and as a servant of the language, why, then, what the poet does all the time is to see what ideas and what words are alive

and, insofar as he can, to go right to the center of the words that represent the things that are vexing us." Finally, Wilbur asserts that most poets are interested in a comparison of things to see whether it unfolds a truth. This is the reason he feels all poetry is "essentially religious in its direction." "Poetry makes order and asserts relations . . . out of a confidence in ultimate order and relatedness." Reprinted: 1990.2.

13 JEROME, JUDSON. *Poetry: Premeditated Art*. Boston: Houghton Mifflin, pp. 168-69, 179-83, 348-49.
   Uses "A World without Objects Is a Sensible Emptiness" and "Love Calls Us to the Things of This World" as examples of stanza forms invented to enhance the meaning of each poem.

*14 *Kirkus*, 15 January, p. 50. Listed in 1971.6, p. 82.

15 MEREDITH, WILLIAM. Commentary on jacket of *Richard Wilbur Reading His Poetry*. Caedmon Records TC 1248.
   Comments that "both in form and in statement, Wilbur conveys his belief that intuitions of order are what hold chaos at bay. It is one of the provincialisms of our time to admire artists who simulate chaos, as though that were an earnest of their seriousness or honesty. But Frost has put it that every poem is a momentary stay against confusion. It is a perilous order that poetry gives us, but the muse does not come bearing security, only inklings of great order." Concludes that "These poems project a lucid vision of the created universe and of its oddest denizen, man. The eye that sees them and the voice that speaks are passionate though the passion is subject to more command than is common today. The ear that hears them is made aware of the music that inheres in the received experience of every poet, though this music is more carefully scored in Wilbur's work than in most poetry today."

16 MONTEIRO, GEORGE. "Redemption Through Nature: A Recurring Theme in Thoreau, Frost, and Richard Wilbur." *American Quarterly* 20, no. 4 (Winter):795-809.
   Contends that Wilbur's vision is that of the romantics, particularly Emerson and Thoreau and Frost. For Wilbur unity with nature comes about by restoring nature's beauty, a function the poet serves through helping the reader see freshly. Says that Wilbur feels "man's problem [is] one of vision," the ability to see things whole. Cites "Junk" as a poem that identifies a concern for the way things degenerate, but also testifies to the ever-renewing power of nature.

Notes that "Digging for China" succeeds in overturning the habitual way of seeing for a new vision of the New Jersey sky. Finds a similar metamorphosis in "The Beautiful Changes." Uses Wilbur's suggestion that he is "a classicist" like William Blake who was able to see truth in a grain of sand as a statement that ties him directly to the romantic vision of Thoreau and Frost.

17 REILLY, JOHN H. "Timeless and Timely." *Christian Century*, 27 November, 1509-10.
     Performance review of *The Misanthrope* performed by the Association of Producing Artists at the Lyceum. Though critical of the performers, argues that "the dialogue is well worth the attention paid to it. Molière's spirit of fun, along with his satirical wit, is left intact in the admirable adaptation by Richard Wilbur. The English version has a natural flow and rhythm which belie the fact that the play was originally written in French."

18 Review of *The Misanthrope. America*, 9 November, pp. 445-47.
     Performance review of *The Misanthrope* performed by the Association of Producing Artists at the Lyceum. Says Wilbur "has done a masterly job. His rhymed verse has the clarity of conversation in a suburban living room."

19 "Richard Wilbur." In *Talks With Authors*. Edited by Charles Madden. Carbondale: Southern Illinois University Press, pp. 181-200.
     Richard Wilbur discusses the function of poetry as that which pulls ideas "down off the plane of abstraction and submerge[s] them in sensibility." In the course of this conversation, done over the telephone, he reads "Seed Leaves," "Beasts," and "Love Calls Us to the Things of This World," and answers students' questions about the poems.

20 WAGER, WILLIS. *American Literature: A World View*. New York: New York University Press, pp. 251-52.
     Lists biographical and bibliographical facts, prizes and awards. Notes that Richard Wilbur is another "younger" poet who has "combined academic, creative, and editorial activities." Describes his poetry as "poised, logical, formal, rhymed, reflective, much concerned with ideas. In it there is no reveling in despair, bitterness, or sarcasm." Suggests that the "Boston-Cambridge group of poets, writing at mid-twentieth century, (including Richard Eberhart, John Holmes, Archibald MacLeish, Richard Wilbur, and Robert Lowell), reminds us, . . . of an even earlier time – that of the group that included Longfellow,

1968

James Russell Lowell, and Oliver Wendell Holmes at the mid-nineteenth century."

21 WAGGONER, HYATT H. "Richard Wilbur." In *American Poets: From the Puritans to the Present*. Boston: Houghton Mifflin, pp. 596-604.

Explores the relationship between Wilbur and the Moderns, Wilbur and the Metaphysical poets, Wilbur and Emerson, Wilbur and Edward Taylor. Claims that Wilbur's "Eliotic conception of the poet's role does not prevent his work from often being closer in theme, and occasionally even in style, to that of romantic and visionary poets of the past." Says "Wilbur's basic assumptions and attitudes and his recurrent preoccupations have much more in common with those of both the American Transcendental and English Metaphysical poets than they have with the dominant patterns of assumption and attitude in Modernist poetry." Sees "The World without Objects Is a Sensible Emptiness" as Wilbur's "rejecting the mystic 'way down,' the 'flight of the alone to the alone,' in favor of the incarnation [and] the poem could also be described as rejecting Poe's 'destructive transcendence' in favor of Emerson's vision of immanent spirit." Sees even further aspects of Emersonian thought in "Attention Makes Infinity" and "The Beautiful Changes." Calls attention to "Love Calls Us to the Things of This World" as "Wilbur's finest effort to bridge the gap between Edward Taylor and Emerson." Adds "Proof" as additional evidence of Wilbur's close ties to Puritan thought. Says "Wilbur's 'reconciling' position is the central fact about his work, not his Impersonal, autotelic theory or his other antiromantic ideas, which often seem defensive in origin." Cites "Junk" as support for this position. Concludes with an analysis of "October Maples, Portland" which brings together all the strands of influences mentioned in the essay. Revised and reissued: 1984.11.

22 WATTS, RICHARD, Jr. "Molière in the Best of Hands." *New York Post*, 10 October.

Performance review of *The Misanthrope* performed by the Association of Producing Artists at the Lyceum. Praises Wilbur's "adaptation" for its quality. Says "it is not merely that his rhymes are ingenious and capture perfectly the spirit of the Molière text. They are also in their own right deliciously witty and unfailingly graceful, and they are constantly a pleasure to listen to for the charm with which they bring back the joy of words to the theater." Reprinted in *New York Theatre Critics Reviews 1968*: p. 217.

23 WEATHERHEAD, A. K. "Richard Wilbur: Poetry of Things." *ELH* 35, no. 4 (December):606-17.

Analyzes Wilbur's use of image and prose statements in his poetry in comparison to the practice of the Moderns. Says that Wilbur's "subject matter . . . works with the premise that ideas must exist in familiar things. The commitment he is anxious to define is one which is delicately balanced between the attraction of a non-physical world on the one hand and a too crass luxuriance in objectivity on the other." Notes the "plenitude of things" in Wilbur's poetry and his attempt to "dispossess himself of things that are cloying" ("A World without Objects Is a Sensible Emptiness," "Grasse: The Olive Trees"). Says "Wilbur also withdraws from before what is too solid and static." ("Grasse: The Olive Trees," "After the Last Bulletins," "Beasts," "Statues"). Finds that in all these poems, "Wilbur, by no means wishing to dispense with his world of sensible, solid objects, counters the fixed, defined, and immobile with their opposites," but he does not go to the other extreme to "espouse abstractions or ideas."

Suggests that for Wilbur the "far away . . . must be balanced by the near at hand and immediate." Cites "Castles and Distances" which "clearly confirms that the good life – the spiritual life, we may say even – flourishes in commitment to defined and immediate things of this world, while the result of dwelling on the far away is evil." Notes influence of Marianne Moore's use of imagery.

Finds that a sense of the "imperfection of the world is ubiquitous throughout Wilbur" ("To Ishtar," "Someone Talking to Himself," "Juggler," "A Courtyard Thaw"). Says that "though [Wilbur] tends to shun the immediacy of crowded fact, [he] maintains a duty to the things of the world that are near at hand and concrete; and in such things he finds a vocabulary for speaking of the unfamiliar or for articulating ideas." In fact, "things define what is not known" ("Advice to a Prophet").

Acknowledges that "although Nature may be fallen in many of Wilbur's poems, it enjoys occasionally the advent of grace, and this changes things" ("Castles and Distances," "October Maples, Portland," "Grace"). Asserts that one could say "that Wilbur conceives of a poem itself as an act of grace." Creates a "formula" to describe Wilbur's art: "a poem of his typically manifests what he here defines as grace. It shows the speaking power of action, of poetic action, by which the form that presents the things of this world simultaneously reflects upon them; his strategy is to work with facts and images subjected to interpretation, not presented bold and bald like a broken bottle in Williams." Cites "Junk," "A Hole in the Floor," "Museum Piece," and "Love Calls Us to the Things of This World" as varying modes of

1968

Wilbur's basic strategy. Concludes, "Wilbur then is conscientiously committed to immediate things, despite the allurements of abstractions and the far-away. But things are imperfect; and if by their means a reality beyond themselves may be grasped, unaided they do not bear meanings. Submitted to the interpretive action of poetic technique, on the other hand, they speak." Reprinted: 1988.18.

1969

1 BENOIT, RAYMOND. "The New American Poetry." *Thought* 44, no. 173 (Summer):201-18

Argues that in spite of the strong influence of Descartes on the modern world, younger American poets appear to be working toward the idea that in the concrete lies truth. Suggests that "contemporary poetry – particularly that of Gary Snyder, William Stafford, Richard Wilbur, and Howard Nemerov – is concerned . . . with letting things be, with letting things reveal themselves; that their poetry marks a significant change in the history of literature that is part of a larger shift in Western culture generally." Says that "the ideal is the real for Wilbur, as it was for Coleridge," yet "insight can only come from a plunge into the concrete" ("A World without Objects Is a Sensible Emptiness"). Finds clear link between Wilbur's aesthetic and "Coleridge's definition of the imagination that reveals itself in the reconciliation of the idea and the image, the general and abstract with the particular and concrete." Establishes a line of thought from Browning through Pound and Eliot to Wilbur: "The line of evolution is toward a pure and purer reconciliation until the idea cannot be distinguished from the image." Says Wilbur is able, through his poetic craft, to change the natural world into a "sacramental reality." What many of his poems do is to "show the eternal through and in the temporal" ("A Prayer to Go to Paradise with the Donkeys"). Asserts that "another phrase to describe contemporary American poetry, instead of a poetry of being, might be a poetry of the secular as sacred." His poems, when studied carefully, reveal the method of the others. More than all the other poets, his poetry "rests upon truth as this hypostasis, 'Where word with world is one / And nothing dies' ("Games Two"), rather than concept or judgment or proposition." Concludes that it is Eliot's "logic of the imagination . . . that . . . contemporary poets find true." Reprinted in part: 1973.1; 1983.18.

2 DAVENPORT, GUY. Review of *Walking to Sleep: New Poems and Translations. New York Times Book Review*, 14 December, pp. 54-55.

Reviews *Walking to Sleep: New Poems and Translations*. Asks "When will this cool mastery collide with a theme worthy of it?" Professes frustration at the lack of passion in Wilbur's work. Says one must describe him as a "gleaner" rather than a "harvester." Contends that "the sure-footed sense of words which makes Mr. Wilbur so good a translator also raises his poems to their calm elegance. Poetic diction is rare in our time, but there is nothing else one can say of Mr. Wilbur's range of words but that they exist within a conscious purity of diction completely free of either the vulgar or the precious. A style so well behaved misses both the native genius of English which Frost caught so splendidly and the more ragged ambiguities of more strenuous demands of language." Concludes that Wilbur's "equanimity of temperament" appears to be part of the reason why his poems' content fail to fit their form.

3 DICKEY, WILLIAM. "A Place in the Country." *Hudson Review* 22, no. 2 (Summer):347-64.

Reviews *Walking to Sleep: New Poems and Translations*. Contends that readers often fail to understand the importance of form to Wilbur's meaning. For him, form is a part of the ceremony, a "means of understanding." "Walking to Sleep" is a long poem that demonstrates the way Wilbur makes form work as a kind of magic. The creating of poems is a way for Wilbur to demonstrate his sense of an ordered world. Argues that to read Wilbur's work intelligently, one must accept the fact that his world view does not allow one to "howl" or to get lost in abstraction – neither extreme is permissible. What he does do is to "celebrate that difficult thing: the simultaneous tenuousness and necessity of civilization."

4 EMERSON, CORNELIA D. "Books by Richard Wilbur." *Hollins Critic* 6, Special Issue (July):5.

Lists brief primary bibliography.

5 HOWES, VICTOR. "Cool Crystals from Wilbur." *Christian Science Monitor*, 31 July, p. 11.

Reviews *Walking to Sleep: New Poems and Translations*. Says this collection shows no change in "the brilliantly polished style which is the Wilbur trademark. What has changed, and what is less obvious, is the focus of the poetry." Says Richard Wilbur is moving toward looking behind the images, "'the vast motive,' the something which 'at the heart / Of creatures makes them branch and burst apart,' the sense of 'the mystery of things that are.'" Defines Wilbur's "typical method" as losing the reader in "dense fact." Finds "Walking to Sleep" a "remarkable poem." Sees this poem and "The Agent" as "promising signs that indicate Mr. Wilbur's continuing achievement" and suggest that "he is moving forward into new territory, widening his perimeters even as he deepens his incursions into those areas he has already secured."

6 JARRELL, RANDALL. "Fifty Years of American Poetry." In *The Third Book of Criticism*. New York: Farrar, Strauss, & Giroux, pp. 329-32.
   Reprint of 1963.13. Reprinted in part: 1983.18.

7 KRAMER, AARON. *Library Journal*, 15 April, p. 1939.
   Reviews *Walking to Sleep: New Poems and Translations*. Says "Richard Wilbur's technical wizardry and imaginative verve are undiminished. Once again the most severe old forms become vessels for his genie. 'Thyme Flowering Among Rocks' is an exquisite rhymed-haiku lyric of the real and the fancied. 'Matthew VIII, 28ff' mocks 'Our trust in the high-heaped table and the full trough.' 'A Late Aubade' is among the cleanest, most delicious sex-poems since Herrick. Like Browning's 'Childe Roland' the title poem rejects a safe 'landscape not worth looking at' in favor of 'long errantry.' Mr. Wilbur's lilacs unfold Lazarus's message; his searocks have been as patiently shaped as man. These poems mark a further intensity of passion and audacity of vision."

*8 MILLS, RALPH J., Jr. Review of *Walking to Sleep: New Poems and Translations*. *Chicago Sun Times Book Week*, n.pp.
   Listed in 1971.6, p. 83.

*9 PRITCHARD, WILLIAM H. "Amherst Authors." *Amherst Alumni News* 22 (Summer):36.
   Listed in 1971.6, p. 83.

10 RATTI, JOHN. "Poets in Contrast." *New Leader*, 9 June, pp. 25-26.
   Reviews *Walking to Sleep: New Poems and Translations*. Argues that Wilbur, the ultimate academic poet, angers the reader with his willingness to merely play with words: "Wilbur is enraging because he seems to wish to say so little with such infinite skill. One wants him to break loose, lose his temper, catch fire." ("Lilacs," "Fern Beds in Hampshire County," "Playboy"). Agrees that "Walking to Sleep" is a "superb, . . . sensitive study of a man's mind searching for sleep around the dark corners of its fears and complications." Finds "The Agent" an example of "the poet's complete mastery of traditional blank-verse narrative form." Praises the translations as excellent, especially the

ballades of François Villon. Concludes that "if there is some anger in this appraisal . . . , it is born of admiration and a certain amount of disappointment. Wilbur has the technical equipment and the insight to burn the faculty club down – and not merely sit by the fireside warming his feet."

11 REEDY, GERALD, S. J. "The Senses of Richard Wilbur." *Renascence* 21, no. 3 (Spring):145-150.

Examines values inherent in the poems of Richard Wilbur. Says Wilbur "calls for a union of ideal and real. . . . He chooses as his own the difficult stance of the nuns, a perfect image of the poet, who must maintain his balance in two worlds, one of surrender to unorganized living, sense-experience, and disorder, the other of an ideal search for form, contemplation, and discipline" ("Love Calls Us to the Things of This World," "A World without Objects Is a Sensible Emptiness," "Epistemology"). Contends that Wilbur's aesthetic includes the idea that "both the conceptually unintelligible concrete and its meaningful use as symbol cannot exist without the other in poetry" ("After the Last Bulletins"). Sees "Year's End" as a poem without hope where "one man struggling against time is not enough. The poem mirrors the oft-felt chasm between the enormous potentiality of modern man and the paltry events which actually occupy him." Says Wilbur's "basic point-of-view is . . . simply an intensified awareness of the world itself."

12 Review of *Walking to Sleep*. *Choice* 6, no. 8 (October):1020.

Reviews *Walking to Sleep: New Poems and Translations*. Says that "in a world gone mad, Wilbur is sane; in a world gone shoddy, he is precise; in a world unrelentingly literal, he is witty; in a world gone callous, he not only feels but evokes a kindred feeling – anger over destructiveness, affirmation of affirmation, grief over good lost. His translations sound strong, and, judging by his Villon, are freshly . . . thought – he is not a padder or an echoer; he is a condenser, a rarity among translators. Making use of forms as divergent as a four-beat alliterative, flexible Sapphics, sonnets, haiku, and closed couplets, he deals with man, nature, God, poetry, death, love, and LBJ. All that in less than 80 pages. Not a scraped together commercial venture, it will be a valuable addition to any modern poetry shelf; recommended even for slim budgets."

13 "Richard Wilbur." In *Directory of American Scholars, II: English, Speech, and Drama*. Vol. 2. 5th ed. New York: Jacques Cattell Press, p. 581.

Lists briefly significant biographic and bibliographic facts.

14 "Richard Wilbur." In *Twentieth Century Writing: A Reader's Guide to Contemporary Literature*. Edited by Kenneth Richardson. London: Newnes, pp. 646-47.

Describes Wilbur's work as "formal and academic." Cites "A Simile for Her Smile" as an example of "the brilliance of the poet's style." Lists several major publications.

* 15 "Richard Wilbur." In *200 Contemporary Authors*. Detroit: Gale, pp. 293-304.

Listed in *Biography Index: A Cumulative Index to Biographical Material in Books and Magazines*, vol. 8, p. 7238.

16 RODWAY, ALLAN. "Richard Wilbur: Beasts in the Elegy Season." In *Criticism in Action: A Critical Symposium on Modern Poems*. Edited by Maurice Hussey. London: Longman's, Green & Company, pp. 11-22.

Explicates "Beasts" and "In the Elegy Season" using New Critical and historical critical principles, borrowing heavily from E. D. Hirsch. Argues that in addition to reading well, an understanding of one's age, one's own assumptions and expectations about poetry, and information about others contribute to a good explication of a poem. Fitting the parts to the whole takes experience and a broad understanding of the nature of poetry. Coherence must "carry the most weight" in determining the rightness of an interpretation of a poem by a poet like Wilbur. Explicating Wilbur's "Beasts" and "In the Elegy Season" makes his case. Reprints "Beasts" and "In the Elegy Season."

17 SCHWARTZ, JOSEPH, and ROBY, ROBERT C. *Poetry: Meaning and Form*. New York: McGraw Hill, pp. 164-67, 408-9.

Reprints "Digging for China" with an explication emphasizing two comparative terms: the literal level of the poem and the "belief in a dream (or promise) of a world nothing like this one." Suggests that when the boy looks up and sees "silver barns," "the fact of belief has given the world a sacramental character." Reprints "Museum Piece" without commentary.

18 TAYLOR, HENRY. "Two Worlds Taken as They Come: Richard Wilbur's *Walking to Sleep*." *Hollins Critic* 6, Special Issue (July):1-6, 8-12.

Reviews *Walking to Sleep: New Poems and Translations*. Argues that Wilbur is moving in a new direction in this book. His subject matter is broader. Unlike so many poets of his generation, he has not made his early work obsolete, but has built on and enlarged it. Not only is he the acknowledged master of technical skill, but he also has control of both traditional and original formal structures ("In the Field," "Advice to a Prophet," "Thyme Flowering Among Rocks"). Says that these poems show Wilbur's metrical precision, his careful use of diction, his mastery of form and metrical patterns, and his ability to move from "image to statement." Concludes this section on form by admitting "some readers have feared that [Wilbur's] well-wrought surfaces contain little more than themselves, and, in the broadest sense, this is true, for his forms and their content are finally inseparable. But his forms are made of words, words whose meanings have been carefully considered; thus the forms themselves become the ideas in Wilbur's poetry."

Sees a continuation of satire and public indignation in this book ("Playboy," "Matthew VIII, 28ff"). Says in "Running" and "Walking to Sleep" Wilbur shows a willingness to allow his personal self come through. Suggests that "it is clear from the movement of ["Walking to Sleep"] that, of the two 'methods' of falling asleep, the second, though risky, is somehow preferable . . . and that something of Wilbur's tendency as a poet is revealed in his preference for the second journey; the wilful rejection of images may be safer, but to take them as they come requires a great imaginative strength and serenity."

Observes that "a look at the eleven translations in this book provides a clue to Wilbur's expanding scope and technique." Suggests that voices "clearly distinguishable" from Wilbur's appear in these poems ("Everness," "Antiworlds"). Concludes that in *Walking to Sleep* Wilbur moves farther and deeper from each of his many points of departure; he moves in more various directions." Reprinted: 1983.18.

19 WALSH, CHAD. "Contemporary Poetry: Variety Is Its Vitality." *Washington Post Book World*, 27 July, p. 7.

Reviews *Walking to Sleep: New Poems and Translations*. Agrees that Wilbur's voice is "quiet, civilized – and at the moment in danger of being shouted down by indignant cries and manic screams." Suggests that "his primary audience is less the present moment than the timeless ear. If quieter times ever come, his voice will be heard more distinctly – though the question does arise: is any future likely to be civilized enough for these well-modulated lines to be completely audible?"

20 WEST, ANTHONY. "*The Misanthrope*, 'faultlessly.'" *Vogue*, January, p. 70.

Mentions Richard Wilbur as translator in passing.

1969

21 WILLIAMS, MILLER. "More Than Jewelry and Crystal." *Saturday Review*, 14 June, pp. 32-34.

   Reviews *Walking to Sleep: New Poems and Translations*. Says Wilbur forces a reader to like what he ordinarily does not because of the unusual power of his word choices. Finds that it is a pleasure to read a poet who enjoys the "devices" of poetry. Claims Wilbur is "among our most innocent poets, and so among our most wise," avoiding the temptation to become too suave or too academic. Suggests that several of his new poems indicate the ability to weave fiction into a poem successfully, though parts of "Walking to Sleep" tend to bore the reader. Praises his translations because they do justice to the originals while they remain poetry in English. Calls them excellent.

1970

1 AMABILE, GEORGE N. "Homo Fecit: Four Essays on the Poetry of Richard Wilbur." Ph.D. dissertation, University of Connecticut, 159 pp.

Discusses in the first three essays the tone, the rhetorical strategies, the literary echoes, imagery, concrete detail, and "modes of coherence" associated with Richard Wilbur's poetry. Analyzes *The Beautiful Changes* as particularly representative of Wilbur's work. Emphasizes the Garden of Eden image as a central metaphor in Wilbur's canon, characteristic of his optimistic view of life. See *Dissertation Abstracts International* 31:1257A.

2 BENEDIKT, MICHAEL. "Witty and Eerie." *Poetry* 115, no. 6 (March):422-25.

Reviews *Walking to Sleep: New Poems and Translations*. Takes these poems as a clear sign that Richard Wilbur has begun to move in a new direction. Instead of giving the reader many surface details, "looking *at*," he presents details in such a way that we are forced to "look *into*." Suggests that this is the difference between a poet of vision and a visionary. "There is a de-emphasis on picture-making, and on the great post-Eliotic mode of the 'objective correlative'; and a fresh stress on a kind of subjective correlative." Sees "Lilacs," "Fern Beds in Hampshire County," and "Seed Leaves" as evidence that the poet is now looking "into" the heart of things. Calls "A Late Aubade" an "exquisite love lyric" representing a new intimacy in Wilbur's work, as does "Running" which is frankly autobiographical. Both "Running" and "The Agent" contribute to the eerie quality by suggesting that the poet may be running off the earth or may become homeless. "'Walking to Sleep' abstracts all these issues. . . . The poem not only exemplifies an altered standpoint, but is about it." Suggests that this collection contains "an uncanny fusion of the witty and the eerie," perhaps a better choice than the ironic mode. Reprinted: 1983.18.

3 BOGAN, LOUISE. "Richard Wilbur." In *A Poet's Alphabet: Reflection on the Literary Art and Vocation*. Edited by Robert Phelps and Ruth Limmer. New York: McGraw-Hill, pp. 419-20.

Reprints of 1947.1; 1956.3; 1983.8.

4 BOYERS, ROBERT. "On Richard Wilbur." *Salmagundi* no. 12 (Spring):76-82.

Repeats the statements found in 1970.5 after saying, "The voice that pulses ever so lightly in Wilbur's verse suggests a refinement of sensibility and a soundness of judgment so satisfying that one is hard-put to discern in it the contours of a man as we have been accustomed to men in our experience. One is stirred by Wilbur's verse, stirred not to feeling but to admiration and to a rather even-headed delight that falls quite short of ecstasy." Further argues that in *Walking to Sleep*, the reader "notices . . . that absence of exhilaration, that slightly tired elegance that impress themselves when the particulars of a vision emerge merely as illustration of an idea, as window dressing for an essentially abstract conception." Quotes a portion of "Walking to Sleep" as an example of poetry that is "fundamentally dishonest." The details of this poem, though "delicious," are unbelievable. Instead one finds a "staged quality, the faint trace of a coyness that is not so much inappropriate as it is boring." Asserts that the injunction to start over in the poem is silly. "Often what [Wilbur] says is inscrutable, impervious to real analysis. His advice, his sense of radical possibility, leaves so much to our imagination that we wonder whether we are dealing with a serious man, or one who makes pronouncements from the proverbial top of his head." Grants that a few poems such as "A Late Aubade," "Matthew VIII, 28ff," "Dodwells Road," and "The Agent" succeed because of "the texture, the density, the peculiar phrasing that strike us as somehow compelling and immediate."

5 _____. "Richard Wilbur." In *Contemporary Poets of the English Language*. 2d ed. Chicago: St. James Press, pp. 1175-76.

Includes date of birth, educational experience, marriage and children, travel to Rome and the Soviet Union, teaching experience at Harvard, Wellesley College, and Wesleyan University. Lists awards such as the Guggenheim Fellowship, Prix de Rome award, Pulitzer Prize, National Book Award, Ford Fellowship, Bollingen Translation Prize, and cites membership in honorary societies as well as honorary degrees. Also lists poetry collections from *The Beautiful Changes* (1947) through *Walking to Sleep* (1969), anthologized poems, literary criticism, translations, and editorial work on Poe and Shakespeare.

Criticizes Wilbur because he does not really care for things, though much of his poetry suggests that he does. "What his verse celebrates is not the hard things of this world, but the imagination that makes possible delight, its own and others', in appropriating things for a variety of spiritual and psychological purposes." Cites "The Beautiful Changes" as a poem that celebrates beauty, but suggests that "Love Calls Us to the Things of This World" reinforces the idea that the poet reluctantly accepts the "punctual rape of every blessed day." Concludes that actually "the hero is not the man who submits but the audacious artist, the visionary," Wilbur's "Juggler." Charges that the tension between what Wilbur says and what he does creates a "fundamental failing in his work which is the sense it evokes of ideas, people, things played with as counters in a not very important game." Suggests that "The Death of a Toad" is a prime example of beautiful poetry wasted on trivial ideas, ones that "dissolve in a kind of absurdity." Says that "it's not that Wilbur doesn't care for the frog, but that he cares for it primarily to the degree that it releases particular imaginative faculties that make for poetry." Asserts that the result is to "make of poetry something less substantial, less fully human, less important than we should want it to be."

6 CUMMINS, PAUL. Review of *Walking to Sleep*. *Concerning Poetry* 3, no.1 (Spring):72-76.

Reviews *Walking to Sleep: New Poems and Translations*. Argues that Wilbur's new collection shows excellence while hinting at new directions for his work. Indicates Wilbur's continuing interest in the dynamic form is demonstrated by the wide variety of forms present in this collection: "Junk," in alliterative Anglo-Saxon verse, two rondeaus, three ballades, a haiku sequence and four sonnets. Cites "A Miltonic Sonnet for Mr. Johnson on His Refusal of Peter Hurd's Official Portrait" as an unusual political poem. Sees "The Proof" as typical of Wilbur's "clever, word-playing but impersonal and rather bloodless poem[s]." Suggests that "The Agent" and "Walking to Sleep" are less typical because of their blank verse form. The latter is rather boring. Finds "A Late Aubade," "Running," and "Playboy" a surprise because of their use of intimate detail from the poet's life and their humor. Locates continuity in the nature poetry, "which sees a dynamic life force in the universe and perceives analogues between the operation of this life force in nature and in man," particularly in "Seed Leaves" and "Fern Beds in Hampshire County." Asserts that the "high point of the volume" is "On the Marginal Way" because of rich descriptions, strong allusions, and classic Wilbur quality: this poem shows Wilbur "at his best – lyrical, passionate, yet superbly controlled, aware of life's inequities and tragedies, yet able to transcend ugliness and to offer us a celebration of the things of this world and a balanced vision of the range of man's potentialities."

7 DeKAY, ORMONDE. Review of *Digging for China*. *New York Times Book Review*, 24 May, p. 42.

Reviews *Digging for China*. Likes Richard Wilbur's *Digging for China*, along with the illustrations, and sees them as representing a publisher's "tour de force – of sorts." Suggests the contrast between the illustrations and the poem are "ingenious and eyecatching."

8 FITZ GERALD, GREGORY, and HEYEN, WILLIAM. "The Window of Art: A Conversation with Richard Wilbur." Edited by Philip L. Gerber and Robert J. Gemmett. *Modern Poetry Studies* 1, no. 2:57-67.

This interview is an edited and abbreviated form of a taped interview done by Gregory Fitz Gerald, William Heyen, and Richard Wilbur on 13 March 1969. Brockport Video-Tape Collection, State University College, Brockport, New York.

Richard Wilbur explains that "form compels, or at least enables, you to write a certain kind of poem." Cites "Junk" as an example of alliterative Anglo-Saxon meter. Amplifies his quarrel with Poe's aesthetic which destroys everything in this world. Insists that art should be a "window, not a door," because he "value[s] the resistance of the world, its independence of the mind, its interaction with the mind." Admits poetry readings have sensitized him to the ways words sound and have caused him to move toward more dramatic poems. Assesses Allen Ginsberg as "a person of great talent . . . who throws it around loosely sometimes." Says he would not be "quite so exhibitionistic, or so loosely Whitmanian." Regards contemporary protest poetry as "pretty awful" and suggests that Yeats's "Easter 1916" is a fine example of a political poem. Admits he reads criticism and reviews about his work but insists on writing his way. Draws a distinction between song lyrics and poetry. Simon and Garfunkel write lyrics; poetry must have "knowledge behind it." Describes his writing process as laborious and slow. Reprinted 1990.2.

9 GLASER, ELEANOR. *Library Journal*, 15 September, p. 3055.

Reviews *Digging for China*. Feels that though this book and the accompanying drawings are well done, it may not appeal to an unsophisticated public.

10 HUGHES, DANIEL. "American Poetry 1969: From B to Z." *Massachusetts Review* 11, no. 4 (Autumn):650-86.

Reviews *Walking to Sleep: New Poems and Translations* as a much better collection than *Advice to a Prophet* in that its tone moves away from the "unction" of the prior collection. Says "Walking to Sleep" is "a major meditation; everything in it stays within itself as the rite of falling to sleep becomes the ritual of the total poem, and unlike any other poem I know by Wilbur, it almost becomes a poem for *use*." Suggests that "For Dudley" is an example of "somber and graceful work [that] is surely still a requirement for readers of poetry today." Declares that Wilbur is still a poet who should be read, that new sounds and variations appear to be entering his work.

11 JOHNSON, KENNETH. "Virtues in Style, Defect in Content: The Poetry of Richard Wilbur." In *The Fifties: Fiction, Poetry, Drama.* Edited by Warren French. Deland, FL: Everett/Edward, pp. 209-16.

Believes it is the reader's and the critic's fault if they are not capable of appreciating Wilbur's kind of poetry. Emphasizes that Wilbur's basic concerns – not his use of traditional forms or his lack of emotional intensity – are his major weakness. Cites "tangible reality" as one major concern ("Driftwood," "First Snow in Alsace," "The Beacon"). Suggests, however, that the reality in these poems is illusive. "A Hole in the Floor" hints of hidden reality, but "The Lilacs" reveals only the reality of "death's kingdom." Asserts that such a "view of reality triggers one primary emotional response in Wilbur: fear" – the emotion depicted in "The Pardon." Says Wilbur then centers his poetry on "man's imaginative powers and . . . a separate ideal realm." Cites "Junk," "For the New Railway Station in Rome," "Grasse: The Olive Trees," and "Clearness" as examples of actual objects being remade by the imagination.

Finds a second major concern of Wilbur's in his effort to maintain a balance between the actual and the ideal world ("Love Calls Us to the Things of This World"). Feels that Wilbur longs most for the ideal world ("In the Elegy Season," "Castles and Distances," "A World without Objects Is a Sensible Emptiness"). Dislikes Wilbur's apparent rejection of unattractive reality ("Stop"). Insists that imagination, for Wilbur, becomes "a refuge . . . a citadel where one can find protection from reality. Yet, his spiritual visions are ultimately judged to be totally subjective, invalid."

Contrasts Keats's firm belief in both the tangible and the ideal world and his certainty that the tangible world contained "messages" for man with Wilbur's apparent inability to see "objects in the tangible world as valid messengers of the ideal world." Contrasts Wilbur with Wallace Stevens and says that the difference is that "Stevens *committed* himself, while Wilbur . . . insists on remaining detached in order to better judge particular experiences as they occur." Wilbur resembles Robert Frost in his need to live in between both worlds. Warns that readers should understand Wilbur is "entangled in the same fundamental problems that we must confront and must work through."

12 LUCAS, TOM. Review of *Walking to Sleep* and *Digging for China. Spirit* 37, no. 3 (Fall):39-42.

Reviews *Walking to Sleep: New Poems and Translations* and *Digging for China.* Suggests that these books are worth reading because of Richard Wilbur's technical skill, the many different verse forms ("The Lilacs," a Miltonic sonnet, "Thyme Flowering Among Rocks," and "Walking to Sleep"), the abundance of fine images and the inferences drawn from them, and the powerful subjects of the expanded consciousness. Cites "The Lilacs," "Fern Beds in Hampshire County," "A Wood," and "Running" as fine examples of Wilbur's ability to "pack the commonplace with feeling and implication." *Digging for China* celebrates a favorite theme of Wilbur's – the ability of the human mind to project "itself to the limits of space." Mentions "In the Field" for its strong connective between the stars of the night and the flowers of the field. Brings up lines from "Walking to Sleep" as a warning about the power of the imagination.

13 MATTFIELD, MARY S. "Some Poems of Richard Wilbur." *Ball State University Forum* 11, no. 3 (Summer):10-24.
      Nominates Richard Wilbur as a legitimate candidate for the label "major" poet because he fits the five conditions set out by W. H. Auden. Most important of these conditions is a continuing process of maturation. Suggests that a survey of Wilbur's first five volumes demonstrates his ability to satisfy all categories of Auden's conditions, especially the latter where he shows that he has grown in a "steady and quiet deepening and mellowing of vision. . . . Wilbur's latest work . . . continues and intensifies his mature vision while extending his range of subject matter and technique." Sees "craftsmanship and conviction" in all five volumes. Observes that "essential characteristics of theme and technique have undergone no major change . . . but have intensified as the poet matured." Sees Wilbur's limitations as "inevitable defects of his qualities: grace may on occasion seem facility, detachment may appear constraint. A scholarly cultivation risks pedantry; delicacy slightness." Finds in each book a "rich variety of form and of subject matter. . . . [Wilbur] confronts the crisis of the modern temper with an unillusioned but affirmative stance which has – if anything – increased in affirmation as he has grown older." Finds influences of Marianne Moore, early Eliot, the English Metaphysical poets, and the French nineteenth century poets as well as many painters in his work ("Objects," "The Giaour and the Pacha", "L'Etoile," "Museum Piece"). Suggests that "one useful key to Wilbur's theory of poetry may be found in 'Ceremony' where the precise formality of the scene contrasts with the 'tigers in the wood.'" Sees two gradual developments surfacing in *Walking to Sleep* – Wilbur's use of more direct language and a shift toward the dramatic poem.
      Analyzes several poems from each volume.

14 ____. "Wilbur's 'The Puritans.'" *Explicator* 28, no. 6 (February):item 53.

Explains the success of "The Puritans" as a result of Wilbur's drawing upon "the resources of diction, musical device, and imagery to make a significant statement in which form is skillfully adapted to meaning." The extended metaphor of the river steamer firing over the water to cause the murdered body of Huck Finn to rise to the surface creates the foundation upon which Wilbur builds, employing "metrical variations for emphasis and impedance, sound-idea correspondences, accent, and stress." Says this poem expresses "a philosophy of commitment, of engagement in the struggle of man" to deal with the "blood-guiltiness" weighing on his conscience.

15 MILLER, STEPHEN. "The Poetry of Richard Wilbur." *Spirit* (South Orange, N.J.) 37, no. 3 (Fall):30-35.

Surveys Wilbur's first five collections of poetry. Suggests that "Wilbur is at his ease and at his best when he is praising – in a genial and lyrical way – the beautiful changes of nature, the ceremonies of the mind's intellection, and the light that emanates from things of this world." His sensibility flourishes within a narrow range of tone and attitude. When the shadows of public and political events fall across his work, his poems often seem banal or trivial. "In *Advice to a Prophet* and *Walking to Sleep* . . . this new tack is a dead end." "Ordered actions" best describe Wilbur's early poems ("Grace," "Museum Piece," "L'Etoile," "Piazza di Spagna, Early Morning"). Contends that the mind is Wilbur's most important subject because it is "always correcting the cave of reality" ("My Father Paints the Summer," "The Bat," and "Praise in Summer"). Acknowledges Wilbur's refusal of the mind's "autonomous visions": "A World without Objects Is a Sensible Emptiness" shows Wilbur turning from the abstractions of the mind to the reality of the world. Interprets "An Event" as an attempt by the poet to order reality which can only last a "flying moment," though such moments appear frequently in the first three volumes ("Love Calls Us to the Things of This World"). Questions the existence of "tigers in the wood" in "Ceremony." Finds the tone of the first three volumes monotonous.

Describes *Advice to a Prophet* as "disappointing." Says *Walking to Sleep* promises new possibilities, especially in the moving elegy "For Dudley," and the sardonic "Matthew VII, 28ff." Praises the light of the imagination in "Complaint" and "Walking to Sleep," where the mind aids one in avoiding the terrors of the journey. Compares Wilbur with Robert Frost: "Frost has the tigers in his woods whereas Wilbur only has feigning ladies in his clearing."

1970

16 OVERMYER, JANET. "A Review of *Digging for China.*" *Poet-Lore* 65, no. 4 (Winter):437.

Reviews *Digging for China*. Says "children should love this book."

17 PATE, WILLARD, ed. "Interview with Richard Wilbur." *South Carolina Review* 3, no. 1 (November):5-23.

Richard Wilbur visited the Furman University campus on February 9-10, 1970. During his visit, he appeared with a panel of students who questioned him about American poetry.

Richard Wilbur says the difference between English and American writers is that "there's always some impulse in the American writer to set out for the frontier in some sense or the other–to head for the savage, the original, the uncivilized, to stand loose from whatever cultural coherences people may try to thrust upon him." Distinguishes between whining and good confessional poetry. Admires John Berryman's unique poetry: Berryman is "writing in about three dialects at once." Calls Marianne Moore and Elizabeth Bishop "great descriptive and more or less overtly moralistic poets." Admires Denise Levertov the most of the Black Mountain School. Thinks the New York School of poets is amusing but not very consequential. Feels that poets must be aware of their culture, but says political poems can be awful: "We want poetry to be as nearly as possible a miraculous precipitation of somebody's whole soul, as Coleridge said. We want it to be honest in the sense that it spills the beans totally, that it says whatever it says with all the reservations, all the qualifications which the speaker must feel. My idea of a fine political poem is Williams Butler Yeats' 'Easter 1916.'" Insists that his poems choose their own form and that rhyme is a great enhancer of meaning, allowing the poet control. Recounts his attempt to write a verse play. Regrets that Coleridge took opium. Says that "the drug experience is shadow boxing, and the business of the poet is to be confronting, with his imagination, these solid objects here." Reprinted: 1990.2.

18 "Poetry." In *Articles on American Literature 1950-1967*. Compiled by Lewis Leary. Durham, N.C.: Duke University Press, pp. 690-700.

Lists general articles on poetry and specific articles on Richard Wilbur's poetry.

19 POULIN, A., Jr. "Contemporary American Poetry: The Radical Tradition." *Concerning Poetry* 3, no. 2 (Fall):5-21.

Argues that the most important distinguishing factor between modernist and contemporary poetry is the consistent use of the personal "I" as opposed to the third person, "he." Finds that the radical tradition is characterized by intimacy between poet and reader, directness and transparency, a lack of wit, dependence on direct experience – the "product of emotion rather than intellect and conscious craftsmanship." Defines the radical tradition as poetry which has become increasingly personalized. Suggests that these poets descend from the Whitman tradition which strongly contrasts to the "traditional mythic method" made popular by T. S. Eliot. Contends that contemporary poets must place themselves within the framework of two extremes – the Whitman or the Puritan tradition. Finds that poets writing in the Whitman tradition are often committed politically and socially, though exhibiting a wide range of religious belief. One of Richard Wilbur's poems testifies to the irrelevance of the existence of God, as do other poets' poems; yet for the most part, this generation of poets finds religious belief impossible. Instead, they lift up the personal and private as a kind of religious experience, priding themselves on being "relevant." Reprinted: 1971.18.

20 PRITCHARD, WILLIAM. "Wildness of Logic in Modern Lyric." In *Forms of Lyric.* Edited by Reuben A. Brower. New York: Columbia University Press, pp. 127-50.

Quotes Robert Frost who suggests that "soundness" in a poem means both the sound of the word and the sense. Contends that a wild line of poetry will exhibit a close correlation between the two. A tame poem is one which contains no revelation or series of revelations, and a tame poet "takes himself so dead seriously that he cannot, evidently, afford to indulge in any recognizable tone of voice, with the result that . . . nobody is speaking to nobody." Asserts that James Merrill, Richard Wilbur, and Randall Jarrell write "wild poems." Concludes that in a poem containing the "wildness of logic" the utterance is deep and playful, made from "gestures of revelation *and* reticence."

21 "Richard Wilbur." In *What the Poem Means: Summaries of 1,000 Poems.* Edited by Harry Brown and John Millstead. Glenview, IL: Scott, Foresman, pp. 279-81.

Paraphrases "A Baroque Wall-Fountain in the Villa Sciarra," "A World without Objects Is a Sensible Emptiness," "Juggler," "Loves Calls Us to the Things of This World," "Still, Citizen Sparrow," "The Beautiful Changes," and "The Death of a Toad" as a method of interpreting each poem.

1971

1 CLURMAN, HAROLD. Review of *School for Wives*. *Nation*, 8 March, pp. 314-15.

Performance review of *The School for Wives*. Says Richard Wilbur has wrought the miracle of rendering the dancelike verse into an English that preserves the shrewd merriment of the original. It is Wilbur's translation – though there are other merits – which makes *The School for Wives* a wholly pleasant occasion at the Lyceum Theatre. "One laughs or smiles with special satisfaction because brightness of mind in Molière takes on the guise of foolery."

2 CUMMINS, PAUL. *Richard Wilbur: A Critical Essay*. Contemporary Writers in Christian Perspective, edited by Roderick Jellema. Grand Rapids: Eerdmans, 47 pp.

Chapter I, "A Tradition and an Individual Talent," assesses Richard Wilbur's critical reputation and recounts his history to date. Chapter II, "New Wine in Old Bottles," elaborates on Wilbur's preference for traditional stanza forms and his use of rhyme, elevated language and puns on the root meaning of words, and his careful inclusion of allusions in his poems ("A Fire Truck," "For the New Railway Station in Rome," "To an American Poet Just Dead," "Juggler," "A Courtyard Thaw," "After the Last Bulletins," "Objects"). Chapter III, "A Public Quarrel with E. A. Poe," compares Wilbur's differing view of the function of the imagination with Poe's. "To Wilbur the poetic experience is not wholly trans-rational; it is largely a process of ordering the disparate elements of experience." Chapter IV, "A Translucent Poetic Universe," joins the philosophy of the paleontologist Father Teilhard de Chardin with the poetry of Wilbur on three bases: their insistence on the plurality of the universe, their understanding of spiritual energy, and their belief in the unity of the cosmos ("Conjuration," "A Wood," "The Giaour and the Pacha," "From the Lookout Rock," "October Maples, Portland," "A World without Objects Is a Sensible Emptiness," "The Death of a Toad"). Chapter V, "Poetry and Happiness," defends Wilbur's consistent habit of portraying the world in positive ways ("A Baroque Wall-Fountain in the Villa Sciarra"). Chapter VI, "'Here at the Fountainside': The Human Condition," centers on two major themes in Wilbur's work – the necessity for people to "work out [their] destiny amid imperfection and ambiguity" ("Beasts," "Still, Citizen Sparrow," "Ballade for the Duke of Orléans") and the paradoxical idea that loss can be gain ("Then," "The Pardon," "For Ellen," "Someone Talking to Himself," "Water Walker"). Chapter VII, "Love Calls Us," uses the poem "Love Calls Us to the Things of This World" to show that "the necessity of the soul's clothing itself with flesh each day is a metaphoric statement of Wilbur's own theory of poetry."

3 DUFFY, CHARLES F. "'Intricate Neural Grace': The Esthetic of Richard Wilbur." *Concerning Poetry* 4, no. 1 (Spring):41-51.
    Analyzes the works of art in Wilbur's early poetry to enable the reader to consolidate a poetics by which Wilbur operates ("Objects," "A Dutch Courtyard"). Finds two principles–that of the "devout intransitive eye" of the poet who chooses to see in order to "guard and gild what's common" and the poet's clear allegiance to the power of the imagination which creates the world. Suggests that "dreams of the ideal or eternal occupy a place in Wilbur's esthetic . . . he lays his strictures on the idealist only when the dream is destructive" ("L'Etoile," "My Father Paints the Summer"). Contends Wilbur "also knows of nightmare." He recognizes that "poetry, to be vital, does seem to need a periodic acquaintance with the threat of Chaos" ("A Hole in the Floor," "Ceremony," "The Giaour and the Pacha"). Examines "Giacometti" as a poem containing most of Wilbur's major themes–man's modern condition, directionless, without imagination, but having a will to "combat intransigent matter, to differentiate, to love and accept the self and the world." Wilbur's esthetic is "a balanced, humanist representationalism which is neither photographic realism . . . nor man-obliterating abstractionism." Reprinted: 1983.18.

4 FARRELL, JOHN P. "The Beautiful Changes in Richard Wilbur's Poetry." *Contemporary Literature* 12, no. 1 (Winter):74-87.
    Posits that "Wilbur's poems envision two kinds of change, disintegrative and metamorphic . . . . Wilbur suggests that a genuine reverence for life can be attained if one has the capacity to see beyond disintegrative change, into the metamorphic and regenerative life of the universe" ("The House of Poe"). Suggests that one can only observe the metamorphosis if one has a moral and intellectual capability. Finds that Wilbur's sympathies lie entirely with the need for being selves that are "amenable to transformation" through change ("Speech for the Repeal of the McCarran Act," "Advice to a Prophet," "Merlin Enthralled"). "Looking into History" affirms the power of metamorphosis as exemplified by the tree which gathers to itself all in order to maintain its "live formality." "The Aspen and the Stream" and "Driftwood" underscore the same reality. The aspen stands beside the stream, open to the changes brought about by its absorbing the living water, changes that may be dark, but which nevertheless testify to its ability to remain alive. "Statues" focuses on children who are "paragons

of the open self, the self that is amenable to transformation." Concludes that Wilbur's ability to create the world where both disintegrative and metamorphic change exist, where the pain of change can be redemptive, marks his work as a high achievement. Reprinted: 1983.18.

5 FIELD, JOHN P. "The Achievement of Richard Wilbur." Ph.D. dissertation, University of Cincinnati, 264 pp.
    Examines Richard Wilbur's "poetic intention" from *The Beautiful Changes* through *Walking to Sleep* as an attempt to more accurately assess his poetic achievement. Shows that Wilbur is not nearly so absent from his poems as many critics have suggested. Contains an extended bibliography. See *Dissertation Abstracts International* 31:3545A.

6 _____. *Richard Wilbur: A Bibliographical Checklist*. Serif Series, no. 16, edited by William White. Kent, Ohio: Kent State University Press, 85 pp.
    Divides the checklist into works by and works about Richard Wilbur. In Section A of works by Wilbur, Field provides descriptive information for each of the volumes of poetry published through *Walking to Sleep*. Section A.2 lists volumes of translations, musical lyrics, and compilations. Two further sections (A.3 & 4) list books edited by Wilbur and a juvenile book of poetry. Section B contains a list of poems published in each collection in the order of their appearance. A further break-down of this section (B.2) includes the publication history of many poems, information gleaned from library holdings and from Richard Wilbur himself. Three sections provide a listing of articles, stories (including translations), and short editorial work (C); a list of book reviews (D); and a list of interviews (E). Field includes a catalog of the holdings of Lockwood Memorial Library at the State University of New York at Buffalo (mostly early manuscripts) and the Robert Frost Memorial Library at Amherst College (F). Items are described by the number of the folder and the contents are carefully itemized. Section concludes with a list of letters, records, tapes, and films (G).
    Divides work about Richard Wilbur into three major categories: books and articles containing critical commentary (A and B), book reviews (C), and biography (D).

7 FUNKE, LEWIS. "Low Costs, High Hopes." *New York Times*, 14 March, Section 2, pp. 1, 26.

Recounts overhearing a conversation of Richard Wilbur telling a caller about his new sport, snowshoeing. Mentions Wilbur's translations of Molière (*The Misanthrope, Tartuffe, School for Wives*) and lyrics for *Candide*. Quotes Wilbur as saying about translation that his procedure is "not so much to delve into any of the scholarship around a play, not to look for a word-for-word sort of translation, but rather thought-for-thought."

8 GILL, BRENDAN. "Crossing the Atlantic." *New Yorker*, 27 February, p. 82.

Performance review of *The School for Wives* produced at the Lyceum Theater. Says "translating French verse, which is syllabic, into English verse, which is accented, tends to play the devil with rhymed couplets; Mr. Wilbur's rhymes, coming at the end of a five-beat line, fall in place a little too quickly for their own good, and I would willingly do without them altogether." Complains about translation of *L'École des Femmes* as *The School for Wives* instead of *School for Wives* which he feels Molière meant.

9 HEWES, HENRY. *Saturday Review*, 6 March, p. 21.

Performance review of *The School for Wives* produced at the Lyceum Theater. Claims that "poet Richard Wilbur has crafted a gorgeous translation of this comic portrait of a forty-two-year-old man who selfishly seeks to marry his teen-aged ward."

10 "In Search of an Audience." *Times Literary Supplement* (London), 21 May, p. 580.

Reviews *Walking to Sleep: New Poems and Translations*. Contends that contemporary poets have a need to become aware of an audience. Though Richard Wilbur's talents are superior, he needs to add more brashness, more bravado, "give his gifts the freedom they deserve." Does not want the poet to "transform himself," but hints "he should be more himself. He should let his audience find him, whoever he decides to be."

11 JAMES, CLIVE. "When the Gloves are Off." *Review* no. 26 (Summer):35-44.

Discusses *Walking to Sleep*. Says that "Wilbur has in fact faded right out: it's doubtful if he is now thought of, on either side of the water, as any kind of force at all." Sees *Walking to Sleep* as "a bit tired." Urges that Wilbur's early work should not be overlooked, however. Begins with *The Beautiful Changes* as the book which "set the level for Wilbur's technical bravura." ("Cicadas," "My Father Paints the

Summer," "Grace"). Says, "as a rule of thumb, . . . the really glaring moments of falsity throughout Wilbur's poetry are brought about when . . . he snatches [for a special effect] and misses" ("The Peace of Cities," "First Snow in Alsace"). Suggests that the war poems, though failures, "demonstrate what kind of pressure it is that makes the successful poems such convincing examples of formal order attained with technical assurance but against great spiritual stress." Grants that a few poems are brilliant successes, though Wilbur's virtuosity often seems like over-kill ("Lightness," "A Plain Song for a Comrade" [*sic*], "A Baroque Wall-Fountain in the Villa Sciarra," "Loves of the Puppets"). Concludes that with *Advice to a Prophet*, Wilbur begins to parody himself. "Wilbur's judicious retreat from raw experience has turned into mere insularity" in *Walking to Sleep* ("The Agent," "Walking to Sleep"). "[Wilbur] is off balance, a condition he is constitutionally unfitted to exploit. While he was on balance, though, he wrote a good number of poised, civilized and very beautiful poems. They'll be worth remembering when some of the rough, tough, gloves-off stuff we're lately supposed to admire starts looking thin." Reprinted: 1974.5; 1980.6; 1983.18.

12 KAUFFMANN, STANLEY. Review of *The School for Wives*. *New Republic*, 8 May, pp. 24-25.
    Performance review of *The School for Wives*. Finds fault with Wilbur's translation. Says it is "an endless series of rhymed iambic couplets, often with feminine endings, that jingle on and on." Calls this "jejune English prosody." Compares this play with Wilbur's lyrics for *Candide*. Says one can "hear the difference between a poet writing light verse in his own tongue and a translator gathering up a lot of little packages while trying not to spill any." Concludes that his "point is not that [Wilbur] could have done better but precisely that he could not."

13 KOLEM, T. E. "The Laughing Cure." *Time*, 1 March, p. 67.
    Reviews the Broadway revival of *The School for Wives*. Says a "large debt of thanks is due Richard Wilbur's deftly idiomatic verse translation. Rendered into pedantic English, Molière's rhyming couplets can drone on with a perishing cumulative monotony. Wilbur makes the meters dance, and the players follow."

14 LASK, THOMAS. "Wilbur's Style Formal, Miss Van Duyn's, Open." *New York Times*, 22 January, p. 20.
    Suggests that Richard Wilbur's work has been known "for its finish, its formal control, for a kind of virtuosity that has been characterized as both elegant and clever." Cites his "unfashionable

interest" in the natural world and his ability to use the past to "illuminate the present."

15 LINDSAY, NOEL. "Two Modern Poets Provide Marked Contrast in Styles." *Daily Journal* (Caracas, Venezuela), 16 September, p. 19.
Contrasts the styles of Thom Gunn and Richard Wilbur.

16 O'MARA, PHILIP F. "The Poetry of Richard Wilbur." Ph.D. dissertation, University of Notre Dame, 317 pp.
Contends that "Richard Wilbur's high critical reputation is based chiefly on his skill in traditional verse forms, and he is often regarded as an esthete." Shows in first chapter that Wilbur's "real views, do not identify artistic accomplishment with self-fulfilment or wisdom. Rather, he sees the proper role of poetry as a subordinate one." Cites nature imagery as a vehicle for Wilbur's thought and his style as part of his meaning. Studies Wilbur's themes, "concentrating on his investigations of the life-world in poems oriented psychologically and in poems of cultural and political critique." See *Dissertation Abstracts International* 31:4787A.

17 PERRINE, LAURENCE. "Dream, Desire, or Dizziness? – Digging in 'Digging for China.'" *Notes on Contemporary American Literature* 1, no. 3 (May):13-14.
Disagrees with Janet Overmyer (1970.16) when she calls the boy's experience in "Digging for China" a dream: it is a physiological event, caused from his having looked into a hole all morning and then suddenly having turned his face to the sun.

18 POULIN, A., Jr. *Contemporary American Poetry*. Edited by A. Poulin, Jr. Boston: Houghton Mifflin, pp. 459-73.
Reprint of 1970.19.

19 RENNIE, NEIL. "Mystic Wisdom." *London Magazine*, June-July pp. 129-32.
Reviews *Walking to Sleep: New Poems and Translations*. Calls these poems a disappointment because, though they employ images of nature in the hopes of investing the poem with a sense of mystical power, the substance is too slight ("Thyme Flowering among Rocks," "Lilacs," "Seed Leaves," "A Wood," "Fern Beds in Hampshire County"). Finds that "Walking to Sleep" "misses the coordinating influence of stanza pattern and rhyme with which Wilbur's technical proficiency controls the motion of other poems." Says "The Agent" is interesting. Grants that the translations are excellent.

1971

20 REXROTH, KENNETH. *American Poetry in the Twentieth Century*. New York: Herder & Herder, pp. 175-76.

Warns that, unlike Theodore Roethke, John Berryman, and Robert Lowell, "Wilbur's danger is facilty." He is able to write good poems too easily.

21 "Richard Wilbur." In *The Penguin Companion to American Literature*. Edited by Malcolm Bradbury, Eric Mottram, and Jean Franco. New York: McGraw-Hill, 1971.

Calls Wilbur "one of the best and most highly regarded of post-war American poets." Gives family background and lists major volumes of poems from *The Beautiful Changes* (1947) through *Walking to Sleep* (1969). Says Wilbur's "elegance, fineness of manner and formality are the distinguishing features of his work, and have made him the target of those who speak for a rawer sort of poetry and who identify him as a leading figure among the 'academic' poets." Describes his poetic method as "the attempt to create out of some impulse toward emotion a revelation of something 'lofty or long-standing,' displaying the essential nature of experience."

22 SERGEANT, HOWARD. "Poetry Review." *English* 20 (Autumn):108.

Reviews *Walking to Sleep: New Poems and Translations*. Says the translations are what are worth reading in this book. Finds that "[Wilbur] appears in this collection to be moving towards some vague Wordsworthian mystique of Nature that is quite unconvincing."

23 SUMMERS, JOSEPH. "Milton and Celebration." *Milton Quarterly* 5, no. 1 (March):1-7.

Writes that Richard Wilbur's "A Miltonic Sonnet for Mr. Johnson on His Refusal of Peter Hurd's Official Portrait" is a twentieth-century transformation of Milton's voice. As such, it gives rise to a hope that this century may yet recognize Milton's great achievement in the best possible way – by responding to his work in similar great works of art.

24 TOULSON, SHIRLEY. Review of *Walking to Sleep: New Poems and Translations*. *Poetry Review* (Summer):208-14.

Reviews *Walking to Sleep: New Poems and Translations*. Says the answer to whether Richard Wilbur has changed in the nine years since he has published a collection of poems is that he "can no more change direction than a tree can." More important is the fact that his "form itself is a natural organic growth, firmly rooted in a strong rhythm that is the source of his confident mastery of all kinds of verse techniques."

Suggests, nevertheless, that Wilbur has "mellowed." His work appears to be taking a new direction as demonstrated by "Junk" and "Lilacs"; the latter is a happier poem. Finds other changes toward an easier mood in "quasi-political poems" ("Shame," "The Agent") and love poems ("Loves of the Puppets," "A Late Aubade").

25 TREASTER, JOSEPH B. "Two Poets Share Bollingen Award." *New York Times*, 11 January, p. 20.

Reports the sharing of the Bollingen Prize (*Walking to Sleep*) with Mona Van Duyn for *To See, to Take*.

1972

1 ADKINS, CARL A. "Richard Wilbur's 'Running' and 'Complaint': Two Self-Portraits of a Young American Artist Nearing Fifty." *Iowa English Yearbook* 22, no. 3 (November):37-41.

Posits that Wilbur has helped himself through the crisis of middle age by writing "Complaint" and "Running." Claims that both poems are heavily autobiographical, indicating that Wilbur is now more willing to let his personal life show in his poetry. "The crux of Wilbur's (or his speaker's) confession in 'Complaint' seems to be the dissatisfaction which he feels as a poet nearing middle-age who believes that he has not yet managed to satisfy himself artistically." Concludes that "as Wilbur the man in 'Running' comes to grips with his loss of physical strength and reassures himself that he may still admire the strength of enthusiastic youth, so Wilbur the poet in 'Complaint' reconciles himself not to a loss of poetic strength but to a continuing struggle for artistic perfection, especially as he responds to the inspiration of Nature."

2 _____. "A Study of Development in the Poetry of Richard Wilbur." Ph.D. dissertation, Kansas State University, 198 pp.

Traces the evolution of tone and theme in *The Beautiful Changes*, *Ceremony and Other Poems*, *Things of This World*, *Advice to a Prophet*, and *Walking to Sleep*. Concludes that Wilbur's later work shows a shift in tone toward fewer formal devices and a slow development of introspection and personal voice. Such a shift helps to invest the later poems with the energy of natural speech, an energy missing from the early poems. See *Dissertation Abstracts International* 33:2359A.

3 BLY, ROBERT. "American Poetry: On the Way to the Hermetic." *Books Abroad* 46, no.1 (Winter):17-24.

Describes hermetic poetry as existing on five levels of descent, each one characterized by an increase in "desire-energy or interior energy or circulating energy . . . libido." Says that Richard Wilbur's poems belong on the first level where "the soul and the invisible world enter, but in which the poet has no faith." Cites "Lamarck Elaborated" as having the typical tone of this kind of poem. Suggests that Wilbur does not believe in the invisible world and is obviously upholding a philosophy that is bad both artistically and morally as is clear in "A World without Objects Is a Sensible Emptiness." In this poem, Wilbur's "desire energy has not been forbidden . . . to move toward the invisible; rather [Wilbur] has allowed it to go out, but has warned it that there is nothing in the world nor in the infinite city of human desire that is worthy of it." Deplores Wilbur's idea that art is a window, not a door because the wall remains between the poet and reality. Says that Wilbur (along with Wallace Stevens) belongs to the practical world of Mark Twain, the first level of hermetic poetry. That is, Wilbur's work lacks spiritual and psychological depth. Asserts that the deepest level of hermetic poetry is that which is totally visionary. Suggests that not many American poets are able to write this kind of poetry.

4 BRODSKY, JOSEPH. "On Richard Wilbur." *American Poetry Review* 2, no. 1 (January-February):52.
    Judges Wilbur's "stylistic and sensual credo" to be found in the voice of the Milkweed in "Two Voices in a Meadow." "[Wilbur's] is a pure, sometimes sardonic voice which speaks as a rule in a regular meter about the drama of human existence, and this narration, conducted according to the rather harsh laws of his *Ars poetica*, acquires an independent value and is transformed into one of those extremely vital 'things of the given world.'" Says that for Wilbur, "attractiveness and beauty are never goals in themselves"; images metamorphose into ideas as in "A Baroque Wall-Fountain in the Villa Sciarra." Contends that "the formal perfection of Wilbur's poems is nothing more than a mask [that] conceals it [character], or rather, underlines it because of the difference between the external features and what is being said." Asserts that the mask is necessary because "it is impossible to speak of life in an open text. . . . The modern art of the mask is the art of creating a scale against which things can be measured." Concludes that "this is all only one idea – the idea that the laws of art, including the laws of an *Ars poetica*, when they are observed, render a greater gain in quality than any breaking of these laws in the name of intellectual freedom or the name of freedom of self-expression." Reprinted: 1983.18.

5 *Craft Interview with Richard Wilbur. New York Quarterly* 12 (Autumn):15-36.

Richard Wilbur discusses his writing process as slow and laborious, requiring rewriting as he goes. Says he agrees with Emerson "that it's not meter but meter-making argument that's important." Urges that "the poet should be wary of the usurping critic in himself, who is capable of concerning himself with ambition, fashion, publication and book reviewers." Has read Joyce, Eliot, Hart Crane, Robert Frost, Wordsworth, Yeats, Baudelaire, Gerard Manley Hopkins, Dickinson, and Auden. Admits to having "dry periods" when he is not writing. Suggests that traditional forms of poetry have no meaning and does not object to "controlled free verse." Says, however, "I think it is absurd to feel that free verse – which has only been with us in America for a little over a hundred years – has definitely 'replaced' measure and rhyme and other traditional instruments. . . . Meter, rhyme and the like are, or can be, serviceable for people who know how to handle them well." Deplores the current fashion in "simplistic political poetry." Suggests that "there are even some good poets, writing in other styles, whom I suspect of having been subtly influenced by the drug cult's notion that vision and self-transcendence are easily come by. It's not so, of course; it's hard and rare as hell to get beyond yourself." Affirms his stand on the writer having "maximum control of his audience" through his skillful use of words. Says that "metaphor, in the small sense and the large, is the main property of poetry. But there are other elements in poetry, and I see no reason why any of these shouldn't be lead dog once in a while." Agrees that his later work has "less gaiety . . . exuberance." Describes his teaching methods for literature and the teaching of writing. Points out that his reason for translating poems is "because someone else has written a poem which you love and you want to take possession of it. . . . You want to speak in the voice of that poem, which perhaps you could not do in your own poetic person." Reprinted: 1974.8; 1990.2.

6 FAVERTY, FREDERICK E. "The Poetry of Richard Wilbur." In *Modern American Poetry: Essays in Criticism.* Edited by Guy Owen. Deland, FL: Everett/Edwards, pp. 227-38.

Reprint of 1959.1 and 1962.6.

7 GRAHAM, JOHN. "Richard Wilbur." In *Craft So Hard to Learn: Conversations with Poets and Novelists about Teaching of Writing.* Edited by George Garrett. New York: Morrow, pp. 41-45.

Richard Wilbur describes methods he uses in teaching creative writing. Feels he can only point students in a good direction. Does not require any particular type of poem, but encourages work with some forms. Encourages students to read widely. Finds that most students have not read Whitman but have read Eliot's "The Love Song of J. Alfred Prufrock" if not his *Four Quartets*. Says he sees too much "polemical writing" in verse. "Usually, they [students] take a while to become discriminating in an aesthetic sense between good protest poems and bad ones."

8 HERZMAN, RONALD B. "Yeatsian Parallel in Richard Wilbur's 'Merlin Enthralled.'" *Notes on Contemporary Literature* 2, no. 5 (November):10-11.

Suggests that "the real focus of the poem ["Merlin Enthralled"] lies in the event itself. History resolves itself into small events, and these are what are important, because it is through small events that human feelings become a reality and not an abstraction." Sees a parallel to Yeats' "Leda and the Swan." However, Yeats' poem conveys a sense of immediacy. Wilbur's poem, though implying that some change has occurred instantly in history, fails to convey any sense of apocalypse.

9 LEVEY, VIRGINIA RHEA MORRIS. "Wonder: Sunshine and Shadow Celebration in the Poetry of Richard Wilbur." Ph.D. dissertation, Marquette University, 212 pp.

Argues that "in his poetry Richard Wilbur asserts and explores the ramifications of a celebration based upon acceptance of both the imperfection and the nobility of human nature." Sees Wilbur's effort as one of combining the "ideal and the mundane based upon the perception of the spirit in the flesh." Asserts that his poetry suggests that "man, living in time, must face loss to know love, accept death to have life, and accommodate the disorder and intransigence of phenomenal reality to perceive mystery, miracle, and myth, the wonder of life." See *Dissertation Abstracts International* 33:318A.

10 MURRAY, PHILIP. "Comment." *Poetry* 120, no. 4 (July):231-32.

Performance review of *The School for Wives*. Thinks that Wilbur's translation was "merrily . . . received by the audience" at the Phoenix Theatre production. Says the play "reads beautifully too, and is a total delight. Wilbur has *re-created* the French original with all the wit, polish, grace, pace, and clarity of a master translator." Cites lines from Act One, Scene One to show how brilliantly Wilbur has succeeded.

11 WOLFE, MARIAN S. "The Poetry of Richard Wilbur: 'An Escape from Personality.'" Ph.D. dissertation, University of Texas at Austin, 302 pp.

Suggests that "Wilbur feels that the poet must use obliquity and distancing to achieve a representation of reality that does justice both to the perceiving mind and to the world." Develops three "means of indirection" used by Wilbur in his poetry: natural landscape as a vehicle for expressing emotion, myth as a "metaphorical world-picture," and arts and artifacts as a way of expressing "his concern with the role of the artist and the nature of the artistic process." See *Dissertation Abstracts International* 33:334A.

1973

1 BENOIT, RAYMOND. *Single Nature's Double Name*. The Hague: Mouton, pp. 127-31.

Reprinted in part from 1969.1.

2 BLUE, MARGARET. *Library Journal*, 15 June, p. 2006.

Reviews *Opposites*. Finds these poems "a poor attempt to present the concept of opposites to young children." Says children will only be confused by them.

3 DILLON, DAVID. "The Image and the Object: An Interview with Richard Wilbur." *Southwest Review* 58, no. 3 (Summer):240-51.

This conversation was transcribed and edited from a tape made on January 31, 1973, in connection with a reading by Mr. Wilbur at Southern Methodist University.

Richard Wilbur talks about his penchant for details in his poetry. "The value of description in poetry is that it should be one side of the big straddle, that it should consist of a continuous, willful adherence to the actual while at the same time the rest of your mind generalizes and connects." Agrees that too many practicing poets, such as those published in *Kayak*, allow "ideas and theories [to] become separated from their experience." Enjoys Robert Herrick, Richard Lovelace, George Herbert, and Thomas Traherne's *Centuries of Meditations* for their creation of a "ligature between the mundane and . . . the abstract." Cites "A Hole in the Floor" as his first dramatic poem, written in 1952. Assents to his statement about forms used as "framing or composition in painting" made in the preface to John Ciardi's *Mid-Century American Poets* some twenty-five years earlier. Insists that though he is "thought to have a quarrel with free-verse poets," he does not. Says he chooses "to write free verse that happens to rhyme or to fall into a

1973

stanza pattern." Discusses the length of "Walking to Sleep," "The Agent," and "The Mind-Reader" as a new direction. Rejects confessional poetry. Prefers instead to "project aspects of myself . . . as characters resembling characters in a play, as milkweed or stones." Suggests, however, that "The Writer," "A Wedding Toast," and "Cottage Street, 1953" are all recent examples of personal poems. Disagrees with those who suggest he is "masking a basic despair." Says that translating poems "stretches" the poet in new directions. Likes Andrei Voznesensky because he "likes to be playful in the midst of his greatest seriousness or passion, and so do I." Describes his writing process as slow, of necessity. Poems must mature in his mind. Thinks the opportunity for publishing poems is ample currently. Finds mixing teaching and writing both good and bad. Thinks the influence of the academy "is going to make for a cleverer poetry" which is both a gain and a loss. Feels A. R. Ammons is "a poet of great stature who has not yet had the applause he deserves." Reprinted 1984.2.

4 ELLMANN, RICHARD, and O'CLAIR, ROBERT. "Richard Wilbur." In *The Norton Anthology of Modern Poetry*. New York: W. W. Norton, pp. 1000-1001.

Introduces several anthologized poems. Suggests that what Wilbur seeks "are complex symmetries, which he composes with 'ceremony.'" Rehearses Wilbur's well-known stand on the use of form (*Mid-Century American Poets* by John Ciardi). Cites two principal interests: "pure, gratuitous verse, as opposed to social protest or religious affirmation" ("Cigales") and the necessity for living "at once in two atmospheres, spirit and its ground in fact" ("Water Walker"). Notes Wilbur's father was a painter and his mother from a prominent journalism family. Describes briefly his early years in New Jersey, his stint of journalism on high school and college newspapers, his education at Amherst College and Harvard, and his teaching assignments at Harvard, Wellesley, and Wesleyan. Though Wilbur works hard to describe "things of this world," another facet of his work is that "sumptuous destitution," borrowed from Emily Dickinson. "It never fully satisfies the spirit which has, like the olive tree, a thirst 'exceeding all excess'" ("Grasse: The Olive Trees").

5 GRAHAM, JOHN. "Richard Wilbur." In *The Writer's Voice: Conversations with Contemporary Writers*. Edited by George Garrett. New York: William Morrow, pp. 75-91.

Recorded at the Hollins Conference in Creative Writing and Cinema, June 15-27, 1970, for John Graham's educational radio program, "The Scholar's Bookshelf." Begins with a brief biography, list of publications and honors, prizes, and fellowships. Describes Wilbur's appearance as "tall, youthfully handsome, graceful, and slowmoving . . . except when he's on the tennis court."

Richard Wilbur discusses the necessity for economy in poetry, despite readers' possible inability to relate to decriptions of nature. Finds the riddle "a fascinating form" because it "describes a concept or a thing without naming it" ("Riddle"). Argues that a poet must not worry about what his audience knows; he must simply "throw it down, and hope it can be picked up." Too much information in a poem is artless ("In the Field"). Suggests that "wit is a part of seriousness, a means of being serious." Contends that a "serious poem is stronger if it allows itself to be wild and absurd and potentially ridiculous at times" ("Playboy"). Explains his method in writing "Walking to Sleep." "As soon as you start to think about something, you furnish it with things, and your [*sic*] furnish any landscape as soon as you start walking along a road, and as soon as you think of a room you start to furnish it." Suggests that a good translator translate "thought by thought." Likes translation because he likes "resistance in art. . . . My sensibility is attracted to the sculpture kind of thing, in which you bang at something that resists you and try to arrive, with its opposition, at something in the nature of an attractive compromise." Wilbur reads "Dead Still" aloud and comments on the challenges involved in translating. Reprinted 1990.2.

6 HASSAN, IHAB. "American Literature." In *World Literature Since 1945: Critical Surveys of the Contemporary Literatures of Europe and the Americas*. Edited by Ivar Ivask and Gero von Wilpert. New York: Frederick Ungar, pp. 36-37.

Includes Richard Wilbur in a group of formalist poets. Lists primary works beginning with *The Beautiful Changes* (1947) and ending with *Walking to Sleep* (1969). Describes Wilbur as being the "epitome of formalist grace. Ceremonial, detached, allusive, a craftsman of beauty and scope, he mastered various complicated verse forms." Asserts that Wilbur's poems began to change with *Advice to a Prophet* (1961). They "exhibited a rougher texture, a new strength, also a new faltering." Concludes that finally, "it seemed as if his temperament was . . . too guarded or fastidious to engage the fullest life of the age." Revised and reprinted: 1973.7.

7 _____. *Contemporary American Literature 1945-1972: An Introduction*. New York: Frederick Ungar, pp. 108-9.

Revision of 1973.6.

8 HEYEN, WILLIAM. "On Richard Wilbur." *The Southern Review* n.s. 9, no. 3 (July):617-34.

Defies New Critical principles and says "the criticism of poetry must be personal." Asserts that poetry is Wilbur's "natural" metier, though at times he chooses elevated language to express his ideas. "Richard Wilbur's voice strikes me as individual, powerful, undeniable, and in poem after poem he makes his taste and feeling for language mine. That taste is for raised, uncommon speech." Argues strongly with those critics who have labeled Wilbur as "too refined." "In Wilbur there is a dramatic confrontation between a center that cannot hold and a center that will. His rage, in a world of vertigo, is for the right word." Rejects the tendency of many contemporary poets to throw out "rhyme, meter, villanelles, repetition, wit, word play, control, complexity, allusion." Says that "there should be no programs, only poets writing the poems that they have to write." Defends Wilbur's "humility in the face of not-knowing" as a virtue. Finds it unnecessary to decide whether or not Wilbur is a "major or minor poet." Compares Wilbur to Theodore Roethke, John Berryman, and Robert Lowell and decides that "Wilbur's work has had to change less; from the beginning the grace, wit, passion . . . . and control of his poems has been unpretentious, usually without apparent strain, less wrenched and self-conscious and forbidding." Suggests that "it has been Wilbur's genius to invest the quotidian with holiness, to conceive of reality . . . as . . . a 'sacramental economy.'" Wilbur is most effective as a "visionary shaper of this world. . . . His language is such that what is recreated is the numina of particulars that I have intimated in my better moments." Concludes that "there is for me in the poetry of Richard Wilbur something always just past the threshold of realization, something elusive, something toward which his formal structures edge and with which they bump shoulders, something that criticism can only hope to graze. This something, I think, is feeling, passion."

9 KUNITZ, STANLEY. "A Sum of Approximations." *Translation 73* 1, no. 1 (Winter):56-61.

Argues that "translation . . . is a sum of approximations, but not all approximations are equal." Illustrates the impossibility of translating word-for-word from the Russian into English. Compares his version of the last stanza of Anna Akhmatova's "Lot's Wife" to Wilbur's. Says Wilbur attempts "something I wouldn't even try to do: he follows the original metrical pattern exactly–ABAB rhymed pentameters." Admits that neither version is very good.

10 LIVINGSTON, MYRA COHN. "The Opposite of Soup Is Nuts." *New York Times Book Review*, 1 July, p. 7.

Reviews *Opposites*. Finds these poems start "the imagination whirling." Thinks that young people will enjoy the humor and the language. Enjoys the poet's personal interjections. Says that these poems "are a reminder that an adherence to form in poetry yields its own rich rewards for the poet as well as reader." Reprinted: 1983.18.

11 MALKOFF, KARL. "Richard Wilbur." In *Crowell's Handbook of Contemporary American Poetry*. New York: Thomas Y. Crowell, pp. 325-31.

Contends that "the sense of agreement that [Wilbur] embodies in his view of reality . . . is not a simplistic faith in the rightness of things; it is rather what Wilbur has called 'the proper relation between the tangible world and the intuitions of the spirit.'" Finds in Wilbur's first five books of poetry (*The Beautiful Changes* 1947 to *Walking to Sleep* 1969) poems which demonstrate his ability to maintain a consistent vision of the complexities of human experience while maintaining a high standard of technical virtuosity. Sees that "the focus for Wilbur is . . . the object itself, never the abstraction alone. But always, or nearly always, the object draws the poet toward another level of being." Acknowledges that "there is a potential monotony in Wilbur's dominant theme, the relation between the spiritual and the material; the real business of his poems, however, is structural rather than thematic." Concludes that though more commonly a poet of celebration, Wilbur, nevertheless, displays his understanding of the darker side of human nature, particularly in *Walking to Sleep*. Contains a short primary and secondary bibliography.

12 O'DEA, MARCIA AILEEN. "He Will Listen Kindly to Creatures Who Teach Him Their Names: A Study of Seven Poems by Richard Wilbur." M.A. thesis, Lone Mountain College, 69 pp.

Asserts that "Wilbur's poems show how he enters with a discerning eye, a patient vision and a warm spirit into the processes of creation and recreation in this world." Central concerns are Wilbur's "respect for life," his appreciation of beauty and harmony made clear through his concrete images, and his desire to lend "an ennobled significance" to "animate and inaimate life." Analyzes seven poems in seven chapters: "The Aspen and the Stream," "Giacometti," "Someone Talking to Himself," "Beasts," "Ceremony," "Grace," and "Love Calls Us to the Things of This World."

1973

13 PRITCHARD, WILLIAM H. "Poetry Matters." *Hudson Review* 26, no.
3 (Autumn):578-97.
    Reviews *Opposites*. Says that "what saves these poems from
coyness, lollipops for the kids, is, along with his usual brilliance of ear,
Wilbur's jaunty and unsaccharine response to the pleasures and
strangenesses of using words."

14 Review of *Opposites*. *The Horn Book Magazine*, August, p. 388.
    Reviews *Opposites*. Calls this a "captivating little book of verse."
Finds that "exploring tempting idiosyncrasies of the English
language – which make irregularities so normal, and nonsense so
logical – the poet plays with synonyms, antonyms, and homonyms.
Twisting words and turning phrases inside out, he tosses off rhymes as
dexterously as he draws his droll, Thurber-like sketches."

15 "Richard Wilbur." In *Cassell's Enyclopaedia of World Literature*. Edited
by J. Buchanan-Brown. Vol. 3: English, Speech, and Drama, edited by
S. H. Steinberg. New York: William Morrow & Co., p. 742.
    Mentions Gerard Manley Hopkins and Wallace Stevens as
possible influences. Says Wilbur is "a fine craftsman whose delicate
observations are occasionally overwhelmed by his preoccupation with
technique. At its best his poetry exemplifies the post-war American
poet's refusal to make the glib statement or the grand gesture while
retaining an absolute fidelity to feeling."

16 "Richard Wilbur." In *50 Modern American and British Poets*. Edited by
Louis Untermeyer. New York: David McKay, pp. 309-10.
    Lists briefly Wilbur's literary accomplishments to date. Says that
"Wilbur's . . . poetry displays the efflorescent images and inventiveness
of a virtuoso. Although designed in definite patterns, the lines are full
of fresh vitality; the taste is immaculate and the choice of form and
phrase unerring." Discusses "Advice to a Prophet," "Digging for China,"
and "The Writer" as poems that reveal "wit and wisdom joined,"
playfulness, and a superb "relation of two images."

* 17 "Richard Wilbur." In *Guide to Modern World Literature*. Edited by
Martin Seymour-Smith. London: Wolfe Publishing, pp. 146, 160.
        Listed in unpublished Hagstrom bibliography.

18 SHARMA, D. R. "Richard Wilbur: An Analysis of His Vision." *Panjab
University Research Bulletin (Arts)* (Chandigarh, India) 4, no. 2
(October):43-50.

Seeks to establish a "correspondence between [Wilbur's] critical stance and creative achievement." Analyzes "Advice to a Prophet" and "The Aspen and the Stream." Says that part of Wilbur's "aesthetic credo" is the assumption that the function of the imagination is to return life to the everyday world, the firm assurance that poetry is not meant to be abstract, and the commitment to writing poetry that is "universal,"–that is, "about everybody." Finds that the poems in *Advice to a Prophet* move away from the dominant form used in the prior three books–the ironic meditative lyric–to the dramatic poem. Mentions two kinds of change, "disintegrative and metamorphic," in Wilbur's work. Concludes that Wilbur rejects limitations that destroy his poetic vision and works to "resolve the content-form dichotomy" familiar to American poets of the middle generation.

19 SMITH, J. F. "A Child's Eden of Verses." *Christian Science Monitor*, 5 September, p. 12.

Reviews *Opposites*. Recommends this book for "a child's Eden of verse." Says that "Richard Wilbur's flair for a clever line rarely flags, and his drawings add more humor to these riddling verses. The kooky logic of *Opposites* . . . is contagious."

1974

1 BEACHAM, WALTON. *The Meaning of Poetry: A Guide to Explication*. Boston: Allyn & Bacon, pp. 10-17, 55-57.

Instructs the reader in methods for discovering Wilbur's ability to control the reader's response through a close reading of "Year's End." Pays attention to the units of time in the poem, the historical facts, the images, metaphors, word usage, metrics, form, alliteration, and sound as contributors to the theme. Includes a copy of a student explication. See 1974.7.

2 BERNLEF, J. "Tussen oog en licht: Over Howard Nemerov en Richard Wilbur [Between Eye and Light: About Howard Nemerov and Richard Wilbur]." *DeGids* [*The Guide*] (Amsterdam) 137, no. 3:217-25.

In Dutch. Treats Howard Nemerov and Richard Wilbur together. Claims that Wilbur and Nemerov do not suffer that much. They do not take the whole world on their shoulders, but keep it at a distance in order to write about it more clearly. That is the criticism which people make of their work: too much at a distance, too intellectual, too academic–which usually means that they know how to give form to something too pretty and witty. Compares a Dutch translation of Nemerov's "The Blue Swallows" and Wilbur's "An Event." Says that

1974

Wilbur is the more original, but both address the same thing: the impossibility for things (nets, cages, webs) to hold on to fleeting images. Finds that Wilbur constantly points to the danger of wanting to flee into idealistic structures ("A World Without Objects Is a Sensible Emptiness"). Stresses that both poets mix analytic (scientific) and mythic modes of thinking: this is what makes Nemerov and Wilbur modern poets. Is not surprised to find that both poets were inspired by René Magritte. Suggests that the problem posed by both poets ("A Hole in the Floor") is an old one for philosophers. Both Nemerov's and Wilbur's solution looks very much like a borrowing from Magritte: both use the image of "eye" and "light." Argues that what the two poets refuse to do is express a preference and choose repeatedly the vacuum which needs to be filled anew at every turn. Charges that poetry is for both poets not a matter of ideas but a need to charge ideas emotionally – ideas which can subsequently be discarded as outdated and sterile.

Suggests that of the two poets, Wilbur is the more lyrical and gentle, the more contemplative who confronts natural phenomena with cultural phenomena. Concludes that these two poets' "unwillingness to arrive at a synthesis makes their poems unfit for people who expect from poetry a substituting religion or an aroused emotional state; but one who enjoys looking for hours at a glass of water will find himself at home here." Includes a select bibliography of Wilbur's works. In addition to poems mentioned above, includes translations of "Juggler" and "Seed Leaves."

3 DACEY, PHILIP. "An Interview with Richard Wilbur." *Crazy Horse* no. 15 (Fall):37-44.
Wilbur talks at length about his personal history, including his ancestor, Samuel Wildbore, his childhood years in rural New Jersey, his college training, his life as a cryptographer for the U.S. Army, his academic experience, and his family life. Discusses the "organic form" his poems take. Recounts the background of "Piazza di Spagna, Early Morning" as a good example of an experience heightened by the imagination. States that "the world is ultimately good and every art an expression of hope and joy. . . . What art needs to do, as Milton said, is to reflect how all things 'Rising or falling still advance His praise,' and in the process to make a full acknowledgement of fallen-ness, doubt, and death." Concludes that "there is something wrong with poems which lack all redeeming gaiety." Defines sincerity as meaning something and as "taking the crafty trouble to embody that meaning exactly and coercively." Feels that the 1960's was a period of

"stupefying" political pep rallies, detrimental to the poet as poetry readings could become. Reprinted: 1990.2.

4 HOWARD, RICHARD. "Comment." In *Preferences: 51 American Poets Choose Poems from Their Own Work and from the Past*. Edited by Richard Howard. New York: Viking Press, pp, 313-16.
    Pairs William Davenant's poem "The Philosopher and the Lover: To a Mistress Dying" with Wilbur's "All These Birds." The two poems are Wilbur's personal choice. Says "it is easy to see why Wilbur prefers this obscure poem for he says he himself is concerned 'with the proper relation between the tangible world and the intuitions of the spirit.'"

5 JAMES, CLIVE. "When the Gloves Are Off." In *The Metropolitan Critic*. London: Faber & Faber, pp. 49-59.
    Reprint of 1971.11. Reprinted: 1980.6; 1983.18.

6 LAMONT, ROSETTE C. "Joseph Brodsky: A Poet's Classroom." *Massachusetts Review* 15, no. 4 (Autumn):553-77, passim.
    Recounts a semester of classes under Brodsky's instruction during which the poet reads Wilbur's "Two Voices in a Meadow" and suggests that the milkweed's statement, "I shall possess the field," is the "bravest." Summarizes Brodsky's theory that writing poetry on the "metaphysical level," that is, beyond personal emotion, is the only acceptable mode. Quotes Brodsky as saying that the beat poets just shout and overwhelm the "quiet voices" like Richard Wilbur's and others'.

7 METZGER, JOHN W. "Imagery in 'Year's End' by Richard Wilbur." In *The Meaning of Poetry: A Guide to Explication of Poetry*. Boston: Allyn & Bacon, pp. 58-59.
    Explicates "Year's End" according to the method suggested by Walton Beacham (1974.1). Follows several dominant images and metaphors in the poem such as snow, people in houses, fossils in stone, and the New Year.

8 PACKARD, WILLIAM, ed. "Craft Interview with Richard Wilbur." In *The Craft of Poetry: Interviews from the New York Quarterly*. Garden City: Doubleday, pp. 177-94.
    Reprint of 1972.5. Reprinted: 1990.2.

9 "Richard Wilbur." In *Directory of American Scholars*. 6th ed. Vol. II: English, Speech & Drama, edited by Jaques Cattell Press. New York & London: R. R. Bowker, pp. 675-76.

1974

Lists Wilbur's college degrees, teaching experience, several prizes and awards. Brief bibliography of primary works begins with *Poems 1943-56.*

10 "Richard Wilbur." In *Literary History of the United States*. 4th ed. Edited by Robert Spillers, et al. New York: Macmillan; London: Collier Macmillan, p. 1433.

Describes Wilbur's poems as those which "exhibit the hard-won excellence of a formality achieved by rigorous exclusions." Grants, however, that this formalism is "a flexible instrument." Suggests that Wilbur's "special intensity results from subjecting his romantic sensibility to the intellectual and spiritual decorum of his forms."

11 STAUFFER, DONALD BARLOW. "The Middle Generation." In *A Short History of American Poetry*. New York: E. P. Dutton, pp. 89, 352, 385-87.

Cites Wilbur's interpretation of Edgar Allan Poe's poetic vision as a "war between the poetic soul and the earthly self to which it is bound." Quotes Wilbur's description in regard to the education of the poets of his generation as saying, "We were led by our teachers and by the critics whom we read to feel that the most adequate and convincing poetry is that which accommodates mixed feelings, clashing ideas, and incongruous images." Describes Wilbur as "an intelligent and gifted man" whose poetry has changed remarkably little over the years, but who is much admired for his ability to use ordinary things to create beauty and freshness. Suggests Wilbur is a master of the use of rhythm, diction, and sound effects, a celebrator of life, and a "brilliant translator." Uses "Cigales," "Lightness," "Altitudes," and "Marginalia" as specific examples.

12 TAYLOR, HENRY. "Cinematic Devices in Richard Wilbur's Poetry." *Rocky Mountain Modern Language Association Bulletin* 28, no. 2 (June):41-48.

Suggests that becoming aware of the cinematic techniques embedded in Wilbur's poems can "remind us of the fact that film has become one of the modern sources of myth." Cites sections of "Castles and Distances" and "Walking to Sleep" as good examples of Wilbur's use of modern myth which "allow him an extreme economy of statement in his efforts to explore the world from which those myths arise, and the world toward which his poems point the way." Specific cinematic techniques such as rapid cutting, montage, fade-out, distortion of technicolor appear also in "Tywater," "Beowulf," "The Pardon," and "Merlin Enthralled." Finds that Wilbur's "muting of cinematic devices in the second part of the poem ["Walking to Sleep"] indicates the poet's attitude toward them: they can be used to narrow the vision in an artificial way, just as the screen presents an artificial world." However, the last lines of the poem suggest that the better way is to allow the imagination free play. Contends that Wilbur appears to feel that "the wilful selection of images may seem safer, but to take all images as they come requires great imaginative strength and serenity."

1975

1 BOGAN, CHRISTOPHER, and KAPLAN, CARL. "Interview: Richard Wilbur." *Amherst Student Review*, 17 March, pp. 4-5, 13-14.

Wilbur discusses his ideas and attitudes during his tenure as editor of the *Amherst Student Review* in the early 1940's. Remarks that Americans expect too much of young people, that "hope ought to be reposed in the proven old." Lists James Joyce, Dylan Thomas, Poets of the Month published by J. Laughlin – New Directions, *The New Yorker*, Gerard Manley Hopkins, Alfred Lord Tennyson, and Edgar Allan Poe as reading he carried around in his barracks bag during World War II. Discusses his interest in Poe at length. Says that Poe may be his "anti-self" because [Poe] was a "world-denier, a denier of the body, and a denier of matter. . . . His more exciting techniques are of erasure, of explosion, of uncreation." Sums up by saying, "I simply cannot finally stomach any kind of idealism or spirituality which is contemptuous toward the body or what we call the material. . . . That's one way of stating my quarrel with Poe. I find myself fascinated with him and opposed to him all down the line." Admits that most poets, even good poets like Yeats, Auden, and Wallace Stevens, end up repeating themselves over and over again. Shys away from talking about his own concerns but allows that the quarrel with Poe is a central one. Describes his writing habits as disciplined. Though he cannot "make" a poem come to him, he'll "sit in a chair for six hours straight and not do anything else. I may not come up with a line, I may not come up with a word, but I can be patient." Feels that translation work is an important contribution to American culture. Dislikes "slovenly free verse," but speaks highly of Walt Whitman and William Carlos Williams. Reprinted: 1990.2.

2 BROUGHTON, IRV. "An Interview with Richard Wilbur." *Mill Mountain Review* 2, no. 2:92-109.

Interviews Richard Wilbur. Wilbur reaffirms his commitment to poetic forms because of the "many effects you can get with them that you can't possibly get without them. He argues that "forced rhyme is no good. Unforced rhyme, even if the rhymes have been used a thousand times, can be effective." Discusses his translation work and his standards for it in detail. Insists that a poet must translate another poet with an awareness of the form in which the original poem is written. Finds that a good translator asks many of the same questions that a good poet asks of his own work. Admits that sometimes criticism which talks "about the heresy of this and the fallacy of that . . . is a little strong, a little arm-twisting, and is likely to be damping to the original sort of poet who's out of step with the fashions of his time." Denies he thinks of his audience as he writes. Discusses the problems involved in collaborating with Leonard Bernstein on *Candide*. Recites a Coventry Patmore poem as one of his favorites. Interprets the poet to mean that "the world is good and will turn out so." Defines poetry "as getting one's various selves to quarrel intelligibly in public." Says he values wit: "When one is making a serious statement, a little playfulness is, if it's done well, a kind of earnest of one's earnestness. If a poem can't stand to be locally amusing, then I suspect it's really not very serious; not as serious as it thinks it is."

Names William Meredith and William Jay Smith as two poets to whom he shows his work regularly. Discusses the fact that it took seventeen years for "The Mind-Reader" to finally gel into a poem, though he doesn't denigrate inspiration of the moment. Admits to having dry periods as well as oases in his writing. Distinguishes the emotional experiences of life from the poetic experience: "Poetry is, to be sure, emotional, but it's emotion at its most precise and understanding. Nothing to which you would say 'Wow!' in ordinary experience seems to me to resemble a poem." Discusses the background of "Cottage Street, 1953." Describes his parents' influences. Indicates that his favorite poetical device is the metaphor about which he says, "Whatever else in poetry is laborious and achieved by will, good metaphors come in a burst. They come to me, at any rate, as happy surprises, not that I won't have been waiting for them. But they do seem like something given." Allows that his dreams play a part in his writing. Enjoys being a light verse writer at times. Admits to feeling "an affinity with Molière's comedy." Argues that "poetry is a matter of life and death, I think, simply because there's no more miserable situation than muteness – being unable to find words for one's sufferings and one's happiness – and so, being inadequate to one's experience." Reprinted: 1990.1.

3 BUFITHIS, PHILIP H. "Richard Purdy Wilbur." In *Encyclopedia of World Literature in the Twentieth Century*. Edited by Frederick Ungar and Lina Mainiero, vol. 4, supp. New York: Frederick Ungar, pp. 398-99.

Covers Wilbur's parents' artistic and publishing backgrounds, Wilbur's college and World War II experiences, his education and teaching assignments, translations, children's books, and first five volumes of poems from *The Beautiful Changes* (1947) to *Walking to Sleep* (1969). Suggests that "at the core of Wilbur's poetry is his view of the natural world. Inherent in that world is . . . the spiritual subsistence that man tries elsewhere to find–in himself, in an idea, in an impalpable God." Says of "The Beautiful Changes," "implicit throughout the poem is Wilbur's belief that, to an eye liberated from the customary way of seeing, nature's essential meaning remains always radiant." Sees wit and "ironic intellections" as saving graces which prevent Wilbur's poems from being heavy or "merely picturesque." Cites Wilbur's statement from "The Genie in the Bottle" regarding the necessary use of formal structures. Calls Wilbur a "lyric poet because sensuous delight is always his poetry's reason for being." Concludes that "few would dispute that Wilbur and Robert Lowell are the two most accomplished poets to emerge in America since World War II."

4 CIARDI, JOHN, and WILLIAMS, MILLER. *How Does a Poem Mean?* 2d ed. Boston: Houghton Mifflin, pp. 148-52.
   Reprints Wilbur's "Still, Citizen Sparrow" as an example of the "effective use of 'double language.'" Suggests categories of adjectives in poetry such as those of evidence, of judgment, philosophical or thinking adjectives, and redundant adjectives. Finds that Wilbur's poem employs more thinking adjectives that open up the "intellectual dimension" of a poem.

5 CRABB, SARAH B. "The Form of Time and Grace in the Poetry of Richard Wilbur." Ph.D. dissertation, Case Western Reserve University, 228 pp.
   Expands on primary concern with "how Wilbur's poetry mirrors in aesthetic design the spiritual and temporal pattern which is its subject." Finds history in "Castles and Distances" as "both revelation and tradition, grace revealed and interpreted through time." Focuses on "Merlin Enthralled" and "Next Door" as poems revealing the myth that is "man's common cultural heritage." "Still, Citizen Sparrow," "The Pardon," and "A Plain Song for Comadre" recreate Wilbur's understanding of grace which carries with it moral responsibilities. Concludes with an analysis of "In the Field," "On the Marginal Way," and "Walking to Sleep" which show Wilbur searching for a "redemptive design in his world; but the speakers, finally, assert their trust in such a design rather than discover its presence." See *Dissertation Abstracts International* 36:1501A.

6 DALY, DANIEL JOSEPH. "Dialectic Poems of Richard Wilbur." Ph.D. dissertation, St. John's University, 133 pp.
   Posits that "the dialectic [poem] represents Wilbur's work at its best." Says this form has the "basic design of argumentation, and given the nature of the ambiguous art, is conclusive." Begins with a prosodic

analysis of the following poems: "The Aspen and the Stream," "Altitudes," "Love Calls Us to the Things of This World," "A Baroque Wall-Fountain in the Villa Sciarra," "Castles and Distances," "Sonnet," "Two Quatrains for First Frost," "Two Voices in a Meadow," "La Rose des Vents," "Gemini," "After the Last Bulletins," "Beasts," "Epistemology," "Museum Piece," "Still, Citizen Sparrow," and "Piazza Di Spagna, Early Morning." Follows the prosodic analyses with descriptive passages which discuss the "poetic war" between the academics and the beats, "Wilbur's use of history, his craftsmanship, and his theory of art and reality." See *Dissertation Abstracts International* 36:5294A.

7 KOLIN, PHILIP C. "The Subtle Drama of Richard Wilbur's 'Exeunt.'" *Notes on Contemporary Literature* 5, no. 1 (Winter):11-13.
    Reprints "Exeunt." Interprets this short poem as an analogue for human mortality. Concludes that "the death of the season has been described in terms reminding us of the death of human life – summer and man both pass away. This great change is writ large in this small poem as Wilbur cautions us – *sotto voce* – and from the proper poetic distance – how so very close the two in fact are."

8 NEJGEBAUER, ALEKSANDAR. "Poetry 1945-1960: Self versus Culture." In *American Literature Since 1900*. Edited by Marcus Cunliffe. London: Barrie & Jenkins, pp. 145-49.
    Charges that some critics have taken the view that Wilbur's poetry is limited by his concern for form and New Critical complexities, but defends Wilbur's poetry as "different – an anachronism in an age of cold war and nuclear threats." Contends Wilbur "is a seer and maker of the beautiful; each of his poems is meant to be, and most often is, a thing of beauty and a source of pleasure." Contrary to the stereotypical notion that Wilbur is fascinated with things and finds clever and elegant ways to write about them, suggests he focuses on the dilemma of "how to live in this world without being degraded by its material nature, how to cultivate the life of the spirit without losing touch with reality." A second focus is the "question of what it means to be a poet." Cites a number of poems in support of this thesis.

9 NEMEROV, HOWARD. "What Will Suffice." *Salmagundi* no. 28 (Winter):90-103.
    Establishes the context in which modern poetry matured as the basis for understanding the theories the middle generation of poets inherited from their elders. Newton's scientific theories removed "mind from the cosmos except as a passive recording instrument." Equally

1975

destructive was Kant's philosophy which denied access to any "ultimate reality." Thus the poet was left with very few options. Suggests poets responded in a variety of ways: one response was imagism – the recording of images without comment. Richard Wilbur's response was to return to myth and legend in order to "see deeply into . . . truth" ("Merlin Enthralled"). Sees "The Great Change" as "not historical only, but primarily metaphysical and psychological; something we have a certain experience of under today's historical conditions, and yesterday's, but also something we should have experienced, though in other terms perhaps, whenever and wherever we lived; a change that can become historical, in fact, only because it is first the experience of every individual at all times." "The Great Change" is that "like the giant forms of mythology and legend these too [the names of supernatural entities] are being driven out of poetry." The great challenge for modern poetry has been to acknowledge the universe as "simultaneously real and transpicuous, physical and mental" without developing a system of religion or ignoring the facts of science. "Wilbur's poem about Merlin is his steadfast and poignant acknowledgment of what magic, and what poetry, are about. It is part of the pathos, maybe, that this acknowledgment can be made precisely and only because magic, and poetry, have gone out of the world." Reprinted: 1978.14; reprinted in part: 1983.18.

10 OLIVER, RAYMOND. "Verse Translation and Richard Wilbur." *Southern Review* 11, no. 2 (April):318-30.
    Deplores the current trend of translators who ignore the form of the original and merely adapt the ideas of the poem to their own form. Asserts that the act of translating helps poets to "get out of themselves." Judges Wilbur as a master translator whose "best work is extremely faithful and it is fine poetry in its own right, achieving a kind of absolute in that it probably cannot be surpassed." Contends that "the goal of accurate verse translation is the equivalence of stylistic effect; one translates form, not language." Wilbur is able to do this and to choose good poems to translate. Compares Wilbur's translation of "Helen" by Paul Valéry, with the original. Finds Robert Lowell's "imitation" of the same poem suffers by comparison. Concludes that though Wilbur pays close attention to the form of the original work, he does not create pedantic translations. Rather, "he shows himself a perceptive critic by picking a good text and deciding which parts of it must be kept and which can be sacrificed; an accurate philologist by grasping the sense of the original; and a good poet by writing a good poem." Analyzes several translations: "Prayer to Go to Paradise with the Donkeys," "Ode to Pleasure," "The Agrigentum Road," "Eight

Riddles from Symphosius," four Spanish sonnets of Guillén and Borges, "Foggy Street," "The Pelican," and Molière's plays. Reprinted: 1983.18.

1976

1 BARNETT, PAMELIA S. "Richard Wilbur and the Painter's Eye." M.A. thesis, University of Houston, 151 pp.

Proposes to "explore in depth those ways in which art has influenced Richard Wilbur's poetic theory, technique, and subject matter." Suggests that "Wilbur's poetic skills of form, praise, analysis, and objectivity must forever link him significantly with the Classical tradition in art." Investigates Wilbur's ties to Classical, Dutch genre, and Romantic painters.

2 BEDIENT, CALVIN. "Books Considered." *New Republic*, 5 June, pp. 21-23.

Reviews *Walking to Sleep: New Poems and Translations*. Determines that Wilbur "is a bell too conscious of its clapper, clapper-happy. Pert but proper, always safe rather than sorry, his poetry is completely without risks, a prize pupil's performance. His ideas are always cut exactly to the size of his poems, he is never puzzled. And the ideas are all sentiments; aware of their potential high-minded emotional value and determined to snuggle into it." Compares Wilbur to Sylvia Plath negatively: "Wilbur's lines appear fusty, and safe as gingersnaps" beside hers ("Cottage Street, 1953"). Considers Wilbur unable to do the work of a real poet.

3 COMMIRE, ANNE. "Richard Wilbur." In *Something About the Author*. Vol. 9. Detroit: Gale, p. 201.

Contains sections PERSONAL, CAREER, WRITINGS, WORK IN PROGRESS, SIDELIGHTS, FOR MORE INFORMATION. Lists major biographical details, prizes and awards, teaching assignments, collections of poetry (*The Beautiful Changes* [1947] to *Opposites* [1973]), editorial and critical work, recordings, and a short secondary bibliography.

4 COOPERMAN, ROBERT. "Brief Reviews." *Denver Quarterly* 11, no. 2 (Summer):142-44.

Reviews *The Mind-Reader: New Poems*. Expresses satisfaction with this collection, but notes two problems: "a paucity or confusion of subject matter" as well as "subject matter and theme . . . trapped within form." Cites "Piccola Commedia" as an example of both these flaws.

1976

Applauds "A Wedding Toast" as a "gem." Sees "The Mind-Reader" as "central to Wilbur's vision."

5 DeMOTT, BENJAMIN. "A Poet's Prose," *New York Times Book Review*, 24 October, pp. 6-7.

Reviews *Responses, Prose Pieces*. Suggests that several ideas appear consistently in most of the pieces in this collection: "among these notions are that a line can be drawn between perverse and appropriate feelings, that solipsism is stupid, that self-restraint and good-humor are not in every instance badges of madness, that indifference to the 'lay and character of the land' is a subjective deformity, that fools alone deny meaning to the term *soul*, that without feeling for generational continuities we're done." Objects a bit to some "posh archaisms ["contemn," "reluct"], some "pricey verbal manners" ["I then begged leave to change the subject"]." Quibbles with Wilbur about his remark that "poetry doesn't prosper when it puts itself wholly at the service of some movement, some institution" because "sensitive middle-class liberalism" is a movement to which Wilbur has dedicated his talent.

6 EDELMAN, JOHN T. Review of *The Mind-Reader: New Poems*. *America*, 21 August, p. 83.

Reviews *The Mind-Reader: New Poems*. Describes the poems in this collection as "refreshing and unique." Applauds Wilbur's continued use of rhythm and rhyme, calling him "one of the most disciplined craftsmen writing today." Suggests that Wilbur's "range in form is matched by a comparable range in theme and emotion . . . [and] a sharply ironic wit." Concludes by saying, "In Wilbur's work, discipline, agility, range and warmly human sensibilities are known and expected qualities."

7 HONIG, EDWIN. "A Conversation with Richard Wilbur." *Modern Language Notes* 91, no. 5 (October):1084-98.

Date & place of interview: 15 October 1975, Middletown, Conn. Richard Wilbur talks about his first experience of translating poems written by his friend, André du Bouchet, a fellow graduate of Harvard. Concedes that "I have to like the poem [chosen to translate] and feel it has something to do with my feelings. . . . Perhaps, also, I like it and am particularly well motivated when I feel the poem represents . . . an extension or stretching of my own emotional possibilities." Describes his role as translator as "putting whatever abilities I have at the service of the person I'm translating." Denies that he ever translates as a mere poetic exercise; instead, suggests that he is "doing something complete, the purpose of which lies within itself." Acknowledges that translating a poem overshadows the next poem he writes, that translating has the possibility of helping the poet grow in new directions. Discusses the ease and difficulty of translating Molière plays in rhymed couplets. Suggests that the couplet is a very flexible form. Relates his surprise at finding *The Misanthrope* was a stageable translation, one which caused him to become more aware of producing speakable lines for actors. Describes his translations as "thought-for-thought" rather than "word-for-word" translations, though he makes every effort to be faithful to the semantic sense of the word and the form of the poem. Feels that a poet often begins a poem by "translating" preverbal intuitions into words. Reprinted: 1985.6; 1990.2.

8 HOWES, VICTOR. "The Civilized Strand of Poetry." *Christian Science Monitor*, 13 October, eastern ed., p. 28.

Reviews *The Mind-Reader: New Poems*. Characterizes this collection as "ecstasy tempered with discipline, as in the best it is." Asserts that Wilbur always writes poems "because he has something to say," that details lend reality and sound and sense enhance each other. Concludes that this book "may be caviar to the general, but will prove solid nutriment to the discriminating."

9 JOVANSKI, METO. "Ričard Vilbar." *Stremež* (Prilip, Yugoslavia) 20, no. 5:403-4.

In Macedonian. Calls Richard Wilbur a representative of the so-called second generation of American poets which came into prominence after World War II. From the years soon after the Second World War till the beginning of the sixties, he was an influential force in the development of the emerging young generation of poets. Sees Wilbur's and Robert Lowell's work as prototypic of the poets of their generation. Notes the characteristics of Wilbur's poems as infused with talent, intelligence, inspiration, and linguistic precision, written in language that resists esoteric verbiage and embraces the vernacular.

10 KUHN, JOHN. Review of *The Mind-Reader: New Poems. Best Sellers* 36, no. 7 (October):288.

Reviews *The Mind-Reader: New Poems*. Finds that "what Roethke called Wilbur's 'mind of grace' continues to work its dependable way among surprisingly right choices, words and verses." Feels that the "thematic reach and disparate images" of "Fourth of July" achieve a "perfect satisfaction at the poem's resolution." Finds "delicious humor" in "Flippancies" and "To His Skeleton." Says that a "Wordsworthian recognition of an underlying harmony both within and

1976

between the mind and outer nature illuminates many descriptive poems." Calls the mind-reader, in the poem by this name, Wilbur's alter-ego.

11 LEIBOWITZ, HERBERT. Review of *The Mind Reader. New York Times Book Review*, 13 June, pp. 10, 12.

 Reviews *The Mind-Reader: New Poems*. Charges that "emergencies are absent in [Wilbur's] poems; he is unseduced by the romantic equation of knowledge and power; he seldom rails at the world. Suspicious of grandiose gestures, of parading the ego, he mediates experience through reason." Further, "Wilbur strives to please more than to astonish, to charm taste rather than to stir passion." Acknowledges that in this book a reader may find enjoyment, like "an old friend whose talk is genial but familiar – and occasionally dull" and that the technical refinement of the poems confirms once again Wilbur's "neoclassical style." Concludes, however, that one finds a "certain affable blandness" in this collection. Castigates Wilbur for refusing to take chances: "one wishes that Wilbur would sometimes risk his mellifluous order and regularity for some of Plath's 'brilliant negative / In poems free and helpless and unjust.'" Welcomes the "rougher texture of the title poem" and wishes Wilbur had written more poems like it. Reprinted: 1983.18.

12 MACK, PERRY D. "Richard Wilbur's Three Treatments of Disintegrative and Metamorphic Change." *Innisfree* 3:37-44.

 Examines "Advice to a Prophet," "Still, Citizen Sparrow," and "Beasts" in order to understand Wilbur's three different uses of the concept of disintegration and metamorphosis – an approach to Wilbur's poems suggested earlier by John P. Farrell (1971.4). Sees Wilbur's treatment of change in "Advice" as disintegrative because it does not look forward to renewal. In "Citizen" Wilbur emphasizes metamorphosis only, looking "past the destroyed career of the outcast politician toward the great public good that he possibly could accomplish if given another opportunity to serve." Finds the "half human, half animal existence of the werewolf" in "Beasts" an example of disintegration and metamorphosis blended together.

13 MADIGAN, MICHAEL. Review of *The Mind-Reader: New Poems. Library Journal*, 1 April, p. 904.

 Reviews *The Mind-Reader: New Poems*. Says that "a final prayer at the end of 'The Eye' comes close to characterizing Wilbur's problem. . . . In many of his new poems, Wilbur still addresses us as if he were the only one alive. How smug 'Children of Darkness' seems in its reduction of the strange to a sunny fact. How self-indulgent 'In Limbo' and the title poem are, the one in its toying with an epistemological puzzle, the other in its demonstration of the limits of the mind. Two poems that will be praised are 'The Writer' and 'C Minor.' In these we hear Wilbur speaking to his daughter or his wife in a tone that gives 'due regard.'"

14 MILLER, R. H. "Wilbur's 'Epistemology.'" *Explicator* 34, no. 5 (January):item 37.

Asserts that "Epistemology: II" has been misinterpreted as a funny image or a "reconciliation of opposites." Interprets "II" as a "clever Johnsonian mock of the self-confident reader." The allusion to the cow is drawn from Boswell's "account of Johnson's attack on an equally repugnant group of philosophers, the skeptics, and specifically David Hume: 'Hume, and other sceptical innovators, are vain men, and will gratify themselves at any expence. Truth will not afford sufficient food to their vanity; so they have betaken themselves to errour. Truth, Sir, is a cow which will yield such people no more milk, and so they are gone to milk the bull'" (*Life of Johnson*, 21 July 1763). Says "the point is not that we become thorough-going skeptics like Hume, reducing all knowledge to a constant flow of impressions, but rather that Johnson, through Wilbur's use of the allusion to Johnson's remark in 'II,' achieves a most ingenious victory over our self-assured rejection of the Truth of the stones in 'I.'"

15 PARK, CLARA C[LAIBORNE]. "The Fastidious Eye." *Washington Post Book World*, 25 July, p. G2.

Reviews *The Mind-Reader: New Poems*. Contends that Wilbur is "a poet of due regard, of the love which enjoins difficult balance between spontaneity and form, passion and precision, our needs and other people's, this world and another." "The Eye," made up of two parts, testifies to the power of the poet's perceptions and challenges the reader's perceptions: "[Wilbur] courts dismissal [in 'I'] as a writer of elegant trivia, while recording his detachment in 24 lines of weightless iambics, in which he throws away passing images each of which could be the substance of somebody else's poem." In "II," the adjectives become charged with power: "hell is the absence of the Spirit's light." Says this "poem . . . turns out to be about how visual and intellectual perception are separate from spiritual perception and moral responsibility, unless we pray for grace to join them."

16 PETTICOFFER, DENNIS. *Library Journal*, 1 October, p. 2066.

1976

Reviews *Responses, Prose Pieces*. Views this collection of essays and addresses and literary criticism by Wilbur as a "disjointed collection of odds and ends." Suggests that libraries on limited budgets should question its value.

17 PHILLIPS, ROBERT. "Poetry: Three in a Bumper Year." *Commonweal*, 10 September, pp. 596-98.
    Reviews *The Mind-Reader: New Poems*. Claims that Wilbur, "writing today much as he did three decades ago, . . . has produced another book which will be read long after the disposable poems of today's more 'with-it' poets are discarded." Regrets that this collection is not longer. Mentions translations ["The Funeral of Bobò" and "Prayer to Go to Heaven with the Donkeys"] as "simple and affecting." Calls "The Writer" and "The Eye" memorable for their ability to remind "us of our inherent humbleness, entreating that we embrace not some, but all creatures." Sees "Cottage Street, 1953" as a criticism of confessional poets who put "most anything into a poem except happiness." By contrast, Wilbur identifies "with his '[A] Black Birch in Winter,' a tree which manages to survive and grow to greater wisdom each year."

18 PRITCHARD, WILLIAM. "More Poetry Matters." *Hudson Review*. 29, no. 3 (Autumn):453-63.
    Reviews *The Mind-Reader: New Poems*. Takes Calvin Bedient to task for his attack on Wilbur's poetry (1976.2). Argues that Bedient is wrong about "Cottage Street, 1953": "I prefer to believe that it ["Cottage"] is humanly admirable, a fresh and compelling gesture of language, and that Bedient (who mans a fire tower in the Angeles Forest, California) can't see the woods from the trees." Contends that Wilbur's work is unique, sometimes "neoclassic," sometimes "baroque" ("Children of Darkness"). Lists "A Storm in April," "The Writer," "In Limbo," "Cottage Street, 1953," "C Minor," "Children of Darkness," and "The Prisoner of Zenda" as his favored choices. Says "[the poems] are not free, not helpless and not unjust. They are good."

19 Review of *The Mind-Reader: New Poems*. *Choice* 13, no. 9 (November):1140-41.
    Reviews *The Mind-Reader: New Poems*. Says that "not all treasure is quickly mined. Contrary to what seems on the surface of Wilbur's poems, his eye is not that of a 'curious angel', but that of a giver of 'due regard.' Sometimes his skill with form and rhyme gets between the eye and mind, and a poem loses immediacy, but such separation is rare. The seemingly playful punning is highly serious, as

in certain metaphysical poems, and expresses qualities beyond the eye, and they in turn give the eye its 'due regard' to all of life."

20 "Richard Wilbur." In *The Face of Poetry: 101 Poets in Two Significant Decades – the '60's and the '70's.* (Photographic Portraits by LaVerne Harrell Clark.) Edited by Laverne Harrell Clark and Mary MacArthur. Arlington, Va.: Gallimaufry, pp. 278-80.

Includes a photograph taken of Richard Wilbur, April 1973, and reprints "Piccola Commedia."

21 SCANNELL, VERNON. *Not Without Glory: American Poets of the Second World War.* London: Woburn Press, pp. 228-30.

Lists poets and poetry connected to World War II. Connects Wilbur with "the school of poetry . . .which would have traced its origins back to the English metaphysical poets of the seventeenth century and would have vigorously rejected any paternity claims from Walt Whitman, eschewing free forms, expansive verbal gesticulations and the exclusive use of the idioms and rhythms of demotic speech in favour of wit, lucidity, grace and traditional prosody." Notes two war poems, "Mined Country" and "First Snow in Alsace." Suggests Wilbur's intent appears to be to "seek for the small redemptions and epiphanies in the vast nightmare of war, to perceive and give permanence to the fugitive moments of beauty and affirmation that gleam ocasionally in the darkness of a world in conflict." "Snow" is less complicated, concentrating on "splendid detail."

22 SCHULMAN, GRACE. "'To Shake Our Gravity Up': The Poetry of Richard Wilbur." *Nation*, 9 October, pp. 344, 46.

Reviews *The Mind-Reader: New Poems* and surveys many poems from earlier collections. Describes Wilbur as a poet who "has conveyed with urgency and power the wonder of ordinary things and of the mind that perceives them." Says "the poet's dominant concern is the creative process that lives in the mind and in the language, waiting to be released": "It takes a skyblue juggler with five red balls / To shake our gravity up" ("Juggler"). Applauds Wilbur's attention to detail: "in Wilbur's poetry, the awareness of physical particularities intimates knowledge of a hidden world of absolute clarity: it recalls Baudelaire's work in its accumulation of facts that betray transcendent reality." Finds "opposite impulses are joined in his poetry" ("John Chrysostom" [1956], "Ceremony" [1950]). Lists most powerful poems from *Things of This World* (1956): "Love Calls Us to the Things of This World," "The Beacon," "For the New Railway Station in Rome," "Speech for the Repeal of the McCarran Act," "Digging for China," "Beasts," "Statues,"

"Apology," "Piazza di Spagna, Early Morning," "A Black November Turkey." Sees the theme in *Things* of "how love heightens the senses and clarifies perceptions" prefigured in "The Beautiful Changes" (1947). Mentions "Walking to Sleep" and "The Mind-Reader" as two long poems which deal with the creative process. Interprets "The Writer" as "one of the best metaphors I know for [Wilbur's] own poetry and for the creative process."

23 SIMON, JOHN. "Translation or Adaptation?" In *From Parnassus: Essays in Honor of Jacques Barzun*. Edited by Dora B. Weiner and William B. Keylor. New York: Harper & Row, pp. 147-57.

Compares Wilbur's translation of Molière's *The Misanthrope* (1955) most favorably with Tony Harrison's adaptation (1973). Wilbur's "line-for-line verse translation" retains the timelessness of Molière's genius; whereas, Harrison's adaptation allows several "damaging contradictions." Decides that "the trouble with modernization [of diction] is that what looks like an equivalent is nevertheless subtly different, and so manages to distort essential meanings." This is true, also, of "loose versification" and "exaggerated cleverness" such as the Marshals' Tribunal set up to prevent dueling being changed to a midnight meeting at Maxim's. Asks, "Does *The Misanthrope* profit from setting its clock three hundred years ahead by way of a supposed Daylight shedding Time?" Answers that it does not. "It is imperative . . . that an Englishing of *The Misanthrope*, along with possible concessions to the present, retain the timeless, old-and-new quality of a classic." Quotes Harrison's adaptation of Alceste's final words to Célemine: "This last humiliation's set me free / from love's degrading tyranny." Concludes "How much more sober, weighty, and correct is Wilbur's: 'Go! I reject your hand and disenthrall / My heart from your enchantments, once for all.'"

24 WOODARD, CHARLES. "Wilbur's 'Still, Citizen Sparrow.'" *Explicator* 34, no. 6 (February):item 46.

Objects to the accepted interpretation of the vulture in this poem as a "representative of rotten politicians." Suggests instead that Wilbur "has his eye on the vulture *as* vulture, not as symbol; the bird's function, then is to consume the 'rotten' carrion. Its ugly function can be forgotten once it is in flight where it is seen as a 'bird of surpassing beauty and freedom.'" Links the vulture and Noah together: "as the vulture's wings rock on the buoying air far above the range of the disapproving sparrows, so Noah's ark rocked, borne up by water, far above the towns and fields of his disapproving neighbors." Views the vulture and Noah as "two terms in a comparison sufficiently far-fetched to constitute a conceit." Concludes with the thought that though Noah was an "object of displeasure to his sparrow-like neighbors, Noah had the courage to endure loneliness, to 'mock mutability' and keep nature's species alive. We are all his copies, bearing the saved essence of the past on the rising flood of time."

1977

1 BROWNJOHN, ALAN. "The Quality Surveyors: Critics on Poetry." *Encounter* 49, no. 1 (July):82-86.

Reviews *Responses, Prose Pieces*. Argues that Wilbur's collection of miscellaneous prose pieces "comes over leadenly and pretentiously." Calls the article on Emily Dickinson a "goodish piece." Finds the book a "limiting sort of manifesto."

2 BURGESS, ANTHONY. "New Poetry." *Spectator*, 6 August, pp. 29-30.

Reviews *The Mind-Reader: New Poems*. Comments that Wilbur's poetry is "full of fine visual surprises," and notes that one poem, "The Eye," is dedicated to two ways of seeing. Relates a story Wilbur told him about searching for the "right word"–"poculum," for the hollow under the lower lip–a real find. Closes by saying, "Most of Wilbur's poems contain finds, or are finds."

3 COOKE, MICHAEL G. "Book Reviews." *Georgia Review* 31, no. 3 (Fall):718-29.

Reviews *The Mind-Reader: New Poems*. Notes that readers have failed to appreciate the fact that over the years "Wilbur has developed a voice more truly Germanic than Gallic, that is to say, an unpretentious sacred voice . . . a voice that addresses itself to and takes effect from the things that have perennial power in and over us, generously binding us to our humanity." Singles out "The Eye" as an example of Wilbur at his best, using the sacred voice in Part II of the poem. "This 'prayer' proves to be a description of less solipsistic uses of the eye and arises dynamically and dramatically within the speaker's psyche." Suggests "In Limbo" is a "sort of counterpart" to "The Eye" because the action takes place in the dark where the eye is useless. Instead, the ear must function as receiver of perceptions. Avers that "the opposition of the licentious ear and the positive eye is effective, but the real power of the poem comes from its final recognition that what surrounds the room is also true." When the speaker turns on the light, the "broken images of the poem like the 'broken dialects' of his person come 'together' not only to 'demand the world' but also to enable 'all [his] selves and ages' to 'parley and atone.'" "The Mind-

1977

Reader" centers on the human being who controls the ear and the eye: "it confronts the problem that the content of actuality as well as the content of the mind cannot be grasped, or retained, or controlled. All, in a sense, is lost." The double irony of the end of the poem is that the cynical mind-reader can read his own mind and knows that he wishes to belong to another world, yet his patrons think they can read his mind and order him another drink.

4 FAERY, REBECCA B. Review of *The Mind-Reader: New Poems*. *Hollins Critic* 14, no. 2 (April):15.
    Reviews *The Mind-Reader: New Poems*. Affirms that Wilbur's "is a poetry of ceremony, of truth shaped by texture. His graceful mastery of words is awesome, and several of the poems in this collection can be read as metaphors for his artistic process; as in the closing lines of 'Teresa,' Wilbur manages to 'lock the O of ecstasy within / The tempered consonants of discipline.'" Suggests that the speaker of "The Mind-Reader" is the poet, writing as "magus."

5 HECHT, ANTHONY. "The Motions of the Mind." *Times Literary Supplement* (London), 20 May, p. 602.
    Reviews *The Mind-Reader: New Poems*. Marks several "virtues that distinguish the poetry of Richard Wilbur": "a superb ear," "a philosophic bent and a religious temper," "an unfeigned gusto, a naturally happy and grateful response to the physical beauty of the world, of women, of works of art, landscapes, weather, and the perceiving, constructing mind that tries to know them." Contends, however, that "most characteristic of all, his is the most kinetic poetry I know . . . his poetry is everywhere a vision of *action*, of motion and performance." Supports his point by citing "pivotal and energetic verbs . . . placed in a rhyming position" in several poems ("Advice to a Prophet," "In the Elegy Season," "Altitudes," "A Baroque Wall-Fountain in the Villa Sciarra," "On the Marginal Way"). Asserts Wilbur has always been "a poet with a gymnastic sense of bodily agility and control." Finds that "time and again in Wilbur's poems this admirable grace or strength of body is a sign of or symbol for the inward motions of the mind or condition of the soul" ("Mind," "The Bat," "A Baroque Wall-Fountain. . . ."). "This poet's recurrent subject is not only the motion of change and transition but how that motion . . . is the very motion of the mind itself." Calls this a "double fluency"–that of "style and subject." Sees a similarity between Wilbur's poetry and the best uses of cinematic film. Feels, however, that "what these poems can do so magnificently that is . . . beyond the range of motion pictures is . . . a transition, or rather, a translation, of outward physical action . . . into a

condition of the imagination; a dissolving of one realm of reality into another" ("Merlin Enthralled"). Quotes the first nineteen lines of "The Mind-Reader" as an example of "the superb visualization of motion, of diminution into irretrievable distances" of which Wilbur is capable. Notes, however, that the entire action is in the mind, is "a metaphor for the imagination, the graceful motions of the mind." Closes by listing other "excellences" such as the translations, the funny poems, the lyrics, the "brilliant" "Fourth of July," and most of all, "The Eye"–a poem which represents "a huge corrective to our self-sufficiency." Reprinted: 1983.18; 1987.4 (as "Richard Wilbur").

6 HIGH, ELLESA CLAY, and ELLISON, HELEN McCLOY. "Richard Wilbur: The Art of Poetry." *Paris Review* no. 72 (Winter):87-105.
   This interview with Richard Wilbur took place in Louisville, Kentucky.
   Richard Wilbur admits that he may now be allowing more personal events into his poetry. Discusses the beat poets, especially Gary Snyder, of whom he says it is "too easy to predict what he's going to say about anything." Admits that a recurring vexation is his inner quarrel between the "lofty and angelic voice" and the "slob voice"–a quarrel he calls "fundamentally of a religious nature." Explains at length his poem, "Cottage Street, 1953," about Sylvia Plath and his characterization of her poems as "unjust." Says she was trapped inside her own "condition of mind"–a severe limitation. Insists that "even the most cheerful poet has to cope with pain as part of the human lot; what he shouldn't do is to complain, and dwell on his personal mischance." Discusses the ongoing argument between Joseph Brodsky and Denise Levertov about how to translate poems from the Russian. Wilbur agrees with Brodsky that if a poem is written in rhyme and meter originally, it should be translated into rhyme and meter. Distinguishes between the ease of translating and the hard work of writing poetry. The first can be done anywhere; the second requires (for him) the right environment. Enlarges on his remark that "men and women have different sensibilities" by saying "I do think that men are capable of greater emptiness and abstraction . . . and I have a feeling that women have their feet on the ground, on the average, a little more than men do, even though men tend to etherealize women in their imaginations, through their affection." Discusses Emily Dickinson's tendency to move toward the abstract in her poetry. Comments on his reluctance to write long poems because he wishes to have at least "one interesting word per line." Says he wrote "The Writer" long after the event of the poem occurred, that he did not write it as a message to his daughter, but that a poem "is a kind of performance; it's a kind of machine of feeling

which other people can use." Describes his writing process as beginning "confidently" with a first line and proceeding from there, rewriting until each line is satisfactory. Says Yeats's books of poetry have "a lot of little poems which are outriders, as it were, destroyer-escorts of the big poems." Declares that he refuses to collect his poems around a single theme. Describes the feelings he has during a dry period: "dead and guilty and ashamed." See companion interview 1977.17; reprinted: 1990.2.

7 HOMBERGER, ERIC. *The Art of the Real: Poetry in England and America since 1939*. Totowa, N.J.: Rowman & Littlefield, pp. 90-94.
    Observes that "Wilbur's undoubted virtues are those of a class and a region, the anglophile East, the Ivy League colleges, the protestant culture of America, discovering in formalism a new and potent mode of social control." Asserts that "by 1962 (in America at least) poetry in the formalist mode seemed a little dated" and that Wilbur was the recipient of much negative criticism because of his reliance on traditional forms: "Wilbur's reputation has scarcely survived the 1950s." Comments on the polished perfection of Wilbur's poems: "formalism was, if not invented, at least perfected by Wilbur." Quarrels with the assumption that Wilbur considers "things of this world" sufficient. Though he belongs, in theory, to the "camp" of Whitman, Pound and William Carlos Williams, "on the side of the 'world of concrete particulars,'" his poems "reflect a continual assertion of the imagination against the 'things of this world.'" Gives examples of Wilbur's acute eye in "Potato," "Place Pigalle," "Cigales," and "Water Walker." The latter unmasks Wilbur as one who wishes only "to observe and praise, to remain completely committed to the here and now." Objects to Wilbur's statement that "the difficulty of the form is a substitution for the difficulty of direct apprehension of the object." Sees his "preoccupation" with form as sufficient explanation for his current disfavor.

8 JAMES, CLIVE. "As a Matter of Tact." *New Statesman*, 17 June, pp. 815-16.
    Reviews *Responses, Prose Pieces*. Describes this collection as a "superlative book." Says these essays and addresses "combine conciseness with resonance, each of them wrapping up its nominal subject while simultaneously raising all the relevant general issues." Mentions "Round about a Poem of Housman's" as an "excellent instance of close reading wedded to hard thinking." Chooses "Poetry and Happiness" as a second example of "another richly suggestive piece of work." Selects "On My Own Work" as necessary reading for a

student of Wilbur's poems. Questions whether Wilbur has "ever really taken that burden up" – referring to Wilbur's idea that "the incoherence of America need not enforce a stance of alienation on the poet: rather, it may be seen as placing on him a peculiar imaginative burden." Values Wilbur's scholarship: "in a few paragraphs Wilbur has not only raised, but to a large extent settled, theoretical points which more famous critical savants have pursued to the extent of whole essays." Contends that F. R. Leavis goes to some lengths to criticize Yeats while Wilbur tactfully says just enough. Agrees with Wilbur's position that one cannot read *Paradise Lost* without a knowledge of classical literature: "If you *did* have to know about those things, then Milton would not deserve his reputation. But you *don't* have to know, since the allusions merely reinforce what Milton is tactful enough to make plain." "Poetry's Debt to Poetry" shows that "["palace revolutions" in poetry] will make their first appeal on a level which demands of the reader no more than an ability to understand the language." Reprinted: 1983.18.

9 KINZIE, MARY. "The Cheshire Smile: On Richard Wilbur." *American Poetry Review* 6, no. 3 (May-June):17-20.

Reviews *The Mind-Reader: New Poems*. Compares Robert Browning's and Wilbur's dramatic poems, especially Browning's Mr. Sludge – to Wilbur's mind-reader – as a means of evaluating "The Mind-Reader." Sees Wilbur's character as one who "holds the romantic melancholy . . . that improbable goals and accidental visitings are the grim but sole measure of our striving." Judges that "the chief imaginative accomplishment of this poem is the rendering of the quirky, subjective mind as a place like the world into which things can disappear. The mind can and does literally absorb the concrete things with which it has engaged so that keys, photos, and ultimately lost eras of the heart reside in a *place* of thought." Warns that "The Mind-Reader" should not be read as confession or autobiography. Observes about Wilbur's poetry in general: "if his poetry as a whole is flawed, in fact, it is so by virtue of his measured, often playful refusal of 'majority,' and of his sense that truths must be perfectly embodied." Sees this embodiment worked out in two ways, "formal grace," and "a movement awry of the plane . . . an implicit swerve of metaphor after the careful links and jumps have been established." Comments that "the mind-reader is a moral version of Edgar Allan Poe's investigator Dupin, to whose flashes of perturbed, random insight Wilbur adds the Christian ethos of social being, pity, and the double sense of likeness to and abandonment by God."

1977

Interprets "The Fourth of July" at length to show the connecting links between each stanza's subject and the concluding lines. Says this poem "is one of the finest and most difficult poems Wilbur has ever written; [it] illustrates the curvature of mind which makes him such an intellectually exciting poet." Wilbur's "ultimate statements in 'The Fourth of July' are, in fact, about the dignity of 'slaves,' the uniqueness of the unnamed, and (in stanza four) the sweetness of the 'natural' Linnaeus."

Concludes with general statements about the translations (most are good except the Russian poems which are as originals, "skittery, messy, and dull"), about "The Writer," where "clearing the sill of the world" represents the "maturation and the discovery of inner wit." Dislikes "The Eye" because of the "false, aimless sound of the language of prayer." Admires "In Limbo" as "a great poem about love." Sees "A Sketch" as further evidence of Wilbur's "pursuing himself into the analogous Creation." Concludes that *The Mind-Reader* is not the best book Richard Wilbur has written. But "poems like 'The Fourth of July,' the title poem, 'In Limbo,' and the continued sure touch and passing flourish of many others, induce in one a great retrospective pride."

10 LAMBERT, J. W. "A Songster in the Wilderness." *Sunday Times* (London), 17 July, p. 40.

Reviews *The Mind-Reader: New Poems* and *Responses, Prose Pieces*. Responds positively to Wilbur's "deft technical skill," listing "springing rhythms and evocative sound," "assonance," and "alliteration." Remarks, however, that technical skill is only "the outward and visible sign of a quick and eager spirit. . . . In a disintegrating civilisation [Wilbur] sees no reason to embrace disintegration, still less to work at his own disintegration." Cites Wilbur's ability to have fun ("The Prisoner of Zenda"), to see "around or through . . . uneventful domesticity ("C Minor"), to write "apt and charming" *vers d'occasion* ("A Wedding Toast"), and to empathize with the artist's panic ("The Writer"). Characterizes "The Mind-Reader" as "a long, Browningesque, darting exploration of creative memory and vision." Says Wilbur's translations are "European echoes . . . finely caught. But it is in the subtle yet straight-gazing poems of his New England homeland that his best qualities shine brightest."

Regards *Responses* as a book that "contains more helpful sense about poets and poetry than whole shelvesful of . . . PhD theses." Allows that Wilbur is "perceptive, if wary, about Emily Dickinson, acute if optimistic about Whitman, excellent on Robert Frost's Crabbewise [*sic*] prosing in verse, – more understanding than most about Housman." Contends that Wilbur "staunchly remains a voice not crying but singing in the wilderness, the burden of his song not overheated anguish but questioning hope."

11 McCLATCHY, J. D. "Dialects of the Tribe." *Poetry* 130, no. 1 (April):41-53.

Reviews *The Mind-Reader: New Poems*. Says of "The Mind-Reader," "This poem of layered insights is the best of Wilbur's recurrent crisp odes which celebrate a rational love that can include and transcend the world, and again confirms his essentially religious imagination – evidenced as well in the book's shorter lyrics which treat natural objects and scenes as emblems of another order." Castigates Wilbur for not having attempted the long poem, and characterizes this collection as one which "reads rather like an anthology of his career." Feels that "something has happened to the familiar voice. Over the years, perhaps because he has increasingly mistrusted himself, the lush extravagance of his early verse has been pared to a more sober and diffident directness." Finds such a tone dull in "A Storm in April" or "Piccola Commedia," but likes "C Minor" and "In Limbo" for their "less assured . . . meanings," their lack of confinement in narrative or "concision."

12 OWEN, GUY. "*The Mind Reader:* New Poems by Richard Wilbur." In *Magill's Literary Annual 1977*. Vol. 2. Englewood Cliffs, N. J.: Salem Press, pp. 505-8.

Reviews *The Mind-Reader: New Poems*. Concedes that critics will probably say that Wilbur has simply repeated himself in this book. Notes, however, new developments such as "a tightening up of his forms," a loss of interest "in the anti-poetic," and a turning away from animal poems. That which is familiar cannot be called "a decline in his art." Says Wilbur "has a way of feeling his way into the poems he translates, always offering new renderings rather than mere translations." Grants that all the poems are "marked by grace, delicacy, wit, and a supple strength. There is always balance and control, never an awkward line or disruptive image." Does see a different "variety of voices." Feels that "What's Good for the Soul Is Good for Sales" and "Cottage Street, 1953" are "ungenerous." Concludes that "Richard Wilbur has rediscovered the language of praise in an age that is bleak and thorny, and he employs it in poems of rare imagination and felicity. Perhaps one should not ask for more."

13 PARK, CLARA CLAIBORNE. "Poetry and Affirmation." *Nation*, 5 November, pp. 469-71.

1977

Reviews *Responses, Prose Pieces*. Comments "it is evident from this prose collection . . . that Wilbur's grace and felicity are not the lucky side effects of brilliance and privilege but earned and profoundly moral qualities, sustained by a faith as real as Eliot's and Auden's, though less explicit." Suggests Wilbur defines "his most serious understanding of the poetic enterprise in 'Poetry and Happiness.'" Finds that "the poetry of happiness is so much rarer than the poetry of misery, self-pity, and the vanity of human wishes that we may suspect that it must be harder to write." Notes that the title reflects Wilbur's attitude toward life: he "respond[s] to life and does not coerce it." Sees in several essays Wilbur's ability to be an "extraordinarily able commentator on the relation of expression and meaning." In the essay on Robert Burns, Wilbur "successfully demonstrates that even the simplest poem has ways of being smarter than we are." The essay on John Housman reflects his regret for the loss of "expertly made popular poetry." Feels his work on Poe has been "as if he felt an obligation fully to realize the world of that dark, anti-self before he could realize his own." Says Wilbur is "penetrating, and merciful, on the misery of today's poets."

14 "Richard Wilbur." In *The International Who's Who In Poetry – 1977-78*. 5th ed. Edited by Ernest Kay. Cambridge (England): International Biographical Centre, p. 455.

Lists teaching positions at Harvard University, Wellesley College, Wesleyan University. Notes memberships in societies, prizes, and awards. Mentions publications beginning with *The Beautiful Changes* (1947), including editorial work on Poe and Shakespeare, contributions to well-known newspapers and periodicals, and anthologies, ending with *The Mind-Reader* (1976). Revised and combined with *International Who's Who 1985-1986*.

15 "Richard Wilbur." In *Who's Who in the Theatre: a Biographical Record of the Contemporary Stage*. 16th ed. Detroit: Gale, p. 1251.

Lists plays written and produced, with dates, and volumes of poetry beginning with *The Beautiful Changes* (1947) and ending with *Walking to Sleep* (1969). Lists poets Wilbur has edited for publication, teaching assignments, prizes and awards, memberships in learned societies, recreations, and home address.

16 SHAW, ROBERT B. "Richard Wilbur's World." *Parnassus* (New York) 4, no. 1 (Spring-Summer):176-85.

Reviews *The Mind-Reader: New Poems* and *Responses, Prose Pieces*. Acknowledges and refutes three common complaints: critics object to the "formal properties" of Wilbur's poetry; they criticize him for "remaining obdurately within the boundaries defined by his earliest successes"; they accuse him of suffering from "arrested development." Debunks all three. Says Wilbur's use of traditonal form is "a calculated means of confronting" the pressures of reality. Says Wilbur has "deepened," a term deserving the designation of development. Says his "intricately patterned poems reflect the discovery of patterns of natural beauty; and the poet's art thus strives to be an adequate analogy to the surrounding creation." Finds memorable Wilbur's "renderings of physical motion" ("Piazza di Spagna, Early Morning," "Running," "Grace," "Juggler"). Denies that Wilbur has avoided negative subject matter ("war poems, political poems," "Advice to a Prophet," "A Miltonic Sonnet. . . ," "On the Marginal Way"). Notes that "Love Calls Us to the Things of This World" is a powerful example of much of Wilbur's work: "[it] takes full measure of all that is meant by incarnation. It achieves a reconciliation of the ideal and the real, the soul and the body, of sudden, otherworldly intuition and steady, continuing observation of 'the world's hunks and colors.'"

Affirms that *The Mind-Reader* "is a solid addition to [Wilbur's] achievement." "His poems are still 'keeping their difficult balance,'" but in a more personal tone ("In Limbo," "The Writer," "Cottage Street, 1953"). Respects Wilbur for being willing to "question motives in the self that most men in middle age leave unexamined" ("The Eye"). Sees "A Sketch" as one of Wilbur's "finer evocations of natural vitality." Finds "Peter" and "Teresa" believable renderings of human saints. Interprets "Children of Darkness" as "natural history with a strong undercurrent of natural theology . . . although its broader concern is with the question why things which seem ugly and maleficent are suffered by the Creator to exist." Considers "The Mind-Reader" "a major effort" complete with a believable character.

Asserts that *Responses* is most welcome to students of Poe and Emily Dickinson. Wilbur's "Poetry and Happiness" and "Poetry's Debt to Poetry" are a "distillation of a lifetime's reading, furnishing discerning views of his predecessors and contemporaries, [and] these pieces cast an oblique but steady light on Wilbur's own poetic themes and stylistic preferences."

17 STITT, PETER. "Richard Wilbur: The Art of Poetry." *Paris Review* no. 72 (Winter):69-86.

This interview took place at Richard Wilbur's home in the Berkshire Mountains near Cummington, Massachusetts, on a Saturday afternoon in March of 1977.

1977

Wilbur describes his friend, André Bouchet, who read his poems and asked permission to send them off to Reynal & Hitchcock who published them as *The Beautiful Changes* (1947). Describes his composition process: "I write poems line by line, very slowly; I sometimes scribble alternative words in the margins rather densely, but I don't go forward with anything unless I am fairly satisfied that what I have set down sounds printable, sayable." Explains that what gets him started on a poem is "a sudden, confident sense that there is an exploitable and interesting relationship between something perceived out there and something in the way of incipient meaning within you." Admits that teaching does get in the way of writing poetry, but likes it anyway. Tries to do physical things such as play tennis, raise a garden, or walk in order to "return to language with excitement. . . . It is good for a writer to move into words out of the silence, as much as he can." Denies that poetry is an "exploration of the self"; rather, he feels that he is "arranging some materials and trying to find out the truth about them. If, in the process, I also find out something about myself, I think it is indirectly done. It is the thing, and not myself, which I set out to explore." Argues that the attempt to tell the truth about oneself often leads a writer to "glamorize" himself too much. Responds to negative criticism by accepting the fact that there are "some critics for whom one's poetry just cannot work because of temperamental differences and distances." Distinguishes between imagination and fantasy: "the imagination is a faculty which fuses things, takes hold of the physical and ideal worlds and makes them one, provisionally. Fantasy . . . is a poetic or artistic activity which leaves something out – it ignores the concrete and the actual in order to create a purely abstract, unreal realm." Objects to Edgar Allan Poe because he is a "fantasist." Suggests that "modern studies of the dream-process are just catching up with some things which Poe noticed and, in his own way, set down" (in the fiction). Argues that he composes in the same way as poets who write free verse and that meter is not rigid – "it depends on how you use it. . . . What matters is the subject and the words which are going to be found for conveying and exploring the subject. The only difference is that I include meters and rhymes in my free-verse proceeding." Agrees that use of formal structures results in "liberating the imagination rather than confining it." Sums up his philosophy this way: "I feel that the universe is full of glorious energy, that the energy tends to take pattern and shape, and that the ultimate character of things is comely and good. I am perfectly aware that I say this in the teeth of all sorts of contrary evidence, and that I must be basing it partly on temperament and partly on faith, but that is my attitude. My feeling is that when you discover order and goodness in the world, it is not something you are imposing–it is something which is likely really to be there, whatever crumminess and evil and disorder there may also be. I don't take disorder or meaninglessness to be the basic character of things." See companion interview: 1977.6; reprinted: 1985.10; 1990.2.

18 THURLEY, GEOFFREY. "Benign Diaspora: The Landscape of Richard Wilbur." In *The American Movement: American Poetry in the Mid-Century*. New York: St. Martins, pp. 35-50.

Compares Wilbur's poetry with English poets. Says his tone is English. Cites "Stop" as representative of all of his work and as comparable to Philip Larkin's "Whitsun Weddings" and Edward Thomas's "Adelstrop," except the English poets are more successful: in this and in many of his other poems Wilbur is closer to English poets' themes than he is to American ideas. Identifies Wilbur and other American poets as being akin to the Jews who have settled in a new land but who constantly long for home: theirs is a "kind of benign diaspora" from which there is no return. Says "Stop" is "typical of Wilbur in a way that could be generalized: its world lacks just that rootedness, the perceptions lack that 'responsiveness and receptivity' which Macha Rosenthal praises in Wilbur's British contemporaries."

Admits that some of Wilbur's early work offers wit and sensibility, "impressive tact," "balance and constraint" ("Beasts"). Claims that this poem "provides . . . a fascinating instance of the interrelationship between English and American poets." Cites Ted Hughes's dependence on Wilbur, though Hughes "took the thing further." Finds echoes in Wilbur's poems of Auden, John Crowe Ransom, Gerard Manley Hopkins, Robert Frost, Baudelaire, Norman MacCaig, Milton, Yeats, Edmund Dulac, Keats, Byron, Thomas Traherne, and Larkin ("Castles and Distances," "Caserta Garden," "June Light," "For Ellen," "A Courtyard Thaw," "A Simile for Her Smile," "A Dutch Courtyard," "Flumen Tenebrarum"). Acknowledges that sometimes Wilbur can maintain integrity in a poem between the "tone, technique and subject."

Criticizes Wilbur because he "has simply failed to engage himself in the scene and consequently failed to engage us, his readers." Contends that Wilbur "has nothing to offer but the observational procedures–methods mastered from the earlier generation of late romantic poets–and the attempt to convince us of universality and importance is hollow. . . . Wilbur, like so many of his contemporaries, simply imitates the technical properties of feeling." Cites "Ceremony" as a poem that is "an elegant and shapely piece of work," but which "on no level . . . convince[s] us of its intellectual or moral integrity." Calls "A World without Objects Is a Sensible Emptiness" a "Traherne

1977

pastiche," one which contains only "sheer vacuity. . . . It is really no more than an effusion, as of a machine that intakes literary grist and turns it out all mixed up, with no fixed point, none of that solid unshakable core of orientation from which the glorious radiance of the seventeenth-century poets emanates." Concludes that "Wilbur has remained a poet without a core . . . and seems to represent a specific mid-century quality. Anglophile, academic, but with a metropolitan poise, correct, but with rushes of gaiety and exuberance that tend to come to nothing–Wilbur embodies better than any other of his contemporaries perhaps a style which we might call, simply, Ivy League."

19 TURNER, ALBERTA T. "Richard Wilbur." In *Fifty Contemporary Poets: The Creative Process*. New York: David McKay, pp. 977, 327-38.
    Reprints "The Eye" along with copies of Wilbur's worksheets of the poem. Appends a letter from Richard Wilbur answering questions sent to him by Turner regarding the process of writing this poem.

20 WOOD, MICHAEL. "Molière in New York." *New York Review of Books*, 8 December, pp. 47-50.
    Reviews *Tartuffe*, *The Misanthrope*, and *The Learned Ladies*. Notes that in *Tartuffe*, the audience becomes aware that the actors are having trouble with some of Wilbur's lines which contain "lumpy" rhythms, and "predictable" rhymes. However, agrees that his translation is admirably rendered for the most part. Approves of Wilbur's choice of rhymed couplets for these three plays. Finds several examples from all three plays of lines that are "gracefully exact versions of intricate originals." Grants that Wilbur "occasionally excels Molière in poise and pointedness." Describes *The Learned Ladies* as a "remarkable achievement" as are *The Misanthrope* and *The School for Wives*.

21 WOODARD, CHARLES R. "'Happiest Intellection': The Mind of Richard Wilbur." *Notes on Modern American Literature* 2, no. 1 (Winter):no. 7.
    Intuits that the cave in "The Bat" is "knowledge itself, including scientific knowledge, but Wilbur is aware how much that cave is subject to alteration by the mind which creates it." Cites "The Fourth of July" as another poem in which Wilbur documents his distrust of matter. Argues that "the interdependency of matter and mind, the former a series of ever-shifting schemata as conceived by the latter through the surges and recessions of intellectual history, makes Wilbur . . . a more skeptical poet than is generally recognized" ("A Hole in the Floor").

"Things do not exist for his mind to make poetry of them, as some critics have charged; rather his mind exists to make poetry, as gracefully as possible, of things whose existence is subject to no final certainty in the 'dream-cache' of the most enlightened head." Posits that a "tribal cave of experience" may also exist for our pleasure. Reprinted: 1983.18.

22 ____. "Richard Wilbur's Critical Condition." *Contemporary Poetry: A Journal of Criticism* 2, no. 2 (Autumn):16-24.

Quarrels with disciples of William Carlos Williams who criticize Wilbur for using his imagination instead of his senses and for ignoring the horror of modern existence. "Lowell and his followers, with their categories of 'cooked' and 'raw' poetry, take it as *a priori* that the good poet will suffer and, further, that good poetry consists precisely in the reporting of this suffering." Such criticism relegates poetry to "immediate sensation and emotion." "Arnold criticized the Romantics for not knowing enough; another generation of critics condemns Wilbur for not suffering enough." Argues that critics have done Wilbur "a very real injustice. Apart from man's mortality, with its attendant suffering, there is perhaps no more tragic situation in his life than the discrepancy between the world he perceives and the world which he knows intellectually to exist" ("Epistemology"). Scoffs at the idea that the senses are more reliable than the intellect. Says that "the play of the individual mind . . . may be as good a model of reality as we have." Sums up by saying that "the uneasy ground of Wilbur's poetry is the irreconcilable oppositions of appearance and knowledge. . . . The perceived world, with its fine gauzy shimmer of fountains and its colored juggling balls, is equally a world of the fine shimmer and juggling of mind." Reprinted: 1983.18; 1988.18.

1977-1978

1 FALCK, COLIN. "The Lettered Life." *New Review* 4, no. 45-46 (December-January): 70-73.

Reviews *The Mind-Reader: New Poems*. Insists that "Wilbur's cut-offness from life's crudities has more to do with unreconstructedly academic assumptions about what poetry ought to look like and deal with than with any philosophical calling-in-question of immediate experience." Sees the elegance and "decorous literariness" of many poems ("Cottage Street, 1953," "John Chapman"). "The range of life-experience that can authentically find its way into these poems is rarely more than a narrow, learned and high-art-ridden one. Life's elemental realities are urbanely gestured at while being left to seem quite remote from the literarily-upholstered world of the poetry itself: as indeed they are."

1978

1 ABAD, GEMINO. *A Formal Approach to Lyric Poetry*. Quezon City, Philippines: University of Philippines Press, pp. 301-4.

Compares Blake's "The Clod and the Pebble" with Wilbur's "Two Voices in a Meadow" to show that, though both present ideas in a dramatic form, the speakers in Blake's poem are presented to the reader by a narrator and argue with each other. In Wilbur's poem, the speakers simply state their own positions, with no narrator intervening; nor do they speak to each other.

2 CHARNEY, DIANE JOY. *Library Journal*, 15 May, p. 1076.

Reviews *The Learned Ladies*. Says that "those who have been led to expect a Richard Wilbur translation to be a masterpiece in its own right should not be disappointed with this. The play is preceded by a valuable introduction. The omission of line numbers is regrettable, but the Pulitzer Prize winning poet's translation effortlessly transcends problems of meter, rhyme, and tone to combine fidelity to the original with the creation of a product that is somehow fresh and new. Molière would approve."

3 COMBS, JOHN. "Richard Wilbur's 'Water Walker.'" *CEA Forum* 8, no. 4 (April):11-12.

Interprets "Water Walker" stanza by stanza. Suggests that "the water walker's experience parallels that of any honest person in our world." Contends that the water stands for all that is comfortable and homely; the air "for some heavenly or utopian existence." The poem centers on the space between water and air "where air mists into water." Interprets stanza six as the poet's reflections on modern suburbia: "the people – with their 'neat plots,' 'trustful houses,' automobiles, children, tricycles, and lawnsprays remind him of the caddis fly's larva: deeply embedded in their 'armoreal' shells, they presume that their secure life in suburbia is really life." Cites Saul/Paul as the prime example of one who chose to leave his safe "water" haven. Says that "exposure to air, a ravishing experience, makes the subject a stranger to both sides of possible dualities: water and air." Forever after, Paul belonged to neither world: "once a person understands that justice is not easily discerned, not merely a matter of law and dogma, not to be glibly expressed . . . he 'cannot go home' but he must live in dilemma, in the struggle where 'air mists into water,' where history is made, in the arena of political involvement."

4 CONTOSKI, VICTOR. Review of *The Mind-Reader*. *Denver Quarterly* 13, no. 2 (Summer):156-57.

Reviews *The Mind-Reader: New Poems*. Observes that "Richard Wilbur's poetry constantly reminds us of our European past and the traditions upon which civilization depends." Suggests that Wilbur "sees the poet not as a holy madman but as a rational teacher in a rational world" ("A Black Birch in Winter," "Children of Darkness"). Finds that Wilbur concludes his poems in "traditional ways, with rational knowledge and wisdom": the fungi in "Children of Darkness" may seem malevolent, but "reason and art show otherwise." Sees finest works on American themes as "John Chapman" and "The Fourth of July." Wilbur "seeks a way to combine the imaginary and the real worlds, the ideal America with what America became, and finds a combination of intuitive and practical knowledge in Copernicus, who risked his 'dream-stuff in the fitting rooms of fact.' This embodiment of ideal and real, of the order of the universe, in the image of a person being fitted for clothes embodies also Wilbur's art – witty, elegant, and civilized."

5 DARLING, CHARLES WALLIS. "Giver of Due Regard: The Poetry of Richard Wilbur." Ph.D. dissertation, The University of Connecticut, 135 pp.

Consists of three chapters: (1) "contends that Wilbur's chief characteristic, that is, his ability to compel our loving attention to the things of this world, is . . . fundamental to an understanding of his poetry"; (2) argues that "Wilbur's apparent need for a kind of ceremonious detachment from the world . . . at the very moment in which he celebrates his closeness to it is a sign of his respect for that world and the caution he feels before the threats of chaos in that world and within himself"; (3) explores the "hypnagogic condition" Wilbur treats in both his prose and poetry as a "specific theme and metaphor by which Wilbur attempts to articulate further his attitudes toward the world and toward form." See *Dissertation Abstracts International* 38:4824A.

6 DONOGHUE, DENIS. "Does America Have a Major Poet?" *New York Times Book Review*, 3 December, pp. 9, 88.

Concedes that the moderns feel a strong need for a "major poet." Defines major poetry as "work . . . done only on a grand scale, with energy so vast that, devoted to other ends, it would seize an empire or set up Murder, Inc. Minor poetry is content with a quiet life and exquisite perfections." Says "the current mood enhances the notion of poetry as a collective act rather than an individual assertion. . . . Grandeur, especially of the bardic kind, is out of phase." Lists Robert Penn Warren, Elizabeth Bishop, J. V. Cunningham, and A. R. Ammons as poets who have chosen quietly to ply their trade. Compares Bishop and Wilbur because "they write poems and let Poetry look out for itself." Avers that "the reader of Wilbur's later poems from *Walking to Sleep* to *The Mind-Reader* finds himself rising to a more urgent and far-reaching occasion than anything provoked by earlier work. After a few years in which his work was overshadowed by glamorously confessional poems, the strength of his talent has come forward again. . . . Wilbur's urbanity is as authentic . . . as, say Alan Dugan's insistence upon making his poems a hoard of destructions. We know they both mean it."

7 LEAVIS, L. R., and BLOM, J. M. "Current Literature 1977, I: New Writing." *English Studies* 59, no. 5 (October):444-68.
     Reviews *The Mind-Reader: New Poems*. Owns that "all the different interests [in the various poems] are held together by an underlying flippancy, apparent in original poems and translations alike." Suggests that "flippancy can be a refreshing quality, but it is disturbing to find in the notes that 'The Funeral of Bobò' which I took to be a tongue-in-cheek obituary for a dog, concerns 'a young woman who was drowned under mysterious circumstances in the Gulf of Finland.'"

8 LEE, L. L. Review of *The Mind-Reader*. *Western American Literature* 12, no. 4 (Winter):321-23.
     Reviews *The Mind-Reader: New Poems*. Says Wilbur is "nearly out of fashion – but still too important to be ignored." Judges that this is not Wilbur's best book. Interprets "The Mind-Reader" as a poem which is "about the creative spirit, the poet, who feels himself into the world of others." It is also "about the problem of existence, of the world." Such a poem marks Wilbur as "a moralist. He urges this need to communicate, to make art, but recognizes the difficulties of morality and the pain of being human" ("The Writer," "For the Student Strikers"). Finds "The Fourth of July" the finest poem in the collection.

9 LINGEMAN, RICHARD. "Sunday Poets." *New York Times*, 13 August, p. D36.
     Recounts Wilbur's and William Jay Smith's good-natured war over who could write the best verse on each other's Sunday edition of *The New York Times*.

10 MARLBOROUGH, HELEN. "New Works by Familiar Names." *Michigan Quarterly Review* 54, no. 2 (Spring):256-62.

Reviews *The Mind-Reader: New Poems*. Asserts that this is not a "major work." Concedes that several poems show examples of "Wilbur's grace and wit" ("The Writer," "The Eye," "A Sketch," "John Chapman," "April 5, 1975"). Finds that "throughout the book we mark a retreat from extravagant desire or praise and a corresponding effort to bring statement into proportion. The possibilities of appalling truth, whether in human arrogance or human destiny, float just beyond the edges of these shapely poems." Declares that "'The Mind-Reader' shows Wilbur's powers undiminished, subdued but strong."

11 McCONNELL, FRANK. "Reconsideration: The Poetry of Richard Wilbur." *New Republic*, 29 July, pp. 37-39.

Reviews *The Mind-Reader: New Poems*. Marks the allusion to Genesis in the last line of "Children of Darkness" as a prime example of Wilbur's ability to employ literary allusion which is "most servicable: a recreation of the texts of our common humanity that reminds us not only how textual, how artificial humanity really is, but also how necessary for life, how paradoxically natural the artificial-seeming texts really are." Reminds the reader that Wilbur "believes that the imagination not only invents the world, but makes that world livable; that intelligence and a sense of form are not just spiritual culs-de-sac but channels of meaningful communication; that language, like the bumblebee, shouldn't work but does." Corrects the notion that Wilbur's poems are full of "easy assurance . . . and *self-confident* sanity for which he is sometimes faulted." Says that he cannot find one poem to support this assumption. "From toadstools to the end of the world, his chosen subjects are unsettling and disorderly, those moments when chaos erupts into the ordinary, and when it is mastered to 'sanity' again because, frighteningly, it *needs* to be." Sees Wilbur's role increasingly as "mediator" between the juggler character of "Juggler" and the bum of "Statues." "If his poetry has made a progress, it is in the direction of . . . rendering keener the sense of 'danger' underlying our serenest assurances of civilization, but maintaining heroically our sense of those assurances as 'rooms,' habitations that, however dangerously, are still habitable" ("A Hole in the Floor").

12 MICHELSON, BRUCE. "Richard Wilbur: The Quarrel with Poe." *Southern Review* 14, no. 2 (April):245-261.

Addresses "the important and pervasive presence of Poe in Wilbur's poetry, his impact on Wilbur's symbolism, his language, and his understanding of imagination." The vortex is a central image for

1978

Wilbur, as it is for Poe. However, where Poe chooses to enter the doomed world of the imagination and thus to take the "vertiginous plunge" [Wilbur's words], Wilbur chooses instead to live on the edges between the "waking and hypnagogic state" ("Marginalia"). Explains that "for Wilbur, a sane man can perceive a 'sublime decor' – illusion, perhaps, or something more than illusion – only when the mind is near some strange edge between the restrained, waking sensibility and the self-loss of deep dream." Emphasizes the concept so vital to understanding Wilbur's work: "Wilbur will not ignore one lasting restraint: that one should not, *must* not give over one's self entirely to a dreaming pursuit of the absolute, if he would not lose himself in the dream-world trap of madness and self-deceit." Suggests that "an imagination that can resist Poe's manic and mystical extremes might indeed experience moments of real insight" ("The Beacon"). Finds an important difference between Poe and Wilbur in their view of the power of the imagination. Poe felt that the imagination *created* reality. In contrast, Wilbur views the imagination as *re*creative: "the essential poetic act' is not one with the creative powers of reality. It is rather the symbolic creation or rediscovery of temporal order and beauty, and, possibly, a momentary perception of something beyond temporality." Examines "The Undead" as an example of Wilbur's ideas about the "pitfalls of the dream." Notes "Merlin Enthralled" as a poem that celebrates "the magnificence that dream can achieve so long as the dreamer-artist maintains his grip against the utter erosion of the waking, controlling, none-too-trusting side of his mind." Reads "Beowulf" as a "poem of Wilbur's own condition, or rather of his plight and the plight of anyone who would follow the changing, subtle edges between waking and dream." The condition that both Beowulf and Wilbur, the poet who insists on being "wise and wakeful," share is isolation. Concludes by saying that "Wilbur's fleeting dream-glimpses of underlying order and the ambiguity of his surface world create together a harmony and a vision which can seem true even to the troubled modern spirit, and stun and excite even the modern imagination." Reprinted: 1988.18.

13 NADEL, ALAN. "Roethke, Wilbur, and the Vision of the Child: Romantic and Augustan in Modern Verse." *The Lion and the Unicorn* 2, no. 1:94-113.
    Claims that Theodore Roethke and Richard Wilbur write out of two central Western traditions in poetry – that of making the complex simple and that of showing the complexity of existence. Roethke leans toward the former, the Romantic, both in his ideas about the world and in the forms he uses. Wilbur is a Neo-Classicist who "strives for

balance, a harmony created by countervailing tensions." Posits that he "achieves his most beautiful moments through affirmation of control, rather than affirmation of escape. Asserts that the concept of change is important to Wilbur, not because it reveals a coming apart of the universe, but because it betrays the underlying order that frames the change and makes it possible" ("The Beautiful Changes," "Boy at the Window"). Suggests that in *Opposites* Wilbur challenges "that capacity [an instinctive capacity for metamorphosis] in children by directing them to the metamorphosis that the meanings of words undergo." Finds that the prosody in *Opposites* is less subtle than in Wilbur's adult poems, perhaps indicating his feeling that children need or enjoy more "overt" rhymes and rhythms and suggesting an Augustinian universe. Concludes that Wilbur, like Roethke, recognizes that childhood is "a privileged state at which the apparent contradictions of the universe are first confronted. . . . For Wilbur, the recognition [of the natural order] is the essential process of coming to grips with the world."

14 NEMEROV, HOWARD. "What Was Modern Poetry: Three Lectures." In *Figures of Thought: Speculations on the Meaning of Poetry and Other Essays*. Boston: David R. Godine, pp. 188-92.
    Reprint of 1975.9.

15 NILES, J. D. "Old Alliterative Verse Form As a Medium for Poetry." *Mosaic: A Journal for Interdisciplinary Study of Literature* 11, no. 4:19-33.
    Argues that the Anglo-Saxon alliterative verse form has possibilities for modern poets. Cites "Junk" as Richard Wilbur's "clever" attempt to revive the old alliterative verse form. Says Wilbur "handles the alliterative line with a good deal of freedom, particularly in his toleration of alliteration on the fourth beat in the line."

16 PINSKY, ROBERT. "Reading: Crowd Scene on Parnassus." *Boston* 70, no. 3 (March): 56-58, 61.
    Refers to "Cottage Street, 1953" in the context of a discussion on how poets relate to each other. Sees "Cottage Street, 1953" as the epitome of a strange meeting of two very different poets, but somehow typical of the way poets live.

17 RAMSEY, PAUL. "Grazie." *Sewanee Review* 86, no. 2 (Spring):294-97.
    Reviews *The Mind-Reader: New Poems* and *Responses, Prose Pieces*. Charges that some critics' fault-finding can be shown false. Indicates, however, that the "counterevidence needs to be selected carefully": "the really first-rate poems, the poems that illumine the

secret places and to which one returns with a deeper gratitude, are fewer than I would wish." Grants that "Piccola Commedia" and "C Minor" are delightful light verse. Claims, nevertheless, that "in most of the poems in the book, skillful as they are, the self-consciousness of control does not vanish or utterly transmute. The arrivals too often arrive too easily, content with their pleasing home." Calls "The Mind-Reader" "one of [Wilbur's] best poems."

Finds *Responses* a collection of "occasional" and sometimes too facile essays. Concedes that Wilbur is "not antitheoretical," however. Says the "prose often pleases." Points out that "Wilbur is at his best 'one on one,' reading poems he likes of poets he likes, such as Poe, Frost, and, in the first-rate essay 'Sumptuous Destitution,' about Emily Dickinson." Admits that "Poetry's Debt to Poetry" is "a very good study of the necessity and dangers of literary emulation."

18 "Richard Wilbur 1921-." In *First Printings of American Authors: Contributions toward Descriptive Checklists*. Vol. 2. Detroit: Gale, pp. 381-85.

Contains photographs of title pages and descriptive bibliographic details to aid the scholar in locating first editions. Begins with *The Beautiful Changes* (1947) and stops with "The Funeral of Bobò" (1974). Includes poetry collections, translations, items privately printed, and works edited or introduced by Wilbur.

19 TAYLOR, DAVID. "End-Words in Richard Wilbur's Poems." *Publications of the Arkansas Philological Association* 4, no. 3:25-32.

Posits that the end-words in Wilbur's poems sometimes form a "loosely syntactical and gnomic poem." Chooses examples fom "Praise in Summer," "In the Smoking Car," "Fall in Corrales," "Two Voices in a Meadow," "Love Calls Us to the Things of This World," and "In Limbo." Suggests that the "technique depends on the logical sequence of lines and Wilbur's habit of placing a line's key word at the end, giving a natural summary element to the end-words." (Example from "In Limbo": "replies, pauses, questionings – together invent breathless world.")

20 TERRILL, RICHARD. "*The Mind-Reader: New Poems* by Richard Wilbur." *Arizona Quarterly* 34, no. 2 (Summer):183-84.

Reviews *The Mind-Reader: New Poems*. Suggests that Wilbur "remains a controversial poet not by changing, but by staying the same in the midst of change." Finds several weaknesses as a result: "high, ornate, diction," "inversion for the sake of rhyme or meter," "phrases . . . consciously poetic," "conventional subject matter," and a "tendency to make broad moral judgment." Notes strengths as the "ability to create a single image that grows larger than its words" ("To the Etruscan Poets"), appropriate similes ("The Writer"), and "a talent for philosophical statement" ("A Wedding Toast"). Argues that "The Mind-Reader" is the "best poem" in the book because Wilbur "is able to bridge the distance usually present in his work. It allows him to be personal while still dealing with things and people outside of himself. It offers surface clarity, but with an obvious emotional conflict."

21 WOODARD, CHARLES. "Wilbur's 'Beasts.'" *Explicator* 36, no. 3 (Spring):6-7.
   Disagrees with Donald Hill's interpretation (1967.4) of the last two stanzas of this poem. Suggests that the "suitors of excellence" would better be understood as "poets, philosophers, creators of myth, who have always been quite as much students of evil as suitors of excellence. . . . Theirs are the dreams which when told break hearts with their revelations of man's dark potential. . . . The true beasts are not the animals in their Darwinian innocence or the man who would deny 'animal' impulses – certainly not the 'suitors' – but those who in all ages stand ready to release their own peculiarly human monstrousness upon the world."

22 YOUNG, VERNON. "Trissotin Exposed in English." *New York Times Book Review*, 2 April, pp. 14, 28.
   Reviews *The Learned Ladies*. Says that "few equal [Wilbur], none . . . surpass him" in translating Molière. Fixes the real test of any translation on the live production where "the contemporary mind may have a keener nostalgia than it likes to believe for metrical symmetry, the suspense of rhyme, the smooth tick-over of dialogue, opposed and synchronized." Sees in Wilbur's translation "a distinct sense of the athletic: the facility with which the poet has marshaled the diction of his characters when fierce and quick in opposition; the overhead serve, the backhand drive; the celerity of the punishing polemic."

1979

1 ALTIERI, CHARLES. "Robert Lowell and the Difficulties of Escaping Modernism." In *Enlarging the Temple: New Directions in American Poery During the 1960's*. Lewisburg, Pa.: Bucknell University Press, pp. 53-77, passim.
   Attempts to "create a limited literary context for the poetry of the sixties in order to provide . . . historical perspective." Deals with Richard Wilbur and Robert Lowell: "my aim . . . shall be less to give an

impartial analysis of their work than to recover the way many younger poets came to view them." Suggests the central idea the poets of the fifties inherited from the New Critics was that of pattern, though the younger poets were unable to sustain the larger vision of the modernists: "the emphasis on imaginative order remains. . . . Prophetic order gives way to reflective private acts of balancing." Asserts that "incarnation provides a doctrinal basis by which an essentially symbolist poetic can assert the value of the mind's orders while insisting that universals are not mere fictions but contain the actual structure and meaning of particular experiences." Finds that "pattern then iluminates [*sic*] flux, but it also leads inexorably to the celebration of contemplative experience ultimately divorced from that flux." Contends that Wilbur's "poetry is based on the tension between the richness of sensory experience and the elaborate patterning of mind. But Wilbur has no metaphysical ground for the dynamic activities of mind exhibited in his poetry, so the poems have difficulty transcending their own elegance and becoming genuine spiritual experiences or witnesses of value." Cites "A World without Objects Is a Sensible Emptiness" as a perfect example of this theory. Criticizes Wilbur because he "does not stand within the oasis of sharply realized particulars; instead his elaborate metaphors and ornate sound play insist on the poem as a space of discourse, a space outside in the desert where the speaker imagines the oasis, reflects on his act of imagination, and arranges it into a kind of verbal clearing – fertile with artificial plants." Argues that what Wilbur fails to do is "follow up the metaphysical implications of the priority he posits for the physical world and of the contradictions between fictive and physical orders with which he plays."

2 BEACHAM, WALTON. "Poetry As Performance: A Conversation between W. D. Snodgrass and Richard Wilbur." *New Virginia Review* I:34-57.

Walton Beacham, Poetry Editor of the *New Virginia Review*, moderated the conversation which was taped by WTGM Radio for National Public Broadcasting (on April 12, 1978) and aired in Tidewater, Virginia, on May 1, 1978.

Moderator opens by saying, "One of the things that Richard Wilbur and W. D. Snodgrass are bringing to life in this part of the 20th century is the return of poetry as performance. They are both interested in the voice with which poetry is presented to an audience, and the ways in which the audience will respond to it."

Wilbur describes his feelings about poetry as performance this way: "I'm a little . . . diffident about my voice as an instrument . . . but [performance] has consequences for the way I write." Says that he "intones" his poems rather than "acts" them, that "if you act a poem very fully, you are going to emphasize some of the words at the expense of others. I think that with a somewhat monotone delivery you deliver more of the words. And it's a little more like encountering the words on a page." Adds that "if a poem is read aloud well, I think it is bound to be a simplification and an enforcement of the interpretation. What you do often when reading a poem aloud . . . what one often does, is to make apparent the simple emotional spine of it."

Snodgrass responds to a question about the formality of a poem Wilbur has just read: "One of the things I hear is a great admiration for the formality of the poem that brings a kind of sub-rational meaning, something that I can't gloss, but it says right away something about his concern for forms, for social forms, commitment toward something of that kind. Also, his concern for a kind of elegance of structure." On another topic, Snodgrass discusses Wilbur's method of translation: "He is faithful to the poem, to the original, in ways I don't try to be. This may be related to the fact that he really reads the language he translates. . . . It seems to me that he tries to get the original all the way . . . to the deepest resonances of the language."

Wilbur says of his translation work that "I don't want the people in any of my Molière translations to remind us for a moment that this is being done in the twentieth century, so I aim . . . at a timeless language, at a transparent language which will make it possible to some extent for the audience to move without struggle into the pure temporal milieu of the play."

Wilbur discusses readers' perception about the lack of pain in his poems. Says "I confess frankly to being an optimist, and I hope not to be a shallow owe. I come out always – not always, but most always – on the 'yes' side of things. I come out saying, 'Nevertheless, it's all right'. . . . Everybody tells partial truths. My part of the truth is to stress what is hopeful."

Wilbur responds to the charge that he writes too much nature poetry by suggesting that though he uses nature imagery, he is really talking about being human and that "we and the birds, we and the trees, are part of one scheme." Describes himself as a more dramatic poet able to incorporate more narrative into his poems than in earlier years.

Snodgrass suggests that he and Wilbur differ in the way they manage the tone of their poems: Wilbur establishes and maintains a single tone while Snodgrass continually attempts to contrast one voice with another. Reprinted: 1990.2.

3 FUSSELL, PAUL, Jr. *Poetic Meter and Poetic Form*. Rev. ed. New York: Random House, pp. 65-66, 73, 99-100, 152-53.

Praises Wilbur's "Junk" as a successful use of Old English versification because of its appropriate subject matter. Notes a dilemma for contemporary poets: "either to contrive new schemes of empirically meaningful repetition that reflect and – more importantly – transmit the color of contemporary experience; or to recover schemes that have reflected the experience of the past." If a poet does the first, he must accept the Christian idea that life has pattern. If he does the second, he must make the assumption that the past can be captured. Concludes that "if Ginsberg and D. H. Lawrence and Hart Crane sacrifice to the first demand, Frost and Auden and Wilbur sacrifice to the second."

4 GROSS, HARVEY. "Paul Fussell: The Historical Dimension." In *The Structure of Verse*. New York: Ecco Press, pp. 40-52.

Notes that Richard Wilbur uses Old English versification for "Junk." Feels the poem is successful because the subject of "the power of good workmanship" is appropriate. Quotes the whole poem.

5 GUSTAFSON, RICHARD. "The Courage of the Quotidian in Recent Poetry." *Poet and Critic* 10, no. 2:26-33.

Suggests that the age of heroic deeds and struggle may be over, that the poet's new challenge has shifted to defining what is required to live today: "the courage of the quotidian may eventually pass from groove to grace." Finds that Wilbur is a poet who has "probed mundane subject matter for whatever mystery might reside there" ("A Hole in the Floor"). Sees both dark and light sides to Wilbur's work which "seem mutually operative in his sense of the beauty and fascination of 'things'" ("Love Calls Us to the Things of This World," "The Beautiful Changes," "Sunlight Is Imagination"). Theorizes that at times Wilbur "seems to suggest a Platonic 'Original' behind all the 'shades,' which must remain hidden because the everchanging light refuses to let us see it without diurnal curtains. He therefore suggests that the *thingness* of things will be forever silent. His vision . . . is rather esthetic in subject; and the challenge is, by sheer craft, to make something perdurable out of the commonplace."

Asserts that "the subjects and forms of recent poetry have their excitement and challenge in the descent from former grand themes of the art – and of course in a dependence on a tighter, carefuller grip on the shaft of the shaping instrument." Recognizes as "courage of the quotidian" Wilbur's ability to "loosen the 'danger' in [his] pretty forest." Says "this daily courage might be called the courage of endurance, but a kind of endurance maybe better understood by the old or the patiently despairing."

6 MATHIS, JERRY WESTON. "The Phenomenology of Movement in the Poetry of Richard Wilbur." Ph.D. dissertation, Northwestern University, 348 pp.

Explores the "movement phenomenon in specific poems by Wilbur," using Roman Ingarden's "phenomenological approach to the strata of literature." Specific chapters deal with (I) "Ingarden's view of the strata of the literary work of art"; (II) "phenomenology of movement in order to isolate and examine movement as it is lived in subjective experience"; (III-VI) "detailed descriptions of movement dimensions of the strata in four poems": "Caserta Garden" (1947), "Year's End" (1950), "The Aspen and the Stream" (1961), and "The Writer" (1976). See *Dissertation Abstracts International* 40:3302A-03A.

7 MICHELSON, BRUCE. "Richard Wilbur's *The Mind-Reader*." *Southern Review* 15, no. 3 (July): 763-68.

Reviews *The Mind-Reader: New Poems*. Notes a new roughness in texture in this collection, more "defiant surfaces," best exemplified by "Children of Darkness." Concedes that "Cottage Street, 1953" will offend some people, but defends Wilbur's treatment of Plath as "gentle and just an observation as anyone who believes can make about anyone who doesn't." Calls the mind-reader of the title poem "a dramatic monologue . . . from the kind of sensibility that Wilbur's almost is – that is, one that hasn't found its way back" (from the dark places of dream). Admits that he finds himself "wishing that this astounding poet would put out something big or flashing enough to turn more heads and absolutely stop all this talk about safety and propriety." Reprinted: 1983.18.

8 MORGAN, MICHAEL W. "Richard Wilbur's 'Conjuration.'" *Concerning Poetry* 12, no. 1 (Spring):81-83.

Analyzes "Conjuration." Sees that this poem encapsulates Wilbur's theme about the "separation between real and ideal." This poem, however, "lets images rather than direct statements carry the theme." For the most part, the poem is "devoted to a novel image for disillusionment – the withdrawal of the ocean at ebb tide. Concludes that finally the speaker "attempts to reconcile, or at least balance, the real and ideal worlds through an act of magic that is also a buried metaphor."

1979

9 ROUTLEY, ERIK. *A Panorama of Christian Hymnody*. Collegeville, Minn.: Liturgical Press, p. 163.

Reprints "A Stable Lamp" which has been set to music as a hymn, first printed in the Lutheran *Contemporary Worship I* (1969). Thinks it may be the first example of "American non-hymnic poetry entering the field of hymnody."

10 SAWYER, ELIZABETH L. "'il faut cultiver notre jardin . . .': The Poetry of Richard Wilbur." A.B. dissertation, Princeton University, 93 pp.

Suggests that "the poet aims not at creating a world outside our own, but at creating a harmoniously balanced one within it . . . of cultivating our own garden." Sees his optimism as "a call to our humanity, an attempt to provoke not common alarm but mutual efforts toward a better world." Notes that Wilbur "takes for granted the conception of two worlds, one here on earth, another timeless and imaginary." Finds his contrasting interests in Poe and Emily Dickinson successfully balance two aspects of his own work. Says that "with Emily Dickinson, Wilbur . . . shares the essentially Romantic belief in the mind's transforming powers." Concludes that "Wilbur's insistence on the individual will, on the human adaptability that allows a synthesis of extremes, reveals a quintessential Americanism in theme as well as voice."

11 SUMMERS, JOSEPH. "Richard Wilbur." In *Great Writers of the English Language: Poets*. New York: St. Martin's Press, pp. 1075-77.

Includes a biographical section listing Wilbur's education, Army service, family, membership in academic societies, teaching assignments, awards and prizes, and home address. Lists poetry publications beginning with *The Beautiful Changes* (1947) and ending with *The Mind-Reader* (1976). Also lists translations of four Molière plays and *Candide*, children's books, and editorial work. Suggests Field (1971.6) and Hill (1967.4) as secondary sources.

Notes that "from the beginning up to *The Mind-Reader* Wilbur's poetry has shown notable continuities." The later poems move toward use of the dramatic voice and a plainer style as well as a "deepening of feeling." Predictably, Wilbur has avoided the confessional mode and free verse. Unpredictably, his superb translation of Molière reveals his affinity for the qualities of the French master: "a humane voice of uncommonly rational common-sense; a use of language that is both familiar and chaste; a witty enemy of the pompous, the gross, and the fanatic; and a juggler, a master of poise and point." Mentions poems that have been surprises ("Junk," "Walking to Sleep"). Wilbur's exploration of the dreamy state between waking and sleeping and his exploration of the activities of the mind in "Walking to Sleep" and "The Mind-Reader" underscore his ability to extend one of his major themes – "the processes, reflections, and creations of the mind." Though he is probably Robert Frost's most natural heir, Wilbur's conviction that "Love Calls Us to the Things of This World" is uniquely his.

12 WALKER, JEANNE COWAN. "'To Hold Creation Whole': Paradox in the Poetry of Richard Wilbur." M.A. thesis, Connecticut College, 130 pp.

Examines "paradox as a central idea and device within Richard Wilbur's poetry." Contends that "paradox is a basic means for revealing the poet's particular vision of the world: life's contrarieties, the shock in attending vying energies from within the spirit of man as well as the forces of outer reality, and the wonders of transformation." Sees three elements in paradox which are revealed in "two recurring themes, innocence-experience and thirst." Finds a "preponderance of paradox [in Wilbur's work] in language and vision."

13 WILLIAMS, ANNE. "Wilbur's 'Beasts.'" *Explicator* 37, no. 4 (Summer):27-28.

Analyzes "Beasts." Finds that this poem "expresses nostalgia for a lost Eden . . . of unconscious animal existence." Points out that "the first two stanzas portray the animal world 'where though all things differ, all agree.' This world is suffused with harmony, a completeness and interdependence between the beasts and nature." Portrays the loss of harmony found in the rest of the poem as parallel to "developing consciousness." Characterizes the werewolf as providing "a modulation between the two modes of being, the 'major' and minor freedom." Meanwhile, the "suitors of excellence" in the final stanzas represent "man, the scholar, at his most conscious and remote from nature." Suggests that "man reads the book of nature rather than experiencing it as the gull does." Finds that Wilbur "distinguishes between 'beasts' and 'monsters'; all beasts belong to nature (man included), but man alone brings 'monsters into the cities, crows on the public statues.'" Concludes that the poem "suggests a grim reversal of the Faust myth enacted in a universe without transcendence: man's striving intellect, imperfect and thus continually failing, leads him to damnation."

14 Z. G. "Richard Wilbur." In *Epica, avanguardia, puzu del*. Edited by Sergio Perosa. Milano: Accademia, n.pp.

In Italian. Notes that Wilbur, an elegant and refined poet, occupies a position in contemporary poetry that is diametrically opposite to that of Robert Lowell. Says his most distinctive passages are his taste for surprising analogy and a long and elaborated similitude, the quest for contrasting effects and musical intonation, the sense of precious detail and a predilection for docile tones. Convinced that "poetry should include every resource that can be made operational," Wilbur has happily known how to assimilate the most unlike influences: the French symbolists, the English metaphysicians, Gerard Manley Hopkins, Wallace Stevens, and Marianne Moore. This availability also represents his most apparent limit, in the sense that it tends to translate itself into a lack of energy, in his whole production, for a real nucleus or for a rigorous logic of development. Quotes Wilbur as saying, "I am not a programmed poet . . . each of my poems is unique to me; each is without connection to anything else I have written." Suggests that this doesn't mean that he lacks precise themes: many of his poems deal with the value of aesthetic experience in a world of confused possibilities. Others deal with problems of cognitive activity while others deal with relations between the tangible world and spiritual intuition, favoring "sensible reality," a spirituality that isn't abstract or a denier of the world.

1980

1 "An Amherst Poet and His Teacher at the White House." *Amherst* 33, no. 1 (Summer):8.

Reports the "launching" of the new U.S. Department of Education by honoring six teachers who had deeply influenced "a half-dozen famous achievers." Richard Wilbur was chosen as one of the achievers; the teacher he chose to honor was G. Armour Craig whose course in seventeenth-century English prose had had a deep and lasting effect on Wilbur's respect for language.

2 CALHOUN, RICHARD. "Richard Wilbur." In *Dictionary of Literary Biography: American Poets Since World War II*. Vol. 5, Part 2. Detroit: Gale, pp. 378-90.

Includes sections on Birth, Education, Marriage, Awards, and Selected Books as well as a selected bibliography of secondary works. Writes biographical section chronologically. Contains a primary bibliography beginning with *The Beautiful Changes* (1947) and including *The Mind-Reader* (1976).

Claims that Wilbur "is consistently a poet of order, of affirmation." His job as a poet, as he sees it, has always been to order his experience, to give his responses to two extremes of disorder: chaos and destruction on the one, and illusions and escapism on the other. His response as a humanist and as a poet is to keep a firm focus on reality as represented by objects, by the things of this world. As a poet he must be modestly heroic, see more, range further than the ordinary citizen." Lists imagination as a corrupting force, "the power of the beautiful to change . . . [to] be used as a buttress against disorder," "the need for contact with the physical world," "the existence of change, mutability," and "the importance of a balance between reality and dream, of things of this world enhanced by imagination" as major themes established in *The Beautiful Changes* (1947).

Indicates that in *Ceremony* (1950) "the concept of mutability . . . is primary." Finds a "new and important theme: whether heroism is possible in a world of disorder." Sees a continuation of the theme of "the need for a balance between the real and the ideal." Notes "first dialogue poem." Describes "A World without Objects Is a Sensible Emptiness" as "a poem with . . . the quintessential Wilbur title."

Selects three poems in *Things of This World* (1956) as Wilbur's very best and as evidence of "an even greater stress on the importance of the use of the real." ("A Baroque Wall-Fountain in the Villa Sciarra," "Love Calls Us to the Things of This World," "For the New Railway

Station in Rome"). Says the "impressive new station becomes a symbol of how man's mind must continually work on things of this world for the imagination to have the power to recreate and to cope with disorder."

Sees in *Advice to a Prophet* a heavy emphasis on "what the imagination can do with apparently mundane things." Notes the negative criticism developing around this book, especially in regard to Wilbur's apparent reluctance to "undertake major experiments in form or to introduce new and socially relevant subject matter." Suggests that Wilbur's work could hardly compete with the "tremendous impact that Lowell had made in *Life Studies*." Concludes that Wilbur "fails in his attempts to indicate more dramatically and more positively how order might be restored, what his personal 'stays against confusion' are, . . . because he seems too exclusively concerned with objects."

Notes poems with recurring themes in *Walking to Sleep* (1961). "Running" "becomes a symbol of aspiration at different stages in life." Finds a clearly discernible movement toward simpler diction and more direct poems in *The Mind-Reader* (1976). Cites as encouraging a "new emotional directness." Praises Wilbur for his consistently good translations.

3 DINNEEN, MARCIA B. "Richard Wilbur: A Bibliography of Secondary Sources." *Bulletin of Bibliography* 37, no. 1 (January-March):16-22.

Supplements John Field's *Checklist* (1971.6). Includes five sections – Books, Articles in Books, Articles in Periodicals, Pamphlets, Dissertations. See also 1990.3.

*4 ERGIN, SEÇKIN. "Modern Amerikan Siiri Üzerinde Bir Çalisma: Robert Lowell, Stanley Kunitz, Richard Wilbur, Theodore Roethke ve Çagdaslari [A Study of Modern American Poetry: Robert Lowell, Stanley Kunitz, Richard Wilbur, Theodore Roethke and Contemporaries]. Edebiyat Fakultesi Arastirma Der Gisi [Faculty of Literature Journal of Research] (Ankara, Turkey) 12, no.2:469-84.

In Turkish. Listed in unpublished Hagstrom bibliography.

5 GARDNER, P. "The Bland Granta – Sylvia Plath at Cambridge." *Dalhousie Review* 60, no. 3 (Autumn):496-507.

Suggests that Plath evokes and dismisses Richard Wilbur's world in "Death of a Toad."

6 JAMES, CLIVE. "When the Gloves Are Off." In *First Reactions: Critical Essays: 1968-1979*. New York: Knopf, pp. 34-44.

Reprint of 1971.11 and 1974.5.

7 JENSEN, EJNER J. "Encounters with Experience: The Poems of Richard Wilbur." *New England Review* 2, no. 4 (Summer):594-613.

Contends that "at the heart of [Wilbur's] achievement is a willingness to face the full implications of our humanness, to confront not merely that paradoxical creature, man, but to encounter as well those structures–both physical and intellectual–that man has created for himself." In "For Dudley Fitts" Wilbur "finds no easy release through anger or rant." "On the Marginal Way" is another poem which "progresses from quiet observation through a tortuous intellectual anguish, ending finally in a sort of religious calm." Finds both poems indicate that "intellect and illusion may permit some temporary refuge, but 'the time's fright' stands ready to seize the mind and senses and to focus them on a world of horrors." "In the Field" asserts "the heroism of being human, the heroism of facing up to the inadequacy of the answers we can discover with all our powers of thought and imagination." Says about "Walking to Sleep" that Wilbur's "vision of man's existence and of his quest for sleep and poetry–rest and creation–must enlarge our sense of Wilbur's capacity as a poet." Embraces Wilbur's vision–"the one that maintains the paradox [that man is both a rational and intuitive creature] and confronts it with full awareness of its extremes"–as the more "daring."

Suggests that a major thread in Wilbur's poems is the idea that "stasis of any sort seems a condition out of nature: the rule of life is movement dictated by the tension of opposites." Sees this concept "imaged in the figure of a walker" ("Water Walker," boys in "Mined Country," girl in "L'Etoile," "Giacometti," "Walking to Sleep"). Other poems carry out the theme of a "cherished and tyrannical dilemma, that we must delight in evanescent things even as we recognize their transience. The world of flux and our longing for patterns are forever in contest" ("Caserta Garden").

Argues that poems in *Ceremony* (1950) "describe the various sorts of ceremonies–of art, of civility, of legerdemain–used to conceal change and disorder" ("Ceremony," "Still, Citizen Sparrow," "A World without Objects Is a Sensible Emptiness"). Notices in "Giacometti" "a tragic awareness, an awareness nearly Shakespearean in its depth of implication, of man's isolation and his awful understanding of how little the traditional forms can help."

Insists that *Things of This World* (1956) and *Advice to a Prophet* (1961) testify to Wilbur's continuing vision of the complexity of man's existence. Sees "Beasts" as focusing at last "upon tragic aloneness and man's inability to locate any source of assurance. . . . The poem's progress . . . is from concord, to decay, to a state of chaos." Concludes by mentioning "The Mind-Reader," "In Limbo," and especially "The Writer" as poems which testify to the unalterable fact that "each of us, finally, is alone." Asserts that in such a world for a poet to "act out our needs or our desires" would seem a "shameless vanity." "He cannot alter our condition nor mitigate our aloneness. What he shares, he must share as a poet, and he does this by helping us to see ourselves as we go on our curious, undirected pilgrimage." Reprinted: 1983.18.

8 JONES, PETER. "Richard Wilbur." In *A Reader's Guide to Fifty American Poets*. London: Heinemann; Totowa, N.J.: Barnes & Noble, pp. 305-10.

Acknowledges that Wilbur's early poems display "a conscious and at times obtrusive wittiness and wordplay that mar the work" ("Lightness"). Recognizes his ability to "lift an apparently banal thought or image, rendering it new and memorable" ("Praise in Summer"). Contends that Wilbur's "meditative argument and counter-argument, his attempt to turn raw events into experience, ensure a balance more complete and resonant than the rhetoric of poets more interested in effect and sensation than full apprehension. Extremity enters the poems only when an experience has changed him: the poem records the change *and* the experience." Sees a movement toward a "controlled but natural style" in later work ("In the Smoking Car"). Defends the use of wit because it "is entirely functional, deepening rather than merely decorating the idea, enhancing and pointing rather than distracting from the meaning." Concludes that "most engaging is Wilbur's communicated sense of wonder and his formal skill. Grace and precision are not academic virtues in his poetry: the academic poet teases out meanings, while Wilbur's task is to discover forms. His is a warm art."

9 KIM, SUNY KON. "The Pulitzer Prize Winning Poet Richard Wilbur." *Literature and Thought* (Seoul, Korea) 4, no. 89:50-53.

In Korean. Contains a brief biographical description. Recounts an interview with Richard Wilbur. Describes Wilbur as a refined and benign human being and as an intelligent and sensitive poet who meditates on the mystery of life and the universe. Says Wilbur attempts, in his poetry, to transform the ugliest object into beautiful objects and the most negative aspects into the most positive. Touches on when Wilbur began to write poetry and why. Also reports Wilbur's defense of his style of poems.

10 KOLDALÁNYI, GYULA. "Richard Wilbur." In *SzavakA Szélbe: Mai Amerikai Köitök* [*Words to the Wind: Contemporary American Poets*]. Budapest, Hungary: Európa Könyvkiadó [Europa Publisher], pp. 347-50.

In Hungarian. Says Wilbur is a poet of the eye, the spirit, and the heart. The order is intentional: the "feelings" permeate into the temper of the creator. The reader realizes his special vision, his inclination to contradictions, his knowing of complicated parables. Notes Wilbur's use of painters and says that his "eye" is inseparable from his spirit. With Wilbur, the spectacle is not just for itself, as with many modernists and Romantics, not even simply Nature, but Human, in the metaphysical, moral, and political sense.

Says a typical Wilbur poem is a big metaphor: the spectacle is written with precision, the complicated changes and intricate structure of the parts of the poem will be the reflection of some kind of human characteristics. Such poems are the unity of the emotions and the abstract which is the eternal essence of metaphorical poetry. Mentions John Donne, Andrew Marvell, T. S. Eliot, Allen Tate, and John Crowe Ransom as influences. Notes Wilbur's preference for difficult poetic forms. Says his choice of forms is based on an esthetic reason. Cites Wilbur's explanation of the similarity of form to the frame of a painting.

Suggests that World War II was a formative influence. Lists a number of biographical facts. Comments on the several excellent translations of Molière.

11 *Literary and Library Prizes*. 10th ed. Revised and enlarged by Olga S. Weber and Stephan J. Calvert. New York & London: R. R. Bowker, pp. 31, 69, 133, 138, 187, 241, 362, 363, 367, 376, 380, 393.

Lists several prizes and awards given to Wilbur.

12 OLIVER, RAYMOND. "Old-English Verse and Modern Poets." *Allegorica* 5, no. 1 (Summer):141-48.

Posits that the modern writer uses Old English poetry in a four-stage continuum: "actual writing in Old English, verse-translation, the imitation of Old English style . . . , and the thematic use of Anglo-Saxon materials." Suggests that "the only poet who has made what strikes me as a superb use of this extraordinary, mannered idiom is Richard Wilbur." In "Junk," Wilbur shows his ability to write contemporary poetry in this old verse form, "carrying with it a tendency to archaism, formality, and slow, ponderous movement."

1980

13 *Poetry Explication: A Checklist of Interpretation since 1925 of British and American Poems Past and Present.* Edited by Joseph M. Kuntz and Nancy C. Martinez. Boston: G. K. Hall, pp. 498-500.

Lists explications of twenty-five of Wilbur's most popular poems.

14 RICHARDSON, KENNETH. *Twentieth Century Writing: A Reader's Guide to Contemporary Literature.* London: Newnes, pp. 646-47.

Contains a Selected Bibliography of work about Richard Wilbur.

15 SOMER, JOHN L., and COOPER, BARBARA ECK. *American and British Literature – 1945-1975: An Annotated Bibliography of Contemporary Scholarship.* Lawrence, Kans.: Regents, pp. 7, 15, 24, 27, 42, 46, 111, 113, 175, 179, 180, 191, 197, 200, 209, 303.

Duplicates some of the bibliographic entries found in Field (1971.6) and Dinneen (1980.3).

16 STERN, CAROL SIMPSON. "Richard Wilbur." In *Contemporary Poets.* 3d ed. New York: St. Martin's Press, pp. 1957-58.

Contains a paragraph of biographical information including birth date, education, military duty, wife's name, teaching assignments, edititorial work, prizes and awards, honorary degrees, and current address. Includes a primary bibliography beginning with *The Beautiful Changes* (1947) through *The Learned Ladies* (1978). A second category lists prose works and books of poetry edited by Wilbur. Cites Field (1971.6) as current bibliography. Contains a brief secondary bibliography of critical studies as well as a short comment by Wilbur about his work.

Suggests that Richard Wilbur "continues to strike that difficult balance between solipsism and scientific objectivity upon which his best poetry depends." Says that critics have chosen to "misunderstand" Wilbur by saying he is "restrained" or "too charitable." The intent of his poems is to "rightly see the tensions which inform our sense of the world, to set isolated moments in a perspective. Wilbur's is a world of balanced discord." Sees strong thematic and tonal relationships between Wilbur's early work and *Walking to Sleep* and *The Mind-Reader.* Reprinted: 1985.9.

17 "Translating Verse: Beyond a Metric Conversation." *Stage-Space* no. 3, pp. 8-9.

Compares the French Alexandrine used by Molière to the English iambic pentameter couplets used by Wilbur. Suggests that a critic feels that "the more serious or darker side of Molière gets lost in translation." Has come to regard Wilbur's translations as "more relentlessly comic than Molière's originals, and therefore as unfaithful to Molière's darker dynamics." Argues that though something may be lost in translation, something is also gained–that is, poetry is gained, poetry in English. Sees Wilbur's "own poetic style . . . which accounts for the more thoroughly comic manner and intensity of his translations, for the comedy without tragic relief." Finds this a celebration "of the genius of Molière."

1981

1 ABBOTT, C. S. "Wilbur's 'Praise in Summer.'" *Explicator* 39, no. 3 (Spring):13-14.

Analyzes "Praise in Summer." Notes that "the praise that the speaker . . . recounts creates a *mundus inversus* in which, through metaphor, up becomes down and solid becomes nonsolid." Indicates that the "final question of the poem, on first reading, may seem to ask whether things should not be described as they are, but it reverts to metaphor like that of the praise." Concludes that "the poem–the praise and the framework in which it is recounted and questioned–appears to be, then, a demonstration of the metaphoric and quasimetaphoric nature of the language into which we transform the world in order to talk about it."

2 BERKE, ROBERTA ELZEY. *Bounds Out of Bounds: A Compass for Recent American and British Poetry*. New York: Oxford University Press, pp. 12, 16-21.

Says "Wilbur's main strength is his skill, a dedicated craftsmanship that has persisted over the years. His attitude is the opposte [*sic*] of that of the makers of shoddy goods which he describes in 'Junk.'" Grants that "his use of this dense form [Old-English alliterative verse] is no mere exercise in style, but an expression of the complexities underlying common tools and the danger when they are badly made." Suggests that at times Wilbur's intense concentration on objects leads to a sense that they are "abstract"–"nowhere in particular." Acknowledges that he has "sometimes been indicted for a lack of passion and disinterest in social issues," but argues that this is not quite the case ("The Pardon," "Advice to a Prophet"). Suggests that there "is a deliberate distance between blunt emotion and the finished poem, but it is the distance of craft, not callousness." Explains in detail the mythological reference to Hephaestus and Wayland in "Junk," concluding that "neither reference is vital to a superficial comprehension of the poem," but they "add resonance and scope." Observes that though Wilbur's "poems do not go off limits with new forms, explosive subjects of forbidden passions, their high concentration of images causes the reader's vision of reality to implode into a new world as wide and surprising as a first look through a microscope."

3 CHAMBERS, ANDREA. "In Winter, U.S. Writing Talent Pools on the Sensual, Timeless Port of Key West." *People*, 23 February, pp. 24-29.

Quotes comments made by Richard and Charlee Wilbur about Key West and its "madcap" atmosphere.

4 COSTA, M. ALLESSANDRA FANTONI. "Richard Wilbur." In *Contemporanei Novecento Americano*. Vol. III. Rome: Luciano Lucarini Editore, pp. 73-98.

In Italian. Contains a biographic and bibliographic section. Discusses Wilbur's view of what poetry should be as presented in "The Genie in the Bottle," "On My Own Work," and "Poetry and Happiness." Praises richness of language, formal control, the passionate perception of the world, and the conceptual sharpness which makes each poem an autonomous artistic object. Mentions poems from *The Beautiful Changes* such as the war poems ("Tywater," "Mined Country"). Classifies poems into categories: poems on love ("Objects," "Sunlight Is Imagination," "The Beautiful Changes"), on tension between life and art ("Caserta Gardens"). Sees in *Ceremony* the theme of the relationship between truth and art ("Juggler," "Epistemology," "Praise in Summer"). Notes that "A World without Objects Is a Sensible Emptiness" is Wilbur's rejection of abstraction. Asserts that "Ceremony" emphasizes the necessity of form for art; the poem veils the truth in order to celebrate it. Says that in *Things of This World* Wilbur celebrates the joyous acceptance of the human condition ("A Baroque Wall-Fountain in the Villa Sciarra" and "Love Calls Us to the Things of This World"). Finds Wilbur is interested in the limits between dreaming and waking ("Mind," "Digging for China," "Merlin Enthralled," "Marginalia"). Thinks *Advice to a Prophet* shows a style more dramatic and robust ("Advice to a Prophet," "Junk"). Hears echoes of Robert Graves in "To Ishtar" and "She" as well as echoes of other poets in other poems. Suggests Wilbur's use of literary allusion is subtle and expert ("Poetry's Debt to Poetry"). Finds that *Walking to Sleep* is not only visual but also visionary and gets back to the intimate correspondence between man and creation ("In the Field"). Cites "Running" and "A Late Aubade" as examples of more personal investment. "Walking to Sleep" ends between the real and ideal with the celebration of the moment of "perfect carelessness" that precedes sleep. Finds that in *The Mind-Reader* the theme of dream and waking is newly centered in "The Mind-Reader" and "In Limbo." Discusses Wilbur's translation work and surveys reviews and criticism to date.

5 DRY, HELEN. "Wilbur's 'October Maples, Portland.'" *Explicator* 40, no. 1 (Fall):60-61.

Analyzes "October Maples, Portland." Centers on "trans-formations – effected by the traditional cleansing elements, fire and water." Finds an important paradox in the words "wash" and "stain" that "neatly reinforce the suggestion that natural beauty may purify and redeem." Explains that "the maples suggest the timelessness of eternal life – either retained in Eden's innocence or regained through Christ's redemption. . . . Wilbur implies that the dying, time-doomed leaves triumph over time in three ways: they ignore it in their 'never so unfallen' identification with the present; they transcend it with their suggestion of Eden and eternity; and they use it to effect both 'lasting' results and an eventual return." Finds that the speaker "is precipitated into a state of worshipful exaltation: he feels himself in a consecrated scene, walking between ranks of temples, and talking with the elect in a holy tongue. If he, so purified, receives a 'stain,' that stain almost certainly amounts to an emblem of redemption – the final purification, or 'washing away' of sin."

6 GOTTIS, DENISE. "Richard Wilbur." In *Contemporary Authors*. Edited by Christine Nasso. New rev. ser., vol. 2, edited by Ann Evory. Detroit, Gale, pp. 665-67.

Contains sections titled PERSONAL, CAREER, MEMBER (awards, prizes, and memberships in professional societies), WRITINGS (poetry, editoral work, plays), WORK IN PROGRESS (poems), SIDELIGHTS (overview of criticism), and BIO-GRAPHICAL-CRITICAL SOURCES.

Gives in SIDELIGHTS a survey of criticism, both positive and negative, from sources dated 1945 to 1980.

7 HULSE, MICHAEL. "The Poetry of Richard Wilbur." *Quadrant* 25, no. 10/170 (October):49-52.

Insists that though Wilbur's mode of writing poetry has gone out of fashion, he should be read, especially for his ability to match subject to language as in "A Fire-Truck." "The passing of the vehicle is followed in all its squalling, skidding clamour, and when it is gone its meaning (a word which I ought perhaps to place beween inverted commas) clicks into place: there has been a (brief) confrontation between cognitive (contingent) and necessary reality, and the true fact of being comes out way ahead of the secondary condition of thinking." Says "this interpenetration of language and subject is Wilbur's most characteristic triumph, and his most characteristic failure, conversely, is made inevitable the moment he grabs over-hastily at such an effect, without the patience to set it up as carefully as he does in 'A Fire-Truck.'" If the reading public rejects his work because they prefer confessional poetry, it is "showing itself to be anti-pluralist."

Cites "Juggler" as a poem where Wilbur is "actually *doing* with words what the juggler is doing with his balls and broom and plate and table. Damn what a show!" Establishes his point with three examples that show the falling sound pattern underscoring the action of the balls, the dense verbs "conveying a vivid sense of action really *happening*," and grammar and punctuation which accentuates the action. Concludes that "Wilbur's craftsmanship is staggering." *The Beautiful Changes* and *Ceremony* contain his best poems. For these he should be appreciated in spite of the fact that his later work has stiffened into a "linguistic pose and a smoothing out of subject matter, an elimination of complexity, of that quasimetaphysical difficulty which made the early Wilbur so rich a pleasure." Reprinted: 1988.18.

8 LEVEY, VIRGINIA. "The World of Objects in Richard Wilbur's Poetry." *Publications of the Arkansas Philological Association* 7, no. 1 (Spring):41-51.

Notes that Wilbur "believes that ideal beauty, which continues to be the object of poetic quests, only exists within the material world." Observes Wilbur's opposition to Poe and other Romantics who would transcend the world and scorn the real. Says Wilbur differs with the Romantics in that "he acknowledges the imperfection of things, not as a transient state, awaiting some resolution which would bring about a nebulous otherworldly perfection, but as a permanent state of things." To separate the perfect and imperfect is impossible: "but must be taken as parts of a whole. Imperfection cannot be avoided without avoiding perfection also and without avoiding an actual life." Finds "the paradigm for this marriage of intuition and sense effected through redeeming love . . . [in] the Incarnation of divine love (abstraction) in the earthly form of Jesus (concretion)." Several consequences grow out of Wilbur's poetic, namely the acceptance of death as a human event, the letting go of the self as imperfect, and the willingness to walk "into the dark" in order to find the light ("Conjuration," "Love Calls Us to the Things of This World," "A Plain Song for Comadre," "A Black November Turkey," "Flumen Tenebrarum"). Asserts that "not only does the transcendentalist ultimately deny the value of the material world of things and degrade human worth, but he also ends by denying even the worth of self" ("The Aspen and the Stream"). Finds in "A World without Objects Is a Sensible Emptiness" Wilbur's "fullest statement of . . . the theme of reconciliation of abstract and concrete, of spirit and flesh." Concludes, "Paradoxically, ideality is purest, or perhaps most nearly possible, only in an impure form."

9   LODGE, SALLY A. Review of *New England Reflections*. *Publishers Weekly*, 27 February, p. 147.
    Reviews *New England Reflections* for which Wilbur wrote the foreword. Comments that his work is "stunning."

10 MITGANG, HERBERT. "Schlesinger Elected Head of Arts and Letters Group." *New York Times*, 28 January, p. C22.
    Recounts the naming of Richard Wilbur as Chancellor of the American Academy and Institute of Arts and Letters. Quotes Wilbur as saying the organization "give[s] material support and recognition to composers, artists and writers who may not have achieved the public acclaim and financial success they deserve. In addition to honoring the country's most distinguished artists, the organization gives some $250,000 a year in cash awards, as well as medals and other honors, to relatively less-known young people."

11 MORLEY, SHERIDAN. "Opinion." *Drama* no. 142: pp. 3, 31.
    Performance review of *The Misanthrope* at the Royal Exchange Theatre (England). Calls Wilbur's translation "sprightly." Praises the translation because it "proved remarkably lively and theatrical: we have got too used to assuming that rhyming couplets are something benighted foreigners can accept in the theatre, but would certainly never suit us. Wilbur's casual, ragtime couplets, with their overtones of the Demon King in Victorian panto, are eminently speakable, and most of the time we forget the rhymes are there, except when their force can be used to make a specific point."

12 NIIKURA, TOSHIKAZU. *America She No Sekai Seiritsu Kara Gendai Made* [World of American Poetry; Establishment to Date]. Tokyo: Taikshukan, pp. 244-45.
    In Japanese. Comments on "Museum Piece." Says that Wilbur's poems contain emotions and complexity proper to poetry and are technically refined. Finds that the subject matter is diverse. Finds the subject of "Museum Piece" interesting because of the contrast between the sleeping guard and the lively dancers in Degas's painting. Notes the humor present in the fact that Degas, who loved beauty and vitality, bought an El Greco, whose religious paintings are like dead corpses, to

hang his pants on at night – a superb ending. Cites Leslie Fiedler's review of the poem (1964.6).

13 *Publishers Weekly.* Review of *New England Reflections, 1882-1907: Photographs by the Howes Brothers.* 27 February, p. 147.

Comments on the foreword to this book. "Richard Wilbur's stunning foreword to this collection of 200 photos (gleaned from more than 20,000 surviving glass negatives) transports the reader to Western Massachusetts in the late 19th century, when the Howeses took to the road to photograph families, school classes, workers in factories, fields, shops."

14 "Richard Wilbur." In *Longman Companion to Twentieth Century Literature.* 3d ed. Burnt Mill, Harlow (Essex, England): Longman House, pp. 572-73.

Notes that "as a poet [Wilbur] was influenced by the Modernists but preferred stricter verse forms because he felt them a stimulus rather than a deterrent. With his verbal sensitivity and aesthetic sense he was able to stand far above the more formless expressions of everyday statement that free verse could encourage." Lists *The Beautiful Changes* (1947), *Poems of Richard Wlbur* (1963), *Candide,* and *The Mind-Reader* (1976).

15 ROSS-BRYANT, LYNN. *Theodore Roethke: Poetry of the Earth . . . Poet of the Spirit.* Port Washington, N.Y.: Kennikat Press, pp. 14-15, 19, 190-91.

Sees allegiances between Roethke's desire to "overcome the gap between things and their significances while paying close attention to both" and Wilbur's similar endeavor ("Seed Leaves," "A World without Objects Is a Sensible Emptiness," "Objects"). Roethke and Wilbur also share a "sense of reality that can be described as magical . . . mysterious and nonrational" ("Objects"). Notes Roethke's and Wilbur's ability to make the boundaries between "reality and dream, depth and transcendence" dissolve ("Thyme Flowering among Rocks").

16 SANDERS, CHARLES. "Wine, Woman, and Wilbur: 'A Voice from Under the Table.'" *Notes on Modern American Literature* 5, no. 4 (Fall): item 27.

Analyzes "A Voice from Under the Table." Quotes Abbé de Vallemont, Pierre de Lorrain, who says the dead can return temporarily and demonstrates by giving instructions on how to make a rose seed reappear as a rose when it is heated in sunlight. Allows that this poem "may be that of the sot to wine and woman, but it is also that of the seer-sorcerer of song. Even though he is 'a horizontal monument to patience,' with 'helpless head upon this sodden floor,' we have to remember that 'raps' and voices from under the table may signify another kind of 'headlines': the séance of the necromancer-poet. On seeing possibly 'real' 'rose carafes conceive the sun,' his own mental vessel becomes as warmly pungent and pregnant: 'My thirst conceives a fierier universe.'" Suggests that the phosphorus ("bringer of light") swallowed by the speaker produces a glow, but it glows in the dark. Thus, the speaker is a kind of martyr who gladly says, "I shall be back for more."

17 WAI, ISABELLA KWOK-MAN. "'Perfection in a Finite Task': Theme and Form in Representative Poems of Richard Wilbur." Ph.D. dissertation, McMaster University, Hamilton, Ont. 251 pp.
     Investigates Wilbur's idea of happiness from five different angles: (1) "true 'happiness' can only be gained through self-exposure to life's endless contradictions and through maintaining a balance between the artist's conflicting responses to these contradictions"; (2) "a poet's vision is to discover the cosmic harmony beneath the apparently fragmented world and, as in a kaleidoscope, to arrange a design which holds the disparate images together"; (3) "Wilbur's mundane commitments counterbalance his spiritual yearnings," resulting in a "dialectic format of ideas" in his work; (4) the artist "gives reality form and pattern"; (5) "the qualities that Wilbur cherishes in poetry – grace and lightness, for instance – are qualities essential to a purposeful existence." See *Dissertation Abstracts International* 42:1166A.

18 ZARANKA, WILLIAM, ed. *The Brand-X Anthology of Poetry*. Cambridge (Mass.): Apple-Wood Books, pp. 306-307.
     Contains two parodies of Richard Wilbur: "Occam's Razor Starts in Massachusetts" by Edward Pygge and "Conceit Upon the Feet" by William Zaranka.

1982

1 BARTEL, ROLAND. "Icarus Poems Since Auden's 'Musee Des Beaux Arts.'" *Classical and Modern Literature: A Quarterly* 2, no. 2 (Winter):95-99.
     Says Wilbur "presents Icarus ("Icarium Mare") as a messenger from the 'undimmed air' to those of us who 'grope like muddled fish.'" He sees the spirit of Icarus exemplified in the lives of those who transcend ordinary limitations by using the fragments of light available to them rather than waiting for spectacular journeys to the sun.

2 DWYER, DOROTHY KURRE. "'Achievements of Place': The Poetry of Richard Wilbur." Ph.D. dissertation, Washington University, 249 pp.

Organizes work in three parts. "Poetic Impulses" examines the four phenomena Wilbur lists as of interest to poets: "the objective fact, the inner experience, the literary past, and the present culture." Suggests that "Wilbur's primary loyalty is to the objective fact, but his best poetry balances between the various extremes." "Persistent Concerns" investigates "ideas which preoccupy him." Sees his poems as an attempt "to reposition himself in and repossess creation. They are 'achievements of place – a place being a fusion of human and natural order, and a peculiar window on the whole.'" "Poetic Vitality" examines Wilbur's "specifically poetic accomplishments: . . . intelligibility, control, assurance and ease, appeals to the whole person, delight in language, variety and elegance, . . . technical and formal elements." Concludes with close readings of "A Fire Truck" and "The Fourth of July" to illustrate Wilbur's concern with "the relationship between thought and action." See *Dissertation Abstracts International* 43:1543A.

3 FREED, WALTER B., Jr. "Richard Wilbur." *Critical Survey of Poetry: English Language Series*. Edited by Frank Magill, vol. 7. Englewood Cliffs, N. J.: Salem Press, pp. 3091-3100.

Contains sections titled Principal Collections (poetry), Other Literary Forms (translations), Editorial Work, Literary Criticism, Achievements (poetic), Biography, and Analysis. Remarks that "Wilbur achieves brilliantly what he sees poetry doing best: compacting experience into language that excites the intellect and vivifies the imagination." Suggests that Wilbur's keen interest in the tension between form and thought, between the known and unknown, between inner and outer lives, between reason and imagination mark him as a poet uniquely aware of the human condition ("Lamarck Elaborated," "Another Voice"). Comments that "Wilbur's poetry contains many examples of contentment, complete happiness, and mature acknowledgement of human limitations" ("Running," "Patriot's Day," "Dodwells Road"). "The voice that Wilbur assumes . . . is often that of a person discovering or attempting to discover something unknown or removed" ("A Hole in the Floor"). Finds that Wilbur likes to work with opposites ("Advice to a Prophet," "Gemini," "Someone Talking to Himself," "The Writer," *Opposites*, dialogue poems, "Water Walker," "A Christmas Hymn"). Suggests that some poems "combine . . . the experience of living life fully and the experience of participating at its edges" ("Boy at the Window," "The Pardon"). Sees "Walking to Sleep" and "The Mind-Reader" as poems which "invite . . . [the] audience to explore the frontier, the wilderness of conscious thought and subconscious ruminating." Concludes that Wilbur's work "focuses on the enlightenment of the human spirit, but never denies the darker impulses or fears which are brought to bear when doubt, resignation, or apathy appear as challenges to the harmony that civilized man strives to achieve." Appends Major Publications other than poetry (plays) and Bibliography (secondary).

4 GILMAN, RICHARD. Review of *The Learned Ladies*. *Nation*, 21 August, pp. 155-56.

Performance review of *The Learned Ladies*. Says "the best thing about the Roundabout Theater's production of *The Learned Ladies* is Richard Wilbur's new verse translation."

5 HART, JAMES D. "Richard Wilbur." In *The Oxford Companion to American Literature*. New York: Oxford University Press, p. 826.

Lists Wilbur's educational experience, his major works, beginning with *The Beautiful Changes* (1947) and concluding with *Andromache* (1982). Says "his cultivated and formal poetry, although influenced by the French Symbolists, Marianne Moore, and Wallace Stevens, among others, is highly original . . . [and often] classic, urbane, . . . witty, and always intellectual."

6 HUGHES, CATHARINE. "Summer Fun." *America*, 25 September, p. 155.

Performance review of *The Learned Ladies* staged by the Roundabout Theater Company in New York. Characterizes Wilbur's translation as "on a par with those he has previously rendered for *Tartuffe*, *The Misanthrope* and *The School for Wives*. Indeed, it is arguably the best aspect of a production that is not without other ample rewards. . . . It is felicitous, funny and apt, a pleasure to the ear and well-nigh perfect opportunity for the player."

7 HULSE, MICHAEL. "Richard Wilbur the Passionate Craftsman." *Quarto* (London) no. 30/31 (July-August):14-15.

Notes that obtaining a copy of any of Richard Wilbur's collections of poems, including Faber's *Poems 1943-1956*, is impossible. Says Wilbur is "disappearing." Places the blame on the "fickle minority of trendy or academic skinflints that passes for a serious reading public." Says such a lack of response to Wilbur is "incomprehensible because there is so much in Wilbur. He perceives beauty; he perceives delusion; he perceives truths, and the way one truth qualifies others; he perceives the constant change in things; and he perceives (this is the excellence that strengthens all his other perceptions) that terrible irony that renders a truth untrue the moment it is spoken, that renders change static and the beautiful unremarkable as soon as their perception is transferred into language." Grants that sometimes Wilbur is bad; that is, "pompous or stuffy." Argues that Wilbur's poetry is relevant to twentieth-century society: "Wilbur's words are never dead on the printed page; those who complain they are pinned butterflies have probably never tried reading the poems aloud." Places Wilbur in a line of poets from Hopkins to A. D. Hope, early Donald Davie, Marianne Moore, Auden or Frost. Says it is a "disciplined, even austere tradition to which Wilbur belongs, though it is no less human for that. It is the tradition of the passionate craftsman."

Asserts that the "quintessence of Wilburism is to ironise precisely . . . white-hot passion in the act of translating it into language." Notes that "some of Wilbur's best poems deal more or less directly with the problem of artistry and the artist, and the created artifact ("My Father Paints the Summer," "Juggler"). Suggests that "Wilbur distances himself from . . . flight [into the unreal world of art] by seeing his own role as that of *commentator on* the world's dreams, *not creator of* dream worlds."

Suggests that Wilbur has "been ignored almost systematically." Thinks the fifties was his decade and that Alvarez's Penguin anthology *The New Poetry* (1962), which ignored Wilbur completely, "was partly identifying, partly shaping taste." Adds that another reason for the public's lack of interest in Wilbur is the poorer quality of his later work. Argues for a pluralism in literature which would make room for a wide diversity of poetic endeavor and urges Faber to reissue a selection of poems.

8 HUMPHRIES, CAMILLA. "Making Things Inviting for the Literary Muse." *Daily Hampshire Gazette* (Northampton, Mass.), 22 September, p. 24.

Reports on the writing habits of several local writers, including Richard Wilbur.

9 LEITHAUSER, BRAD. "Reconsideration: Richard Wilbur, America's Master of Formal Verse." *New Republic*, 24 March, pp. 28-31.

Concurs that "Richard Wilbur is almost unanimously acknowledged to be one of the few living American masters of formal verse. Such unanimity is unusual in a world as diffuse and factional as that of contemporary poetry, and it bespeaks perhaps not only a deserved admiration but also a suspicion that the role is not widely coveted." Observes that critics have too often been willing to "scant the contents for the package or equate a 'conservative' use of old forms with a conservative or narrow outlook." Objects to this narrow assessment of a "man of large, lively and mettlesome intellect." Finds that "the major tension in his work is the contrary, dissociative tug beween the ideal and the actual, and the shuttling role the mind must play between the spirit's hunger for visions and the body's physical hungers." Admires the brilliance of poems in *The Beautiful Changes* (1947) and *Ceremony* (1950), but asserts that with *Things of This World* (1956), Wilbur's "distinctive voiceprint had emerged." Lists characteristic traits of Wilbur's work such as "breadth of language," "an elevated grandness of both subject and style," "formal elevated lightness" kept in bounds by a finely tuned ear and use of the colloquial, and a "sense of proportionality," that is, control of the poem. Admits that Wilbur has perhaps lost his ability to surprise the reader and attempts at times to "be too articulate about what he confesses is ultimately ineffable." Concludes, nevertheless, that "praise should be sung in full voice" for a poet whose work "shows little sign of depletion." Reprinted as "Richard Wilbur at Sixty": 1983.18.

10 LITTLER, F. "Wilbur's 'Love Calls Us to the Things of This World.'" *Explicator* 40, no. 3 (Spring):53-55.
    Analyzes "Love Calls Us to the Things of This World." Suggests that "the carefully expressed paradoxes of the last stanza of the poem are the key to the poem's theme. Wilbur presents an affecting version of the ideal world through his images of angelic laundry, but this world is evanescent, seen only for a moment under the light of false dawn. Though man desires and needs the world of spirit, he must yet descend to the body and accept it in 'bitter love' . . . because this is the world in which man has to live. In contrast to St. John's plea [1 John 2:15], to avoid the world and the things of it, Wilbur would have us accept them, though we should also retain the capacity to perceive the world of the spirit in the everyday."

11 MICHELSON, BRUCE. "Wilbur's Words." *Massachusetts Review* 23, no. 1 (Spring):97-111.
    Contends that "Wilbur's use of language – especially his famous word-play – has everything to do with his most urgent reasons for being an artist, that it is as daring an experiment in poetry as we have seen in the past three decades. Wilbur's language . . . is an attempt to use words as magical, incantatory, creative forces. His famous word-play is in fact the very essence of his imaginative transcendence of the world, as well as his reconciliation *with* the world. If we cannot understand this, the paramount seriousness of Wilbur's word-play, we cannot appreciate what Wilbur is doing." Argues that "Wilbur's word-play . . .

expresses his conception of our ontological condition, his role as a careful, insightful nature poet, and his idea of the recreative power of language itself." Cites "The Regatta" (1947) as an early example of serious word-play. Wilbur creates the moment of imaginative vision, and immediately recognizes "the method of the poem itself, of the 'trick' of the poet's language, the 'trick' of making a regatta on a windy afternoon work as a metaphor for the human condition and the grounds of human hope." Sees word-play in "Year's End" (1949) as having "a new task to perform. The object now is to transform 'ends of time' into events of both destruction *and* conservation, and to suggest in that duality something of the mystery of eternity." Finds that "Love Calls Us to the Things of This World" (1956) "marks an important development in Wilbur's relationship with words, for here he succeeds as never before in making his word-play look easy. . . . Wilbur's theme in 'Love Calls Us' is not a new one in his poetry; what *is* new is the grace with which he uses his rich language, a grace which shows that he has reconciled the play of words with that spontaneity and excitement which sacred play, ceremony, ought to have." In "In a Churchyard" (1969) the "word-games are now more difficult and less obtrusive, the flow of one loaded utterance into the next being not rapid and easy as before, but deliberate, hindered, slow." Admits that "reverberating words turn up " less frequently in "The Mind-Reader" (1976), but when they do, "they reveal the mind itself and its fatal mistake. . . . Word-play in the poem is meant as homage to a powerful consciousness gone wrong . . . and used to illustrate isolation from life." Concludes that "living as we do in a time which confounds crudeness with passion, drabness with authenticity, and coherent, thoughtful art with superficiality, we can easily forget that artifice and intensity can have much to do with one another." Reprinted: 1983.18.

12 REIBETANZ, JOHN. "What Love Sees: Poetry and Vision in Richard Wilbur." *Modern Poetry Studies* 11, no. 1-2 (Spring-Autumn):60-85.
    Explores the course of Wilbur's poetic "evolution by following the progress of his concern with the process of seeing . . . devoting considerable initial attention to his early poems, for by showing so clearly the basic presuppositions of his art, they provide a basis for comprehending more recent work as it develops and modifies these presuppositions." Establishes the poet's basic beliefs: "that love is more powerful than hatred; that nature is a source of values and of reassurance; and that there is a strong creative urge in both man and nature which constantly seeks and finds expression in images of grace and plenitude." Finds two distinguishing differences between Wallace Stevens and Wilbur's vision in *The Beautiful Changes*: (1) the poems

are not about facts but about "what man's minds can make of them"; (2) "Wilbur views the present moment through the lens of tradition." Though these poems are hard to see as a "direct encounter with the present," they are evidence of "personal needs and creative principles that are at the heart of Wilbur's later poetic triumph." Asserts that in his first two books, Wilbur is "aspiring toward something lacking in the visionary world of pure imagination, and the imperatives show both that he feels its necessity strongly and that he realizes he has yet to achieve it." Allows that "as Wilbur seems to have realized, his task was not the ultimately futile one of trying to efface his ideas – his vision – in order to express things more directly; rather, he needed to bring the vision more into play with things, widen it so that it could comprehend more of the world around him." Two early poems about "birds are unusual . . . because they give Wilbur's love and his vision a solid base in the world of 'raw event'" ("In a Bird Sanctuary," "Still, Citizen Sparrow").

Sees a "new interpenetration of imaginative vision and perceptual reality in 'Love Calls Us to the Things of This World.'" Suggests that Wilbur has "found that, insofar as he is a poet, he can satisfy his need for love by training his imaginative vision on the world: he can bring the whole man into the poetic experience, and needn't retreat into a closed garden in order to exercise this way of seeing." Rounds out discussion by demonstrating that "one of the greatest pleasures offered by Wilbur's more recent poetry has been the gradual realization and fulfillment of this wider sense of community [elsewhere described as a shared vision]. Cites the influence of Poe, Augustine, and Thomas Traherne on Wilbur's formation of his poetics. Traces the growth of Wilbur's vision through the rest of his work, concluding with "The Eye" which he describes as "Wilbur's most explicit framing of the relationship between love and vision that has proved essential to his mature poetic achievement." The poem "moves us squarely from Eliot's sad formula for detachment to Wilbur's own postulate for involvement and happiness."

13 Review of *The Learned Ladies*. *Variety*, 28 July, p. 76.

Performance review of *The Learned Ladies* produced at the Roundabout Theater in New York. Comments "A solid translation in rhymed couplets by Richard Wilbur, and an agreeable cast, turns the evenning [*sic*] which begins a trifle slowly, into a joyous occasion."

14 ROBINSON, EDWARD. "Professionalism and the Religous Imagination." *Religious Education* 77:628-41.

Suggests that part of religious education should involve the training of the imagination. "If we are really going to open ourselves up . . . to those infinite possibilities that life is continually confronting us with, we need to use all the imagination we have got. And more." Asserts that "whatever else art and poetry may or may not be, at the heart of them is the ability of the artist, the poet, to enter so deeply into his or her own personal experience that the essential truth, the inner reality of it, can then be expressed in a form that will be valid not just for him or herself but for all of us." Cites Wilbur's "Two Voices in a Meadow" as an example of how poems enrich a person's experience. Argues that one must "recognize the vital part that art and poetry have to play in any true communication of spiritual realities."

15 SIMON, JOHN. Review of *The Learned Ladies*. *New York*, 26 July, p. 43.

Performance review of *The Learned Ladies* produced at the Roundabout Theater in New York. Calls Wilbur's translation "a marvel . . . more than which no poet dramatist could dream about." Contends that "if anything, the translation is more gnomic and lapidary than the original." Criticizes a line of the play where Martine says "I wouldn't talk your *jargon* if I could." Says "something like *lingo* would be more within her ken."

16 STAMELMAN, RICHARD. "The Art of the Void–Giacometti, Alberto and the Poets of Ephemere." *Esprit Createur* 22, no. 4 (Winter):15-25.

Comments that Giacometti tried all of his life to represent absence palpably. He gives "form and density to absence itself." French poets such as Yves Bonnefoy, Jacques Dupin, and André Du Bouchet have been interested in his work because his sculptures represent "the presence of death and disintegration in the world and . . . testify to having themselves been touched directly by the finitude of being." Says Giacometti's figures always stand very close to the void which is always present in his work, yet "the impossible reality Giacometti and Bonnefoy both seek . . . is an instant of furtive and unpossessable plenitude." Affirms that both the poets and the artist found it was impossible to capture reality. As soon as it became a presence, it was pressed into nothing by the terrible pressure of the surrounding absence. Introduces a part of Richard Wilbur's "Giacometti" by saying, "The result is a poem as minimal and vulnerable to extinction as a Giacometti statue, a representation 'shaved and scraped / Of all but being there.'"

17 STEEGMULLER, FRANCIS. "'I Love You Still', Said Hermione."
New York Times Book Review, 26 December, pp. 6-7.

Reviews *Andromache*. Concedes that in translating this difficult
French playwright Wilbur has met "the challenge courageously and
well, and it will be interesting to see whether American audiences rise
to this unfamiliar, grand occasion." Questions, "Was the infinite
attention markedly accorded by Racine to every word of his verse – it is
one of his supreme characteristics – perhaps among Mr. Wilbur's
reasons for choosing to translate a Racine play?" and "Has he begun
with this early play to give us hope of more?" Says "Mr Wilbur's
felicities are many; I could object to few of his renderings, and for
fewer still could I propose improvements."

1983

1 BARNES, CLIVE. "*Misanthrope* Witty & Clear in Any Language."
New York Post, 28 January.

Performance review of a revival of *The Misanthrope*. Says that
"last night at the Circle in the Square, there opened a brilliant
production of *The Misanthrope* that was pellucid in its language, clear
in its sentiment and even spontaneous in its witty rhyming. It had the
verbal gloss of an original.

"We owe all this to Molière's remarkable translator Richard
Wilbur, who by some process, which surely has as much to do with
alchemy as literature, can take Molière's plays and transform them into
living English, while preserving the original sense and sensibility."
Reprinted in *New York Theatre Critics Reviews 1983*: p. 387.

2 BEAUFORT, JOHN. "Molière's Comic Genius at Work on Broadway:
The Misanthrope." *Christian Science Monitor*, 2 February.

Performance review of revival of *The Misanthrope* produced at
the Broadway Circle in the Square, New York City. Comments that the
cast "treats Richard Wilbur's felicitous verse translation with all of the
verve and grace it merits." Quotes from Wilbur's introduction to the
play, implying that not only is the actual language of the play in
excellent taste, but also Wilbur has caught the essential meaning.
Reprinted in *New York Theatre Critics Reviews 1983*: p. 388.

3 BRESLIN, JAMES E. B. "The New Rear Guard." In *From Modern to
Contemporary: American Poetry 1945-1965*. Chicago: University of
Chicago Press, pp. 23-52, passim.

Uses Wilbur as the outstanding example of the typical poet of the
fifties. Explains that "a cautious conservatism made these younger

poets [of the fifties] different from the rebels who had preceded them; it made them the new rear guard." Charges that Wilbur accepted the label of "New Formalist," but in doing so, he "left no ground to stand on. [Wilbur] affirms the revival of traditional forms but, of course, he does not want to repudiate the moderns so he tips his hat in the direction of experimentalism, which he then deftly redefines as–traditionalism. His statement dramatically reveals how the poets of Wilbur's low-profile generation tried to counter strength with skill, energy with expertise." Cites Allen Tate's perception that meter was "an image of some moral order" as a theory fully accepted by the middle generation of poets. "What was crucial in the poetics of the 'new period' . . . was the assumption of a *tension* between form and content." Cites Wilbur's theory that "the difficulty of the form is a substitute for the difficulty" of direct perception as "a curious version of the theory of 'imitative form.'" Says Wilbur "insists upon separating the formal and the temporal. . . . It was this conception of poetic form as autonomous, timeless, abstract, and therefore prior to its specific occasion–a form, moreover, that very likely will call attention to itself *as form* –that established authority in the late forties and early fifties."

Examines Wilbur's *The Beautiful Changes* for supporting evidence. Suggests Wilbur was "attracted by the New Criticism's poetics of tension and his secular and more playful verse sustains, rather than struggling to resolve, the contradictions of contemporary experience. . . . Wilbur really is at home in a world without absolutes." Cites several poems which substantiate this claim. Says Wilbur is "like the caddis fly in 'Water Walker' who knows both air and water but finally inhabits neither; he is a poet of beautiful changes, an elusive figure who can freely explore opposed perspectives because he is finally committed to neither. . . . By refusing such passionate and unequivocal commitment, Wilbur frees his imagination to make the circling, playful movements of his poems." Argues that "a Wilbur poem, then, becomes a verbal conjuring, a series of light, quick, beautiful changes, and its intricacy of form becomes both part of the feat and a reminder that the poem, while creating the illusionary presence of 'mastery,' remains a fictive construct." Concludes that "Wilbur writes like a man who is at home in a social and historical present which never enters his poetry. His poems occupy a *literary* space in which they carry on their quarrel with the symbolic figure of Poe. . . . The result is a poetry that seldom challenges its readers–or itself."

4 BRUSTEIN, RICHARD. *"The Misanthrope."* *America*, 19 February, pp. 22-23.

Performance review of a revival of *The Misanthrope* at Circle in the Square in New York City. Notes that "the show enjoys a distinct advantage in Richard Wilbur's clear, witty, pungent rendering which, like the best translations, is a supreme work of art on its own."

5 DEVLIN, D. Review of Wilbur's translations of four Molière plays. *Drama* no. 147:52-53.

Reviews Molière plays. Calls these translations "excellent."

6 GILMAN, RICHARD. Review of *The Misanthrope*. *Nation*, 19 February, pp. 217-18.

Performance review of a revival of *The Misanthrope* produced at the Circle in the Square, New York City. Affirms that Wilbur's "lovely, witty rendering survives. Like his other Molière translations, this *Misanthrope* is a fusion of accuracy and justifiable liberties, the latter taken in the interest of lively contemporariness. Among the rhymes I jotted down (getting the rhymes right is one true test of a translator's success) were 'Alceste' and 'second-best' and 'I'm not so interested as you suppose / in Célimène's discarded gigolos.'"

7 GUTCHESS, ELIZABETH DENVER. "Four Translators 'After' Pound: Studies of Richard Wilbur, Robert Lowell, Robert Bly, and Galway Kinnell." Ph.D. dissertation, University of Notre Dame, 153 pp.

Suggests that Ezra Pound's "work in translation might have issued some new kinds of poetic license to later American translation. But the thing which seems more sturdily influential in his work is its strong stand for accuracies of all kinds. . . . So his influence actually ramifies, and every specific, technical legacy exists within some deeply individualistic or deliberate dissociation from his work as a whole."

Asserts that "'after' Pound, Wilbur sees and uses lyric translation as good exercise in exact articulation. But unlike Pound's truly pragmatic assumption of foreign *personae*, Wilbur's seem to speak for themselves, even at variance with his own themes, in some glorious sense of play, like philosophical versions of his riddles." See *Dissertation Abstracts International* 44:752A.

8 HAGSTROM, JACK W. C. "The Role of Course Descriptions in Bibliographies of Twentieth Century Authors (With specific references to Richard Wilbur)." *Notes on Contemporary Literature* 13, no. 3 (May):8.

Contends that course descriptions should be included as part of the canon of twentieth-century authors such as Richard Wilbur. "No claim can be made for their importance *per se* compared with the first appearance of a poem or a piece of fiction; however, a valid claim can and must be made for their inclusion in a bibliography that attempts to represent a complete compilation of an author's work."

9 HUGHES, CATHARINE. "A 'Bridge' Too Many." *America*, 30 April, p. 342.

Performance review of a revival of *The Misanthrope* produced at the Circle in the Square, New York City. Describes the play as Richard Wilbur's "splendid verse translation."

10 JACKSON, RICHARD, ed. "Richard Wilbur, 1979: The Mystery of Things That Are." In *Acts of Mind: Conversations with Contemporary Poets*. University, Ala.: University of Alabama Press, pp. 140-45.

Richard Wilbur comments on an apparent "metaphor system" in his poems that "distinguishes ownership as a passive and possession as an active, more imaginative mode of relation to the world": "I think one job poetry has to do today is to combat the neutrality of so much of our environment. The poet can be like the Aspen ["The Aspen and the Stream"], and the poem can be his exercise in taking possession, by observation and feeling and form, of some part of the world. The poem can help us embrace the world more intensely than we would do normally." Contends that "language for the poet is surely always a language of desire. . . . This reminds me of one of the early Yeats observations to the effect that it is the business of the poet to remember Eden." Responds to a question about "In a Churchyard" which talks about "Pooling the mystery of things that are" by saying, "I am very attracted to accurate description ["Thyme Flowering Among Rocks"]. . . . I think one effect of that kind of exhaustive description is to take you beyond the object you usually perceive. You go away from the object as you do in a metaphor, but you do so by going into it. You reveal a world that ordinarily lies beyond human perception and you imply a further beyond." Suggests that the best metaphors are those that surprise one with their "linkage, the interpenetration of things." Admits he likes very much to use a word with its present and past meaning. Objects when critics explain that "a poem means this or that. A poem is not a static thing but rather always a dramatic striving after some conclusion – not necessarily, I suppose, *the* truth, not necessarily a yes or no, but some kind of conclusion, some kind of concrete sounding of a subject. The striving is part of the truth itself." A poem's meaning cannot be permanently fixed.

Suggests that his concern with the dialectic between "seeing and creating, reality and vision" grows out of an interest in the five senses "and in the ranking of those senses, for example, in medieval theology.

There the eye is supreme, the most spiritual. And I have always been interested in the way certain poets rebel against the eye. . . . Among modern poets, I have always linked Williams and D.H. Lawrence as advocates of the lower senses. Charles Baudelaire is more visual, and this emphasis suggests a certain distance or detachment." Discusses "The Eye," "The Beacon," and "In Limbo." Says as far as "The Mind-Reader" "is a poem about the mind and its dealings with the world, it is about the poet. . . . I think of it being, more importantly, a poem about the mind of God. When one considers the agony of the mind reader, one thinks of the unimaginable tolerance with which the deity is willing to listen to us all, be aware of us all. There is an utter incapacity of the human mind to tolerate what God would tolerate."

11 JEROME, JUDSON. "Minor Masterpieces." *Writer's Digest*, March, pp. 62-64.

Contends that Richard Wilbur is the "greatest living American poet today." Though this claim may seem outrageous given the many fine poets now writing and given the fact that Wilbur has produced no "great work," he is nevertheless worthy of this title. Says that "great poetry somehow challenges the universe and strives mightily in ragged failure." Mentions "Two Voices in a Meadow" as an example of the "passive stasis" that seems to have come over the poets of Wilbur's generation. Argues for "major modes" in poetry: "if poets are ever to escape their stereotype as dilettantes, they will have to bite off and chew hunks of life as intractable as those novelists take into their great jaws." Comments that "most poets writing today could not write effectively in the longer forms because they can't write good metered verse." Concludes that "the problem is not that Wilbur lacks profundity. Rather that he *uses* profundity-as he does music, harmony, wit, rhetoric, and all other resources of language-as a kind of decoration in poems that back off and seem too modest to assert. Matter is there-but, as in a diplomatic dinner party, so swathed in manner that it is lost on the naked eye."

12 ____. "Poetry Notes." *Writer's Digest*, February, pp. 60-61, 71.

Analyzes Wilbur's "Advice to a Prophet." Says it "is a poem that will endure, though it is uncharacteristic of much of his work." Its loose measure, yet formal "tightness" add strength. Rhyming adds power also, and the language is more than mere decor. The poem describes accurately what the world would be like after a nuclear war. "This poem is gentle, quiet, caring-proof that rhetoric need not be associated only with strident harangues." Affirms that Wilbur avoids the sentimental in favor of a hard look at where man would be without nature. Insists that Wilbur "is uniquely qualified among modern poets . . . to meet the challenges of longer forms, such as he has not yet tried."

13 KISSELL, HOWARD. *The Misanthrope. Women's Wear Daily*, 2 February.

Reviews a revival of *The Misanthrope* at Circle in the Square, New York City. Mentions reprint of this play in *Four Comedies*. Says that "few events in the theater in recent years have provided as much cause for rejoicing as Richard Wilbur's translations of Molière's plays. They reflect a sensitive ear for the nuances of Molière's comedy and language, which one would expect of a poet as accomplished as Wilbur. What is unexpected is Wilbur's theatrical acumen. The works never seem like translations. They never require you to 'make allowances.' They seem as fresh and immediate as if they had been written yesterday . . . . In some ways his translation of *The Misanthrope* is the most impressive of the four recently published in a handsome edition by Harcourt, Brace, because it is Molière's most difficult play." Reprinted in *New York Theatre Critics Reviews 1983*: p. 388.

14 KUNITZ, STANLEY. "Stanley Kunitz on Richard Wilbur." *Envoy*, no. 43:2.

On December 14, 1983, Stanley Kunitz introduced Richard Wilbur with the following address. The reading, held at the Solomon R. Guggenheim Museum, was part of the *Ten Poetry Readings 1982-83* series sponsored by the Academy of American Poets.

Observes that "what Wilbur stands for in my mind is a certain grace of spirit, inseparable from the formal beauty of his verse." Notes that Wilbur "has been a staunch defender" of the limits necessary for good art. Quotes Wilbur's remarks about the artist imposing or discovering a pattern in the world and the idea that "limitation makes for power: the strength of the genie comes of his being confined in a bottle." Says "one of the genies [Wilbur] has let out of the bottle is the spirit of Molière." Concludes by saying that "Wilbur's mind has a cleansing sanity and wit that make it possible for him to view the world, despite its burden of suffering and tragedy and evil, as a place of fortuitous joys and blessings and miracles, not the least of which is the gift of life itself. And he has taught us, by precept, that life is not, as some would have us believe, for the sake of poetry, but that poetry is for the sake of life. And he has conducted himself, in his work as in his days, with honor and decency and dignity. For which he deserves our applause."

15 RICH, FRANK. "Stage: *Misanthrope* at Circle in the Square." *New York Times*, 28 January.

Performance review of the revival of *The Misanthrope* produced by Circle in the Square, New York City. Mentions "Richard Wilbur's great rhymed-verse translation" in passing. Reprinted in *New York Theatre Critics Reviews 1983*: p. 386.

16 "Richard Wilbur." In *Oxford Companion to American Literature*. 5th ed. New York: Oxford University Press, p. 826.

Includes biographical and poetic summaries and lists *Walking to Sleep* (1969), *The Mind-Reader* (1976), and *Seven Poems* (1981).

17 ROMANO, A. C. "Arthur Koestler and Richard Wilbur: The Sage and the Poet—on Human Creativity." *Journal of Creative Behavior* 17, no. 2:125-30.

Finds that Richard Wilbur's ideas about the creative imagination closely follow Arthur Koestler's theories of creativity: "the maker and the seer share a common vision." Says "Mind" "is a masterful restatement and realization of Koestler's (1964) major thesis about the creative act. . . . Wilbur's 'graceful error' is Koestler's bisociative act, and the correction of the cave is the intersection of two matrices." Finds that "A Hole in the Floor" "explores the realm of the unconscious, the working of which Koestler terms 'thinking aside' or 'underground games.'" Quotes Koestler as saying, "Language can become a screen which stands between the thinker and reality. This is the reason why true creativity often starts where language ends." It is also the action Wilbur describes in his poem. Likens the "buried strangeness" of Wilbur's poem to "the working of the unconscious . . . the nourishment for the conscious mind, the source to enliven the plants of rationality with wilder blooms."

18 SALINGER, WENDY, ed. Introduction to *Richard Wilbur's Creation*. Ann Arbor: University of Michigan Press, pp. 1-21.

Suggests that the "ideal for the new generation of poets [poets of the fifties] was a virtuoso craftsmanship. . . . Their instincts were toward preservation, perpetuation: the entrenchments of tradition, the securities of the academic job, the grant, and so forth." Admits that Wilbur accepted these values too. Contends that "the constraint of craftsmanship in Wilbur's case produced some dazzling effects." Positions Wilbur in a generation which inherited the ideas of William Carlos Williams and Walt Whitman, yet finds that "for Wilbur *things* are irrepressibly suggestive—have 'legerity'. . . . While Wilbur holds the imagist reverence for things . . . Williams' objects have a bare simplicity to which Wilbur can't confine himself – because his deepest instincts are metaphoric." Finds that "mind" is a problem for Wilbur: "one cannot render *things* totally free from *ideas*. . . . The resolution of these dichotomies has always been an implicit part of Wilbur's vision even as he has struggled with them." Notes that "in Wilbur's later poetry there is a growing directness, a simplicity of tone which, I think, is the voice of this reconciliation of the pull of things with their spiritual/intellectual suggestiveness."

Observes that Wilbur's voice and themes have not been fashionable for the last several decades, yet his "reverence for life," his complex awareness of good and evil, beauty and love, and his fundamentally "religious" stance, make him a "poet of serious, contemporary concerns." Defends Wilbur as major poet who fulfills Auden's five requirements, especially the idea that a major poet must grow. Suggests that Wilbur has grown by "pursuing the *difficulty*" in his work. Concludes by discussing Wilbur's "linguistic genius . . . because it is unrivaled." Asserts that "our sense of language and our sense of reality are inextricably bound. This is the great mystery and joy of writing. This mystery has always been at the heart of Richard Wilbur's work. [Wilbur] writes *about* it as well as *from* it." Suggests that "it is easy to see . . . that the word-and-world correspondence in Wilbur's poetry is a manifestation of the intimate connection he sees between self and world. . . . We see that *he* is not the world, but his medium is the articulation of his relation *to* the world." Concludes that Wilbur "has always been praised for his virtuosity but too often praised and *dismissed* because of it. This is a mistake. In the best poems, Wilbur's virtuosity is one with his vision. It is a function of intimacy, not formalism." Includes a bibliography of works by and about Richard Wilbur.

Reprints of 1947.1; 1948.5; 1948.9; 1951.1; 1951.8; 1951.10; 1951.15; 1952.5; 1956.6; 1956.15; 1956.23; 1956.24; 1962.8; 1962.12; 1962.13; 1962.14; 1963.13; 1967.4; 1967.11; 1969.1; 1969.18; 1970.2; 1971.3; 1971.4; 1971.11; 1972.4; 1973.10; 1975.9; 1975.10; 1976.11; 1977.5; 1977.8; 1977.21; 1977.22; 1979.7; 1980.7; 1982.9; 1982.11.

19 SHAFARZEK, SUSAN. *Library Journal*, 15 December, p. 2301.
Reviews *The Whale and Other Uncollected Translations*. Says that this book "is a must buy."

20 VERNER-CARLSSON, JAN, ed. "Richard Wilbur." In *USA Poesi*. Göteborg, Sweden: Forlegat Café Existens, p. 839.

In Swedish. Contains a brief statement regarding Wilbur's poetic achievements and a short bibliography of works through *The Mind-Reader* (1976).

21 WATT, DOUGLAS. "A Mild *Misanthrope*." *Daily News*, 28 January.
Performance review of a revival of *The Misanthrope* at the Circle in the Square, New York City. Says *The Misanthrope*, "which opened last evening, is hardly scintillating Molière. But it is good to hear once more Wilbur's excellent verse translation after having last listened, almost a decade ago, to Alec McCowen and Diana Rigg grapple with Tony Harrison's later version in that updated 'Gaullist' presentation. . . . A halfway decent *Misanthrope* is better than none at all, and it is impossible not to take satisfaction in Bedford's vigorous, incisive performance and in Wilbur's felicitous translation." Reprinted in *New York Theatre Critics Reviews 1983*: p. 386.

22 WILLIAMS, PAUL O. "Richard Wilbur: Poet of Order and Detachment." *Christian Science Monitor*, 12 January, p. 20-21.
Analyzes several poems as a means of judging Wilbur's worth as a poet. Assesses Wilbur's achievements: "in a time of prevalent free verse, often wispy in form and shattered in semantic content, Wilbur has persisted in writing in fairly traditional verse forms. But he has made his voice distinct by its intensity and virtuosity." Sees the intensity in the first stanza of "The Beautiful Changes" where the combination of "traditional and recent techniques" and the "intricate music" of internal rhymes and alliteration create a pattern of echoes. Finds a "triple pun on the word 'shade'" an example of Wilbur's "intellectual virtuosity." Mentions "Junk" and "Juggler" as other examples. Finds that "for Wilbur, experience gains order through thought and imagination, which can alter the appearance of the rockiest barriers ("Mind"). . . . The 'correction' is often a means of managing one's life through perceptions of order, not constructing a philosophy." Concludes that "Wilbur's warmth also infuses his work. He is a poet on the side of man."

23 "Writers and Wrongs: W. D. Snodgrass, Richard Wilbur, and Aidan C. Mathews in Conversation." *Crane Bag* 7, no. 1:122-26.
Mathews interviews Snodgrass and Wilbur. On political poems, Wilbur says "he can perceive injustice, and react to it; but my sense of it is now more theological than political." He objects to the "self-indulgence" of many militant movements. Grants that "protest poetry becomes wearisome when it sounds like football rally chants, a ra-ra for the home-side. But political poetry, at its best, is strong and

delicate. The model might be Yeats's 'Easter 1916,' a long-delayed and deliberately problematical piece." Wilbur compares his situation with the Russian poets who risk much to tell truth: "Over here, we find it easy to believe – as I firmly do – in a transcendental realm that requires and rewards courage. Over there, it's harder to answer the door."

On the loss of religious faith among poets Wilbur says, "As a fairly orthodox Christian, I'm interested in the relations between faith – isn't belief rather different? – and the imagination. It seems to me that it would be impossible to accomplish today what George Herbert achieved in his day: to house the entirety of one's being in this world within the diction and doctrine of one's faith, to accommodate everything inside one's experience of faith." In answer to the question, "Isn't faith more an amorous vacuum than a solid outpost?" Wilbur replies, "Perhaps so. I tend to think of faith as a proper response. . . . I care about ebullience in doing. My poetry can't be codified, it doesn't arise from an axiomatic set. I want simply to celebrate the radical joyousness of this world." Rejecting the notion that the "apostolic zeal of the ideologue or the humanitarian . . . is a working substitute," Wilbur suggests that "it may help to realise that one is asked to celebrate the world, not to verify it. The world is sufficient before I ever trouble myself to say so. It's not raw material waiting for the artistic kiss of life to revive it. . . . But for me the good poem is also – even always – a way of stating the unbearable in a bearable manner: language heightened toward exactitude, speech made honest."

On the role of the poet in his poems, Wilbur concludes that "When the Spirit moves you, you tend not to talk about it or to atomise it. You speak out of it gladly. You speak the world. And you enter into union with it. The poem solemnises that union."

1984

1 BLAKE, PATRICIA. "'Couriers of the Human Spirit': Translators Give New Life to Foreign Literature." *Time*, 19 November, pp. 118, 120, 122, 126-27, passim.

Reviews *The Mind-Reader: New Poems*. Suggests that interest in translation in the United States has risen dramatically in recent years. Lists several prominent writers who have translated prominent novels. Asserts that "perhaps the most successful translations by a major American poet are Richard Wilbur's renditions of Molière."

2 DILLON, DAVID. "The Image and the Object: An Interview with Richard Wilbur." In *American Poetry Observed: Poets on Their Work*. Chicago: University of Illinois Press, pp. 285-95.

Reprint of 1973.3.

3 ECONOMOU, GEORGE. "Pelagic Wanderings." *American Book Review* 7, no. 1 (November-December):20.

Reviews *The Whale and Other Uncollected Translations*. Criticizes Wilbur for putting together a collection "whose contents are as diverse and attenuated as this one's." Suggests that "Wilbur does not show much sympathy for the text from the *Middle English Bestiary* that provides his book's title when he edits out four key moralizing verses from the poem's *Significacio*. Such liberties may be taken, it appears, with an anonymous medieval Christian poem but not with a contemporary poem like Brodsky's 'Six Years Later,' whose wooden and wordy version here presumably keeps good faith with its original." Calls Wilbur's translation of "A Song" by Vinícium de Moraes "riveting and startling beauty."

4 FJELDE, ROLF. "Lost in Translation." *Theatre Communications* 6, no. 2 (February):1-4.

Applauds the apparent "signs of change in American theatre," indicating that instead of using the old two-step method of translating a play into flat prose and then asking a writer to prepare a stageable script, more theater companies are using scripts written by experienced translators. Says "out of the latter, the Poet's Theater of Cambridge, Mass., in 1955 came a work that was pivotal in its encouraging example to theatre translators hoping for an authentic classic repertory stage in America second to none: the first of Richard Wilbur's rhymed couplet texts of Molière, *The Misanthrope*, buoyed by his inimitably adroit and felicitous verse."

5 FREEDMAN, SAMUEL G. "The Translators vs. Adapters: Foreign Plays Spark Debate." *New York Times*, 4 January, p. C13.

Recounts the problems involving the use of "translations" of plays done by writers who do not speak the original language as well as plays done by those who simply "adapt" from an English translation. Suggests that translators who are familiar with the languages they translate are most uncomfortable with such a loose use of an original writer's work. Quotes Wilbur as saying, "It's a very muddled situation. . . I don't think of the translators as a union being scabbed on, but I worry about the fidelity of adaptations to the originals."

6 GWYNN, R. S. "Wilbur's Techniques of Translation." *Sewanee Review* 92, no. 4 (October-December):644-49.

1984

Observes that "good poetic translation must make the best of a bad compromise between languages in the same way that treaties between nations must weigh the numerous variables that separate one culture from another." Notes the several translations present in most of Wilbur's collections of poetry. Suggests that *The Whale* enhances Wilbur's "reputation as a master of the translator's art." Says, "That Molière has proved eminently actable is no surprise; that he should be equally readable testifies to Wilbur's ability to turn couplet on couplet so that succeeding lines seem simultaneously unexpected and inevitable." Finds that though Racine's *Andromache* "is not likely to reinvoke the rage for snuffboxes and perukes, . . . Wilbur's translation does give Racine his day in court . . . and allows us to accept or reject his [Racine's] theory and practice of tragedy on its own terms." Admits that translating Racine is a nearly "impossible" task. Grants that "if Wilbur has not quite accomplished the impossible in giving us an *Andromache* that measures up to what we expect of great tragedy, the fault is not in the translation, which is excellent on all counts." Compliments Wilbur: "The best translations of poetry should be impersonal only in the sense that the translator's own voice is so effectively submerged in the translation that he writes himself into the persona of a Racine or a Molière and allows the original to speak to us as he might have done. Such is Wilbur's accomplishment."

7 HART, RICHARD HOOD. "The Lyric As Fictive Rhetoric: Skeptical Deconstructions of Poems in the Major British Tradition." Ph.D. dissertation, University of Texas at Austin, 250 pp.

Describes Wilbur's work as combining "both formalist and deconstructionist principles for reading lyrics." The major premise is that "an internal, fictional rhetoric operates between a lyric speaker and listener analytically apart from and prior to the rhetoric that connects a poet with readers." Says Chapter 1 "considers how lyric texts relate to lyric fictions and how figuration intertwines with persuasion in the lyric." Chapters 2, 3, 4, and 5 focus on poems selected to demonstrate paradox, syllepsis, internal tension in the apostrophe, and the function of allusion, especially in the poetry of W. B. Yeats and Richard Wilbur, whose "biblical allusiveness . . . almost recover[s] moments of sacramental vision." See *Dissertation Abstracts International* 45, no. 3:849A.

8 KODAMA, SANEHIDE. "Richard Wilbur's 'Genie in the Bottle.'" In *American Poetry and Japanese Culture*. Hamden, Conn: Archon Books, 1984. pp. 162-66.

Sees "Thyme Flowering Among Rocks," written as a series of haikus, as a synthesis of Japanese and American sensibilities. Just as the haiku poets attempt to do, Wilbur has created a world "where the hereness suggests universality and nowness eternity." The allusion to the Japanese haiku poet, Matsuo Basho (1644-94), shows Wilbur's sensitivity to the delicate balance struck between dream and reality by haiku poets.

9 ROSS, LAURA, ed. *Theatre Profiles 6*. New York: Theatre Communications Group.
    Lists places and performance dates for Richard Wilbur's translations of Molière.

* 10 SPANGENBERG, D. F. "Padda en akkedis, oor: Twee gedigte van Richard Wilbur en Ernst van Heerden" ["'Toad' and 'Lizard': On Two Poems by Richard Wilbur and Ernst van Heerden]. *Standpunte* (Johannesburg, South Africa) 37, no. 3 (June):28-33.
    In Afrikaans. Listed in *MLA International Bibliography of Books and Articles on the Modern Languages and Literatures,* items 84-1-11140 and 84-2-16438, 1984 (computer search).

11 WAGGONER, HYATT H. *American Poets from the Puritans to the Present*. Rev. ed. Baton Rouge: Louisiana State University Press, pp. 591-600.
    Revision of 1968.21.

1985

1 BIXLER, FRANCES. "Richard Wilbur: 'Hard As Nails.'" *Publications of the Arkansas Philological Association* 11, no. 2 (Fall):1-13.

Agrees with critics who see "high seriousness" in Wilbur's work. Argues that Wilbur "has demonstrated his ability to give a theme of consequence faithful articulation. The theme of seeing runs through his canon like a golden thread." Suggests that the "devout intransitive eye" of the poet enables objects to "speak." Poems such as "Poplar, Sycamore" and "Praise in Summer" directly refer to what the eye does. Again and again, in a variety of voices and situations the poet affirms the dependence of the eye on the object. Contends that for Wilbur the eye also is necessary in that it transforms the object into something new. "A Black November Turkey" suggests that seeing the world in its objective quality is a choice that may render the eye merely utilitarian; whereas, seeing beyond the thing reveals another world. Concurs that it is the poet who can see with a clear eye as evidenced in "A Plain Song for Comadre" and "Love Calls Us to the Things of This World." Both poems reveal the unseen love resident in the actions of Bruna Sandoval and the subject of "Love. . . ." Concludes that "Wilbur's stature as a major poet of the twentieth century can no longer be considered doubtful. He is a fine craftsman; and he is a serious thinker, capable of sustaining a powerful theme over more than thirty years of poetic endeavor. . . . For this reason, we can describe his work, like the 'holy things' in 'A Plain Song for Comadre' as 'Hard as nails.'"

2 BOLD, ALAN. "Richard Wilbur." In *Longman's Dictionary of Poets*. Burnt Mill, England: Longman, p. 305.

Notes a few biographical facts about Wilbur's education and teaching assignments. Lists several prizes and awards. Comments that "his work investigates, often with an ironic wit, the relationship between the individual and the civilization that surrounds him."

3 BUNGE, NANCY. "Richard Wilbur." In *Finding the Words: Conversations with Writers Who Teach*. Athens: Ohio University Press, pp. 171-81.

Interviews Richard Wilbur. Wilbur discusses the loss of vocabulary and "easy speech" which contribute to a poet's facility with language. Grants that poetry may have become "in good part sub-literary nowadays." Thinks that poetry became confused with rock lyrics which mean "shapelessness and want of grammar and any old kind of rhyming if one rhymed at all." Finds a return to a core curriculum a heartening sign that more students may be exposed to a wider variety of disciplines. Thoroughly disagrees with the notion that the past is irrelevant to today. Admits that "it's hard to be a poet in a culture with no strong sense of community [as in America]." Suggests that too many poems "are now being written which are their own paraphrases."

Says he teaches Milton by concentrating heavily on this poet's technique: "you cannot understand that 'L'Allegro' and 'Il Penseroso' are serious poems unless you worry the structure to death and discover the ideas implicit in the structure." Reads aloud in both literature and writing classes to "give a sense of [the poem's] measure as well as of its meaning."

Discusses the problem created by so many writing programs proliferating around the country which foster mediocre "creative writing students" who end up imagining themselves poets, are supported by universities who encourage them to think of themselves as poets, and who fill the little magazines with "quantities . . . of bad poetry, depressing poetry." Thinks poetry would be better served if poets had to earn a living some other way than through writing poetry. Closes by saying many gifted students are writing good poetry today, and "a course in writing can be stimulating and salutary. As for anyone's taking *two* such courses, or three, at the cost of neglecting Geology or Latin, I have my doubts." Reprinted: 1990.2.

4 HALLBERG, ROBERT Von. "Tourists." In *American Poetry and Culture 1945-1980*. Cambridge, Mass.: Harvard University Press, pp. 62-92, passim.

Takes note of the large amount of traveling done by American writers in the 1950s. Says that because of this heavy traveling, "three conventional poetic subjects dominated the decade; animals, . . . the fine arts, and travel." Quotes from Wilbur's "A Baroque Wall-Fountain in the Villa Sciarra" as an example of a poet who must ask a moral question, not just describe. Cites "Marché aux Oiseaux" (1949), "Wellfleet: The House" (1948), "Piazza di Spagna, Early Morning" (1955), and "A Baroque Wall-Fountain in the Villa Sciarra" (1955) as Wilbur's contribution to travel poetry. Uses the faun ménage in "A Baroque Wall-Fountain" to demonstrate how poets "establish authority over a subject." Suggests that Wilbur's celebration of the building of the Rome Termini ("For the New Railway Station in Rome," 1955) stands in sharp contrast to his lack of any comparable poem on a civic American project. Comments that "Wilbur could play at being a Roman and speak on behalf of its traditions: those first-person plural pronouns could be said to rest on the sense that all westerners have a claim to representation in the Foro Romano, and for a moment it seems that bella Roma is Wilbur's and he, hers." Characterizes "Piazza di Spagna" as a "snooty gesture toward others [monuments]." Finds that "only an American poet attends to the ritual significance of St. Paul's bells" [Wilbur's "Bell Speech," 1947].

Suggests that "affluence and a favorable exchange rate . . . give a tourist a sense of power." Finds that Wilbur addresses this problem in "Marché aux Oiseaux": "So powerful is the need to be regarded as beneficent that the mighty will reduce the victims of their magnanimity to helplessness." Concludes that "the adequacy of American high culture was in serious question after World War II . . . . For poets to feel upon them the questioning eyes of fellow citizens, as well as of Europeans, was natural, and to concentrate their energies on those types of poems that display taste, sophistication, intelligence, and inventiveness was, after all, responsible. The still greater responsibility of writing critically as well as patriotically, these poets have managed admirably."

5 HECHT, ANTHONY. "The Pathetic Fallacy." *Yale Review* 74, no. 4 (Summer):481-99.

Establishes that John Ruskin's famous dictum in regard to the pathetic fallacy rests on a false premise by citing examples first from Homer and Shakespeare's *I Henry IV* and *As You Like It*. Of Duke Senior's speech he says, "It is a mode characteristcally [sic] religious . . . and premised on the conviction that the whole purpose and majesty of God is made legible in the most minute, as well as the most stunning and conspicuous, parts of his creation." So too is a quotation from Psalm 19. Finds equally powerful examples of "the world as a holy cipher and mute articulator" in George Herbert, Donne, and Robert Herrick as well as fiction writers such as Dickens, Conrad, Dostoevski, Hawthorne, Joyce, and Mann. Cites an example from Hardy's *Return of the Native*, which demonstrates the rich use of the human element when describing nature.

Disputes Ruskin's claim that the best poets are able to do away with the subjective and objective states: "the objective is straightforward, factual, visual; the subjective is evaluative, secret, and interior. The objective world is nothing but random data without the governing subjective selection and evaluation; the two are halves of a single act of cognition. . . . Thus stated, it would seem that the pathetic fallacy was almost unavoidable." Suggests that "objectivity is a condition that can be approached only by canceling our humanity and by advancing toward a state that strongly resembles insensibility or death." Cites Frost's "The Wood-Pile" as an example of objectivity and subjectivity working in harmony to create meaning. Concludes by reprinting Richard Wilbur's "Advice to a Prophet" where he finds many resonances mentioned earlier in regard to Homer and Shakespeare. Asserts that in Wilbur's poem and in all the other cited works, "there is the beautiful and undoubted fact that metaphor is not merely our mode of expressing *ourselves* but of expressing the world, or what we are able to know of it. And metaphor is not merely the gadget of poets; it is virtually unavoidable as an instrument of thought."

6 HONIG, EDWIN. "Richard Wilbur." In *The Poet's Other Voice: Conversations on Literary Translations*. Amherst, Mass.: University of Massachusetts Press, pp. 79-83.
    Reprint of 1976.7. Reprinted:1990.2.

7 "Richard Wilbur." In *International Who's Who 1985-86*. 49th ed. London: Europa Publications, p. 1610.
    Contains exhaustive list of prizes and awards given to Wilbur as well as list of primary publications from *The Beautiful Changes* (1947) through *Andromache* (1982). Includes leisure interests and current address.

8 SEYMOUR-SMITH, MARTON. *The New Guide to Modern World Literature*. New York: Peter Bedrick Books, pp. 162-63.
    Describes Wilbur as a "purely technical skilful poet." Criticizes him as "graceful, learned, civilized – but he cannot allow himself to mean as much to his readers as they would like. He cannot be wild. His discretion, his control, insists on decorum. He observes well, writes beautifully, translates exquisitely; but it is all just a little too good to be true." Laments this lack in Wilbur. Suggests that "perhaps a British critic put his finger on the trouble when he suggested that Wilbur's poetry may not cost him enough." Concludes that he "belongs to a tradition of very highly competent conventionality."

9 STERN, CAROL SIMPSON. *Contemporary Poets of the English Language*. 4th ed. New York: St. Martin's Press, pp. 926-28.
    Reprint of 1980.16.

10 STITT, PETER. Interview with Richard Wilbur. In *The World's Hieroglyphic Beauty: Five American Poets*. Athens: University of Georgia Press, pp. 39-54.
    Reprint of 1977.17. Reprinted:1990.2.

1985

11 ____. "The Sacramental Vision of Richard Wilbur." In *The World's Hieroglyphic Beauty: Five American Poets*. Athens: University of Georgia Press, pp. 9-38.

Insists that "in order to appreciate Wilbur's poetry fully, the reader must enter *its* world, and this requires more of a willing suspension of disbelief than is the case in reading most contemporary poetry." Grants that Wilbur "stands apart from his poetic age in a number of ways–he is an optimist among pessimists; he has a classic objective sensibility in a romantic, subjective time; he is a formalist in the midst of a relentless informality. The underlying worldview that predetermines these characteristics is traditional and religious; admitting the existential primacy of material reality, Wilbur yet believes in a spiritual reality as well, and his goal as a poet–and, one feels, as a man–is to bring these two realms together into a unified whole." Cites as "crucial" the Christian idea that "through Christ, the Christian God gave physical manifestation to pure spirituality, thus uniting the two contrasting realms. And this is the way Richard Wilbur would have the two appear in his poetry, as in the universe he inhabits–together, in interaction with one another, neither one alone." Notes the frequent appearance of the idea of chaos consistently portrayed as water or the sea and spirituality portrayed as light. "Wilbur's ideal is a union of the two realms, a mingling of them, so that we deal with a spiritualized reality. The tension that exists in a Wilbur poem is between these two poles." Locates the "spiritual element in Wilbur's vision and art" outside of man: "It will be most useful to define God through one of his primary attributes–creative intelligence–for through this term we can define also that which is divine in mankind." It is this "creative intelligence" which aids the poet in "discovering" the evidence of the spiritual in the universe. Another word for "creative intelligence" for Wilbur is imagination.

Establishes another important concept for Wilbur as the idea "that sleep is allied with the spiritual realm, or provides a way into it, and waking is allied with the material, the everyday." Finds that "motion is an important attribute of most of the poems so far cited showing the presence of the spiritual within the material." Asserts that "a careful reading of several poems shows that Wilbur's injection of motion into a scene is his way of imagistically indicating the presence of the spiritual within the material." Argues that "it is . . . through the use of metaphor that Wilbur's poetry technically accomplishes what he has conceived as true of the world in a philosophical sense." Finds an understanding of Wilbur's definition of "grace" central for accurate reading. Wilbur reverses the scripture in "Grace," by saying "flesh made word / Is grace's revenue." Sees this as a clear sign that "it is the poet's function, in his attempt to read God's mind, as it were, his attempt to match God's creative intelligence with his own pale version of the same thing, to change that manifest grace back into words."

1986

1 DACEY, PHILIP, and JAUSS, DAVID, eds. *Strong Measures: Contemporary American Poetry in Traditional Forms*. New York: Harper & Row, pp. 1-16.

Defends the purpose in compiling this anthology as helping to "foster a more balanced view of poetry, one that recognizes that both traditional and open forms are indispensable resources for contemporary poets. We hope to accomplish this aim by doing for contemporary traditional verse what Donald Allen's *New American Poetry* and Mezey's *Naked Poetry* and *New Naked Poetry* did for contemporary free verse: provide a showcase for its practitioners' finest work. By doing so, we hope to encourage future anthologists to present a more balanced picture of this period's poetry, one which would highlight the finest achievementss in both free and formal verse." Reprints Wilbur's "Junk," "Piazza di Spagna, Early Morning," "A Late Aubade," and "Year's End." See Chronology for Wilbur's Foreword.

2 HELD, LUCAS. "Wilbur Returns with a Poetry Lesson." *Middletown (Conn.) Press*, 4 October, pp. 1, 24.

Reports Wilbur's returning to Wesleyan University for a poetry reading. Quotes several critics' comments about Wilbur. Lists Wilbur's reading and musical tastes. Describes his view of the decline of language, especially as it has influenced the role of poets and poetry.

3 HOLDEN, JONATHAN. "Postmodern Poetic Form: A Theory." *Style and Authenticity in Postmodern Poetry*. Columbia: University of Missouri Press, pp. 9-32, passim.

Creates a taxonomy for postmodern American poetic forms consisting of poems moving from the communal to the impersonal. Asserts that "the anxiety which [postmodern American poetic form] reflects is anxiety with respect to poetic *convention*: what kind of discourse seems suitable for verse (without sounding obsolete) and what does not? . . . Poets have increasingly turned to nonliterary analogues such as conversation, confession, dream, and other kinds of discourse as substitutes for the ousted 'fixed forms,' substitutes which in many cases carry with them assumptions about rhetoric that are distinctly antimodernist." Argues that "postmodern formal strategy consists . . . not only of extending the range of formal analogues, but

1986

also of clearly favoring 'communal' analogues such as confession and conversation over such impersonal analogues as the 'fugue,' the 'ideogram,' and the 'vortex.'" Locates other poems at the opposite end of the continuum toward "greater impersonality." Calls these, "Poems whose forms are based upon what might be regarded as 'literary' analogues: narrative poems. . . ; dramatic monologues. . . ; and late-modernist 'essay' poems such as Richard Wilbur's famous 'Love Calls Us to the Things of this World.'" Defines these poems as ones in which "the poet has removed himself fully as a character, and we are conscious of him only as a peripheral presence, as 'The Author'" Contends that poems written in these forms allow the poet much more freedom from "the ethos of the author."

4 HOLLANDER, JOHN. "Ballade for Richard Wilbur." *New Republic*, 26 May, p. 40.
    Conducts a kind of *riposte* with Richard Wilbur in this poem, a ballade, in response to some of Wilbur's ballades.

5 KAUFELT, LYN MITSUKO. *Key West Writers and Their Houses*. Englewood, Fla.: Pineapple Press, pp. 138-39.
    Pictures the Wilburs's Key West home with the comment that the Wilburs's "earliest home was once a bordello managed by a Key West historical figure named Singapore Sadie. Now they live in one of the small Conch houses . . . in deliberately unpretentious Windsor Compound. It is in the Solares Hill Section of Old Town, a half block from David Jackson's house."

6 MICHELSON, BRUCE. "Richard Wilbur." In *Contemporary Authors: Bibliographical Series*. Vol. 2. Detroit: Gale, pp. 335-68.
    Contains a Primary Bibliography of Books, Selected Essays, a Selected Story, Translations, Edited Books, and Recordings. Lists in Secondary Bibliography Bibliographies and Checklists, Selected Interviews, Critical Studies: Books, Critical Studies: Collection of Essays, Critical Studies: Major Articles, and Book Sections. Concludes with a Bibliographical Essay that evaluates some secondary material. Says that Wilbur's "essential problem . . . may simply be this: in an age in which 'serious' poetry is supposed to have a raw, offhand look, Wilbur's formal, intricately crafted works are out of step with fashion and liable to the charge of mannerism." Laments the lack of a good book-length study of Wilbur's work. Suggests that "there has been an evolution in the way his work has been understood, a movement away from the notion that Wilbur's poems are treatises and toward the recognition that any ideas they suggest are a *poet's* ideas."

Recommends that anyone interested in reading Wilbur criticism should read with guidance. Provides informative insights into several important critical articles.

7 PASTON, LINDA. "Poet-to-Poet: A Conversation between Richard Wilbur and Linda Paston." Columbia, Md.: Howard County Poetry and Literature Society.

Sponsored by the Howard County Poetry and Literature Society, videotaped by Cable 8 TV Studio of Howard Community College in Columbia, Maryland in the fall of 1986.

Converses with Richard Wilbur. Each poet reads several poems aloud and comments on various aspects of writing poetry. They discuss the naming urge all poets have. Wilbur says, "I feel that if I don't know that that's philodendron, I have less control over it. I assume it's philodendron. Somehow, if I have a thing by the name I almost have it by the scruff of the neck." Wilbur argues that poets "ought to write out of all the words that are in and out of the dictionary." He describes his writing method: "I start talking in poems. I find some words that are interesting and that have a kind of rhythm, and they constitute a first line. We know where to break, when to start another line. And after a while a stanza appears, if it's going to appear; if it's a freer sort of poem that won't happen." Paston and Wilbur discuss the fact that many younger poets are returning to writing more formally. Wilbur suggests that "many writers must feel that, for them at any rate, the possibilities of free verse have been exhausted." Session ends with Paston reading a poem. Reprinted:1990.2.

8 "Richard Wilbur." In *Contemporary Theatre, Film, and Television*. Vol. 3. Detroit: Gale, pp. 388-89.

Contains sections Personal, Education, Vocation, Career, Related Career (translator, teacher, poet, critic), Writings, Plays Produced, Plays Published, Books, Member, Awards, Sidelights (recreation), Addresses. All sections are brief.

9 "Richard Wilbur." In *The Reader's Advisor: A Layman's Guide to Literature*. 13th ed. Vol. 1. New York: R.R. Bowker, pp. 284-85.

Quotes the *New York Times* as saying, "A seemingly effortless craftsman, Mr. Wilbur reveals a fine lyrical gift, a searching wit and, in his translations, a sympathetic kinship to the works of others." Notes briefly Wilbur's education and teaching assignments, some prizes and awards, some translations, and books of poetry.

1986

10 ROBERTSON, NAN. "A Musical Collaboration in Homage to America." *New York Times*, 2 January, p. C16.

Reports on "On Freedom's Ground: An American Cantata." Recounts the events leading up to the collaboration of William Schuman, composer, and Richard Wilbur, poet, on the cantata commissioned by eight well-known symphony orchestras on the subject of America. The cantata was planned to celebrate the centennial of the Statue of Liberty. Says Schuman "asked Mr. Wilbur to write a text after failing to find inspiration in the words of Thomas Jefferson, Walt Whitman or Emma Lazarus."

11 ROBINSON, EDWARD. "Enfleshing the Word." *Religious Education* 81:356-71.

Cites the lines "All that we do / Is touched with ocean, yet we remain / on the shore of what we know" ("For Dudley") as Richard Wilbur's rendering of the human condition. Suggests that "the Word needs a continually new enfleshment in every generation, and that this may even require a discarding of old forms, a willingness to let them die, to give room for new life." Finds that "the creative imagination is that human faculty which opens up the possibility for understanding some of the mystery of life." Urges that poetry, music, and painting be considered participatory art in order that each person's imagination may be renewed. Infers that Wilbur's poetry has this power.

12 TURCO, LEWIS PUTNAM. *Visions and Revisions of American Poetry*. Fayetteville: University of Arkansas Press, p. 135.

Writes about postmodernism in American poetry. Mentions that Wilbur, along with Anthony Hecht and Howard Nemerov, was one of the poets "who turned for models to the English Renaissance and the metaphysical tradition of Donne . . . and began to write a poetry of elegance."

13 WRIGHT, WILLIAM. *Lillian Hellman: the Image, the Woman*. New York: Simon and Schuster, pp. 266-72.

Recounts Hellman's working and quarreling with Leonard Bernstein and Richard Wilbur over *Candide*. Narrates several scenes where all three are together, attempting to collaborate. Provides some insight as to why *Candide* was not as successful as it might have been.

1987

1 DISCH, THOMAS. Review of *Tartuffe*. *Nation*, 2 May, pp. 585-86.

Performance review of *Tartuffe* produced at the Theater Project at R.A.P.P., New York City. Says "Molière's play has been a serviceable vehicle for a few centuries already, and Richard Wilbur's translations are also a sure thing."

2 GLOVER, RAYMOND F. "A Stable Lamp Is Lighted." In *A Commentary on New Hymns: Hymnal Studies 6.* New York: Church Hymnal Corporation, pp. 12-13.

Explains the origin of the text for the hymn "A Stable Lamp is Lighted" as the poem "A Christmas Hymn" (*Advice to a Prophet*). Suggests that the "text expresses the paradoxical meaning of Christmas through its emphasis on the harsh reality that implicit in the birth of Christ are his death and resurrection; the three are intertwined and cannot be separated."

3 HAMMILL, SAM. "Recent Press Books." *Fine Print* 13 (October):185-87.

Comments on the techniques of Harry Duncan, publisher for Wilbur's *Lying and other Poems* (1987). Says that "this is an exquisite little book." Describes it in detail, noting that Duncan's choice of type, paper, graphic design, and Joanna caps greatly enhances the poems.

4 HECHT, ANTHONY. "Richard Wilbur." In *Obbligati: Essays in Criticism.* New York: Atheneum, pp. 130-39.

Reprint of 1977.5.

5 HUMPHRIES, CAMILLA. "Wilbur Back in Cummington: Poet Laureate Pleased about Appointment." *Daily Hampshire Gazette* (Northampton, Mass.), 20 April 1987, pp. 1, 10.

Reports on Richard Wilbur's being appointed Poet Laureate of the United States in April 1987.

6 MARIANI, ANDREA. "Roma nella letteratura americana del Novecento." *Studi Romani* (Rome) 35:172-91.

Asserts that Richard Wilbur, among others, admires the new monuments in Rome such as the new railway station; he does not want to be identified with the old. In "A Baroque Wall-Fountain in the Villa Sciarra," he describes a baroque (really rococo) scene and shows his American anxiety by suggesting that the plain fountains of Maderna more aptly symbolize human life. Identifies "A Baroque Wall-Fountain" and "For the New Railway Station in Rome" as links with American transcendentalist philosophy.

7 McCLATCHY, J. D. "Richard Wilbur: A Note and a Conversation." *Four Quarters* 2d ser. 1, no. 1(Winter):23-27.

Includes critical commentary and record of an interview with Wilbur. Notes *humility, concentration,* and *gusto* – Marianne Moore's "three standards for art, poem or painting" – in Wilbur's poetry. Says "the way Wilbur's poems search, not so much for meaning as for understanding, is a wonder. . . . His is that rational love that wants both to include and transcend the world – an essentially religious imagination which treats natural objects and scenes as emblems of another order."

Relates Wilbur's description of the difficulty in translating Racine's *Andromache*: "the translator is bound, in rendering Racine, to try to match the author's expressiveness of sound in a general way, . . . but to seek to duplicate the sound-patterns of particular passages is to play a losing game." Wilbur asserts that "rhyme and meter are part of the music [of Racine's play], which in turn is part of the meaning." He notes that a major problem in translating *Phaedra* was conveying the "veiled utterance of courtly innuendo. . . . Degrees of obscurity and degrees of understanding are not easy to translate with exactitude, but to make the attempt is fascinating work."

Wilbur observes, in regard to an apparent resurgence of formal verse in America, that "it may be . . . that certain bromidic ideas about form are losing their power over us. The idea, for example that meter and stanza are intrinsically repressive and right-wing, whereas free verse is liberating and democratic. The idea that free verse is forever original and venturesome, that it is somehow 'experimental' to imitate Pound or Bill Williams decade after decade. The idea that formal poetry's heightening of language, its power to make strong emphases, rhythms, and closures, will betray the poet into saying things that his honest prose self wouldn't say." Wilbur insists that he never chooses a form and then fills in the lines; rather, the subject chooses the form. "Such finding of form is based on much reading, hearing, and writing, but it happens almost instinctively."

8 MOLOTSKY, IRVIN. "Richard Wilbur Is Named Nation's Poet Laureate." *New York Times,* 17 April, p. 26.

Reports that Richard Wilbur was "named today the poet laureate of the United States." Notes that Wilbur, appointed by Librarian of Congress, Dr. Daniel J. Boorstin, "succeeds Robert Penn Warren, who became the nation's first poet laureate last year." Mentions that the appointment is a one-year, renewable term and that the duties are largely those chosen by the poet himself, though he is occasionally asked to "deliver lectures and to advise the Library of Congress on its literary programs and recommend new poets to be recorded in the library's archive."

9 "New Poet Laureate." *Amherst* 39, no. 4 (Summer):5.
Reports on Richard Wilbur being named Poet Laureate of the United States in April 1987.

10 PERKINS, DAVID. "Richard Wilbur." In *A History of Modern Poetry*. Cambridge, Mass.: Belknap Press of Harvard University Press, pp. 383-87.
Acknowledges that with *The Beautiful Changes* (1947) Richard Wilbur "captured this audience [students of the New Criticism] almost at once and held it for twenty years. . . . Like the high Modernists and the New Critical poets of the 1920s and 1930s, he was formal, witty, and impersonal; he kept his subject at an emotional distance and activated very diverse attitudes toward it. But his texture was less dense than theirs." Argues that "Ceremony" (*Ceremony*, 1950) "has his characteristic note, with its combination of sophisticated civilization – paintings, Europe, ballet – and decent affections, its playful yet serious wit, its fresh, apt, sympathetic descriptions, reflective intelligence and formal skill." Grants that in recent years Wilbur has "developed a plainer style and, in some poems, a greater emotional intensity." Suggests that translating Molière's plays may have enhanced his ability to write in the dramatic mode. Concludes, "In his plainer style he can be nobly eloquent, as in his poem on the death of Dudley Fitts ("For Dudley"). And whether in his dramatic lyrics or his meditative utterance he is still a master of elegance and wit."

11 SHAW, ALAN. "*Phaedra* in Tact." *Hudson Review* 40, no. 2 (Summer):225-33.
Reviews *Phaedra*. Concedes that "of the three arts that [Wilbur's] versions [of Molière and Racine's plays] excel in – the art of translation, the art of versification and the art of writing for the stage – it would be hard to say which current literary fashion cares least about, or is most ignorant of." Demonstrates Wilbur's "tact" in translating *Phaedra* by comparing his lines with the identical lines translated by Robert Lowell. Asserts that Wilbur's lines render the character as created by Racine far more accurately. Argues that it is Racine's "strategy to understate things and constantly to use – we might as well say it – clichés." Any translator must follow the original writer's strategies. Wilbur attempts to do so. Grants that Lowell is a fine poet, but that Wilbur seems much more able to employ tact when translating, and thus avoid losses that ruin the play. Notes that "poets like Pasternak

have given, in their own languages, more than one example of tactful, metrical and speakable translations of verse drama; Wilbur's are almost the solitary example of this kind in English." Affirms the excellence of Wilbur's use of rhymed couplets because "they are a part of [Racine's] rhetoric, almost a part of his grammar. It is as if language, in his hands, grows another conjugation, one that cuts across, sometimes reinforcing, sometimes qualifying or contradicting, the human grammar. For this grammar is not the grammar of the impassioned individual; it is the grammar of something larger against which that individual struggles and is measured."

*12 STOKES, GEOFFREY. *Village Voice*, 28 April, p. 1.
       Listed in *Access*. Edited by John Gordon Burke and Ned Kehde, vol. 13. Evanston, Ill.: John Gordon Burke, 1988, p. 1013.

 13 Van DIEMA, D. "Richard Wilbur." *People Weekly*, 5 October, pp. 91-92, 97-99.
       Writes an informal survey of Richard Wilbur's life and thought. Notes that many famous poets of Wilbur's generation "are gone, . . . out of the running [for Poet Laureate]. Unlike Wilbur, they could not find the exquisite balance; to understand enough of turmoil to be a major American poet of the 20th century and to stay sane enough to reap rewards." Recounts Wilbur's early success. Suggests that "at 35, Wilbur had it all, in a profession where some of the best never get any of it." Mentions the "golden" period the Wilburs experienced and the later darker time when Charlee "had four miscarriages" and Aaron, the fourth child, became autistic. Tells of the "toll" Wilbur experienced in the deaths of so many of his fellow poets. Asserts that Wilbur's "stability should not be confused with tranquillity [sic]. . . . When it comes to the crunch, Wilbur simply refuses to let his intimations of evil get in the way of his belief in good." Quotes Wilbur as saying, "I'm never shaken from the mental belief that there is a God, and He means well. . . . Sometimes I believe everything that the catechism says that we ought to believe, and sometimes I don't believe any of it, and much of the time I'm in between. But a belief in God and God's mercy is unquestioned, really."

 14 WEIR, EMILY HARRISON. "Richard Wilbur: A Masterful, Modest Poet Laureate." *NewsSmith* (Northampton, Mass.) 2, no. 3 (Summer):3.
       Reports Richard Wilbur's appointment as Poet Laureate in April, 1987. Includes various quotations from critics as well as a general listing of his writings. Compares him to other poets such as the

Beats and the confessional poets, especially Robert Lowell. Mentions response of former students. Notes Wilbur's comments about his wife's ability to be an excellent critic of his work. Concludes with Wilbur's rueful admission that fame brings with it some drawbacks.

1988

1 "Afternoon Delight: Brian Bedford and Friends Reading Great Scenes from Molière." Columbia, Md.: Howard County Poetry and Literature Society.

Sponsored by the Howard County Poetry and Literature Society, videotaped by Cable 8 TV Studio of Howard Community College at the Smith Theatre in Columbia, Maryland on May 3, 1988.

Bedford gives Richard Wilbur the credit for reviving interest in Molière's plays. Wilbur contrasts translating Racine, who he feels has "qualities of belief and feeling . . . that put him back in the seventeenth century, amongst the stern Jansenists and those who believe that we have no free will" and translating Molière who does not possess any of these qualities. Wilbur comments on the difficulty of translating the French Alexandrine into the English pentameter line which creates "built-in infidelity. . . . You're taking a language which moves in gentle waves and putting it into a language which comes down hard on its stressed syllables." Says the most important part of translating is to "get the tone of it right. And secondly . . . one sets aside the idea of word-for-word fidelity, because that makes you write in a language which does not exist anywhere. But one insists upon a thought-for-thought fidelity and it is possible." Reprinted:1990.2.

2 BARNARD, NANCY. "Wilbur's 'A Late Aubade.'" *Explicator* 46, no. 4 (Summer):37-39.

Analyzes "A Late Aubade." Finds that she, the reader, is "forced to fill the place of the woman addressed [in the poem] because of the speaker's use of 'you.'" Admits to a high level of exasperation because of the trivializing of the woman in the poem. "The woman has been said by the speaker to prefer lying in bed and kissing, to studying, shopping, gardening, lunching, training a dog, and listening to a lecture. Now [in the last lines] she's told that if she must do something else, as long as she's up, she can go get some food – of the speaker's choosing. I know that an aubade can express reluctance at lovers' separations; but if this is a complimentary love lyric, I would prefer something else to the reading of love poems. I also have a subversive suspicion that the woman addressed in this poem might feel the same way."

1988

3 BROWN, ASHLEY. Review of *New and Collected Poems*. *World Literature Today* 62, no. 4 (Autumn):660.

Reviews *New and Collected Poems*. Grants that "Richard Wilbur is one of the finest poets of our time." Notes that forty years have passed since Wilbur's first collection, *The Beautiful Changes* (1947), appeared. Finds that "the new poems include at least a dozen that are as good as any of the familiar anthology pieces; Wilbur has never lost his touch for turning almost any occasion into something civilized. Especially worthy of praise are the five poems that make up a cantata called 'On Freedom's Ground,' done in collaboration with the composer William Schuman."

4 BROWNE, MICHAEL DENNIS. "The Poem Behind the Poem." *A View from the Loft* 10, no. 7 (February):4, 16-17.

Analyzes "The Writer" as an example of a successful attempt on the part of the poet to write "the poem behind the poem." Contends that "most poems fail to generate their true subjects, the subjects often implicit in the poems' opening phrases, even as early as the title." Suggests that "articulation of the authentic problem surfaces in this poem, insists itself into the final lines, because the poet takes up the proposition of sound that he offers himself, intuitively, at the poem's beginning." Insists that "it takes two to parent a poem and that many of our poems seem to fail their early potential because we don't manage to generate the second emotion, or subsequent ones. One reason for that failure is the lack of charge in our words." Comments that in "The Writer," "the screened, authentic problem is transformed into utterance which from now on will be dissolved in the poet, will become a part of who she is and how she sees the world. There is no mistaking the force of such discoveries; they cannot be faked and there is not [sic] going back from them."

5 BUTTS, WILLIAM. "An Interview with Richard Wilbur." *Esprit* 4, no. 1 (Fall):1-8.

Butts says, "Richard Wilbur, winner of the Pulitzer Prize for Poetry and the National Book Award, stands as tall amid the melee of modern poetry as he does in the flesh. The poise and authority of his highly structured verse in an array of traditional forms have made him the despair of many a modernist, but few would deny that Wilbur's mellifluous voice of reason is charged with a wit and intelligence difficult to match. He recently completed his term as our nation's second poet laureate. The following interview was conducted by mail."

Wilbur talks about the farm upbringing he had which influenced his love of nature. Expresses pleasure at having produced "actable versions" of Molière and Racine, but regret at having allowed himself to become diverted so completely from writing original poetry, though he sees definite benefits growing out of having done translations such as broader vocabulary and ability to modify style and technique. Suggests teaching and writing are both "hard, enjoyable tasks" which have been mutually beneficial.

Says the best way to write poetry is "to be frequently idle, and thus available to the impulse should it come." Denies knowing where his work is going next. Denies belonging to any "school or phalanx" of poetry and admits that "those who spurred me on in the first place – my immediate American elders, and a host of poets, of all times and tongues – are still my main prompters." Gives advice to young poets to "read the poetry of all ages . . . not to succumb to any one influence, but to take pleasure and prompting from a hundred sources."

Comments that "I don't pretend not to read my critics, and it matters to me what they say. If a criticism is intelligent, I am pleased to have had the attention of an intelligent person, even if he gives me a hard time. If all my critics denounced me, I think that I would be somewhat disheartened and would write somewhat less. When I am praised by someone I respect, it makes me want to write more. No criticism, however, has had the effect of making me strive to please by writing this way or that; I am stuck with my own tastes, themes, and capacities."

Disagrees strongly with the notion that "metrical writing tempts one to make strong closures, and that strong closures are fraudulent in an age of doubt and confusion." Replies that "poets are not bound to conform to anyone else's notion of the age, and that a few iambs and trochees never led an able poet to say more than he meant." Reprinted:1990.2.

6 CONANT, MICHAEL. "The Farm Boy Who Became Poet Laureate." *Seattle Post-Intelligencer*, 9 May 1988, pp. C1-2.
    Reports the awarding of the Robert C. Bunn Prize to Richard Wilbur. Describes his physical appearance, his teaching, and books of poetry. Quotes several remarks about the role of poet laureate. Includes brief bits of biography. Notes that Wilbur "feels there's been a resurgence of interest in poetry. Some of it comes from the 'Vietnam unpleasantness' when young war protesters wrote a lot of bad poetry that read much like a Bobby Dylan song." Says Wilbur also senses "a new popularity of poetry readings. . . though most people would rather hear poetry than read it." Quotes Wilbur as saying, "There's something therapeutic in writing poetry. You begin by 'submitting yourself' to something common – the English language – discover a 'general

1988

humanity' about yourself, and in the end hope your poetry will be accessible to everybody."

7 DISCH, THOMAS. "Rhyme and Reason: Reading Poetry for Pleasure." *Washington Post Book World*, 22 May, pp. 1, 14.

Reviews *New and Collected Poems*. Laments that Richard Wilbur "if he were not, for the time being, America's poet laureate . . . could lay claim to the unenviable title of being the country's most neglected poet of the first rank." Insists that "there is nothing in *New and Collected Poems* a publicist might latch onto and ballyhoo: no hints of scandal or suicide notes, no howling jeremiads, nothing *newsworthy*." Concludes that "the new poems, composing a fifth of this volume, are solidly Wilburtian, the grandest of the lot being the libretto for a long, lilting patriotic cantata, 'On Freedom's Ground,' which would alone entitle him to the peppercorns and all other emoluments of laureatedom."

8 GARRISON, D. Review of *New and Collected Poems*. *Choice* 26, no. 8 (October):319.

Wilbur's latest, fullest volume belongs in every undergraduate library. Finds that Wilbur "has proved himself an accomplished practitioner of verse forms and the elegant, decorous line of imaginative power. His phrasing at its best, brings to language an intellectual liquidity; at its less than best, a decency of manner and idea. As he has said of Auden, his own is a 'civil tongue / In a scattering time.' The only serious quibble with this otherwise fine volume is that it contains no index of either titles or first lines."

9 GRAY, PAUL. "A Testament to Civility." *Time*, 9 May, pp. 84-85.

Reviews *New and Collected Poems*. Says that Wilbur has the ability to be a "messenger between outer and inner worlds, to specify and make memorable what everyone already knows or to give narrow personal experience the breadth of shared impressions. This dedication to communal speech is visible through *New and Collected Poems*, making the book a singular testament to civility." Mentions "Leaving" as "moving adroitly from the specific to the universal." Sees in "On Freedom's Ground" an example of the way Wilbur's poems "always allow animal and vegetable kingdoms their tumultuous integrity. Their energy is a cause for celebration, and so, equally, is the power of the human mind to absorb, assimilate and assort all these phenomena." Notes that the poet laureate thinks that the American public enjoys reading and hearing poetry. Wilbur's occasional poems should add to their reading enjoyment.

10 GUILLORY, DANIEL L. Review of *New and Collected Poems*. *Library Journal*, 1 June, p. 116.

Reviews *New and Collected Poems*. Says "that nature and imagination are the two poles of Wilbur's creativity is evident in this volume's opening poem, 'The Ride,' in which Wilbur rides an imaginary horse in his dreams and, upon awakening wants to give it 'some hay, some water to drink, / A blanket and a stall.' The poem could be taken as a metaphor for Wilbur's best work, which always leaves the reader with a strange vividness and a painful sense of loss." Finds this collection "a fitting tribute to the poet laureate of the United States."

11 GWYNN, R. S. "Double Agents." *Sewanee Review* 96, no. 2 (Spring):297-305.

Reviews *Phaedra*. Quotes Wilbur's comment on "the difficulty of rendering only one of Racine's hallmarks – 'the celebrated sonority' of his verse. 'Since French does not sound or move like English, a translator who sought to duplicate the "music" of certain famous lines in *Phaedra* would in the first place fail, and, second would doubtless slight the matter and tone, which are primary in all writing. What one must do, I think, is to try throughout for equivalent effects of significant sound and pacing in the key of English, and remember always that one is seeking to be worthy of a magnificent ear.'" Notes that Racine's narrow vocabulary and the "absence of any equivalent tradition of rhymed tragedy in English" are two more reasons why translating Racine presents large challenges. Finds Wilbur's translation much more acceptable than Robert Lowell's (1961) because Wilbur's "is more in keeping with the tactful elevations of Racine's language." Concludes "if ever there has been an ear worthy of Racine's, it is Wilbur's own."

12 HECHT, ANTHONY. "Master of Metaphor: The Achievement of Richard Wilbur." *New Republic*, 16 May, pp. 23-32.

Reviews *New and Collected Poems*. Argues that "this new work bears all the hallmarks of excellence that have stamped Wilbur's previous work: a kinetic imagination that is rare among poets, as well as an unusually rich and fertile gift for metaphor." Cites "An Event" with the lines "They roll / Like a drunken fingerprint across the sky!" as a superb example of this gift. Says this metaphor is "breath-takingly vivid, accurate, and most astonishingly, *in motion*." Claims that Wilbur then "throws it [the metaphor] away. Or in any case declares that this is only one, and perhaps an imperfect, way to formulate what may in the end defy formulation." Contends that "this *sprezzatura* would be reckless in another poet. But Wilbur's government of his enormous resources is what makes this poem (as well as many others) a triumph over its local details, and an amalgamation that is wonderfully greater than the sum of its parts." Moreover, it is "refreshing in the work of so accomplished a poet to encounter an acknowledgment of 'the defeat of words.'"

Disagrees with George Bernard Shaw's notion that "a painter, a composer, an author, may be as selfish as he likes without reproach from the public if only his art is superb." Asserts instead that "the work of art bears some important imprint of the spirit and inmost life of its maker." Cites "Still, Citizen Sparrow" and "A Wood" as showing two sides of the personality of the man behind the poet. Insists that "it is an index . . . of Wilbur's growth as an artist that his eye has become increasingly ample over the years." His use of puns indicates his ability to do the serious play required of all good poets, and his ability to appreciate and translate widely different poets indicates the breadth of his reach. Notes that his lyrics for the cantata written for the celebration of the centennial of the Statue of Liberty demonstrate his ability to take unusual risks and succeed. Finds "The Ride" a continuation of Wilbur's exploration of the "relationship between dream and waking." Sees the translation of "A Part of a Speech" by Joseph Brodsky "as no small accomplishment . . . to have translated a poem from the Russian that allows the influence of the 17th-century poet [John Donne] to exhibit itself in a modern and modulated way." "'Mirabeau Bridge' is as miraculous in its poise and fragility as the original." "'A Fable' is a deftly funny poem." "Trolling for Blues" marks a return to the theme of "An Event." "All That Is" is notable for its wit and thoughtfulness. Judges "Lying" to be "the best poem in the collection" because of its movement from simple lying to the "feigning" which is art. The poem ends with three such lies – metaphor, that is. Concludes "there is nobility in such utterance that is deeply persuasive, and throughout Wilbur's poetry we are accustomed to finding this rare quality, usually joined to wit, good humor, grace, modesty, and a kind of physical zest or athletic dexterity that is, so far as I know, unrivaled."

* 13 HOWE, RANDALL. "America's Prized Poet." *Berkshire Eagle*, 4 June, pp. 10-11, 17.
      Listed in 1990.3; p. 149.

  14 JEROME, JUDSON. "The Poetic Catalog: Exercises for Learning How to Handle Accentual Meter in Poetry." *Writer's Digest*, May, pp. 10-14.

Uses Richard Wilbur's "Junk" as an example of how to write in accentual meter and as an example of the poetic catalog.

15 KENNEDY, X. J. "The Coiled Fury of His Chosen Reticence." *Los Angeles Times Book Review*, 9 October, p. 5.

Reviews *New and Collected Poems*. Affirms that "there is more to Wilbur and his poetry than a respectable, polished exterior . . . and that today, in a stampede back to traditional forms, [younger poets] have rediscovered him." Acknowledges that "with Wilbur any change has been slow and nonviolent. How firmly he has persisted in what he does so well, refusing to cut his coat to passing fashion. He has devoted himself to shaping not a career but individual poems, and he has made them to last." Argues that "his new work displays new virtues. For one thing, his recent poems are more easily speakable – a result, I suspect, of his translating so much of Molière. More often now, the poems tell stories. Moreoever, the gifts Wilbur has always had – an impeccable ear, an eye for a metaphor today shine brightly as ever." Notes the "sheer variety" of Wilbur's achievement – literary criticism, children's books, editions of Shakespeare and Poe, translations of Molière and Racine and numerous poets, and lyrics for *Candide* and "On Freedom's Ground." Says, "Wilbur is the opposite of Poe, that hater of nature who imposed his inexorable will upon language and reality." Defends Wilbur against the charge of his lacking passion by saying, "The charge ignores what George Garrett has called the 'coiled fury of his chosen reticence,' for Wilbur's poems seem the winners of fierce wrestling matches. A rage for symmetry struggles with an urge for truth."

16 RAETHER, KEITH. "Richard Wilbur: Words Put World in Order for Poet Laureate." *News Tribune* (Seattle, Wash.), 8 May 1988, pp. E1, E7.

Reports on the awarding of the Robert C. Bunn Prize to Richard Wilbur by the Seattle Public Library.

17 Review of *New and Collected Poems*. *Booklist*, 15 April, p. 1387.

Reviews *New and Collected Poems*. Says "the new poems [in this collection] consolidate him as the poetic voice of cultivated suburbia. He is most congenial as a translator. . . and as a writer of light verse." Concludes Wilbur "is ever the consummate craftsman and a pleasure to watch at work even when, lamentably frequently, he belabors unremarkable observations with historical references and special vocabulary."

1988

18 "Richard Wilbur." In *The Chelsea House Library of Literary Criticism.* Edited by Harold Bloom. Vol. 7, *Twentieth Century American Literature.* New York: Chelsea House, pp. 4276-89.

    Reprints of several critical articles: 1968.23, 1977.22, 1978.12, 1981.7.

19 "Richard Wilbur." In *Waterstone's Guide to Books.* 2d ed. London: Waterstone & Company, p. 1283.

    Lists *Walking to Sleep* (1969). Comments that "as an antidote to the excesses of modernism and post-modernism on the one hand, and of 'confessional' poetry on the other, Richard Wilbur developed a witty and elegant style of verse which returned to a direct sensual apprehension of the world and a distinctly Keatsian sense of its beauty. The conventional forms and genial middle-style tone of his short lyrics relate Wilbur most directly to Robert Frost, but his concern with the relationship between material reality and intellectual perfection, and his use of what he describes as 'the single meditative voice balancing argument and counter-argument, feeling and counter-feeling' reveals the pervasive influence of Wallace Stevens. Wilbur has also translated Molière for the American stage and edited the poetry of Edgar Allan Poe."

20 "Richard Wilbur." In *Who's Who in America 1988-1989.* 45th ed. Vol. 2. Wilmette, Ill.: Marquis Who's Who, pp. 3304-3305.

    Mentions Richard Wilbur's educational experience and teaching assignments. Lists publications beginning with *The Beautiful Changes* (1947) through *New and Collected Poems* (1988). Lists prizes and awards as well as home address.

21 RICHMAN, ROBERT, ed. *The Direction of Poetry.* Boston: Houghton Mifflin, pp. xiii-xxi.

    Describes the poets included in this anthology as "united in their use of metered language. This is the principal feature of the poetry here, and the central trait of the 'movement' being surveyed in this book." Asserts that "not since the fifties has such a large number of the most gifted younger poets chosen to make the mastery of metrical form a test of their achievement. Among other things, the publication of this anthology invalidates the countless critical judgments, expressed in the sixties and seventies, of the death of metrical verse." Reprints Richard Wilbur's "Lying," "Transit," and "The Catch."

1989

1 COULTHARD, A. R. "Poetic Justice in Wilbur's 'A Game of Catch.'"
Notes on Contemporary Literature 19, no. 5 (November):5.
Suggests that this early short story is "an excellent parable of
aggression." It "illustrates that in the ritual of revenge, nobody wins."
Interprets the outcome of Sho's determination to break up the game of
catch between Monk and Glennie as a victory that "has separated him
from his friends. . . . The proud avenger has caught only himself."

2 GERY, JOHN. "The Sensible Emptiness in Three Poems by Richard
Wilbur." *Essays in Literature* (Macomb, Ill.) 16, no. 1 (Spring):113-126.
Treats the idea of a "sensible emptiness" in "A World without
Objects Is a Sensible Emptiness," "Advice to a Prophet," and "In the
Field." Says that "Wilbur's sense of annihilation, or nothingness, has
changed . . . becoming not only darker but increasingly aligned to his
notion of the necessary modesty of the human spirit in relation to the
ineffable." Finds that "A World without Objects. . ." resembles Wilbur's
early nature poems in that it "looks to the physical world as the place
from which the spirit garners meaning." Says that "Advice to a Prophet"
shows a change "in emphasis from understanding the things of this
world by imagining sensible emptiness to understanding that same
emptiness by imagining the things of this world." Suggests further that
this poem "becomes increasingly preoccupied with our perception of
the world more than with the things in it, so that even though nature
itself is prominent both as the source of the heart's understanding and
as the source of our physical existence, the annihilation of nature is a
meaningless concept unless it is rendered in terms of the human
experience of it." Argues that "In the Field" uncovers Wilbur's
acknowledgement that "even nature itself, put under the threat of
annihilation, cannot finally provide meaning, circumscribed as it is by
its own potential absence from both our perception of it and from
existence itself." Interprets the "night" section of the poem to mean that
"last night 'we could not say' whether or not the sky has anything to say
to us. It is not that it is waiting for a language to be developed to
decipher its meaning; it is simply not available to meaning at all." Sees
that finally this poem reaches "an apocalyptic vision of the ultimate
finitude not only of our language and ourselves but of what we
experience . . . of nature itself." Summarizes by saying that "unlike in 'A
World without Objects. . .' in which imagined annihilation is presented
as that experience beyond our sensual one which ultimately allows us
to value and praise the sensible fullness of everyday living; and unlike
'Advice to a Prophet,' in which it is through our linguistic ability to

value and praise that sensible fullness that we can come to grasp the horror imagined annihilation promises; in 'In the Field,' imagined annihilation itself takes precedence over our language, our sensible experience, and nature itself."

3 HAMILTON, IAN. "A Talent of the Shallows." *Times Literary Supplement* (London), 15-21 September, p. 999.

Reviews *New and Collected Poems*. Argues that "Cottage Street, 1953," in its urbane judgments of Sylvia Plath, is really intended to "measure . . . the distance between Sylvia Plath's kind of poetry and his own. For all his modesty, which seems genuine, [Wilbur] knows very well that the decline of his reputation since the mid-1960s has been in large part a consequence of Plath's post-humous appeal." Describes Wilbur as a poet "grown used to being thought of as exemplary, as embodying qualities of cultivation and humane subtlety that had been imperilled by the war." Says that "much of the time, what the poet 'wants to say' is very simple indeed, something like: Look what the imagination can contrive when it is genuinely free" ("Cicadas"). Attributes Wilbur's early success to "his zestful mood and the delighted quickness of his eye and ear" which "made a virtue out of a seeming paucity of subject matter." Asserts that Wilbur turned to translation because he "had begun to scratch around for things to take off from" ("Seed Leaves"). Says that "in middle to late Wilbur there is an almost constant sense of skills that have become habitual, enabling the poet to drone on rather prettily, to keep talking so long as the rhyme supplies hold out." Quotes the first three stanzas of "Icarium Mare" and comments that "there are so many irritating details here (accidental repetitions, ugly rhymes, hideous archaisms, arch inversions and so on) that it seems superfluous to take issue with the pleased-with-itself tone in which the whole thing is served up. The poem goes on for a further five stanzas and does not improve." Admits that a few poems are "likeable" ("The Ride," "Leaving," "The Catch"). Concludes that "Wilbur seems to have accepted some time ago that in choosing to be a poet of the 'shallows' (as he puts it in his Sylvia Plath poem) he has under-extended his considerable talent." Uses "The Writer" as further evidence of this point.

4 HOWARD, BEN. "Incarnate Lights." *Poetry* 154, no. 2 (May):99-112.

Reviews *New and Collected Poems*. Comments that "for all their luminous transparency, the poems of Richard Wilbur enact an unending spiritual drama. Within the confines of Wilbur's shapely stanzas, the claims of the spirit vie with those of the body, and the soaring imagination, dreaming of 'the sky's blue speech,' confronts the impurities of daily experience." Confirms that "this distinguished collection reaffirms Wilbur's position as one of the pre-eminent formalist poets of the postwar period." Finds that this "compendium reveals . . . a central, recurrent figure and a dominant emotional tone. The figure is that of energy harnessed or constrained–the starling trapped in a room, the juggler defying gravity, the heaving sea and its trammelling tides. . . . The dominant tone is one of restrained exaltation." Notes that "over the years Wilbur's formal style has remained remarkably consistent, deepening rather than changing. At the same time, one can detect a slow drift from self-conscious artifice toward greater simplicity and candor." Suggests that "the most complex and beautiful of the new poems" is "Lying." Concludes, "In the speech of their eloquent witness, ordinary objects take on a spiritual radiance, and the discontinuous worlds of body and spirit, word and thing, achieve a delicate accord."

5   HUDGINS, ANDREW. Review of *New and Collected Poems*. *Hudson Review* 41, no. 4 (Winter):743-44.

 Reviews *New and Collected Poems*. Praises Wilbur as a "master. . . . In the seemingly effortless play of syntax over meter and rhyme he has few equals in our time. But the great ease, the technical mastery of his poems, sometimes lapses over into the subject matter, as if to imply the world itself can be similarly mastered." Finds that such a result is not intentional but comes from Wilbur's "classical or neoclassical view of poetry as something consructed beautifully, as the end result of reflection and art and not, as in the romantic view, as part of the process itself." Uses "The Writer" to show that "Wilbur himself is aware of the dilemma." Concludes that *Collected Poems* is chock full of work of enduring value." Cites "Juggler" as a source of information about how Wilbur views his role as an artist. "As a juggler who triumphs over gravity and the world's weight, no one in our time is better than Richard Wilbur."

6   KENNER, HUGH. "Whatever Spins Around." *National Review*, 2 September, pp. 48-49.

 Reviews *New and Collected Poems*. Comments that "What [Wilbur] has long since arrived at is an enviable sureness, an evenness of performance that doesn't lapse, that seems not to fumble for rhymes, that can draw syntax out the length of several stanzas or else box it in crisply. The quotidian doesn't bore him, and he's untempted by bardic postures" ("C Minor"). Contends that "for all its deftness it's unambitious verse: verse unpropelled by any such radical originality as that of Wilbur's countryman William Carlos Williams."

7 LOGAN, WILLIAM. "America's Laureate: An Elegant 'Poet of Light' Who Also Has Weight." *Tribune Books* (Chicago), 24 July, p. 4.

Reviews *New and Collected Poems*. Criticizes Richard Wilbur because he continues to write poetry that indicates he would rather "intimate than be intimate." Compares Wilbur, an untroubled poet, with Robert Lowell. Admits "it would be a mistake, however, to believe that a poet of light is one without weight." Finds that "in the autumnal poems, newly collected here, sadness and death are the suffusing themes, played against nature and its annual rebirths."

8 McPHILLIPS, ROBERT. "What's New about the New Formalism." *Crosscurrents: A Quarterly* (Westlake Village, Calif.) 8, no. 2:64-75.

Argues against critics who would characterize the new formal poems of the 80s "as derivative, as retreats to the allegedly stale and stodgily 'academic' formal poetry of the 50s against whose strictures the Beat, Confessional and Deep Image poets emerged." Describes the poets of the 50s as a group who wrote poems noted for their irony, poetic distance from the subject, use of cultural artifacts, use of classical allusions and foreign-language titles, and "baroque diction." Mentions John Hollander, Anthony Hecht, and Richard Wilbur, in particular, as exemplars of poets writing in this vein. Contends that "these are not the values and virtues of the 80s formalist poets who are as likely to be found in the business world as they are in the university, and whose inspiration derives not from the academy but from the quotidian world and the desire to write about emotion directly and memorably."

9 MIDGETTE, ROCKY. "Reading Richard Wilbur." *Amherst Spectator* 5, no. 3 (Winter):15.

Writes a sardonic poem alluding to several images in Wilbur's poems.

10 MOLE, JOHN. "Old Year Poetry Choice." *P[oetry] N[ation] Review* 16, no. 5:8-10.

Reviews *New and Collected Poems* (English edition). Says, "Pigeon-holed far too readily as Big Chief Paleface or (in Randall Jarrell's words) as the progenitor of 'the tea-party or grey-flannel poets' of American academe, Richard Wilbur deserves to be read afresh entirely on his own terms as a poet of consummate elegance and graceful accuracy. Yes, he can be lured at times into the excessively rococo by his sheer agility, and yes, there is plenty of 'suave bombination' (his phrase, and rather good one) when the sound is turned up too loud and the sense is muffled, but the nearly 400 pages of *New and Collected Poems* can easily accommodate these authentic lapses and still come out on top. 'Not that I don't like Wilbur, but one is enough' wrote Jarrell. Given the present state of the craft, can we afford such reservations?"

11 MOLOTSKY, IRVIN. "The U. S. Poet Laureate in the Role of the Performer." *New York Times*, 7 March, p. C12.

Reports on a poetry reading by Richard Wilbur. A mature poet laureate reads poetry aloud and answers questions, charming his audience. Says he showed himself to be "gracious and witty."

12 ODELL, JOSHUA. "Poet Takes Refuge in Language Itself." *Los Angeles Times Book Review*, 31 July, pp. 3, 6.

Reviews *New and Collected Poems*. Says Wilbur "is a major poet of our time." His poems "clearly show a continued evolution in style from an ornate elegance found particularly in . . . *The Beautiful Changes* toward a simple, direct and crisp verse." Admits that "Wilbur's work has not enjoyed the popular appeal that perhaps it could given its clarity and grace . . . its accessibility to any reader." Calls *New and Collected Poems* "the best book of poetry published this year."

13 PAYNE, MARJORY SCHEIDT. "'Giver of due regard': The Religious Vision of Richard Wilbur." Ph.D dissertation, University of Rochester, 260 pp.

Investigates the nature of Wilbur's "religious vision and traces the continuity and development of that vision throughout his volumes of poetry. Introduces Wilbur as a poet whose 'religious vision' is characterized by an imprint of orthodoxy and an indebtedness to religious poets of the past, a contemporary, 'existential' quality; and a common-sense humanism." Sees *The Beautiful Changes* and *Ceremony* as demonstrative of Wilbur as the Christian humanist. Finds that *Things of This World* and *Advice to a Prophet* argue "the poet's growing confidence in the goodness of this world, despite experiences of loss." In *Walking to Sleep* and *The Mind-Reader* the poet "looks less frequently up a vertical axis to the heavens; rather, he peers down into the psyche and into the sometimes savage roots of natural creatures to probe the mysterious source of all freshness." See *Dissertation Abstracts International* 50 (July):136A.

14 *Poets & Writers Magazine*, July-August, p. 42.

Notes that "Richard Wilbur of Cummington, Massachusetts won the 1989 Pulitzer Prize in poetry for *New and Collected Poems*."

15 RADEMAN, CHAD L. "Poetry Reading Attracts Students." *Amherst Student*, 29 November, p. 3.

Reports on a poetry reading given by Richard Wilbur during his week-long visit to Amherst College as the 1989 Robert Frost Library Fellow.

16 ____. "Wilbur '42 Visits as Frost Fellow." *Amherst Student*, 15 November, p. 3.

Reports on Richard Wilbur's being appointed the 1989 Robert Frost Library Fellow by Amherst College and his activities which grew out of this appointment.

17 REEVES, GARLAND. "Wilbur Raises His Voice for Rhyme & Meter." *Birmingham* (Ala.) *News*, 12 March, p. 1, 6F.

Describes Richard Wilbur as "tall, tanned and lean, with a voice as gently cultured as an English garden, [his] very being is fragrant with the perfume of courtly poet. But beneath the suit and tie, the urbane gentleness and erudite speech, wildness hides." Notes the awarding of the Grand Master Award by Birmingham-Southern College to Wilbur. Reports his conversation with the writer on the role of form, meter, and rhyme in the writing of poetry. Mentions that "Wilbur has been interested in the cadence of language and its effect on poetry for years, and though it might not seem so on the page, the natural, regional cadences of the poet often become of paramount importance."

18 "Richard Wilbur." In *Guide to American Poetry Explication: Modern and Contemporary*. Edited by John R. Leo, vol. 2. Boston: G. K. Hall, pp. 464-68.

Lists bibliographical information on explications of several of Wilbur's poems.

19 "Richard Wilbur." In *International Authors and Writers Who's Who*. 11th ed. Cambridge: Melrose Press, p. 916.

Lists Education, Publications (from *The Beautiful Changes* [1947] to *Phaedra* [1986], including editorial and critical work), Honours, Memberships, Agent, and Address.

20 "Richard Wilbur." In *The Writer's Directory 1988-90*. 8th ed. Chicago: St. James, p. 1007.

Lists names and current addresses of contemporary writers.

21 RICHMAN, ROBERT. "Benevolent Possessions." *New York Times Book Review*, 29 May, p. 2.

Reviews *New and Collected Poems*. Says "this book reminds us that [Wilbur's] verse expresses a very clear and thoughtful view of life." His verse is "more than an Eden of beautiful language." Cites "An Event" as a poem which displays Wilbur's "willingness to examine the difficulties of his esthetic viewpoint." Sees "Worlds" as a comment on the theme of "*possession and ownership*" of the world. Observes that Wilbur "is preoccupied with the correct 'possession' of nature because the transaction holds the possibility of spiritual release" ("Piazza di Spagna, Early Morning"). Finds that "nothing in Mr. Wilbur's *oeuvre* argues more eloquently for the value of ordinary life than poems such as 'Running,' 'A Late Aubade,' 'For Dudley,' and 'The Writer.'" Quotes "The Writer" in full. Concludes that "there is much to be said for a poet who refuses against all odds to allow his vision of hope (as manifested in the elegance and attractiveness of the verse) to die. If it were not for writers like him, future students might wonder if there were no poets in the late 20th century who championed beauty (as unlikely a cause as it may have been) or who were capable of rising above all the despair and doubt. Fortunately, we do have Richard Wilbur, and I am confident our age will be deemed the better for it."

22 RUTSALA, VERN. "Déjà Vu: Thoughts on the Fifties and Eighties." *American Poetry Review* 18, no. 5 (September-October):29-35.

Compares the new conservatism of the eighties with the similar, yet different conservatism of the fifties. Suggests that Richard Wilbur – highly respected for his work during the fifties and the newly appointed Poet Laureate of the United States – is "an obvious link with the fifties." Wilbur's poetry seemed in the fifties to be "the kind of poetry one *should* write, a poetry of light and air." Sees the emergence of *The New Criterion* and discussions of "metrical illiteracy" among poets as evidence of a return to ideas about poetry current in the fifties. Suggests that the shift toward New Formalism indicates a return to conservatism by the literary establishment.

23 STUTTAFORD, GENEVIEVE. "Forecasts." *Publishers Weekly*, 18 March, p. 64.

Reviews *New and Collected Poems*. Says that "Wilbur is a poet for whom intellect serves as an antenna, filtering signals from an inscrutable world to create lyrical structures informed by wit and irony." Finds that this "omnibus displays Wilbur's many facets as nature poet, mordant commentator on social mores, philosophizer and as a translator adept at capturing the varied moods of poets as different as Voznesensky, Borges and Jean de la Fontaine." Says "the new material is mostly minor, though it confirms him as a versatile craftsman."

24 "Taylor Poetry Award Goes to Richard Wilbur." *New York Times*, 20 January, p. 23.

Reports on Richard Wilbur's being given the Aiken-Taylor Award for Modern American Poetry. The annual award is $10,000 and is administered by the *Sewanee Review* and its publisher, the University of the South in Sewanee, Tennessee, and is a recognition of a "contemporary American poet for the work of a substantial and distinguished career."

1990

1 BROUGHTON, IRV, ed. "Richard Wilbur." In *The Writer's Mind: Interviews with American Authors*. Vol. II. Fayetteville, Ark. & London: University of Arkansas Press, pp. 127-61.

Reprint of 1975.2. Reprinted: 1990.2

2 BUTTS, WILLIAM, ed. *Conversations with Richard Wilbur*. Literary Conversations Series, edited by Peggy Whitman Prenshaw. Jackson & London: University Press of Mississippi, 261 pp.

Reprints of 1962.4; 1964.9; 1966.6; 1967.3 (partial); 1968.12; 1970.8; 1970.17; 1972.5; 1973.5; 1974.3; 1975.1; 1976.7; 1977.6; 1977.17; 1979.2; 1985.3; 1986.7; 1988.1; 1988.5.

3 DINNEEN, MARCIA. "Richard Wilbur: An Annotated Bibliography of Secondary Sources, Continued." *Bulletin of Bibliography* 47, no. 2 (June):143-50.

Lists supplementary material to an earlier bibliography (1980.3).

4 HARRIS, PETER. "Forty Years of Richard Wilbur: The Loving Work of an Equilibrist." *Virginia Quarterly Review* 66, no. 3 (Summer):413-25.

Review *New and Collected Poems*. Acknowledges that Wilbur's "poetry celebrates the power of metaphorical language to divine the human implications of natural patternment, and it affirms the capacity of strict metrics to contain both the dictates of civility and the promptings of joy." Notes that "Wilbur has remained steadfast to his commitment . . . to the indissolubility of form and value." Finds Wilbur demonstrates his ability as an "equilibrist" in poems that create "a yearning for a formal perfection beyond the depredations of time and an equally strong impulse to harrow the pleasures of the physical world." Allows that Wilbur's "work takes no particular position on formal religion, but it does seem to lean a bit, at times, in the direction of granting the archetypes a metaphysical rather than a merely psychological existence." Finds an example of the "seminal reciprocity between nature and spirit in 'Fern-Beds in Hampshire County.'" Says that in "Advice to a Prophet," Wilbur "shows his mastery of all the elements of poetry that interest him: the musical, the lyrical, the metaphorical, the descriptive, the dialectical, even the high rhetorical, to which he rises in the peroration that ends the poem." Regards love as the "central value in his work." Asserts that the new poems in this volume "show him near the top of his powers" ("The Ride," "Alatus," "Lying"). Concedes that "whatever else he believes, Wilbur trusts that we all lie in the lap of an immense intelligence." Finds little pathos except in the translation of Joseph Brodsky's "Six Years Later" and "Leaving." Looks at "Trolling for Blues," "Shad-Time," and "Hamlen Brook," as poems where "Wilbur angles after metaphysical insight and aesthetic delight." Judges *The Mind-Reader* (1976) as the "most urgently moving volume." Cites "Cottage Street, 1953" and "The Writer" as evidence. Analyzes both extensively. Suggests that the conclusion of "The Writer" exposes "through explicit statement, the fundamental impulse that drives Wilbur's scrupulous decorum. The finding of the right analogy for his daughter's situation is both the measure of the quality of his love and of the quality of his poem." Craftsmanship, in this instance, becomes a kind of "exemplary categorical imperative with existentialist overtones: either we are exacting in our search for what is right and, thereby, affirm life or we are seduced by fatal ease and become, symbolically, unquickened."

5 HILE, KEVIN. "Richard Wilbur." In *Contemporary Authors*, edited by Hal May and James G. Lesniak, new rev. ser., vol 29. Detroit: Gale Research, pp. 450-56.

Contains sections headed Personal, Addresses, Career, Member, Awards & Honors, Writings, Sidelights, and Interview. Sidelights section reviews chronologically a number of literary assessments by key Wilbur critics. See Jean Ross (1990.8) for annotation of Interview.

*6 HOUGEN, JOHN BYRON. "The Poetry of Richard Wilbur: Ecstasy within Discipline." Ph.D. dissertation, University of Virginia.

Listed in 1990.3, p. 150. See *Dissertation Abstracts International* 50 (January):2053A.

7 HULSE, MICHAEL. "Richard Wilbur's Dreamt Land." *Poetry Durham* no. 25:28-32.

Comments on the philosophical / religious "core" found in "A World without Objects Is a Sensible Emptiness" and "A Baroque Wall-Fountain in the Villa Sciarra." Suggests that "at its best, Wilbur's poetry reestablishes an emotional and aesthetic wholeness, or an appearance of wholeness, out of the experience or awareness of fracture." Mentions Valéry's definition of poetic emotion as "an intricate thing of correlatives checked and balanced." Says these two poems of Wilbur's are fine examples of this kind of poetic emotion. Quotes from Traherne's *Second Century*, "Meditation 65" as a means of refuting Geoffrey Thurley's argument against "A Sensible Emptiness . . ." (1977.18). Interprets this passage as the starting point for Wilbur's poem. This work suggests that "the things of this world, in delighting our senses and inspiring love, provide us with a sense of purpose and belonging in the world." Sees this theme running throughout Wilbur's poetry. Finds that "the poet's wit consists in positing Traherne's 'Sensible Emptiness' literally . . . and examining the implications." Concludes that in this poem "Wilbur rejects philosophical games and urges belief in Christ." Acknowledges that "in the post-Cartesian and post-Einsteinian world, Wilbur's belief in the things of this world can occasionally give the impression of epistemological over-simplification." Argues, however, that "it is precisely here, in [Wilbur's] understanding of knowledge of the world and of the way that knowledge relates to final belief, that we discover the core Thurley claimed was absent from Wilbur."

Suggests that the charge of "over-simplification will not survive careful reading." Sees the reference to a "dreamt land" in "A World without Objects" as central to portraying human longing for sensuous fullness. However, the adjective "dreamt" is crucial in that it acknowledges that this land is not "of this world." Rather, it speaks of death. Concludes that "in Wilbur's work perception is not absolute but relative; understanding is gained at the cost of misunderstanding . . . [and] knowledge and belief are neither simple nor simply achieved. Wilbur is an honest doubter, a pained believer." His gift is to be able to "think in verse."

8 MERRILL, JAMES. Introductory Remarks for the Academy of American Poets. New York: Sea Cliff Press, n.pp.

Introduces Richard Wilbur by recalling how he, as a younger student, first met him at Amherst. Describes in metaphorical terms the measurement of Wilbur's poetry. Says "in our time the golden cubit of Cummington, Massachusetts, exactly equal in length to the right forearm of our poet, has become the nearest thing we have to a national standard. The measures produced by this means have never cheated us of a single syllable, nor has the thumb of untested feeling ever brazenly tipped the scale." Closes with a riddle especially written for the occasion.

9 ROSS, JEAN W. Interview with Richard Wilbur. In *Contemporary Authors*, edited by Hal May and James G. Lesniak, new rev. ser., vol 29, pp. 453-56.

Wilbur responds to a question about his wide vocabulary by saying, "I can't think offhand of any poet whose work I like in whom I don't find a keen pleasure in the words of our common language, and also in the historical roots of those words, the etymologies of those words, and in the uses which they've had in other and earlier hands." Wilbur finds that poetry and painting are both very visual arts and have "affinity" for each other. Admits that he does not have a sense of his audience so much as a sense of addressing some "condition of the language." Using certain words implies the existence of a certain audience. Describes the way a poet digs into his deeper self: "When you're writing on all eight, you write with reaches of your own nature and depths of your own experience which aren't readily available to you at ordinary times. And one way to commune with the deeper and stranger parts of one's self . . . is by taking advantage of the irrational suggestions that adherence to certain formal demands can make." Grants that writing poetry grows harder as he grows older in that he does not wish to write the same poem twice, but finds his interests are often the same as those he had as a young poet. Believes that "the proper function of criticism is to tell somebody else who might be about to read what you've just read what you see in it and what he just possibly might miss if he read with a little less care or experience than you have read with. It's mostly a matter of appreciative mediation, I think." Admires the work of some of the older confessional poets, but feels that too much recent poetry has been sloppy, "bar stool ramblings." See Kevin Hile (1990.5) for related material.

10 STEELE, TIMOTHY. *Modern Poetry and the Revolt Against Meter.* Fayetteville and London: University of Arkansas Press, pp. 280, 289.

Argues that the "free verse" movement triumphed by doing away with meter; but in so doing, the range of American poetry has been greatly diminished. Recognizes that poets like Richard Wilbur have been practicing traditional versification "brilliantly." Argues that "versification, as it has been understood for millennia, is for the majority of contemporary poets an irrelevant matter." Rejects the notion that poets must abandon meter and asks that poets "be allowed to chart their own courses." Suggests that "the fluid character of language insures that conventional meters are continually renewed." This then ensures that though forms may be recognizable, a "pleasing feature of a fine contemporary poem in meter is this: it enables one to hear a voice which – in its phrasing and the rhythm of its thought – is distinctively of one's day and yet which at the same time recalls the cadences and shapes of speech that characterized earlier masters working at earlier stages in the language." Wilbur's "The Mind-Reader" is such a poem.

1991

1 BIXLER, FRANCES. "Richard Wilbur: A Review of the Research and Criticism." *Resources for American Literary Study*, forthcoming. 55 pp.
    Surveys and evaluates critical work, including reviews of Wilbur's major publications, from 1947 to 1991. Contains sections Bibliography, Editions, Manuscripts and Letters, Biography, Criticism (Collections, Full-length Studies, Shorter Studies). All sections are arranged chronologically where appropriate. Contains brief biographical notes at the beginning of each decade. Concludes that "in general, criticism of Richard Wilbur's work has begun to mature, though it has not yet shown itself capable of grasping fully the large vision of the poet."

2 LANCASTER, JOHN, and HAGSTROM, JACK W. C. *Richard Wilbur: A Descriptive Bibliography* (working title). (Work in progress.)
    Describes in a comprehensive manner all publications of which Wilbur is sole or contributing author (including translations and works for the theater), and lists (with less detailed descriptions) his contributions to periodicals, blurbs provided to promote other poets' work, translations into other languages of his poems, and recordings. Contains a section detailing the publication history of each poem, which will include information on manuscripts and anthology appearances.

3 MICHELSON, BRUCE. *Wilbur's Poetry: Music in a Scattering Time*. Cambridge: University of Massachusetts Press, forthcoming.
    Discusses a number of poems in detail, many of which have not been closely read before. Suggests that "Richard Wilbur is a 'darker' and more complex poet than most reviewers and critics have been willing to grant, and that his famous or notorious optimism is tempered with long looks into the abyss." Contains a chapter on Wilbur's longer poems, a review of his famous quarrel with Poe, and speculations on what "constitutes true experimentation, real chance-taking, in an academicized postmodern world."

Finding List

1 AMERICAN ACADEMY OF ARTS AND LETTERS LIBRARY (New York, New York)
   Manuscript Collections of the American Academy of Arts and Letters Library (New York) contain correspondence and literary manuscripts pertaining to the American Academy of Arts and Letters and to the National Institute of Arts and Letters. Wilbur has papers in this collection.

2 AMHERST COLLEGE LIBRARY (Amherst, Massachusetts)
   The bulk of Wilbur's papers have been placed in the Special Collections and Archives of this library. Materials there fall into four groups: I – Poetry; II – Translations and Adaptations; III – Prose; and IV – Miscellaneous. Folders have been prepared for each poetry collection, together with worksheets and typescripts. Also, folders for individual poems contain correspondence and Wilbur's notes relating to the poem. Likewise folders containing worksheets and typescripts for each edition of the plays and prose pieces have been established. Some material has been placed in the library by the poet but may not be consulted without his permission.

3 LIBRARY OF CONGRESS (Washington, D.C.)
   The papers of Joseph Warren Beach (1891-1955) in the Manuscript Division of the Library of Congress include correspondence between Beach and Wilbur.

4 LOCKWOOD MEMORIAL LIBRARY (State University of New York at Buffalo)

The Poetry/Rare Books Collection at this library contains a complete set of the first editions of Wilbur's work. Manuscripts of poems, mostly early ones, can also be found here. Included in the folder for each poem are various versions, corrections, notes, and fair copies.

Index

Bestiary, A
-commentary on, 1959.1
-reviews of, 1956.6
BIXLER, FRANCES, 1985.1;
1991.1
"Black Birch in Winter, A,"
1976.17; 1977.12; 1978.4;
1980.2
BLACK, IRMA SIMONTON,
1963.3
"Black November Turkey, A,"
1957.13; 1963.13; 1967.4;
1976.22; 1981.8; 1985.1
BLAKE, PATRICIA, 1984.1
BLOM, J. M., 1978.7
BLUE, MARGARET, 1973.2
BLY, ROBERT, 1967.1; 1972.3;
BOGAN, CHRISTOPHER,
1975.1; 1990.2
BOGAN, LOUISE, 1947.1;
1951.2; 1956.3; 1970.3
BOGARDUS, EDGAR, 1957.2
BOLD, ALAN, 1985.2
BOSQUET, ALAIN, 1960.2
"Boy at the Window," 1957.18;
1960.2; 1971.4; 1978.13;
1982.3
BOYERS, ROBERT, 1970.4, 5
BRESLIN, JAMES E. B., 1983.3
BRODSKY, JOSEPH, 1972.4;
1983.18
BROUGHTON, IRV, 1975.2;
1990.1
BROWN, ASHLEY, 1988.3
BROWNE, MICHAEL DENNIS,
1988.4
BROWNJOHN, ALAN, 1977.1
BRUNS, GERALD L., 1964.1
BRUSTEIN, RICHARD, 1983.4
BRUSTEIN, ROBERT, 1965.3
BUFITHIS, PHILIP H., 1975.3
BUNGE, NANCY, 1985.3; 1990.2
BURGESS, ANTHONY, 1977.2

BUTTS, WILLIAM, 1988.5;
1990.2

C

"C Minor," 1976.13, 18; 1977.10,
11; 1978.17; 1989.6
CAHOON, HERBERT, 1951.4
CALHOUN, RICHARD, 1980.2
CAMBON, GLAUCO, 1962.3;
1963.4
Candide
-commentary on, 1956.17, 25;
1959.5, 8; 1986.13
-reviews of, 1956.1, 5, 7, 10, 19,
25
CARGILL, OSCAR, 1954.1
"Caserta Garden," 1949.1;
1966.2;1967.4; 1977.18;
1979.6; 1980.7; 1981.4
"Castles and Distances," 1951.6, 9,
14; 1953.1, 3; 1960.8;
1965.18; 1967.4, 11;
1968.23; 1970.11; 1973.23;
1974.12; 1975.5, 6;
1977.18
"Catch, The," 1989.3
"Ceremony," 1948.7; 1949.1;
1951.6, 8, 9, 14; 1951-
1952.1; 1955.3; 1961.11;
1966.2; 1967.4; 1968.7;
1970.13; 1971.3; 1973.12;
1975.8; 1976.22; 1977.18;
1980.2, 7; 1981.4; 1987.10
Ceremony and Other Poems
-commentary on, 1952.5;
1953.2; 1954.2; 1955.3;
1956.15; 1963.4; 1965.18;
1967.4; 1970.15; 1972.2;
1980.2, 7; 1981.4; 1982.9;
1989.13
-reviews of, 1950.2, 4; 1951.1, 2,
3, 4, 5, 6, 7, 8, 11, 12, 13,

"Sunlight Is Imagination," 1949.1;
 1963.4; 1967.4; 1970.13;
 1979.5; 1981.4
"Superiorities," 1948.5; 1967.4
SUTTON, WALTER, 1965.19
SWALLOW, ALAN, 1948.10
SWENSON, MAY, 1957.17;
 1964.15

T

Tartuffe
 -commentary on, 1967.4; 1971.7
 -reviews of, 1963.10, 16; 1963-
 1964.1; 1964.2, 11, 12;
 1965.4, 7, 9, 10, 11, 13, 16,
 20, 21, 22; 1966.4
 -reviews of revivals, 1977.20;
 1983.13; 1987.1
TAUBMAN, HOWARD, 1965.20
TAYLOR, DAVID, 1978.19
TAYLOR, HENRY, 1969.18;
 1974.12; 1983.18
"Teresa," 1977.12, 16
"Terrace, The," 1951.1; 1957.15;
 1965.18; 1970.13
TERRILL, RICHARD, 1978.20
"Then," 1951.9; 1955.3; 1971.2
theses (M.A.) on Richard Wilbur,
 1966.1; 1973.12; 1976.1;
 1979.12
Things of This World
 -commentary on, 1961.11, 12;
 1963.4; 1965.18; 1966.3;
 1967.4; 1970.15; 1972.2;
 1980.2, 7; 1981.4; 1982.9;
 1989.13
 -reviews of, 1956.3, 4, 6, 8, 11,
 12, 14, 15, 16, 18, 20, 21,
 23, 24; 1956-1957.1;
 1957.2, 4, 9, 10, 13, 18;
 1958.7
THORP, WILLARD, 1961.15

THURLEY, GEOFFREY,
 1977.18
"Thyme Flowering Among
 Rocks," 1969.7, 18;
 1970.12, 13; 1971.20;
 1981.15; 1983.10; 1984.8
"To an American Poet Just Dead,"
 1951-1952.1; 1963.4, 17;
 1966.2; 1971.2
TOBIN, JAMES E., 1957.18
TOERIEN, BAREND J., 1962.27
"To His Skeleton," 1976.10
"To Ishtar," 1967.4; 1968.23;
 1981.4
"To the Etruscan Poets," 1978.20;
 1980.2
TOULSON, SHIRLEY, 1971.24
translation
 -criticism of, 1956.1, 2, 6, 11,
 22; 1959.1; 1962.1, 4;
 1963.16; 1964.9; 1969.18,
 21; 1971.7; 1972.5; 1973.9;
 1975.10; 1976.7, 23;
 1980.2, 17; 1981.4;
 1982.15; 1983.7; 1984.1, 4,
 5, 6, 9; 1987.7, 11; 1988.1,
 5, 11, 12, 15; 1989.23
translations of
 "Beasts," 1955.2
 "Ceremony," 1961.10
 "Death of a Toad, The,"
 1962.27
 "Digging for China" 1962.27
 "First Snow in Alsace," 1961.10
 "Love Calls Us to Things of
 This World," 1961.10
 "Museum Piece," 1961.10
 "On the Eyes of an SS Officer,"
 1961.10
 "Piazza di Spagna, Early
 Morning," 1961.10
 "Sunlight Is Imagination,"
 1961.10

FAULKNER UNIVERSITY
Library Services